LOYAL LOCHABER

AND ITS ASSOCIATIONS

HISTORICAL, GENEALOGICAL, AND TRADITIONARY

BY

WILLIAM DRUMMOND-NORIE

Member of the Gaelic Societies of London and Glasgow

ILLUSTRATED BY NUMEROUS REPRODUCTIONS OF

OLD AND RARE PRINTS, PHOTOGRAPHS, &c., &c.

With an Introductory Poem

By ALICE C. MACDONELL OF KEPPOCH

Bardess to the Clan Donald Society

GLASGOW

MORISON BROTHERS, 52 RENFIELD STREET

1898

TO

DONALD CAMERON, Esq.

OF LOCHIEL

XXIVth CHIEF OF CLAN CAMERON

THE WORTHY REPRESENTATIVE AND DESCENDANT

OF A LONG LINE OF HEROIC ANCESTORS OF WHOSE DEEDS

Lochaber

MAY WELL BE PROUD

THIS VOLUME IS BY KIND PERMISSION

RESPECTFULLY DEDICATED

PREFACE.

IF any apology is needed for this unpretentious volume, it will be found in the recent completion of the West Highland Railway, and the further opening up of the country by the new line to Mallaig, great engineering undertakings which are destined to effect material changes in the beautiful and romantic district of Lochaber.

Until recently, the only practical means of communication between Lochaber and the outer world has been by steamer from Glasgow, or by coach from Kingussie, both routes involving a considerable expenditure of time and money, which, in these days of rapid and economical travelling, are important considerations, especially to those who can only afford a brief absence from their duties.

Much as I dislike the intrusion of the "personally conducted" into the sublime solitudes of Lochaber, and to hear the deafening screech of the railway whistle echoing from the granite sides of Ben Nevis, I cannot but admit that out of evil good may come.

The student of Nature will have a new field for meditation among the hills and glens, the lochs and rivers of this most beautiful spot on God's earth; the poet new themes of inspiration in a land teeming with the legends and traditions of a past age; the artist will, among the picturesque scenery of Loch Linnhe or Loch Eil, find fresh subjects for his brush; and the historian and antiquarian will here discover food for reflection and research among the ancient dwellings and strongholds of departed chieftains, or amid the dolmens, brochs, and cairns of a prehistoric race.

Apart from these somewhat sentimental reasons, I believe that the new railway enterprises will prove important factors in promoting the future welfare of the Highland crofters and fishermen, who will now have the opportunity, so long denied them, of disposing of the produce of land and sea in the great markets of Edinburgh and Glasgow, which will be brought within a few hours' journey.

The great alterations that must necessarily ensue when these undertakings are completed, will, I fear, obliterate many historic landmarks, and introduce a foreign element among the Highlanders of the district, who up till now have retained all the sterling good qualities of their Celtic ancestors, pure and unadulterated. Proud, reserved, but hospitable to a fault; of splendid physique and appearance, they fully deserve the title of "nature's gentlemen"; and I take this opportunity of offering my tribute of thanks for the many acts of kindness and hospitality I have received at their hands.

It is no small part of my reward in connection with the task of compiling this volume, to have found so many willing hands ready to assist me in my undertaking. I have first to tender my respectful thanks to Her Majesty the Queen, by whose gracious permission I have been enabled to insert several extracts of local interest from her "Highland Journal"; and I cannot pass over without grateful acknowledgment the very great help I have received from Mrs MacDonell of Keppoch and her two talented daughters. Much valuable information has been placed in my hands by these ladies, which

cannot but prove of interest to my readers, and I am
sure that all Highlanders will appreciate the charming
verses, written specially for this work by Miss Alice
MacDonell (Bardess to the Clan Donald Society), not
only on account of their intrinsic merit, but still more
from the fact that they are composed by a direct
descendant of the famous Alasdair MacDonell of
Keppoch, whose heroic death at Culloden will never
be forgotten by his fellow-countrymen. To Mr Tom
MacKay, of Inverness and Glen Nevis, I am indebted
for many curious traditions and stories of by-gone days
which find a place in these pages; and to Mr Andrew
Scott and Mr Patrick Honeyman, of Glasgow, for several
of the most beautiful photographs with which they are
illustrated.

It has been my endeavour to collect, in the compass
of this volume, all that is of most interest in the
authentic history and traditionary lore of Lochaber,
and to rescue from possible oblivion its many old-world
stories and quaint legends, which another generation
will probably have forgotten amid the inrush of the
questionable civilising influences of Sassenach tourists.

This work does not pretend to any high standard
of literary merit, nor does it by any means exhaust
all that could be written respecting the history and
traditions of the district. Many subjects have been
practically untouched, such, for instance, as the Bards
of Lochaber and their poetry; the detailed history and
genealogy of the various smaller clans and septs of
the district; and a full account of the progress of the
Christian Church in Lochaber, from the time of St
Columba and the Culdees to the present day, each of
which would fill a volume of no small dimensions.
Much has already been done in this direction by such

able and scholarly writers as Alexander MacKenzie, the well-known clan historian, Dr Fraser-Mackintosh, and Dr Alexander Stewart ("Nether Lochaber"),[1] whose works are monuments of patient research, well worthy of careful study by all who are interested in the Highlands and the Highland people.

My own task has been less ambitious, being merely an attempt to awaken the interest of the general reader in the history of a typical Highland district; and with that object in view I have approached the subject in a lighter vein, and have woven into the local narrative brief descriptions of those great historical events which, although occurring far beyond the limits of Lochaber, were yet fated to have a marked effect upon the destinies of its inhabitants. For my Jacobite sympathies I make no apology. To all honest seekers after the beautiful in Nature, I say in all sincerity, come to Lochaber with a reverent spirit and admire the glorious scenery, and recruit your health with the life-giving breezes that are wafted over many a league of ocean and purple moorland, laden with the scent of the heather and the pungent odour of the seaweed. It is for you I write; and if my poor words can lend additional charm, or add a further interest to this land of poetry and romance, or help to throw any light upon its past history, my object will have been accomplished and my labour will not have been in vain.

W. DRUMMOND-NORIE.

GLASGOW, 1898.

---

[1] Dr Cameron Lees' book on Inverness-shire has been published since this work was written.

CONTENTS.

PART I.—INVERLOCHY.

CHAPTER I.

PAGE

Inverlochy in Pictish times—The building of the city and stronghold of Inverlochy by King Ewin II.—News of a Roman invasion brought to King Ethodius at Inverlochy—Donald of the Isles usurps the throne, and is murdered at Inverlochy—Assassination of King Gonranus—King Donwald drowned in the Lochy — Traditionary visit of the Emperor Charlemagne to Inverlochy—King Eocha (Achaius) receives the Frankish ambassadors—Dress and weapons of the Picts—Origin of the royal arms of Scotland—The St Andrew's Cross adopted as the national badge—Ancient dress of the women of Inverlochy — Lochaber described by Boetius—Derivation of the name Lochaber—Macbeth's castle at Loch Debhra — Chronicle of St Berchan — Place-names — Banquo, Thane of Lochaber—Revolt of the MacDonalds—Origin of the Stuarts—Murder of Banquo by Macbeth — Story of Fleance — Erection of the castle of Inverlochy — The Comyns in Lochaber — The Red Comyn slain at Dumfries by Robert Bruce—Traditional origin of the Camerons—The Mackintoshes — Battle of Invernahavon — Quarrel between Davidson of Invernahavon and Cluny MacPherson—Rout of the Camerons, .   .   5

CHAPTER II.

The Clan Donald and its branches—Alasdair Carrach, I Chief of Keppoch—Donald of the Isles claims the Earldom of Ross—Battle of Harlaw—James I. of Scotland—His captivity in England—Alexander of the Isles invades Lochaber—He is summoned before the king at Inverness—Inverness burned by the MacDonalds—The Lord of the Isles sues for pardon at Holyrood—Imprisoned at Tantallon Castle—Donald Balloch takes the field—First battle of Inverlochy—The king takes the field in person—Story of the Earl of Mar and O'Birrin—Liberation of Alexander of the Isles—The Cameron lands bestowed upon MacLean of Coll—Ailein nan Creach — Battle at Corpach between the Camerons and MacLeans—The MacMasters of Ardgour—Ewen of the Feathers—Murder of MacMaster—The MacLeans become possessed of Ardgour, .   .   21

CHAPTER III.

PAGE

Lordship of Lochaber forfeited to the Crown—The Gordons in Lochaber—Origin of the family—Restoration of Inverlochy Castle—Treaties made with the local chiefs—"Ranald of the Hens"—Battle of Blàr nan leine —Defeat of the Frasers—Stories of Ranald "Galda"—Capture and execution of Keppoch and Lochiel—"The Black Tailor of the Battle-axe"—Attack on Ruthven Castle by Angus Mackintosh—Battle between the Camerons and Mackintoshes—The Earl of Argyll claims the lands of the Camerons—Jealousy of Huntly—Dissensions among the Camerons —Lochiel takes vengeance upon the traitors, ...   34

CHAPTER IV.

Historical retrospect—Charles I.—Act of Revocation—Attempt to force the English Liturgy upon the Scottish Presbyterians—The National Covenant —Montrose—His early history—His jealousy of Argyll—Character of Argyll—Imprisonment of Montrose—Montrose goes over to the king—Argyll raids the West Highlands—"The Bonnie Hoose o' Airlie,"   .   47

CHAPTER V.

Montrose returns to Scotland—The Highland army—Aberdeen sacked by the Irish—Hatred of the Campbells by the loyal clans—Argyll arrives at Inveraray Castle — Descent of Montrose and the Highland army upon Argyllshire — Slaughter of the Campbells — Flight of Argyll—Montrose proceeds to Kilcumin—Argyll invades Lochaber with a large army of his clan — Montrose determines upon a strategic movement—Arrival of the Highland army in Glen Nevis—Description of the rival forces—"Iain Lom," the bard of Keppoch—His genealogy and history —Friendship of Montrose for Iain Lom—The bard prefers the pen to the sword—Poem, "The Battle of Inverlochy,"   53

CHAPTER VI.

Description of the battle of Inverlochy—Rout of the Campbells—"The Campbell's Stone"—Death of Auchenbreck—Montrose sends a message to king Charles—Flight of Argyll from Inverlochy—Apparent cowardice —Curious explanation from "Britanes Distemper"—Future career of Montrose—His capture by the Covenanters—The last scene on the scaffold—Present condition of Inverlochy Castle—Description of the surrounding scenery—Ben Nevis—Probable derivation of the name,   63

CHAPTER VII.

Charles II. crowned at Scone—Cromwell invades Scotland—Battle of Worcester, and escape of Charles to France—General Monk endeavours to force the Highland chiefs to submission — Humorous account of General Dean's expedition to the Highlands—Monk determines to build

PAGE

a fort at Inverlochy—The fort completed—Description of its position—
Sir Ewen Cameron of Lochiel—His early days—He joins the Royalist
forces under Glencairn—Gallant conduct at Braemar—His hatred of
the Sassenach intruders, ... 72

CHAPTER VIII.

Colonel Bryan sends two sloops of war to Loch Eil—Anger of the Cameron
chief—He decides to fight the English troops—Bravery of Alan Cameron
—The fight at Achdalieu—Deadly combat between Lochiel and the
English commander—Narrow escape of Lochiel—Anecdote of Lochiel's
visit to London—Lochiel joins the army under General Middleton—
Desperate skirmish between the Camerons and the English near Inverlochy—Lochiel agrees to a treaty of peace with the English—Amicable
meeting of Lochiel and the officers of the garrison, . . . 77

CHAPTER IX.

Restoration of Charles II.—Argyll throws himself upon the king's mercy—
His execution—The effect of the Restoration upon the Covenanters—
Death of Charles II. and accession of James II.—The Prince of Orange—
The Keppoch Murder—Iain Lom vows vengeance against the murderers—
He appeals to the MacDonald chieftains for assistance—The bard fulfils
his vow—" Tobar nan Ceann," 86

CHAPTER X.

The Clan Chattan—Coll of Keppoch—His ancestry—Mackintosh disputes
Keppoch's right to the Lochaber estates—Battle of Mulroy (*Meall Ruadh*)
—Desperate encounter between Mackenzie of Suddy and MacDonald of
Tulloch—Death of Mackenzie—" The red-haired Bo-man "—Defeat of
Mackintosh—The fight for the standard—Description of the battle by
a tobacco-spinner's apprentice from Inverness—His future career—
Mackintosh a prisoner—Arrival of the Macphersons—Mackintosh re-
leased and escorted to Moy—Dress of the Highlanders of the period—
James II. renders himself obnoxious to the Protestant party—Imprisonment
of the bishops—Birth of a prince—William of Orange lands at Torbay—
King James retires to France, ... 92

CHAPTER XI.

Bonnie Dundee—His youth and education—Supernatural powers attributed
to Dundee—Created Viscount Dundee—" Iain Dubh nan Cath "—Rising
of the Highlanders—Coll of Keppoch besieges Inverness—Dundee arrives
at Inverness—General Hugh MacKay of Scourie—Appointed by the Prince
of Orange as Major-General of the forces in Scotland—Inverness pays
indemnity to Keppoch—Quarrels in the Highland army—Advance of
General MacKay to Forres, ... 104

CHAPTER XII.

PAGE

Lochaber in 1689 A.D.—Sir Ewen Cameron of Lochiel and king James II.—
Characteristic anecdote—Lochiel and the Sheriff of Inverness—Overtures
made to Lochiel by the rival commanders—The gathering of the clans at
Moy—Macaulay's description of the muster—The Highlanders difficult to
control—Lochiel refuses to adopt the new method of warfare,   .   .   III

CHAPTER XIII.

Dissensions in the camp at Moy—Old feuds break out—Quarrel between
Glengarry and Lochiel—MacKay advises the Government to establish a
strong garrison at Inverlochy—The witch "Gormshuill"—The wreck of
the "Florida"—Dundee writes to MacLeod—Expected arrival of Irish
troops at Inverlochy—The character of Dundee—Killiecrankie—Heroic
death of Dundee—The victory largely due to the advice of Lochiel and
Glengarry—Narrow escape of Lochiel—His contempt for luxury,   .   117

PART II.—FORT WILLIAM.

CHAPTER XIV.

General MacKay granted permission to build a fort at Inverlochy—He proceeds
to Lochaber—Iain Lom—Lochiel deplores his inability to attack MacKay
—The erection of Fort William, and its effect upon the district—The
"Craigs" burial-ground—Submission of the Highland chiefs—MacIain
of Glencoe remains obstinate—Events that led up to the Massacre of
Glencoe—The massacre, ...   127

CHAPTER XV.

Jacobite sympathies of the Lochaber chiefs—Breadalbane suggests the employment of Highlanders as soldiers—Death of James II. at St Germains—
Proclamation of James III.—His recognition by Louis XIV. as king of
Great Britain and Ireland—Death of William of Orange—Accession of
Anne—The Crown settled upon the Electress of Hanover—Anger of
the Jacobite party—Hunting match in the Highlands—Schools in Fort
William—Death of Iain Lom—Anecdote of Iain Lom and the Marquis
of Argyll—Death of Anne—The Elector of Hanover proclaimed king
as George I., ...   137

CHAPTER XVI.

Effect of the accession of George I. upon the Lochaber chiefs—The Earl of
Mar—His overtures to the Elector of Hanover—His dismissal from the
Court—"The Standard on the Braes of Mar"—The chiefs at first refuse
to take up arms—Attack on Fort William by the Highlanders under
General Gordon—The Lochaber clans join the forces under Mar—The
battle of Sheriffmuir—Death of the captain of Clanranald—Loyal speech

of Sir John MacLean—Rob Roy at Sheriffmuir—Visit of Rob Roy to
Fort William — He intercepts the despatches in Glen Dochart — John
Cameron of Lochiel unpopular—Mar's incapacity as a general,   .   .   146

CHAPTER XVII.

Landing of James VIII. (The Chevalier) at Peterhead—Strange vision of
Lochiel—Second-sight—Description of Sir Ewen Cameron's appearance
at this period — His reply to the English officer — Description of the
Chevalier — Disappointment of the Highlanders — Departure of the
Chevalier and the Earl of Mar, ...   155

CHAPTER XVIII.

End of the Rebellion of 1715—The Highlanders ordered to surrender their
arms — Lochiel, Keppoch, and Clanranald remain obstinate — They
eventually yield—Only worthless arms given up—Lochaber in peace—
Death of Sir Ewen Cameron of Lochiel — His character — Donald
Cameron succeeds his grandfather—Sir Ewen's posterity—Character of
Donald Cameron of Lochiel—General Wade's report on the Highlands
in 1724—The Creach—Tasgal money—Last feudal execution in Scotland—"Domhnull donn" and Lochiel—Power of the chiefs—Lochiel
endeavours to improve the moral status of his clan,   .   .   .   160

CHAPTER XIX.

State of the Highlands in 1724—Marshal Wade sent to Inverness by the
English Government — His suggestions for improving the condition of
the Highlands—He recommends the formation of a Highland militia—
Commissions granted to Highland gentlemen — Lochiel suspected of
corresponding with the Chevalier—Alan Cameron sent to Lochaber—
The Black Watch—Marshal Wade commences road-making—The new
roads disliked by the Highlanders — Captain Burt — His letters — His
description of Fort William—Amusing account of an ascent of Ben
Nevis—Pathetic story of the famine in Fort William, .   .   .   167

PART III.—THE "FORTY-FIVE."

CHAPTER XX.

Retrospective notes—Marriage of the Chevalier—Birth and early years of
Prince Charles Edward—Alan Cameron's mission to the Highland
chiefs—The Chevalier's letter to Lochiel—Death of George I. and accession of George II.—The Chevalier dissuaded from attempting a *coup
d'état*—Coll of Keppoch at the Chevalier's Court—His death—Friendship of Prince Charles for Alexander of Keppoch—Lochaber the cradle
of the "Forty-Five"—Lochiel pledged to assist the Jacobite cause —
Lochaber expectant, ...   177

CHAPTER XXI.

PAGE

The "Forty-five"—Arrival of Prince Charles in the Highlands—Lochiel
embarrassed—Cameron of Fassfern endeavours to dissuade Lochiel from
meeting the prince—Lochiel and Prince Charles—The rising of the
Lochaber clans—The MacDonalds—Keppoch strikes the first blow—
The skirmish at High Bridge—Surrender of Captain Scott,   .   .   183

CHAPTER XXII.

The prince arrives in Glenfinnan—His disappointment at the absence of the
Highlanders—The Camerons and MacDonalds of Keppoch join the prince
—The story of Jenny Cameron, ...   189

CHAPTER XXIII.

The standard raised in Glenfinnan—Enthusiasm of the Highlanders—Prince
Charles no "Pretender"—MacLeod refuses to join the prince—The
prince at Fassfern—He proceeds to Moy—The Highland clans continue
to come in—The retreat of General Cope from Corrieyairack—The
prince's toast—Cluny MacPherson comes in—The prince determines to
march to Edinburgh, ...   195

CHAPTER XXIV.

Loyalty of the Lochaber chiefs—Lady Mackintosh raises her husband's clan
for the prince's service—Prince Charles at Holyrood—Prestonpans—
Lochaber gentlemen slain—News reaches Lochaber of the prince's march
to Derby — The garrison at Fort William strengthened by General
Campbell — Retreat of the Highland army — Battle of Falkirk—
MacDonald of Tirnadris taken prisoner — Lochiel and Dr Cameron
wounded—Accidental death of young Æneas MacDonell—The prince
arrives at Moy Hall—The rout of Moy—Prince Charles at Inverness—
Fort Augustus surrenders to the prince—Preparations for the siege of
Fort William, ...   202

CHAPTER XXV.

Description of Glen Nevis—The "Clach Shomhairle"—Cana grass—The
burial-ground of the Camerons of Glen Nevis—"Tom-eas-an-t-slinnein"
The septs of Clan Cameron—The Camerons of Glen Nevis—Glen Nevis
House—Highland hospitality, ...   213

CHAPTER XXVI.

The rocking stone—The hill of evil counsel—The massacres of the MacSorlies
—Escape of the young heir—His adventures—His meeting with Lochiel,
and ultimate restoration to his estates—Vitrified fort,   .   .   .   221

CHAPTER XXVII.

The legend of Deirdri, ... 227

CHAPTER XXVIII.

Description of Glen Nevis continued—"Acha-nan-con"—Achriabhach—The
Falls—Murder of a chieftain by Iain Beag MacAindrea—Further traditions
of Iain MacAindrea—Grand scenery of the glen—The "Cave of Somerled"
—Curious traditions connected with the cave—The Upper Falls of Nevis, 236

CHAPTER XXIX.

Detailed account of the siege of Fort William—The siege raised—Kilmallie,
its history and traditions—"Annat," probably of Druidical origin—
"Ailein nan Creach"—Grant of lands in Lochaber—Alan consults the
oracle of the "Tau Ghairm"—The Cat's Pool—Alan erects the seven
churches—Alan starts on a pilgrimage—Tor Castle and its traditions—
The parish of Kilmallie—Corpach—"Domhnull nan Ord," . . 241

CHAPTER XXX.

Prince Charles at Inverness—Advance of the Duke of Cumberland—Lochiel
arrives with his clan—The battle of Culloden—The Lochaber clans at
Culloden—Fatal error of Lord George Murray—Anger of the MacDonalds
—Desperate charge of the Camerons and Mackintoshes—Iain Mòr
Macgilvra—The MacDonalds refuse to fight—Appeal of Keppoch to
his clan—His heroic death—"Keppoch's Candlesticks"—The curse of
Keppoch—Lochiel wounded at Culloden—Culloden fatal to the Stuart
cause, ... 251

CHAPTER XXXI.

Brutality of the Duke of Cumberland after Culloden—"The Butcher"—Lady
Mackintosh taken prisoner—Her meeting with the Duke of Cumberland
in London—Flight of Prince Charles to the Highlands—The prince and
Lord Lovat—He arrives at Invergarry Castle—Sufferings of the Highlanders after Culloden—Privations of the prince—Money sent from France
—Meeting of the Highland chiefs at Murlaggan—Lord Loudoun ordered
to Fort Augustus—The hiding of the treasure—Lochiel and Dr Cameron
retire to Badenoch, ... 260

CHAPTER XXXII.

The Duke of Cumberland marches to Fort Augustus—A reign of terror in
Lochaber—Burning of the chiefs' houses—Brutal treatment of the
unarmed Highlanders—English troops in Glen Nevis—Disgraceful scenes

PAGE

at Fort Augustus—The duke visits Fort William—A tragic incident at
Fort William—Mrs Grant of Laggan—The wanderings of Prince Charles
—Fidelity of the Highlanders—Edward Burke—Flora MacDonald,   .   268

CHAPTER XXXIII.

Prince Charles returns to Lochaber—The prince and the farmer's wife—
Donald Cameron of Glenpean assists the prince—Dugald Roy Cameron's
son murdered by Captain Grant of Cnoc-ceanach—Death of Major Munro
of Culcairn—Wretched condition of the prince—Peter Grant guides
Prince Charles to Achnasaul—Lochiel endeavours to communicate with
the prince—Dr Archibald Cameron and the Rev. John Cameron start
for Loch Arkaig—Dr Cameron meets the prince's messenger and returns
with him to Lochiel—He again sets out for Lochaber—The prince's
friendship for Lochiel, ...   274

CHAPTER XXXIV.

Description of Loch Arkaig and its neighbourhood—Ach-na-carry—The
Mackintosh's Island—Prince Charles hides in a cave in the Black Mile—
Approach of the redcoats—Toilsome flight of the prince—Dr Cameron
conducts the prince to Lochiel at Mellaneuir—Meeting of the prince and
Lochiel—The regret of Cluny Macpherson that his clan was absent from
Culloden—Magnanimous speech of Prince Charles—Generosity of Sir
Stewart Thriepland, ...   283

CHAPTER XXXV.

Glenaladale watches for the French ships—Arrival of two French men-of-war
in Loch-nan-Uamh—Glenaladale sets out to convey the intelligence to the
prince—The prince and his followers cross the Lochy at Mucomer—The
Camerons of Mucomer—Prince Charles at Glen Camgharaidh—Mrs
Grant's eulogy on Lochiel—Character of Dr Archibald Cameron—Cameron
of Torcastle—Letter of Prince Charles to Cluny—Prince Charles's last
night in Lochaber—" Lochaber no more "—Embarkation of the fugitives
—Vain regrets—" Will ye no come back again ? ".   .   .   .   289

PART IV.—LOCHABER AFTER THE "FORTY-FIVE."

CHAPTER XXXVI.

The victims of the rebellion—Donald MacDonald of Keppoch—His defiant
attitude at his trial — Executions at Kennington Common — Horrible
barbarities—Anecdotes of MacDonald of Tirnadris told by Bishop Forbes
—He refuses to plead guilty—His loyalty to the cause—Execution of
Tirnadris and Kinlochmoidart at Carlisle—Bill of Attainder passed—
Names of the proscribed chiefs, ...   299

CHAPTER XXXVII.

PAGE

Lochaber desolate—"Rebel hunting"—Hugh Cameron of Anoch taken—
"Sergeant Mòr"—His career—Treachery detested by the Highlanders—
Act of Indemnity passed—Lochaber chieftains excluded from the benefits
of the Act—Disarming of the Highlanders—The Highland dress proscribed
—Indignation of the Highlanders—Amusing evasions of the Act—Act for
the abolition of hereditary jurisdiction—The Duke of Argyll receives
£21,000 compensation—The estates of the Jacobite chiefs forfeited, . 306

CHAPTER XXXVIII.

The Jacobite exiles—The Cameron chieftains at St Germains—John Cameron
of Lochiel accompanys Prince Charles to Fontainbleau—Reception by the
French king—Generosity of the French Government to the exiles—Young
Lochiel advises the prince to risk another expedition—The treaty of
Aix-la-Chapelle fatal to the Stuart cause—Its effect upon Prince Charles
—Death of John Cameron of Lochiel—Donald Cameron, "the Gentle
Lochiel," succumbs to an attack of brain fever—Poem in his praise—
Charles Cameron succeeds to the chieftainship of the clan—Account of
Dr Archibald Cameron's career, ... 313

CHAPTER XXXIX.

Colin Campbell of Glenure appointed factor on the forfeited estates in Lochaber
and Appin—His unpopularity in the district—Alan Breck Stewart—
Eviction of James Stewart of the Glen—Murder of Glenure—Alan Breck
suspected of the crime—Reward of £100 offered by the Lords Justices—
James Stewart arrested and imprisoned at Fort William—His trial at
Inveraray—A packed jury—The verdict—His execution at Ballachulish—
Probable guilt of Alan Breck deduced from the evidence—"Salm
Sheumais a Ghlinne"—Mrs Grant's (of Laggan) account of the crime, . 319

CHAPTER XL.

English garrisons posted in Lochaber—General Wolfe at Culloden—He
refuses to obey a barbarous order of the Duke of Cumberland—Dislike
of the English officers for the Highlands—Arrest of Dr Archibald
Cameron at Inversnaid—A brave Highland lassie—Trial of Dr Cameron
in London—Horrible sentence—The doctor conveyed to the Tower—
His wife pleads for pardon—Scene at the execution—The doctor's letters
—His last message to his son—The execution of Dr Cameron an act of
unnecessary severity—His last resting-place in the Savoy Chapel—
Memorial window, ... 326

CHAPTER XLI.

John Cameron of Fassfern and Alexander Stewart, W.S., of Banavie arrested
and imprisoned at Fort William—Committed to Edinburgh Castle—
Fassfern liberated on bail, but afterwards rearrested on a charge of

PAGE

forgery—His trial and sentence—William Pitt recognises the merits of
the Highlanders—Letters of service issued for the raising of Highland
regiments—Popularity of military service among the Highlanders—Pitt's
tribute to Highland courage—Fraser's Highlanders largely officered by
Lochaber gentlemen—Uniform of the regiment described—Tact of the
War Office authorities in respecting the Highland customs—Captain
Donald MacDonald killed at Quebec—Ranald MacDonell of Keppoch—
Legitimacy of Angus, chief of Keppoch, questioned—His parentage and
history—He abdicates the chieftainship in favour of Ranald—Keppoch
House—The story of "*A' bhaintigearna bheag*"—John of Keppoch and
Prince Charles, ...   335

CHAPTER XLII.

Death of the Old Chevalier (James VIII.)—Marriage of Prince Charles to
Louisa of Stolberg—Unhappy result—Melancholy condition of the prince
—His *liaison* with Clementina Walkinshaw—A vindication of the prince's
character—His daughter Charlotte attends him in his last illness—His
death and burial in St Peter's, Rome—Prince Henry succeeds his brother
—His death in 1807—Accession of George III., and its effect upon the
Highlands—Loyal Lochaber—Lochaber, the nursery of the Highland
regiments—Duncan MacPherson of Cluny—Story of his birth—Lochiel's
return to Lochaber—Characteristic remark of an old Highlander—Lochiel
receives a captain's commission in the 71st Regiment—The Camerons
refuse to embark without their chief—Death of Charles Cameron of
Lochiel—Restoration of the forfeited estates, ...   343

CHAPTER XLIII.

Keppoch's claim to his estates disputed by the Crown—He is allowed to reside
at Keppoch on payment of a nominal rent—Alan Cameron of Errachd—
His ancestry — "*A' bhanntrach ruadh*" — Duel between Errachd and
Murshiorlaich—Death of Murshiorlaich, and flight of Errachd—He joins
the Royal Highland Emigrant Regiment—He returns to Lochaber and
raises the Cameron Volunteers—Ranald of Keppoch assists in bringing in
recruits—History of the Errachd tartan—Pibroch of Donald Dhu,   .   352

CHAPTER XLIV.

Brief sketch of the history of the "Cameron Highlanders"—War Office
interference—Indignation of Errachd—The Camerons in the West Indies—
Deplorable condition of the regiment—Recruiting in Lochaber—Egmont-
op-Zee—The 79th brigaded with the 92nd Regiment—John Cameron of
Fassfern—The Camerons in Egypt—Proposed abolition of the kilt—
"*Am Breacan Uallach*"—Colonel Cameron's arguments in favour of the
kilt—He carries his point—Errachd retires from the active command of
the regiment — Colonel Philip Cameron — Heroic death of Captain
Alexander Cameron at Busaco—Colonel Philip Cameron slain at Fuentes

PAGE

d'Onor—Errachd retires from the army with the rank of lieutenant-general—His death—His descendants—Glorious record of the Camerons—Disbandment contemplated by the authorities—A second battalion wanted, ...   359

CHAPTER XLV.

The birthplace of John Cameron of Fassfern—Inverscadale described—Ewen MacMillan—John Cameron's early years—He joins the army—The raising of the Gordon Highlanders—The Duchess of Gordon's original method of recruiting—Huntly visits Fassfern—A captain's commission offered to John Cameron—He joins the Gordons with a hundred of his clansmen,   .   369

CHAPTER XLVI.

1815 A.D.—Napoleon the would-be dictator of Europe—The Powers determine his overthrow—The night before Waterloo—Colonel John Cameron at the Duchess of Richmond's ball—The 92nd ordered to the front—Quatre Bras—Charge of the 92nd—Colonel Cameron mortally wounded—The death scene—Impressive funeral at Kilmallie—Heraldic honours—Baronetcy conferred upon Ewen Cameron of Fassfern—Anecdote of Colonel Cameron and the Turkish (?) pasha, ...   374

CHAPTER XLVII.

Famous military heroes of Clan Cameron — Sir Alexander Cameron of Inverailort—Sir Duncan Alexander Cameron at the battle of the Alma—"We'll hae nane but Highland bonnets here!"—Death of George III.—George IV. ascends the throne—His appearance in Highland dress at Holyrood—A Sassenach Highlander—Accession of Queen Victoria—Loyalty defined—The Queen visits Lochaber—The Prince Consort—The royal party at Ardverikie, ...   381

CHAPTER XLVIII.

Sir Duncan Cameron of Fassfern—His philanthropic actions—His death in 1863 — Mrs Cameron Campbell of Monzie — Dr Alexander Stewart ("Nether Lochaber")—Description of Nether Lochaber—The road from Fort William—Beautiful scenery—Onich —"Sliochd a ghamhna mhaoil Duinn"—A quaint lullaby—View from Onich Pier—Cameron of Callart in the '45—Curious tradition of the Isle of St Mun—The ss. "Chevalier,"   .   388

CHAPTER XLIX.

The Caledonian Canal—James Watt employed to survey the ground—Telford's estimate accepted by Parliament—The canal opened for navigation in 1822—Public rejoicings in Lochaber—Traffic suspended—Reconstruction of the canal in 1847—The West Highland Railway—Its probable effect upon Lochaber—The Crofters Act and the Deer Forest Commission,   .   396

d

CHAPTER L.

PAGE

The present Lochiel and Lady Margaret Cameron—The Keppoch lands pass
to the Mackintosh—Angus of Keppoch—The present representatives of
the MacDonells of Keppoch—Lord Abinger purchases the Inverlochy
estates from the Earl of Aboyne — Queen Victoria's second visit to
Lochaber — Triumphal arch at Keppoch — Enthusiastic reception—The
Queen at Inverlochy — She visits Lochiel at Ach-na-carry — Jacobite
sympathies of the Queen—A royal speech—Conclusion,   .   .   .   402

APPENDIX, ...   413

ADDENDA, ...   461

INDEX, ...   479

LOCHABAIR GU BRÀTH.

(LOCHABER FOR EVER.)

IN all thy moods I love thee,
    In sunshine and in storm;
Lochaber of the towering bens,
    Outlined in rugged form.
.Here proud Ben Nevis, snowy crowned,
    Rests throned amidst thé clouds;
There Lochy's deep and silvery wave,
    A royal city shrouds;
Whose waters witnessed the escape
Of coward Campbell's dastard shape,
    Disgrace eternal reap:
Whilst fair glen Nevis' rocks resound,
With " Pibroch Donald Dubh " renowned,
    From Inverlochy's keep.
Grey ruined walls, in latter years,
    That saw the great Montrose,
MacDonell's, Cameron's men led forth,
    To victory 'gainst their foes.
Oh! Lochaber, dear Lochaber,
    The rich red afterglow
Of fame that rests upon thy shield,
    Unbroken records show.
" *O, Lochabair, mo Lochabair fhein gu bràth.*" [1]

Lochaber, on thy heather hills,
    The fame of heroes rest;
Each name in Scotia's annals famed,
    Found echo in thy breast:
Historic Keppoch, desert now,
    Speak from thy ruined mound,
The days when Claverhouse, noblest chief,
    Thine aid and shelter found.

[1] Oh, Lochaber, my own Lochaber for ever.

Tell how the hot MacDonell blood,
Impetuous as the mountain flood,
 The first for Charlie bled.
'Tis writ where high o'er Spean spans
The bridge where triumphed first the clans,
 Scott's white horse captive led :
Whilst stately Spean, tumbling Roy,
 Eternal requiems sing,
For those around whose honoured names,
 Both faith and honour cling.
Oh, Lochaber, dear Lochaber,
 You played a losing stroke ;
But your failure, oh how greater !
 It was lost for honour's sake,
" *O, Lochabair, mo Lochabair fhein gu bràth.*"

In all thy moods I love thee,
 Thy far off classic days,
When Ossian mused by dark Loch Treig,
 The home of prisoned fays.
How green Strath-h-Ossian's fairy saw,
 The dark-eyed lad from Skye ;
His stately limbs, his hunter's bow,
 In wild confusion fly.
Around her grouped her timid fawns,
Dilated fear upon them dawns,
 They feel the snare :
As graceful poised with honeyed speech,
The hunter strove the fay to reach,
 Sweet fay beware !
The antlered herd around her grouped,
 With quiet and trustful eye,
They knew their queen would ne'er condemn
 Her loving friends to die,
 For all the dark-eyed lads from Skye.
Oh, Lochaber, dear Lochaber,
 Thy wooded glens and braes,
Teem with the tales of chivalry,
 That speak of other days.
" *O, Lochabair, mo Lochabair fhein gu bràth.*"

In all thy moods I love thee,
  But I think I love thee best,
When the moon is rising slowly
  Behind Beinn Chlinaig's crest;
To list the plaintive owlet calling,
  When the woods are very still,
The gentle plash of waters falling,
  Ringing, rhyming, down the hill;
So rich with flowers the river braes,
Whose honeyed perfume scents the ways,
    Sweet lingering on the air.
Wild purple bloom the heather shows,
O'er hanging rocks the rowan grows,
    Where scarce a foot may dare:
Enough it is among thy braes,
  To dream, to breathe, to live;
With the soul's repose of trustfulness,
  Whate'er the future give;
Across the hazy distance,
  Thy children look and long,
For thy spell is found resistless,
  And their hearts beat true and strong.
" O, Lochabair, mo Lochabair fhein gu bràth."

ALICE C. MacDonell
  of Keppoch.

INTRODUCTION.

"For Lochaber no more, Lochaber no more;
We'll maybe return to Lochaber no more."
—ALLAN RAMSAY.

LOCHABER! Unsympathetic indeed is the man, be he Highlander or Lowlander, Gael or Sassenach, who does not experience a thrill of pleasurable emotion, tinged perhaps with sadness, when this name falls upon his ears; what visions of lofty mountains lifting their mighty summits to the clouds does it not conjure up before the imagination; we see as in a dream, stretches of purple moorland, dotted here and there with snow-white sheep; blue sparkling lochs embosomed among the hills, reflecting in their mirrored surface the brown sails of the fishing boats; turbulent rivers rushing merrily along over rocks and pebbles, making sweet music as they go to join the sea; foaming cataracts tumbling noisily from deep corries in the mountain sides, sending up clouds of smoke-like spray, in which all the colours of the rainbow gleam; wee murmuring burns, where the brown trout love to dwell, flowing between banks all thick with ferns and foxgloves, their tuneful voices helping to swell the great harmonious Lobgesang to the Almighty.

If this is the vision, how much more beautiful is the reality. Let us take our stand upon the great green hill of "*Meall-an-t-suidhe*," that forms as it were the first step in the toilsome ascent of giant Ben Nevis, and is appropriately named "the hill of sitting or resting"; here let us pause for a few moments and survey the magnificent prospect that lies before us. The air around is fragrant with the scent of wild thyme and bog myrtle, with which the ground at our feet is covered; great clumps of

A

purple heather, growing here in wild luxuriance, give the one
touch of local colour that is wanted to harmonise with the tints
of the surrounding vegetation. Among the heather the bees go
humming merrily as they extract the honey from its tiny bells.
The sheep are grazing lazily in the shade of the great lichen-
covered boulders, or, perched upon some inaccessible crag,
nibble the short sweet grass they have discovered in the clefts
of the rocks, regardless of the precipice yawning at their feet.
A great silence, like the silence of some immense cathedral, is
all about us, broken only at rare intervals by the shrill scream
of an eagle, as it swoops down from its rocky eyry upon its
unsuspecting prey in the glen beneath; this and the occasional
harsh crow of the grouse cock among the heather, are the only
sounds that fall upon our ears.

The very air is still on this calm September day, and as we
rest in the shadow of the everlasting hills, far above the turmoil
and strife of the world below, our whole being thrills with the
pleasure of mere existence, and we realise, perhaps for the first
time in our lives, what a great gift is life, and how much we
have to thank our Creator for its possession. Gaze out upon
the splendid panorama that is unfolded before our astonished
eyes, and as we glance from one prospect to another, each one
more beautiful than the last, let us try to learn something of the
history and associations of "the land where Ossian dwelt, and
Coila's minstrel sang," a veritable *tir nam beann nan gleann's
nan gaisgeach*,[1] full of the romantic myths of a past and nearly
forgotten age, when the world was younger and less prosaic
than in this enlightened nineteenth century. What care the
money-grubbers in our great cities for shadowy legends of the
brave chieftains who lived and died among these mountains;
or the heroic stanzas of the warrior bard's description of the
mighty battles where Fingalian heroes met in all the glorious
panoply of war, making the hills and glens resound with the
clash of their weapons? This is indeed an age devoid of poetry
and sentiment, when gold, gold, gold, is the chief aim and

[1] Land of mountains, glens, and heroes.

object of existence; the great god Mammon is set up in our midst like the golden calf of old, and we jostle and struggle among the ever-surging crowd of humanity to catch some of the golden pieces thrown among us by those that minister in the temple of the false god; crushing and treading under our feet the weak and the maimed, the widow and the orphan, lest perchance one coin may slip from our grasp; feverish and excited, we pass onward to the goal of our ambitions, to find at last that the fruit of years of scheming and toil, like Dead Sea apples, turns to ashes in our mouth.

Here above the struggling multitude, and alone with God's beautiful creation, we can forget for a few brief moments our poor mundane affairs, in the contemplation of all that is grand and soul-stirring in nature; and while, gentle reader, you are thus engaged, let me act as your guide, philosopher, and friend, and with story and verse, while away an hour or so of what I trust will not be time ill spent.

of a ferocious breed, of which some were known to exist as
late as the sixteenth century.   Probably the first building
erected on the site of the present ruin was simply a rude hut
or hunting-lodge, where the king and his nobles might find
shelter when they came here deer-stalking; a primitive shooting-
box, in fact.   This theory is borne out by the local traditions,
which without this interpretation could only be considered
mythical—that the original castle was built by the Picts in a
single night.   When, however, we consider that it was the
constant practice of that ancient people to build their houses
of turf and wattles, there is nothing improbable in the story,
as doubtless one of the long summer nights of these latitudes
would amply suffice for the purpose.

The old chroniclers, Fordun and Hector Boetius, have much
to say respecting the early history of Inverlochy, and although
a great deal that they have written on the subject must be
rejected as pure fable, there is doubtless some probability of
truth underlying the various graphic descriptions they give of
the building of this ancient stronghold.   Boetius tells us that
King Ewin, the second of that name, not only built a castle, but
a city at Inverlochy, some years before the commencement of the
Christian era.   Hollinshed thus translates from the original
Latin : " After this he (King Ewin) visited the west parts of
his realme, and at the mouth of the Lochtey (Lochy) he builded
a citie, which he named Ennerlochtey, infranchising the same
with a sanctuarie for the refuge of offenders.   This citie afterwards
was much frequented with merchants of France and Spain, by
reason of the great abundance of samons, herrings, and other fish
which was taken there.   The old ruins of this citie in parte
remaine to be seen to this day."

We hear no more of Inverlochy until the year 180 A.D., when
the same chronicler describes how word was brought to King
Ethodius, who was then living there, that the Romans had
broken down the wall of Adrian, and had made a great raid into
Scotland under their commander Victorine, and were carrying
death and destruction in their wake.   Later, in the year 273 A.D.,

Donald of the Isles landed in Ross with a large following of islandmen, and having overthrown the army of King Donald, the third son of Athires, in a pitched battle, proclaimed himself king. For a while he held his own by force of arms, but eventually fell a victim to the conspiracies of his enemies, who, taking him by surprise, murdered him one night at Inverlochy.

About two centuries and a half after this event, we are told by Fordun (a more reliable chronicler than Boetius), that King Gonranus, having completed his thirty-fourth year on the throne, was ensnared into an ambuscade at Inverlochy by his nephew Eugenius and put to death.[1] Another catastrophe occurred in close proximity to the ancient castle in the year 647 A.D., when, if Boetius may be believed, King Donwald, then in the fifteenth year of his reign, "being got into a bote to fish in the water called Lochtaie (Lochy), for his recreation, his chance was to be drowned, by reason the bote sank under him."

The old stronghold of Inverlochy is brought into special prominence in connection with the traditionary visit of the illustrious Carlovingian emperor, Charlemagne, to the Pictish king Eoghan mac Aodh (Eocha IV., Latinised as Achaius), in the ninth century, and it is still believed by many that a treaty was signed here by the two monarchs, and was witnessed by no less than sixteen members of the great family of Comyn. This story is now proved to have been a fable; but there is little doubt that although Inverlochy was not honoured by the presence of the mighty Charlemagne in person, his ambassadors visited the place when they came over from France on a mission to King Eocha, with the purpose of persuading that monarch to enter into a treaty for the mutual protection of the two nations against the depredations of the English.

Hollinshed, quoting from Hector Boetius, who flourished in Dundee in the fourteenth century, writes: "There were sent therefore from Charles unto Achaius certaine ambassadors to bring this matter to pass; who arriving in Scotland and coming into the king's presence declared effectualie the sum of their message,

---

[1] Fordun's "Scotichronicon," lib. iii. cap. xxiv.

showing that the conclusion of such a league should be no less
to the wealthe of the Frenchmen, than of the Scots."

The Frankish ambassadors were received with the greatest
honours by Eocha, and after a lengthy discussion, and many
long speeches on the part of the Pictish counsellors, the treaty
was agreed upon and signed with due ceremony. The proceedings terminated by a great banquet, and the guests were
afterwards invited to take part in a royal deer hunt, during
which they probably visited Lochaber, where game of all kinds
was plentiful.

The contrast between the Frankish nobles and their Pictish
allies must have been striking and picturesque. The former,
clad in all the bravery of rich armour and splendid apparel,
bejewelled and emblazoned with the heraldic devices of their
respective families, and armed with magnificent weapons from
the famous forges of Spain. Fresh from the great conquests
they had helped their sovereign to achieve in Europe, where he
had just founded the kingdom of the Franks, they must have
excited the curiosity and admiration of the warlike tribes among
whom they were now going to enjoy the pleasures of the chase.

Although the Picts[1] could not compare with the Franks in
the splendour of their habiliments, they could yet attract
attention by the quaint picturesqueness of their national garb,
and the muscular development of their limbs. They were clad
for the most part in a parti-coloured garment folded round the
upper part of the body, and fastened at the shoulder by an
ornamental brass pin or brooch of large dimensions. The ends
of this ancient form of *breacan an fheilidh* were gathered in at
the waist by a leathern belt, and fell in folds as far as the knee,
leaving the lower part of the legs bare; but as some protection
against the thorns and thick undergrowth of the forests, many

[1] I may state here, that I consider the name "Picts" a misleading appellation
as applied to the ancient inhabitants of Caledonia. It is clearly of Latin origin, and
was never adopted by the people themselves, who were then, as they are now,
"Albannach," speaking a language practically identical with modern Gaelic. The
so-called "Pictish" language is, in my humble opinion, a myth.

of the Picts wore *cuaran, i.e.,* sandals of cow or deer hide with
the hair inside, and drawn neatly round the foot with thongs of
the same material. Their heads, of shaggy uncombed hair, were
mostly uncovered, but some wore caps or bonnets (*boineid*) of
woollen cloth, sometimes conical, but more often flat. Those
parts of the body that remained naked were covered with
designs pricked into the skin and stained with some vegetable
dye—a national custom which some centuries before had caused
the Romans to give them the name of *Pictus* or painted, by
which they have always been known to history. Among themselves they were simply *Albannach,* inhabitants of Albyn, a name
still retained by their descendants, the modern Highlanders.

For weapons they carried bows and arrows and the long
double-handed sword (*claidheamh mòr*), in the use of which they
were thoroughly proficient. Some bore spears (*lann*) for use in
hunting the wolf and wild boar, and nearly all had daggers or
dirks (*biodag*) thrust in the waist-belt. Slung over their backs
were small circular shields or targes of brass, bronze, or leather,
ornamented with metal bosses of a more or less elaborate workmanship, according to the rank of their owners.[1]

The Pictish chieftains could only be distinguished from their
more humble followers by the superior quality of their clothing
and weapons, and by the costly brooch or fibula with which
their mantles or plaids were fastened. Many of these brooches
were very beautifully chased with quaint designs of Celtic
ornament, and were set with crystals and precious stones of
great value. A few of the more important chiefs wore chain
mail of exquisite workmanship, over leather jerkins, and had
flowing mantles of several colours reaching to their feet; while
for head-gear they wore helmets (*clogaid*) of brass or bronze
adorned with an eagle's wing.

[1] Ossian, describing the shield of the chief of Atha, says, "Seven bosses rose on
the shield; the seven voices of the king, which his warriors received from the wind
and marked over all their tribes. On each boss is placed a star of night"
("Temora," book vii.). The stars which were represented by the seven bosses,
were, Cean-mathon, Col-derna, Ul-oicho, Cathlin, Reul-durath, Berthin, and
Tonthena, and were doubtless connected with some ancient astrological superstition.

After spending some weeks in feasting and other amusements, the ambassadors returned to France ; and King Eocha, to show his sense of the importance of the treaty he had just signed, sent his brother William and four of his nobles, with a considerable retinue, to acquaint Charlemagne of his assent, and, as the story goes, he "did augment his armes, being a red lion in a field of gold, with a double trace seamed with *floure delices* ("fleur de lis"), signifying thereby that the lion should thereby be defended by the aid of the Frenchmen." Boetius also states that it was during the reign of this monarch that the St Andrew's Cross was adopted as the badge of Scotland.

There appears to have been a general belief among the older Scottish historians that a city of some considerable importance had existed in remote times by the shores of the river Lochy in Lochaber, where a considerable trade was carried on with foreign countries. Lesly, Bishop of Ross, who lived in the sixteenth century, referring more particularly to the ancient inhabitants of Lochaber, says that their women "were clothed with purple and embroidery of most exquisite workmanship, with bracelets and necklaces on their arms and necks, so as to make a most graceful appearance." [1]

"*Ad Louchæ ostia sita olim erat opulentissima civitas Inverlothæ appellata, ad quam Galli, Hispanique comercii causa frequentius trajecerant.*"

Camden in his "Britannia" also refers to this ancient castle or city, and compares it to Carthage, it having been, like that place, reduced to ruins. He also quotes some verses by a contemporary poet, Johnston, as follows :—

> "Two stately forts the realm's old guardians stood,
> The first great walls of royal builders prov'd ;
> Their lofty turrets, on the shores were shown,
> One to the rising, one the setting sun.
> All round, well stock'd with fish, fair rivers lay ;
> And one presents a safe, and easy bay."

---

[1] Translation from the Latin by Donald M'Nicol, A.M., Minister of Lismore, in his "Remarks on Dr Samuel Johnson's Journey to the Hebrides," 1779.

The two strongholds here described were the castle of Inverness on the east and Inverlochy on the west coast, the "safe and easy bay" having reference to Loch Eil.

A further and more complete account of Lochaber is given by Hector Boetius, and is thus translated by Hollinshed in 1585 A.D.:—"Beyond Lorne is Lochquhaber, heretofore a portion of Murray land (Morayshire), verie riche in mines of iron and lead, and no less beneficiall to the countrie in all kinds of cattell. There are likewise manie woods, manie lakes, and manie rivers; but two of them are most notable for the plentie of samons, and other delicate fish, as well of the salt, as the fresh water, which be there taken and almost without anie travaill; neither is there anie where else in all the Ile such store. The one of them is named Lochtie (Lochy), and the other Spanze (Spean), but upon what occasion these names were given to them, I find as yet no certaintie. . . . In the mouth of Lochtie likewise was sometime a riche toune named Inverlochtie, whither the merchants of France and Spain did make theire dailie resort, till at last it was so defaced by the warres of the Danes, that it never was able since the said time to recouver her prestine renoune. But whether the negligence of the due repaire of the towne, proceedeth of the slouth of our people, or hatred that some envious persones doe beare to cities and walled townes in our countrie, as yet is uncertaine."

Boetius's explanation of the meaning of the name Lochaber, affords conclusive proof that he did not understand the Gaelic language. He says, according to his translation, "Lochquhaber took the name of a great meare of water, into which the river of the Quhaber falleth and passeth through the same." To those of my readers who, like Hector Boetius, "have no Gaelic," I will pause to explain, that the name of the beautiful and historical district of Lochaber is derived from *Loch* ("lake") and *Aber*[1] ("confluence"), *i.e.*, the loch at the confluence of two

---

[1] Some authorities say the word should be *Eabar* ("a muddy place"), and certainly this has some probability of truth, as the place where the loch existed is of that character. Alexander MacBain, M.A., of Inverness, is of opinion that Lochaber is derived from *Loch*, "lake," and *Apor*, an old Gaelic word meaning "marsh."

rivers. The rivers in this case being either the Lochy and the Nevis, or the Lochy and the Spean. The loch itself no longer exists, but its waters are said to have covered the whole of the tract of boggy land that extends from the west side of the Lochy beyond the suspension bridge to Corpach and Banavie, and which is now known as the Corpach Moss. Some of the oldest inhabitants say they can recollect the last remnant of this once large sheet of water disappearing after an abnormally hot summer. In John Speeds map of Scotland, dated 1630, Loch Linnhe is not shown, but the arm of the sea which stretches from the island of Mull to Inverlochy ("Everlothæ" he calls it) appears as Loch-Aber; and as further bearing upon the subject, there is a place marked on this map on the Ardgour or Morven side, called "Quhabyr," which may perhaps be identified with the small Loch-nan-Gabhar, near Salachan.

After the reign of Eocha IV., who died in 833 A.D.,[1] the historical references to Lochaber, or Inverlochy, are few and far between, and it is not until the eleventh century that any important event worthy of being recorded occurred there. The unfortunate King Duncan I. ascended the throne of Scotland 1034 A.D., upon the death of his grandfather Malcolm II. At this time his kinsman Macbeth (or Macbeda) was Maormor of Moray, and ruled in almost independent state a large portion of the northern and western Highlands. The Maormordom of Moray at that period appears to have extended to the borders of Lochaber, and probably comprised some portion of that district. There is a tradition still extant, that Macbeth had a stronghold on an island in the centre of Loch Lundavra,[2] a small lake which lies between Fort William and Callart on Loch Leven, and that it was at this place that he was murdered in 1057.

Mrs MacKellar, late bardess to the Gaelic Society of Inverness, in proof of this story, quotes the Chronicle of St Berchan [3]

---

[1] These dates are of course approximate.

[2] This loch gives its name to a family of Camerons, called the Camerons of Lundavra.

[3] See Appendix II.

(*Trans. Gaelic Society*, vol. xvi. p. 267), which states that Macbeth was killed at his habitation of Deabhra; and Skene says this was a lake in the forest of Mamore, on an island of which there was a castle of Mamore, and refers in support of this theory to the names of the places in the immediate neighbourhood, viz., *Gleann Righ* ("The King's Glen"), *Abhainn Righ* ("The King's River"). Following up this line of reasoning, Mrs MacKellar makes the name of the loch *Loch-da-rath*, and the castle *Dun-da-rath*, and mentions there being two apparently artificial islands still remaining. From personal investigation I must admit there is every probability of truth in this statement. Further evidence as to the identity of Dun-da-rath with Lundavra will be found in the "Scots Acts of Parliament," vol. ii. pp. 241-249, when James IV. grants a life-rent of Mamore and castle on the island of Dundavray to one of the Stewarts of Appin. The whole of this district teems with interest to the antiquarian, and much may be learnt from the local place-names, many of which are clearly of Druidical, or at least clerical, origin.

Blarmachfhuildaich, as it appears on the maps, but pronounced *Blar-mac-Cuilteach*, means "the field of the son of the Culdee"; *Blar-nan-Clèirach* and *Meall-nan-Clèirach*, respectively "the field of the Clerks" and "the hill of the Clerks"; *Blar-mac-Druidheachd*, "the field of the son of the Druid." There is no more conclusive evidence of the antiquity of the Gaelic language than is afforded by such names as these.

While Macbeth was Maormor of Moray, the government of Lochaber was in the hands of his kinsman Banquo, and, if the old chroniclers are to be believed, he found his vassals somewhat unruly. We are told that having aroused their ire by the severe punishments he had inflicted, they broke out into open rebellion against his authority, under the leadership of one MacDonald ("the merciless MacDonwald"[1] of Shakespeare). A severe fight ensued, in which Banquo was wounded, and, finding himself completely overpowered, he fled from Lochaber

---

[1] "Macbeth," Act i. Scene 2.

to lay his grievances before King Duncan, and implore his assistance. The king, having heard the story, despatched one of his officials to the disaffected district to summon the insurgent chief to appear before him, and answer for his crime. Instead of obeying the royal command, MacDonald treated it with scorn, and slew the messenger. The king, enraged at this insult to his authority, ordered Macbeth and Banquo to proceed at once into Lochaber at the head of a strong body of men-at-arms, and enforce obedience among his rebellious Highland subjects. The two nobles therefore departed on their errand, and, arriving in Lochaber, gave battle to the insurgents. MacDonald, seeing that he was likely to be overcome, sought shelter with his family within the walls of a castle, and when he found that the day was lost, he slew his wife and children, and lastly himself. Upon Macbeth entering, he found the heap of slain, and so cruel was his nature that he ordered the dead man's head to be cut off and sent to the king, and put a great number of the rebels to the sword without mercy.

It has been claimed for Banquo, Thane of Lochaber, that he was the progenitor of the great Stuart dynasty; and although grave doubts have been cast upon the authenticity of the tradition by many of the leading Scottish historians, it is worthy of a place in any work that professes to give a full account of the historic district over which he ruled, and its appearance in these pages, therefore, needs no apology.

After the murder of Duncan, Macbeth's guilty conscience made him afraid lest the prophecy of the weird sisters should come true, and that Banquo might supersede him.

> " Our fears in Banquo
> Stick deep ; and in his royalty of nature
> Reigns that which would be fear'd : 'tis much he dares ;
> And, to that dauntless temper of his mind,
> He hath a wisdom that doth guide his valour
> To act in safety. There is none but he
> Whose being I do fear ; and, under him,
> My genius is rebuked."

These are the words that Shakespeare puts into the mouth of the regicide, and in the end Macbeth determined to put his rival to death, and with that object invited him, together with his son Fleance, to a supper. The unsuspecting Banquo accepted the invitation, and was slain by the hired assassins of the unscrupulous king; but Fleance escaped into Wales, where he made his abode, and being a youth of noble bearing, and gifted with many knightly accomplishments, he soon attracted the attention of the prince of that country. Becoming enamoured of the prince's daughter, he got her with child, and thus brought down upon himself the wrath of her father, who slew him and cast off his erring daughter, who "had loved not wisely, but too well."

The fruit of this fatal amour proved to be a boy, who received the name of Walter, and grew up of great strength and courage, and developed many qualities worthy of his noble lineage. The circumstances of his birth were unfortunately known to his companions, who took a cowardly delight in taunting the unprotected lad with his illegitimate origin. So keenly did he feel these insults that he fled to Scotland, where, having attained to man's estate, he performed great deeds of valour, and was afterwards appointed Steward of Scotland, and became the progenitor of that remarkable family who for centuries ruled the destinies of Britain. For other and more authentic accounts of the origin of the royal House of Stuart, I must refer my readers to one of the many histories of that brave but unfortunate race.

The probable period of the erection of the castle we now see in ruins before us, was the latter end of the thirteenth century, during the stormy times of the wars between Bruce and Baliol, the latter, as all readers of history know, being supported by the powerful assistance of King Edward I. of England. At this time the great family of Comyns were Lords of Lochaber and the neighbouring district of Badenoch. Originally an English family of Norman descent from Northumberland, they acquired great power in Scotland, and flourished in strength from

1080 A.D. to 1330 A.D. Sir John Comyn, who was appointed ambassador from Alexander II. to Louis IX. of France, was the first of his name known as the Lord of Badenoch ; his son John was one of the nobles who, swore to support Queen Margaret, daughter of Alexander III., on her succession to the throne, and was one of the six regents who arranged her marriage with the eldest son of the English king, Edward I., and upon her death, in 1290 A.D., became one of the competitors for the Scottish Crown by right of his descent from Donald III. He was known and feared as the Black Lord of Badenoch, and lived in regal state among the mountains of Lochaber. To this chieftain may be ascribed the building of Inverlochy Castle ;[1] and he was doubtless assisted in the task by the English king, who had erected many similar fortresses in Wales to keep in awe his troublesome Welsh subjects. As we survey the scene, a brilliant shaft of sunlight rests for a moment upon the crumbling masonry of the two remaining towers, the more prominent of them still bearing the name of the Comyns Tower, and thus handing down to the present time the name of the once powerful' rulers of this beautiful district. It was the son of the Black Lord of Badenoch, by his wife the sister of Baliol, who became famous, or infamous, under the name of the Red Comyn, and it was he who incurred the wrath and animosity of Robert Bruce, which ended in his violent death in the Greyfriars Church in Dumfries. History relates that they met before the high altar of the church, and high words were given on both sides, until the fiery temper of Bruce could stand the insults no longer, and in a sudden burst of passion he drew his dagger and stabbed the Comyn, and without waiting to see if the wound was mortal, rushed to the door of the sacred building ; here he met Kirkpatrick of Closeburn, and James de Lindsay, two powerful barons, who, astonished at seeing their leader with a bloody weapon in his hand, asked Bruce what had occurred. Scarcely

---

[1] It is stated that he had two galleys, larger than any to be seen in the Isles, anchored near his castle : *quod juxta castrum Johannes Cumin in Lochaber duæ magnæ galeæ fuerunt etc.* (Stevenson's "Hist. Doc.," vol. ii. p. 190), quoted by Lady Middleton.

able to speak, owing to the excitement he was labouring under, Bruce answered, "Bad tidings, I doubt I have slain Comyn."

"Doubtest thou?" said Kirkpatrick, "I'll mak siccar" (*i.e.*, sure), and with these words the two barons hastily disappeared through the door and dispatched the dying Comyn, as he lay drenched in his blood at the foot of the great altar. From this act the Kirkpatricks assumed as a crest a hand holding a dagger, and as motto the words "I mak siccar." It is to this incident that Sir Walter Scott makes reference in the song, " The Brooch of Lorn," viz. :—

> " Vain was then the Douglas brand,
> Vain the Campbell's vaunted band,
> Vain Kirkpatrick's bloody dirk,
> Making sure of murder's work."

After the slaughter of their chieftain, the Comyns of Lochaber took up arms to avenge his death, and after a desperate battle at Barra in 1308, they were defeated by Bruce, their estates forfeited, and their chief outlawed. Tradition states that the last of the Comyns of Lochaber fled from Inverlochy along the shores of Loch Lochy and Loch Oich to where Fort Augustus now stands, and the place where he was buried is still known as " *Cille - Chuimein.*" Thus a great name faded away from Lochaber, the place knows it no more, and, with the solitary exception of the tower before mentioned, there is nothing to call to mind the days when the name of Comyn made the land tremble.

Among the more important Celtic tribes or clans that dwelt in Lochaber at this period were the Camerons and the Mackintoshes, the latter clan forming part of the great Highland confederacy known as the Clan Chattan. According to their own written tradition, the Camerons traced their descent from one of the Danish kings who had visited Scotland in the time of Fergus, and who, from a malformation of the nasal organ, had been nicknamed "Camshron," or "crooked

C

nose." This story is purely mythical, and cannot be supported by any trustworthy evidence. It is more probable that the Camerons were directly descended from the ancient Picts, and had dwelt in Lochaber from prehistoric times. In the eleventh century Angus Cameron, one of the chiefs of the clan, had married Marion, the daughter of Kenneth, Thane of Lochaber, and sister of Banquo, and this event may be taken as the first authentic record we have of the early ancestors of this distinguished family, whose deeds will occupy considerable space in these pages.

The Mackintoshes were not originally a Lochaber clan, if their own MS. history is to be taken as correct, as they are there stated to have been descended from Shaw or Seach, one of the sons of MacDuff, Earl of Fife, and held lands in Strathearn. It was by the marriage of Angus MacFerquhard, sixth chief of Mackintosh, with Eva, only child of Dougal Dall MacGillechattan, in 1291, that the Mackintoshes acquired with the chieftainship of Clan Chattan their Lochaber estates, among which were the lands of Glenlui and Loch Arkaig; and it was in connection with these lands that the sanguinary feud arose in 1370 between the Camerons and the Clan Chattan, which continued with more or less vigour until the seventeenth century. Many traditions exist respecting the origin of the quarrel, but the one most generally accepted as correct by the best authorities is as follows.

Sometime during the reign of Robert II., probably between the years 1380-90, William, chief of Mackintosh, after many fruitless attempts to collect his rents from the Camerons, who had possessed themselves of a large portion of his territory in Lochaber during the absence of his father Angus in Badenoch, became exasperated at their utter disregard of his rights, and determined to levy them by force. He therefore mustered a strong body of his clansmen, and placing himself at their head, made a sudden descent upon the Camerons,[1] and carried off a

---

[1] The chief of Clan Cameron at this period was Allan IX. of Lochiel, known as MacOchtery (*Mac ochdamh triath*, son of the eighth chief).

large number of their cattle in lieu of payment. This method
of rent collection did not at all suit the warlike Camerons, and
they very shortly took steps to wipe out the indignity they
had suffered. Headed by one of their chieftains, Charles
MacGillonie (of the Strone or Invermailie branch), the clan, to
the number of about four hundred, marched into Badenoch,
hoping to take the Mackintoshes by surprise. The foray was,
however, of too important a nature to be kept a secret, and
Mackintosh got wind of the approach of the attacking party
sometime before they reached Badenoch. On receiving this
intelligence, he called upon the other septs of the Clan Chattan
to assist him in defending his property against the invading
Camerons, and fixed a place named Invernahavon (*Inbher na-
h-abhainn*), at the junction of the rivers Spey and Truim, for
the rendezvous. On the appointed day, the powerful clan
MacPherson, and the smaller sept of Davidsons (*Clan Dhaibhidh*),
arrived with a numerous following, and proceeded to take up
their position in battle array, and hold themselves in readiness
for the expected attack.

And here one of those foolish and injudicious quarrels for
precedence took place, which so often have to be recorded by
the chronicler of Highland history. These disputes (of which
the fatal one on Culloden field furnished a striking example)
arose in the first instance from an inordinate pride of birth,
and intolerance of any superior authority on the part of the
Highland chieftains. Their independent spirits could not brook
the least restraint, and any interference with their prerogatives
or hereditary privileges, however much the force of circumstances demanded it, was considered in the light of a serious
insult, which only blood could avenge. In this instance the
quarrel arose between the chiefs of MacPherson and Davidson
on a question of precedency. Mackintosh, as captain of Clan
Chattan, assumed, as a matter of course, the command of the
centre of the line, but upon Davidson of Invernahavon forming
up his clan on the right wing of the army, Cluny MacPherson
uttered an indignant protest, asserting that the position

belonged to him by prescriptive right, and appealed to Mackintosh to support his claim. Mackintosh refused to do so, and decided in favour of Invernahavon,[1] much to the annoyance of Cluny, who was so offended at the slight, that he withdrew his clan from the field just as the Camerons were seen approaching. The defection of the MacPhersons at this critical moment was most unfortunate, as the Camerons now outnumbered their opponents by nearly two to one; but it was too late to patch up the quarrel now, and the Mackintoshes and Davidsons had to withstand the onset of MacGillonie and his bold warriors as well as they could.

The battle now began, and the consequences were most disastrous for the Davidsons, as we are told that they were nearly all slain by the Camerons. Mackintosh and his clan were hard pressed, and would probably have met the same fate as their comrades, had not Cluny, forgetting in the excitement of the moment all that had taken place, joined in the conflict. This considerable accession of numbers completely turned the scale, and in a few moments the Camerons were utterly routed, and few escaped the swords of the MacPhersons. MacGillonie fled towards Ruthven, and was killed on a hill a few miles from that place, which still bears his name.

Many writers assert that the remarkable combat which took place at the North Inch of Perth, before King Robert III. and his Court, in 1396, so quaintly described by Andrew Wyntoun, was the outcome of the dispute at Invernahavon; but whether this be so or not, there is very little doubt that some of the contending clans in 1370 were also among the combatants in 1396.

---

[1] This historical fact appears to me to afford very strong evidence in support of the claim of Mackintosh to the chieftainship of Clan Chattan. Although Cluny objected to Mackintosh's decision at Invernahavon, why was that chieftain called upon to settle the dispute if he was not acknowledged to be the head of the clan?

CHAPTER II.

AMONG the staunchest supporters of Bruce during his struggle for the Crown was the powerful Lord of the Isles, Angus Og, who, with his MacDonald clansmen, had helped in no small degree to win the day at Bannockburn.[1]   In return for such valuable assistance, Bruce bestowed upon him the Lordship of Lochaber, and from this period down to the present day, the great Celtic family of Clan Donald have been closely associated with the beautiful district which forms the subject of this history.   Angus Og was succeeded by his son John, who was fourth in succession from Somerled.   By a special papal dispensation in the year 1342, John was permitted to marry his cousin Amy (Ami nic Ruari) of the Siol Cuinn, the wealthy heiress of the North Isles.   This lady bore him four children.   (1) John, who predeceased his father ; (2) Godfrey of Uist and Garmoran ; (3) Ronald, from whom are descended the families of Clanranald and Glengarry ; and (4) a daughter Mary, who first married one of the MacLeans of Duart, and afterwards MacLean of Coll.   About the year 1357, John of the Isles divorced his wife Amy, and married Lady Margaret Stewart, daughter of Robert, High Steward of Scotland, who, after the death of David II. in 1370, ascended the throne as Robert II.   The children of this marriage were (1) Donald, who succeeded his father in the Lordship of the Isles ; (2) John, usually known as John Mòr Tanastair, ancestor of the Earls of Antrim ; and (3) Alexander, commonly called Alasdair Carrach (or Crafty), to whom was granted the Lordship of Lochaber.   This famous chieftain became the progenitor of the family of Keppoch in the Braes of Lochaber, of whom much will have to be written in the course of this work.

[1] Bannockburn, as all Scotsmen know, was fought on 24th June 1314, and here, as elsewhere, the Highlanders of Lochaber distinguished themselves by their courage. In addition to the MacDonalds mentioned above, large contingents of the clans Cameron, Mackintosh, and MacPherson, under their respective chiefs, were present, and materially assisted the cause of Bruce on that memorable day.

Donald of the Isles had united himself in marriage with
Margaret, daughter of Sir John Lesley, by his wife Euphemia
Ross, sole heiress to the Earldom of Ross, owing to the
failure of the male line.   At her decease, Margaret's brother
Alexander succeeded to the title.   He married a daughter of
the Duke of Albany, and had issue one daughter, Euphemia,
who, upon her father's death, became a nun, and renounced
all claims to the earldom and estates in favour of her uncle
John Stewart, Earl of Buchan.   When this became known to
the Lord of the Isles, he immediately laid claim both to the
title and estates in right of Margaret his wife.   The Duke of
Albany, who was Governor of Scotland, naturally objected to
the pretensions of the Highland potentate, and supported the
Earl of Buchan.   Donald, whose wrath was now aroused,
determined to assert his rights by the sword, and ordered his
brother, Alasdair Carrach, to lay waste the valley of the
Ness ; these instructions were faithfully carried out, and miles
of country were devastated by the Lochaber men.   So serious
was the outbreak, that the Earl of Moray, who governed the
district, found it necessary to make terms with Alasdair Carrach,
and on 5th September 1394, a treaty was signed between them,
in which they "bind themselves to support each other"; and
all the Church lands and possessions of the Regality of Moray
were put under the Lochaber chief's protection for seven years.

Long before that period had expired, Alasdair had claimed
rights of ownership, and had even gifted some of the Church
lands to his friends, and the keeping of the Castle of Urquhart,
with the possession of certain lands in the parish, to his
faithful follower, Charles MacLean, a son of Lochbuie.   The
bishop of Moray complained to the Crown, and Parliament
made a feeble show of authority by imprisoning Alasdair
Carrach, and appointing Donald of the Isles his warder.   This
punishment was of course a mere farce, and it was not long
before we hear of Alasdair committing fresh depredations in
the north.   He robbed the canonry of Elgin, and destroyed the
town by fire, and shortly after was fighting by the side of his

brother Donald, at Dingwall, against Angus Dubh MacKay and the Sutherlandshire clans. He was again successful, Angus Dubh being taken prisoner[1] and his brother Roderic slain.

After this victorious progress, the Lord of the Isles, flushed with success, resolved to carry war into the eastern counties, and after halting at Inverness to muster his army, marched through Moray, accompanied by his brother, Alasdair Carrach. No opposition was met with here, and they proceeded through Strathbogie and Garioch, which were laid waste with fire and sword. Donald had often threatened to burn the town of Aberdeen, and he would undoubtedly have done so on this occasion, had it not been protected by a powerful army under the Earl of Mar, officered by some of the bravest noblemen and gentlemen from Angus and the Mearns. Finding, therefore, the town too strong to assail, Donald, with his Highlanders and Islesmen, halted at the village of Harlaw, on the water of Ury, and waited the arrival of Mar. On the eve of St James, 25th July 1411, the two forces arrived within fighting distance, and with a terrific shout the Highlanders, who had eagerly watched the approach of their enemies, rushed forward with tremendous impetuosity, and for a time carried everything before them ; but they had to face a magnificently equipped force, well armed and disciplined, and led by such stout warriors as Sir James Scrymgeour, Sir Alexander Ogilvy, Sir Alexander Irving of Drum, and hosts of steel-clad knights. The fight went on until nightfall, when, after fearful slaughter, both forces withdrew, leaving over fourteen hundred dead on the field, among whom were the chiefs of Mackintosh and MacLean, who fought under the standard of the Lord of the Isles ; whilst on the side of the Earl of Mar, Sir James Scrymgeour, Sir Alexander Ogilvy, Sir Thomas Murray, Sir Alexander Irving of Drum, Sir William Abernethy of Salton, and many other gentlemen of rank met a similar fate. The battle was a drawn one, but the result was, if

[1] Angus Dubh MacKay afterwards married a sister of the Lord of the Isles. Iain Abrach MacKay was a natural son of this chief.

anything, in favour of Donald; he, however, did not follow up his advantage, and it is idle to speculate on what might have been had he done so. The actual outcome was, that Donald of the Isles had to swear fealty to the Scottish Crown, and give up his claim to the Earldom of Ross. Alasdair Carrach returned to his stronghold of Tor Castle in Lochaber, where we hear of him from time to time as a staunch supporter of his brother in his various difficulties, political and otherwise. Donald died in 1425, and was succeeded by his son Alexander, who was but a lad at the time of his father's death.

James I., the third Stewart, son of Robert III. and Annabella Drummond, is now on the throne. Taken prisoner at an early age by the English in 1405, he had, when confined in Windsor Castle, received all the advantages of the society of princes and nobles of his own age, and doubtless vied with them in all their knightly sports and occupations. Naturally of a pensive and studious disposition, he had every opportunity while at Windsor of gratifying his craving for literature, and it is greatly to the credit of the English monarchs, Henry IV. and V., that no trouble or expense was grudged to provide the education befitting one who was to rule the Scottish people. To beguile the weary hours of his captivity, he read and re-read the poems of the first of English poets, Chaucer, and soon, with boyish ambition, began to write verse himself, and this of no mean order; inspired by the charms of the noble damsel who was afterwards to share his throne in the rude north, and to take her part as an unwilling witness in that last tragic scene at the Abbey of Blackfriars at Perth. All this is matter of history and outside the scope of my present purpose, which is to deal with Scottish history so far only as it touches Lochaber.

It is now the year of our Lord 1429; James I. has sat on the throne of Scotland for twenty-three years, ruling justly and wisely, and finding a few hours to spare, when not occupied by the affairs of state, to follow his favourite pursuit of verse making. His rest is rudely disturbed by the news that the

Highland caterans under Alexander, Lord of the Isles, and Earl of Ross, are laying waste Lochaber with fire and sword, and he must perforce leave his poetry and gird on his armour and go forth to chastise these troublesome Highlanders who set his kingly authority at defiance. A parliament is hastily summoned at Inverness, which the king attends in person, and Alexander is summoned before him. The wily chieftain promises to reform, and, after a nominal punishment of a few days, is set free; but as an example to others, several of the lesser chiefs are summarily executed. Justice having been done, the king returns to Perth, and before the last struggling remnants of his retinue are out of the town, Alexander, forgetful of his promises of amendment, returns with a large body of MacDonalds, and destroys the town by fire. We may imagine the wrath of James at this proceeding, and vowing vengeance against the clan and its chieftain in particular, he plans an expedition for his destruction. Alexander, feeling now assured that he has aroused the lion, and seeing no chance of escape, has recourse to that mother wit with which every Highlander, ancient or modern, is well provided.

It is now Easter, the king and queen are at Holyrood engrossed in those devotions which the Catholic Church imposes upon her followers at this holy festival. While the ceremony of the mass is in progress, a noise is heard without, and, like an apparition, the figure of a Highland chieftain appears, clad in the picturesque garb of his race, and pushing aside the kneeling courtiers, throws himself at the king's feet, and implores pardon in the name of Him who died upon the Cross; and such is the superstition of the age, and the glamour of the sacred surroundings, that, in the presence of the Host held aloft by the hands of the officiating priest, James grants the life of his inveterate enemy. A few days later the great gates of the castle of Tantallon close upon Alexander, and he troubles the king no more.

"*Le roi est mort, vive le roi.*" Alexander is secure in Tantallon, but his young cousin, Donald Balloch, son of

D

John Mòr Tanastair, with a brave determination to protect the hereditary rights of his clan and family, immediately raised the standard of his chief at Carnich, a small island in Loch Sunart, and called upon the neighbouring clans to join him in attacking the forces sent by the king under the command of the Earls of Mar and Caithness, which were encamped around the castle of Inverlochy. MacIain of Ardnamurchan, Allan, son of Allan of Moidart, and his brother, Ranald Bàn, promptly answered the summons, and brought in over six hundred followers, mostly *daoine-uaisle* or gentlemen, many coming in their own galleys and biorlinns. With this force, Donald Balloch set sail for Inverskippinish, two miles south of Inverlochy, where he awaited a favourable moment for a descent upon the king's army, meanwhile sending word to his uncle, Alasdair Carrach, to hold himself in readiness for a combined attack upon a preconcerted signal.

On the king's side Mar had not been idle, having strengthened his force by a large accession of Highland chiefs and Lowland noblemen, among the former being Huntly, Fraser of Lovat, Malcolm Mackintosh (*Calum Beag*), captain of Clan Chattan, Donald Cameron (*Domhnull Dubh MacAilein*), chief of Clan Cameron, Grant, and MacKay of Strathnaver; but at the time of the battle, Lovat was away collecting men and provisions in Sunart and Ardnamurchan. Upon the approach of Donald Balloch and his Islesmen, Alasdair Carrach, with two hundred archers and the remainder of his clan, took up a position upon the steep hill overlooking the castle of Inverlochy, and awaited the moment when the king's army being engaged with his nephew, he could swoop down upon the unprotected flank. So little did Mar comprehend the dangerous position in which he was placed, that he was actually playing a game of cards in his tent with Mackintosh whilst Donald Balloch was disembarking his men but a short distance away. Huntly, however, with keener military instinct, fully realised the necessity of immediate action, and expostulated with the players at their folly in wasting time at such an important juncture. Mackintosh is said to have exclaimed: "We will play this game out, and do with the enemy what we please afterwards, for I know very well the doings of the big-bellied carles of the Isles," and even went out of his way to insult Huntly, by saying that though he (Huntly) should assist the enemy, he would defeat them both; an insult which caused Huntly to withdraw his clansmen and become a mere spectator of the fight.

Whilst these foolish boasters were sowing discord in the ranks of the Royalists, Donald Balloch and his followers had landed from their galleys, and taken up a strong position in front of the king's forces, which had now been put into some sort of order. The front of the Islesmen was commanded by MacIain of Ardnamurchan, John MacLean of Coll, and his kinsman, Lachlan Bronneach; the main battle by Ranald Bàn and Allan, son of Allan of Moidart; whilst other important posts were assigned to MacDuffie of Colonsay, MacQuarrie of Ulva, and MacGee (MacKay) of the Rhinns of Isla.

At a given signal, Alasdair Carrach and his gallant MacDonalds poured down the hill like an impetuous torrent, driving everything before them with irresistible fury, hacking and slashing with *claidheamh mòr* and Lochaber axe, whilst showers of arrows from his archers carried death and devastation into the massed body of the enemy farther afield. Donald Balloch and his Islesmen had meanwhile attacked the Royalists in front with such tremendous ferocity, that resistance was unavailing, and in spite of all the efforts of the old chief of Clan Cameron, who had fought at Harlaw, and the vigorous protests of Mar, the king's army was completely routed, leaving nearly a thousand dead upon the field, amongst them being the Earl of Caithness, with sixteen of his personal retinue, and many knights and barons from the Lowlands.

Donald Balloch followed up his victory by a descent upon the lands of the Camerons and Clan Chattan, which he ravaged with fire and sword, but news reaching him that king James was advancing in person to Lochaber at the head of a powerful army, he fled to Ireland, where he married the daughter of

Conn O'Neill (son of Hugh. Bhuidhe O'Neill). The king, after a triumphal progress through Lochaber, proceeded to Dunstaffnage, on Loch Etive, and held a trial of as many of the insurgent leaders as he had been able to secure; several were executed, and the lands of others forfeited. Alasdair Carrach, for the share he had taken in the rebellion, was dispossessed of · his estates in Glen Roy and Glen Spean, which were bestowed upon Malcolm Mackintosh, captain of Clan Chattan, as some compensation for the loss he had sustained. It was this circumstance that led to the great feud between the Keppoch MacDonalds and Mackintoshes, which continued until the end of the seventeenth century.

There is still extant in Lochaber an interesting story in connection with the flight of the Earl of Mar from Inverlochy after the death of his colleague, the Earl of Caithness. Weary and footsore, almost dead from want of food, he got as far as Glen Roy, where he met a poor Highland woman, who, taking pity on his destitute condition, and of course quite ignorant of his identity, charitably shared with him the small portion of meal she had; the earl, having no utensil to mix it in, took off his shoe, and going to a small burn known as *Allt-acha-na-beithe*, he filled his shoe with water, and having stirred the meal into it, ate the mixture with a degree of pleasure that astonished the poor woman, saying at the same time in Gaelic,—

> " Is math an cocaire an-t-acras,
> 'S mairg ni tailleas air biadh ?
> Fuarag eorn a sail mo bhroige
> Biadh is fhearr a fhuair mi riamh."

Which may be expressed in English as " Hunger is the best of cooks; who would despise the most frugal meal. I never had anything so good as barley crowdie in my shoe."

After partaking of this simple food, which temporarily assuaged the pangs of hunger, he reached a place some distance up the glen named Beggich, where resided an Irishman by the name of O'Birrin (possibly O'Brian), who, with the hospitality for which his race is celebrated, welcomed the wounded stranger, and, having no food to offer him, killed his solitary cow, and having cooked a portion of the flesh, gave it to the earl. After eating heartily of the good fare provided for him, the earl, overcome with fatigue, fell into a sound sleep, and his kind host covered him as he slept with the warm hide of the recently slaughtered animal. Whether from the virtue in the hide, or the effects of the nourishing food of which he had partaken, the earl arose from his slumbers refreshed and strong, and shortly after took his departure, previously informing his host of his name and rank, and promising that in the event of danger or difficulty he would come to his assistance.

O'Birrin soon had an opportunity of proving the earl's good faith, as, shortly after his noble guest had departed, some of the neighbouring MacDonalds having heard of the occurrence, and enraged that their foe should have escaped their clutches at Inverlochy, threatened him with violence. Fearing they would take his life, O'Birrin bethought him of his friend the earl, and decided to flee to him for succour. He reached the earl's residence at Kildrummie at an inopportune time, as that nobleman was entertaining his friends at a banquet. For a long time the servants resisted O'Birrin's entreaties to be allowed to see their master, but at length he prevailed upon one of them to take his message to the earl, who immediately left the table, excusing his absence to his friends in Gaelic verse, thus—

> " S' ionmhuinm leam na bheil a muigh,
>   O'Birrin's a Bhaggach ;
>   Thug mi oidche na thigh,
>   Air mhoran bidh's air bheagan aodach."

Which being interpreted, is—

> " Dear unto me is O'Birrin of Beggich,
>   Who stands at my threshold ;
>   I stayed a night at his dwelling,
>   With plenteous food and scanty clothing."

Taking him by the hand, he led him into the castle, where he was amply provided for during the remainder of his lifetime.

Notwithstanding the flight of Donald Balloch, the Camerons' had yet to discover that their misfortunes had only just begun, for upon the restoration to liberty of Alexander, Lord of the Isles, from the dungeons of Tantallon, who, having sworn fealty to king James, had been appointed Justiciar of the kingdom north of the Forth, they found themselves deprived of their lands by their feudal superior as a punishment for their desertion from his standard at Inverlochy.

His first step on regaining his freedom was to bestow the lands of the Camerons upon his staunch adherent, MacLean of Coll. This chieftain was the son of Lachlan MacLean of Duart in Mull, and had obtained the Island of Coll and the lands of Quinish from the Lord of the Isles, as a reward for his services. Upon proceeding to take possession of his newly acquired property in Lochaber, he experienced considerable opposition from the Camerons, who offered every resistance in their power to the intruder, but without success, and for some years MacLean usurped the place of the exiled Donald Dubh.

At length the day of reckoning came, for Alan (*MacDhomhnuill Duibh*), the Cameron chief (better known as *Ailein nan Creach*), having sworn to support the cause of Celestine of the Isles, Lord of Lochalsh, received from that chief a charter of the lands of Loch Arkaig and Loch Eil, with remainder to the heirs male procreated between him and his wife Mariot, daughter of Angus (*Aongas na Feairte*), second chief of Keppoch.[1] He at once commenced hostilities against the MacLeans with such energy that he soon regained the possession of most of his patrimony.

A decisive battle was fought between the Camerons and MacLeans at Corpach on Loch Eil, in which the latter clan were utterly routed, and their chief (John, the son of John Garbh) slain.[2]

---

[1] Appendix III.

[2] The spot where he fell is pointed out on the Ardgour shore of Loch Eil, near a large boulder known locally as "*Clach Mhic Iain.*"

The exact date of this conflict is not known, but there is little doubt that it took place during the reign of James III. (1460-1488 A.D.), and from that period until the "Forty-Five," the Camerons of Lochiel remained in secure possession of their ancestral territory, and furnished a long line of redoubtable chieftains to the whole clan. In a later chapter I shall have occasion to refer to the different branches of Clan Cameron, and the origin of the assumption of the chieftainship by the Lochiel family.

Although the MacLeans had suffered defeat and been driven from the Cameron lands by the rightful owners of the property, they still retained considerable influence in the immediate neighbourhood, owing to the territory they had recently appropriated in Ardgour (*Ard-gobhar*, "Height of the Goats"), on the opposite side of Loch Eil. This beautiful and extensive district, which stretches from Drumsallie, near the head of Loch Eil, to a short distance beyond Corran on Loch Linnhe, had for generations belonged to the MacMasters, a small clan or sept of obscure origin, who had held it from the Lords of the Isles. Tradition states that the chief of the MacMasters at this period (anterior to 1480 A.D.) had given offence to his feudal lord by the use of an insulting epithet on the occasion of an interview that had taken place between them, and that the Lord of the Isles had threatened to punish MacMaster for his temerity by expelling him from the lands of Ardgour. For some reason or another, no immediate steps were taken, and MacMaster returned to his dwelling at Clovullin (*Cladh a Mhuillin*), in the fond belief that his crime had been overlooked or forgotten. This, however, was not the case, as we shall see.

At the great battle of Harlaw in 1411, Hector MacLean (*Eachann Ruadh nan Cath*, "Red Hector of the Battles") had commanded the right wing of the Highlanders and Islesmen under Donald, Lord of the Isles, and was slain by Sir Alexander Irving of Drum. He had married a daughter of the Earl of Douglas, who bore him several sons, among whom was one named Ewen. At the time of his father's death, Ewen was an

infant, and the Earl of Douglas constituted himself the guardian
and protector of his fatherless grandchild, and brought him up
with his own family. As soon as he could handle weapons,
young Ewen was trained in the art of war and other manly
exercises, in which he soon became proficient. His first
military exploit occurred at Dunbarton, where he greatly
distinguished himself under the leadership of the Duke of
Albany, and young as he was he challenged the leader of the
royal forces to single combat, and after a desperate struggle
overcame and slew him. Owing to the fact that Ewen MacLean,
after having killed his opponent, appropriated the head-covering
of the dead warrior, which was ornamented by three feathers,
he was dubbed by his Highland comrades *Eobhan nan iteag*
("Ewen of the Feathers"). After this event, Ewen sought his
fortune in Ireland, but returned later to Ardtornish when he
heard that the Lord of the Isles was engaged in making grants
of lands to those chiefs who had supported his cause during
the late troubles. Young MacLean is said to have crossed from
Ireland in a galley with sixteen followers, among whom were
some bearing the names of Boyd and Livingstone. Upon his
arrival at Ardtornish, Ewen sought an interview with Lord
MacDonald, which, having been granted, he boldly asserted
his claim to a share in the division of property. The great
chieftain, pleased though he was at the bold spirit displayed
by MacLean, was somewhat embarrassed, as all the available
land had already been divided among the earlier claimants,
and he reluctantly had to admit his inability to grant the
request, but added that if Ewen wanted land, he had a good
sword and a stout arm, and could take it, and, moreover, offered
to lend him the assistance of a body of men to aid him in the
enterprise. The idea seemed to please the dauntless Ewen, but
he refused the proffered help of the chief's warriors, stating
that the men he had with him were quite sufficient for the
purpose, provided the Lord of the Isles would tell him where
to go, and grant him permission to retain the lands when he
had won them.

Suddenly calling to mind the insult he had received from MacMaster of Ardgour, and glad of the opportunity of inflicting condign punishment upon a rebellious vassal, Mac-Donald turned graciously to Ewen and said, "the spirit of your brave father is in you, and you deserve a reward; go therefore and take the lands of '*Fiuch!*' '*Fiuch!*'" (Anglice, "pshaw!")[1] — this being the objectionable interjection used by MacMaster which had aroused the wrath of the proud Hebridean potentate. A little further explanation followed, and Ewen and his bold followers set sail for Loch Linnhe, filled with the most sanguine expectations of success in their somewhat questionable expedition.

Late at night they arrived at Clovullin, and having landed, proceeded to the dwelling of MacMaster, where Ewen knocked loudly, and demanded food and lodging for himself and men. The Chief of Ardgour, having been probably awakened from his slumbers, was in anything but a conciliatory mood, and he refused the request in most insulting terms. These words were the last he was to utter, for they had scarcely left his lips when Ewen, drawing his sword, decapitated him on the spot. Thus *Eobhan nan iteag* became possessed of the lands of Ardgour, and his descendants from that time have taken the patronymic of *Mac ic Eobhainn*. The son and heir of the slain chief was known as "the Fox," and after the murder of his father, he sought the shelter of a wood in the neighbourhood, where he remained all night, but was afterwards captured by MacLean and slain. The spot where he was buried is still known as *Carn an t-sionnaich* ("the Cairn of the Fox"). The rest of the MacMasters fled across Corran Ferry to Inverlochy, where many of the name may still be found, while their places were filled in Ardgour by the Boyds and Livingstones, who had come from Ireland with MacLean, and to this day several families of their descendants flourish in that district.

---

[1] Another version is "*Falbh! nach leum thu'n garradh far is iosaile*" ("Off! canst thou not leap the fence where it is lowest"), and the hero, instead of Ewen, is said to have been Donald, son of Lachlan Bronneach.

E

CHAPTER III.

AFTER the events just chronicled we hear little of Lochaber and its turbulent inhabitants for some time. The campaign of Alexander of the Isles, in which he was assisted by his Keppoch kinsmen, resulted most disastrously, and in the year 1493 the historic Lordship of the Isles was forfeited to the Crown, and Donald (III. of Keppoch) was thus deprived of all legal claim to his Lochaber lands.[1] During the next twelve years the country was the scene of local feuds and clan dissensions, in which MacDonalds, Camerons, and Mackintoshes were all involved; but the most serious event that disturbed the peace of the district was the insurrection of Donald Dubh of the Isles, in order to recover his lost inheritance. Donald Glas (VI. of Keppoch) supported his kinsman, and carried fire and sword into the lands of Clan Chattan; Badenoch was laid waste, and the town of Inverness destroyed by fire. The king (James IV.), now thoroughly alarmed, raised a powerful army, and called upon the Earls of Argyll, Huntly, Crawford, and Marshall, with Lord Lovat and many other noblemen of note, to lead it against the rebellious islanders. For two years the war went on, and for part of the time the king led his army in person. At length Donald Dubh was made prisoner, and confined in Edinburgh Castle, where he remained for a period of nearly forty years. These energetic measures broke the back of the rebellion, and for a time at least peace reigned in Lochaber.

In the year 1505 [2] Alexander Gordon, third Earl of Huntly, was invested with full power in the disaffected district; and as from thenceforward the family of Gordon were closely associated with Lochaber, a brief account of their origin may not be out of place.

The family is undoubtedly of very considerable antiquity,

[1] Appendix IV.
[2] The deed of grant is dated Edinburgh, 22nd March 1505, *vide* Appendix V.

for as far back as the reign of Malcolm III. (1058-1093 A.D.)
we hear of one Richard Gordon, who was said to have slain
an enormous wild boar near the forest of Huntly, for which
deed he was rewarded with a grant of lands by the king,
and was empowered to carry arms, viz., three boar's heads,
or, on a field azure; and later, in 1199 A.D., tradition states
that Bertram de Gordon, at Chalons, shot the fatal arrow
that mortally wounded the English king, Richard Cœur
de Lion.

In the reign of Alexander III., Adam Gordon married his
cousin Alicia, who was heiress to an immense fortune which
she brought to her husband, who, however, did not live long
to enjoy it, as shortly afterwards he went to the Crusades
with Louis of France, where he was slain.   It is from his
grandson Sir Adam, that all the Gordons were descended.
In 1402 A.D., another Sir Adam Gordon fought, and was
slain at Homildon, and the male line became extinct: his
only daughter married a Seton, and their son Alexander
assumed the name of Gordon, and became a favourite of
James I. and James II., and was created Earl of Huntly
by the latter monarch in 1449 A.D.   The Gordons were now
as powerful in Lochaber as their predecessors the Comyns
had been in earlier times, and about 1511 A.D. the then Earl
of Huntly, by the king's instructions, set to work to restore
Inverlochy Castle, which had at this period fallen into decay.
A moat 40 feet broad was dug around it, the massive towers
were strengthened, and a strong force of armed Gordons with
their chief took up their abode within the fortress, ready for
any service that the unsettled state of the district might
demand of them.   Treaties offensive and defensive were
entered into with the neighbouring clans; and among other
chiefs of Lochaber who signed documents of this character
we find Ewen M'Alan Cameron (*Eobhan MacAilein*), XIII.
of Lochiel, binding himself to the Earl of Huntly to be
"his leill, trew, ane fald man and servand," and with his kith
and kin to take part with the earl in all his just actions and

quarrels with all men.[1] This was in May 1543, and it is evident that Lochiel did not consider the bond as binding on his conscience, as one year later, in 1544, he was in arms against Huntly at the battle of *Blàr nan leine.* Here he fought on the side of the MacDonalds of Clan Ranald against the Frasers, headed by their chief, Hugh, fifth Lord Lovat, whose cause Huntly supported. The origin of the dispute which led to this sanguinary battle was as follows:—Alexander Alanson (*Alasdair MacAilein*), second son of Alan MacRuari (IV. of Clan Ranald), dying in 1530, left a natural son, commonly known as Iain Moidartach (John of Moidart), who having arrived at man's estate, obtained by false representations a charter of his father's estates from the Crown to the exclusion of the legitimate heir, Ranald, son of Alan MacRuari by his wife Isabella, daughter of Fraser of Lovat. Ranald had been brought up by his grandfather among the Frasers, and was hence called Galda ("stranger") by his own clan.

When Ranald came of age, he went with a few of his friends to take possession of Castle Tioram and assert his rights to the chieftainship. Great preparations were made for his reception, and many bullocks were slaughtered to provide a feast worthy of the occasion. Observing the unwonted excitement, and being told its cause, he remarked, "There is no necessity for so much extravagance; a few fowls might serve us." These harmless words were at once taken up by his clansmen, instigated by Iain Moidartach, and misconstrued into a reflection upon the hospitality of the clan. So indignant were they, that all sorts of insulting epithets were hurled at the unfortunate lad, among which was *Raonuill nan cearc* ("Ranald of the Hens"), a name which stuck to him as long as he lived. Deeming it useless to remain, Ranald departed with his friends to report the insult to his grandfather and take steps for punishing his rebellious vassals. Immediately upon

---

[1] Several charters of land were granted to *Eobhainn MacAilein* and his son Donald about this period, *vide* Appendices VI. and VII.

his departure, Iain Moidartach was unanimously elected chief,
and preparations were made to protect the clan from the
vengeance of the Frasers.

Maclain of Ardnamurchan and his son, *Raonuill Mòr*[1]
(VII. chief of Keppoch), and *Eobhan MacAilein* of Lochiel,
who were friendly to Iain, were asked for their support,
which was willingly given. Hearing that the Frasers were
on the move, Iain and his allies spread themselves through
Stratherrick and Abertarff, wasting and destroying everything that came in their way: they raided Glenmoriston and
took possession of Urquhart Castle on Loch Ness. News
of the disturbance soon reached Huntly, and he at once
proceeded against the insurgents, accompanied by nearly the
whole of the Frasers; the Grants of Strathspey and Glenmoriston, and a strong contingent of the Clan Chattan. The
MacDonalds of Keppoch and Glengarry made a show of
submission, and Urquhart Castle was given up to Huntly.
Ranald Galda was put in possession of his patrimony, and
everything being apparently happily settled, Huntly departed
with the Clan Chattan, whilst the Frasers and Grants marched
northwards. They had to pass up the Great Glen, through
which the Caledonian Canal now runs, and when near the
Church of Kilfinnan, at the southern end of Loch Lochy, they
found themselves face to face with the whole forces of the
enemy. The month was July, and the heat was so intense
that the combatants stripped to their shirts before commencing
the action, from which circumstance the battle is known as
Blàr nan leine, or "Battle of the Shirts." The fight was a
desperate one, and continued all through the long summer day
until nightfall, when sheer exhaustion on the part of the
victorious MacDonalds and Camerons brought it to an end.
The Frasers were nearly exterminated by their relentless foes,
and we are told that Lord Lovat, with his eldest son and over
eighty gentlemen of the clan were slain. Utter recklessness

[1] It is from this chief the MacDonalds (or MacDonells) of Keppoch derive their
patronymic of "*Mac Mhic Raonuill.*"

of life was shown on both sides, and many prodigies of valour were performed. Two gigantic Highlanders challenged each other to single combat with their huge double-handed swords; both fought magnificently for a long time, and neither gained any advantage. At length one cried out, *"Am bheil thu an gobha?"* ("Art thou the smith?") *"Tha mi! Am bheil thu an gobha?"* ("I am! Art thou the smith?"), queried the man addressed, to which the other replied, *"Tha mi"* ("I am"). Instantly throwing away their weapons, they grasped each other in a grip of iron, with brawny limbs intertwined, the muscles standing out like cords; for a few moments they stood thus, gradually drawing near to the edge of the loch, until at last, locked in a deadly embrace, they fell over into the deep water and perished.

The young heir, Ranald Galda, greatly distinguished himself by his conspicuous bravery during the battle, he having engaged in a hand to hand fight with a famous old swordsman called *Iain Ruadh Beag* ("little Red John"). As they were fighting, Iain's son passed by, and the old man finding himself hard pressed by Ranald, he called out, *"Is coma leam suaicheantas duine òg 's e teicheadh"* ("I hate to see the badge of the young fugitive"). *"Ceum air aghaidh d an t-sean duine, mac an air aite an athar"* ("Step forward, old man"), replied the lad ("let the son take the place of the father"), at the same time placing himself in front of Ranald Galda, who soon had him at his mercy. Seeing this, the father, thinking to alarm his son's antagonist, cried out, *"Cha bhi mu'r brath foille dhuit, sin iad air do chul thaobh"* ("Take warning, young man, behind you"). The ruse succeeded, for Ranald turned his head for a moment and was cut down by his assailant, who left him for dead on the field. The wound was not mortal, but owing to weakness, due to loss of blood, he was unable to escape, and fell into the hands of his enemies, who carried him to a small inn at Laggan, where he was laid upon a rough bed, and his wounds tended by one of the MacDonalds, who professed a knowledge of surgery. While he lay here suffering intense pain from his wounds, he could hear the MacDonalds and Camerons in their cups, boasting of their exploits on the field of battle, and making mocking allusions to the vanquished Frasers. Ranald could stand these taunts no longer, and in spite of the pain the movement caused him, he sat up in his bed, his head all swathed in a bloody bandage, and addressing his foes, who, at the sound of his voice became sobered, he scornfully remarked that if he were only as well and strong as he had been in the morning, he would rather encounter the whole of those in the room in mortal combat than the one brave man he had fought with that day. At this remark the MacDonalds were exceedingly irritated, and vowed speedy vengeance against the wounded lad. On the pretence of bringing about his recovery, they called in one of their clansmen who had some knowledge of medicine, and, having given him secret instructions, sent him to the young chief's bedside. Ranald appears to have been suspicious of the man's intentions, and at first forbade his proffered assistance, but the pain, which was now becoming unbearable, caused him to yield himself to the doctor, who at once proceeded to dress his wounds. Whilst apparently engaged in this merciful occupation, the treacherous MacDonald thrust a needle into Ranald Galda's brain, but, quick as the action was, Ranald had time to snatch his dirk from his belt and stab the villain to the heart before he died.

There is a totally different version of this story current in the Highlands, which is to the effect that Ranald Galda was killed in fair fight by young Ranald MacDonell of Strontian, who, seeing his father in danger of being worsted by that hero, and being called upon for his assistance, shouted out, " *So mar bu chòir a bhi, am mac a dol 'an ionad an athar* " (" This is as it ought to be, the son in the place of the father "), rushed into the fray and attacked Ranald Galda, and soon overcame him.

Huntly, upon hearing the news of the defeat, was greatly enraged, and having called in the assistance of the powerful Earl of Argyll, they obtained a decree of outlawry against

Iain Moidartach, and then proceeded to attack him by sea and land. By a ruse he was captured and imprisoned, but soon after made his escape and retired to his mountain fastness, from whence he laughed at all attempts to secure him. Lochiel and Keppoch were less fortunate, for, owing to the treachery of Mackintosh, both were taken prisoners and executed at Elgin, in the year 1547, by order of the Earl of Huntly, and their heads stuck over the gate of the town.

For some years after the battle of *Blàr nan leine*, comparative peace reigned in Lochaber, save for an occasional skirmish between the rival clans of that unsettled district, who were continually raiding each other's territory on some slight pretext or other, and affording Huntly plenty of employment in settling their disputes and inflicting punishment upon the more unruly members of his troublesome neighbours.

Sometimes he came into direct collision with them, as in 1591 or 1592, when Angus Mackintosh, the chief of that unique confederation the Clan Chattan, at the head of a great number of his followers, attempted to surprise the garrison of Ruthven Castle in Badenoch, belonging to Huntly, but without success: and we read in an old MS. history of the Gordons, still preserved in the Advocates' Library, how Angus, " finding this attempt could neither by force nor fraud have successe, he retires a little to consult how to compass his intent. In the meantime one creeps out under the shelter of some old ruins, and levels with his piece at one of the Clanchattan *cloathed in a yellow war coate* (which amongst them, is the badge of the Cheiftaines or heads of Clans), and piercing his body with the bullet, stricks him to the ground and retires with gladness into the castle. The man killed was Angus himself, whom his people carry away, and conceille his death for manie yeirs, pretending he was gone beyond the seas."

Upon the execution of Ewen Cameron of Lochiel (*Eobhan MacAilein*), the chieftainship of the clan passed to his grandson Ewen Beg (*Eobhan Beag*), owing to the death of his eldest son Donald. Ewen died or was assassinated about 1554, and was succeeded by his uncle Donald (*Domhnull Dubh MacDhomhnuill*), who only lived to command the clan for ten years, and died about the year 1564. John (*Iain Dubh*), Donald's brother, married a daughter of the Chief of Mackintosh, with issue two sons, the eldest of whom, Alan (*Ailein MacIain Duibh*), became the sixteenth chief of Lochiel.[1]

It was during the early years of Alan's chiefship that we first hear of the famous *Taillear Dubh na Tuaige* ("the Black Tailor of the Battle Axe"), whose doughty deeds are renowned throughout Lochaber. He was a natural son of *Eobhan Beag* the fourteenth chief, by a daughter of MacDougall of Lorne; and the tradition still extant is, that MacDougall, enraged at the seduction of his daughter, surprised and captured the father of her child, and after confining him for some time in the castle of Inch Connel, Loch Awe, put him to death with the assistance of one MacArthur. The child, then known as Donald MacEwen (*Domhnull MacEobhainn Bhig*), was sent to Blar na Cleireach, near Loch Lundavra, where he was nursed by a tailor's wife, from which circumstance he was called *An Taillear Dubh*. He grew up a powerful man, with limbs and sinews of iron, and during the many battles and skirmishes with the Mackintoshes proved himself a splendid warrior.

Many stories are told of his prowess, of which the following is one. Mackintosh, who was still hard at work trying to bring the Camerons under his subjection, had invaded Lochiel's territory with a force of two hundred chosen men of Clan Chattan, and had reached the head of Loch Eil without meeting any opposition. Here he rested for the night, and on the following morning crossed the side of *Beinn an t-Sneachda*, and proceeded in the direction of Loch Arkaig. He had not gone far on the road when Lochiel, with a hundred and twenty Camerons, was seen occupying a strong position on the brae side, prepared to defend his property at all costs.

[1] Appendices VIII., IX., and X. throw some interesting light on Lochaber history at this period.

F

There was a few moments hesitation, and then the Camerons swept down upon their foes like an avalanche of destruction, shouting their war cry, and dealing such terrible blows with their huge swords, that in a few moments the beautiful green sward was red with blood, and strewn with the bodies of dead and dying Mackintoshes. The Black Tailor stood on a small knoll and swung a gigantic axe, which clove skulls and sheared off heads as though they had been thistles, until he could no longer move for the heaps of slain that were piled around him; then, leaping from the hillock, he rushed among the Chattan men and mowed a path clean through their ranks until he regained his clansmen. The Mackintoshes, brave as they were, turned and fled from the ferocious Camerons and their invincible champion, who now pursued them round the head of Loch Eil to the Ardgour shore, where Mackintosh halted, and, standing upon a great boulder by the water's edge, formed his men around him in a position of defence. The Camerons, headed by Lochiel and the Black Tailor, soon came up with them, and once more the slaughter began. With dauntless courage Mackintosh, who was armed with an immense double-handed sword, stood his ground, cutting down every man who came within the reach of his weapon, and hurling derisive taunts at his enemies. At length the Black Tailor cut his way to where the Mackintosh was defending himself so bravely, and faced him. In an instant the Clan Chattan chief aimed a mighty blow at his adversary, but it was deftly avoided by the Cameron warrior, who, raising his great axe, struck Mackintosh to the ground.

The wound, however, was not mortal, and with fearful execrations against the Camerons, the Chattan men raised their injured chief on their shoulders, and, still pursued by their relentless foes, retreated with him to *Bun Garbhain*, where, overcome with fatigue, they had to halt. Again the deadly strife was renewed, until few of the Mackintoshes were left alive, and these few fled across the hills to Cona Glen. The chief and his son were taken prisoners and left in charge of some women, whilst the Camerons still pressed on after the fugitives, determined that if possible not one should escape their vengeance. Night was now coming on, and the wretched remnant of Mackintosh's men, thinking they had outstripped their enemies, lay down in a small hollow called *Cuil nan Cuileag*, where they fondly hoped to sleep. It was a vain hope, for they had scarcely time to throw themselves on the ground when the Black Tailor with his terrible weapon leapt into their midst, followed by a party of Camerons. The Mackintoshes sprang to their feet and made a last desperate stand, but it was of no avail, and they were cut down one by one until not a man remained alive.

The Camerons, satisfied with their bloody work, returned to *Bun Garbhain*, where they had left their wounded prisoners. There they spent the night, and early the next morning started for their homes, carrying their wounded with them. Lochiel was now in a dilemma, for his mother was a Mackintosh, and had a character for being a woman of ungovernable temper, who hated her son's clan with a deadly hatred; it was therefore no pleasant task to face her with the story of the Mackintosh defeat. The Black Tailor, however, cared nought, and Lochiel dispatched him to Achnacarry with the tidings. Upon arrival he presented himself to the lady, who welcomed him heartily and asked his news. He replied, "*Gun robh bian cait an diugh air plang, agus rogha's taghadh air peighinn*" ("A cat's skin might be had that day for a plack, and the choicest for a penny"). Understanding his meaning, but dissembling her anger, she bade him enter and take some refreshment, but first requested him to leave his axe outside. "*Far am bi mi fhein bidh mo thuagh*" ("Where I am myself, there will be my axe"), replied the Tailor. This remark so irritated her, that taking her young child from the cradle she threw it into the fire, showing by this action her hatred even of her own Cameron offspring. Horrified by this fearful deed, the Black Tailor raised his axe and shouted, "*A bhean a rug an leanabh, tog an leanabh*" ("Woman who bore the child, take up the child"). So terrible was his aspect that she caught up her child, who was but slightly burned, and made her peace with the Tailor. When Lochiel returned he found his mother in a reasonable frame of mind, and handed over his wounded prisoners to her care. When they had fully recovered they were allowed to depart, after giving Lochiel a written promise not to invade his territory again.[1]

A more serious outbreak of feudal hostilities disturbed the peace of Lochaber in 1613 A.D.,[2] and was productive of far-reaching consequences to Clan Cameron. The trouble arose, in the first instance, from the arbitrary attempt made by the Earl of Argyll to possess himself of the lands of *Ailein MacIain Duibh*, sixteenth chief of Lochiel, with a view to weakening the power and influence of his rival the Earl of Huntly. He based his claim to this property upon the fact that one of his ancestors, who lived in the reign of James V., had received from that monarch a grant of the territory in question. The dispute was not in this instance settled by the *argumentum baculinum*, but rather by the *argumentum ad ignorantiam;* for the crafty Argyll, being assured that an armed invasion of the Cameron district would probably end in disaster, adopted the less heroic but safer course, of instituting legal proceedings in Edinburgh for the recovery of his alleged rights, trusting to the ignorance of Lochiel—whose acquaintance with the tortuous course of an action at law would necessarily be limited—to enable him to bring his action to a successful issue. The result showed that he was right in his surmise; for upon Lochiel's arrival in Edinburgh to defend his property from the clutches of *Mac Cailean Mòr*, he very unwisely allowed himself to accept the suggestion of his opponent, and agreed to submit

---

[1] Between this period and 1613 there are many entries in the Register of the Privy Council of Scotland relating to the efforts of the Government to extirpate the Clan Gregor by the assistance of the Lochaber chiefs. That the task was not a congenial one may be judged from Appendices XI. and XII.

[2] Appendix XIII.

the dispute to arbitration. In the end, the arbiters decided in favour of Argyll, and Lochiel, making the best of a bad bargain, consented to hold his ancestral estates as a vassal of the earl. This arrangement was resented by Huntly, who clearly saw that unless he could break up this new and unexpected alliance, his power in Lochaber would be merely an empty name. He therefore endeavoured by every possible means at his disposal to induce the chieftains of the other branches of Clan Cameron to refuse allegiance to Lochiel, now that he had allied himself with the enemy of their race. By dint of insidious arguments and other more questionable methods of persuasion, Huntly. was so far successful that he won over the Camerons of Glen Nevis, Errachd, and Kinlocheil to his side, and they agreed to support him in any hostilities that might ensue between the Gordons and the Campbells.

When Lochiel heard of the disloyal behaviour of his clansmen, his annoyance was extreme, and after a vain attempt to enforce their submission, he returned to Edinburgh to take counsel with his lawyers, and learn from them the extent of his legal authority over his mutinous kinsmen and tenants. Before he had been many days in that city, news reached him that a plot was in course of formation against him, and that his life was in danger. This intelligence caused him to set out at once for Lochaber, with the stern determination of punishing the conspirators, and rooting out the germs of sedition from among his clan.

The Camerons of Strone, Letterfinlay, and Callart were as yet loyal to their chief, and to these faithful adherents Lochiel now appealed, to aid him in breaking up the conspiracy. The would - be assassins, the better to carry out their fell purpose, had appointed a rendezvous in a remote spot, where they had invited Lochiel to meet them, and discuss terms of reconciliation. They had, however, reckoned without their host, for Lochiel, getting wind of their murderous plans, had proceeded early to the place of meeting, attended by a large

body of well-armed Camerons, and after having concealed
them behind rocks and clumps of heather, awaited alone the
approach of the traitors. They were not long in coming,
and as the leader of the party came up, Lochiel suggested
that the conference should be held farther up the glen.
Ignorant of the fate that was in store for them, the whole
body of rebellious Camerons followed Lochiel into the deep
recesses of the ravine, their coward hearts rejoicing as they
saw in this movement only a better opportunity of effecting
their bloody purpose. But as they drew near the spot where
the loyal Camerons lay in ambush, Lochiel gave the signal
whistle, and

> " Instant, through copse and heath, arose
> Bonnets and spears and bended bows ;
> On right, on left, above, below,
> Sprung up at once the lurking foe." [1]

Caught in the snare they had laid for their chief, the conspirators received a well-merited punishment ; twenty of
their number being slain in the first few minutes, and eight
taken prisoners. Justice having been satisfied, Lochiel did
not follow up his advantage, but allowed the fugitives to
escape to their homes without further molestation. For his
share in this affair,[2] and also for the part he took in conjunction
with Alexander, chief of Keppoch (*Alasdair nan Cleas*), in the
rebellion of Sir James MacDonald of Islay in 1615, he, together
with his son Allan, were outlawed by the Privy Council at
the instigation of Huntly, who was authorised to pursue and
arrest him ; and a few years later Mackintosh obtained a commission for himself and several other chiefs against Lochiel,[3]
but before it could be put in execution, Mackintosh died.
Eventually the earl of Argyll came to the rescue, and, owing
to his powerful influence, the sentence of outlawry was recalled
and the Cameron chiefs pardoned. Keppoch, having previously
submitted, escaped without punishment.

[1] Scott's " Lady of the Lake," Canto V. ix.
[2] Appendix XIV.   [3] Appendix XV.

CHAPTER IV.

WHILE these petty hostilities are disturbing the peace of the remote West Highlands, stirring events are occurring in the great world without, destined to leave their marks on the pages of the history of Scotland for all time. The romantic tragedy of the life of Mary Stuart has been played out to its bitter end at Fotheringay Castle; one continual succession of heart-stirring incidents, from that first scene at the old palace of Linlithgow, to the last scene of all at Westminster Abbey, when, with all the pomp and circumstances that became her royal position, she is laid to rest beside her implacable cousin, Elizabeth of England. The years roll by, the son of Mary Stuart, James VI., has in his person united the kingdoms of Scotland and England, and after a reign of fifty-eight years, sleeps by his mother's side at Westminster, and his son, Charles I., reigns in his place. And now once again the dogs of war are let loose in Lochaber, and the old castle is, as of yore, the centre of the conflict.

To understand the circumstances that again brought the tide of battle surging around the grim old fortress, we must take a hasty glance at the history of the period, and learn something of the great personages who took an active share in this memorable engagement. When in 1625 A.D. Charles I. succeeded to the dual throne of Scotland and England, he had not forgotten his father's favourite project of effecting the same reforms in the Church of Scotland that had already been brought about in the Church of England, viz., the restoration of the Episcopacy, with all the dignity and honour that belonged to it in times past. The mass of the Scottish people had no objection to bishops as their spiritual rulers, and even the Presbyterian clergy could give no logical reasons for refusing to serve under them, as, by another name, they formed part of John Knox's original scheme of church government. But with the proud Scottish nobles it was quite another matter; they certainly had no wish to see the establishment of a powerful ecclesiastical hierachy in the realm, that might eventually despoil them of the estates that many of their number had acquired by questionable means at the time of the Reformation. Since that period the principal noblemen had received the tithes formerly given to the Church, on the understanding that they were to support the Reformed clergy. This privilege was of course grossly abused, even during John Knox's lifetime, and he is said to have observed, "I see two parts given to the devil, and the third must be divided betwixt God and the devil." Charles now determined by one vigorous measure to sweep away these abuses, and an Act of Revocation was passed before he had been a year on the throne, which practically gave the entire control of the tithes to the Crown, and, with the funds thus placed at his disposal, Charles decided to endow the new bishoprics. We may imagine the nobles would not stand quietly by and see their ill-gotten gains slipping from their grasp without a struggle, and a deputation was immediately sent to the king, who, now becoming aware of the powerful opposition he had aroused, must needs dissemble, and agreed to modify the obnoxious Act, and in its stead issued a commission known as the Commission of Surrender of Superiorities and Tithes, which for a time quieted the slumbering discontent of the aristocracy, and gave satisfaction to a large number of the small landowners, who had for years past suffered severe exactions at the hands of their temporal rulers. Had Charles stopped here all might have gone well, as he was affectionately regarded by the majority of his Scottish subjects; but the ill-advised action of his favourite prelate, Archbishop Laud, in endeavouring to force the Liturgy of the English Church upon the Presbyterian clergy, served to arouse the slumbering discontent of the extreme section of the Reformed Church, which was soon fanned into action by the intrigues of the nobility, who were only too glad of the opportunity afforded them to foment a quarrel which could only lead to their further aggrandisement. The storm

soon broke, and within a year of the abortive attempt to read
the new form of service at St Giles, Edinburgh, 23rd July 1637,
the Presbyterians had bound themselves by a solemn oath to
eradicate Prelacy and to defend their Church, with their lives
if need be, against all her enemies. This bond was known
as the National Covenant, and was signed by rich and poor
alike throughout the realm of Scotland.

It is outside the scope of this work, interesting though
the subject may be, to describe all the great events which
followed on the signing of the Covenant; suffice it to say,
that the whole kingdom was soon in arms against its rightful
king, who, by his obstinacy and procrastination, had brought
matters to this pass. And now, like a meteor flashing brilliantly
across the sky on a winter's night, leaving a train of shining
sparks in its wake, so across the dim pages of history we see,
as it were, written in characters of fire, the name of Montrose,
a name feared by king and Covenanters alike; for true to his
convictions, both parties in the State had felt the strength of
his iron hand, and had used his military skill and intrepid
courage to good purpose.

It may here be worth while to digress from our narrative
for a few moments to glance rapidly at the part that Montrose
played in Scottish history, and, as after events will show,
Lochaber has every reason to be interested in all that pertains
to the Great Marquis, who left his mark upon the traditions of
that district for ages.

Born in the year 1612 at Montrose, James Graham inherited
all the traditional qualities of his heroic ancestry. His father,
the fourth earl, was not greatly distinguished in the service of
the State, and appears to have preferred a quiet country life,
and the peaceful pursuits of golfing, reading, and archery,
devoting much of his time to the care of his children. As is
often the case, Montrose more nearly resembled his celebrated
grandfather, who had held, under James VI., the important
offices of treasurer, chancellor, and viceroy, and whose fiery
spirit had frequently led him into serious brawls and feuds with

his neighbours. Montrose's mother was Lady Margaret Ruthven, daughter of the earl of Gowrie, and granddaughter of that old Lord Ruthven who was a grim actor in the terrible scene at Holyrood, when Rizzio fell at his mistress' feet, wounded unto death by the daggers of the jealous nobles. The early days of Montrose were passed at Glasgow, where he acquired his knowledge of the classics under the supervision of his tutor, William Forrett, and it is interesting to notice, as bearing upon his after life, that his favourite books were Xenophon's "Hellenics," "Seneca," and Raleigh's "History of the World." His father died in 1626, and the young earl, then in his fifteenth year, became a student at St Andrews, and, after the usual course of studies, in which he showed great proficiency, left the university, and shortly afterwards, 10th November 1629, married Magdalene, daughter of Lord Carnegie of Kinnaird. A description of his personal appearance at this period of his life, portrayed by the hand of Patrick Gordon of Ruthven, cannot but prove of interest. We learn that he was possessed of "a bodie not tall, but comely and well compossed in all his lineamentes; his complexion meerly whitee, with flaxin haire; of a stayed, graue, and solide looke, and yet his eyes sparkling and full of lyfe; of speache slowe, but wittie and full of sence; a presence graitfull, courtly, and so winneing upon the beholders, as it seemed to claime reuerence without seweing for it. . . . He did not seeme to affect state nor to claime reuerence, nor to keep a distance with gentlemen that ware not his domesticks . . . for his winneing behauior and courteous caryage got him more respect than those to whom they ware bound both by the law of nature, and by goode reason to haive gieun to it." Such was James Graham, Earl of Montrose, when he takes his place in the forefront of the history of these troublous times as the champion of the Covenanting body, at whose hands he was eventually to suffer an ignominious death.

It would be quite impossible, in the small compass of this work, to give anything approaching a detailed account of the

romantic and adventurous life of the Great Marquis, whose
brilliant achievements would fill a volume ; the subject has
already been most ably and exhaustively treated by
Mr Mowbray Morris in his recent book, to which I am
indebted for several of the facts given here.

Although Montrose had thrown in his lot with the
Covenanters, and had been placed by them in supreme
command of all the military forces at their disposal, his fiery
and independent spirit could not long brook the noticeable
preference shown by the heads of his party to his feudal
enemy, the Earl of Argyll, who was at this time probably
the most powerful noble in Scotland, and had only recently, at
the age of forty, succeeded to the immense estates of his father
in Argyllshire. Up to the present Argyll had been careful
not to identify himself with either party, but now, seeing the
opportunities the approaching hostilities would afford him of
taking summary vengeance upon his enemies under the guise
of patriotism, he determined to join the Covenanters, who, of
course, received such a puissant ally with open arms. Of a
cool and crafty disposition, he took every opportunity of
forwarding his own ends, while apparently devoted to the
interests of his party.

Montrose, on the other hand, was frank and open, and
although he had a somewhat arrogant bearing when in the
society of his equals in rank, he was most courteous and
affectionate to his inferiors. Skilled in the art of war and
all the latest improvements in military science, and possessed
of an unyielding purpose when once his mind was made up,
he maintained the honour of his party at every engagement
with the enemy. Notwithstanding these brilliant victories
over the Royalist forces, the Estates, influenced by Argyll,
were only lukewarm in their praise, and Montrose, fretful
under the supposed insult, and indignant at his treatment by
Argyll, who had now assumed almost dictatorial powers,
placed himself in communication with the king, who, with
little effort, induced him to promise his support in the future.

Shortly afterwards a document was signed by Montrose and several other noblemen, among whom were Mar, Almond, and Erskine, pledging themselves to unite in the royal cause. The knowledge of this having reached the ears of Argyll, Montrose was arrested and imprisoned in Edinburgh Castle, where he remained during King Charles's visit to that city, in August 1641. It was doubtless a source of bitter mortification to the king to have to admit his powerlessness to liberate Montrose from the clutches of Argyll, but such was the power of that crafty noble, that it would have been madness to attempt it; he, however, found means to communicate with the imprisoned earl, who informed the king that a plot had been formed against the royal person, in which both Argyll and Hamilton were implicated. Charles at once resolved to arrest the two noblemen mentioned, but having heard of his purpose they both fled. Eventually they were recalled to court, and, as an act of policy, the king advanced the Earl of Argyll to the dignity of marquis. Meanwhile, Montrose obtained his freedom, and now went boldly over to the king and joined his army in England, accompanied by several loyal Scottish noblemen, among whom were Crawford, Nithsdale, Reay, Ogilvie, and Aboyne. Montrose was hastily commissioned as Lieutenant-General of the Royal forces in Scotland, and a few months later, in May 1644, received his patent of marquis.

Events followed rapidly; the Marquis of Argyll had taken full advantage of the powers conferred upon him by the Committee of Estates, and after raiding the West Highlands as far as Lochaber, where he found ample opportunities of inflicting severe punishment upon his ancient enemies, the MacDonalds of Keppoch, he returned to Forfarshire, and learning that Lord Ogilvie was still absent in England, destroyed the " bonnie hoose o' Airlie " under circumstances of almost fiendish brutality.

CHAPTER V.

MONTROSE having returned to Scotland by circuitous paths, and carefully disguised, arrived at Blair in Athole, where he was soon joined by Alasdair MacDonell, son of Coll Mac Gillespie MacDonell (*Colla Ciotach*), chief of *Clann Iain Mhoir*, or MacDonalds of Isla, Kintyre, and Antrim, who was at the head of a body of fifteen hundred Irish, sent by the Earl of Antrim to support the royal cause. The men of Athole did not at first take kindly to their Irish allies, and but for the presence of Montrose, would probably have come into collision with them. Such, however, was the influence and tact of their great leader, and such the enthusiasm with which they regarded him, that all differences were soon forgotten in the excitement of the preparations for the march into the enemy's country. The royal army in Scotland now consisted of a body of untrained Highlanders and half-savage Irishmen, and accompanied with all the impedimenta of women and children. Badly armed, without cavalry or ammunition, success would have seemed impossible to anyone but Montrose, whose sanguine temperament and inflexible purpose nothing could daunt. As time went on, and victory after victory was assured to him, his little army grew in strength and efficiency, and, after the fall of Perth, he found himself at the head of a substantial force, well armed and equipped, with plenty of ammunition, and a welcome addition in the shape of fifty well-mounted troopers under the command of their leader, Nathaniel Gordon. Aberdeen was the next city to feel the power of the Great Marquis, and terrible were the scenes enacted on that awful 13th September 1644, when, owing to a promise made by Montrose in the earlier part of the day, on seeing a drummer boy wantonly slain by the Covenanters in cold blood, the city was given over to the tender mercies of the wild Irishmen, who slew and plundered all they could lay hands upon, regardless of age or sex.

And now Argyll was to learn by bitter experience what it was to have made an enemy of the relentless Montrose, who was now in a position to pay back with interest all the indignities that had been heaped upon him during the last few years. The race of Diarmid had few friends in the Highlands, and their chief, *Mac Cailean Mòr* (the Gaelic name for the Marquis of Argyll), had incurred the enmity of the most powerful of the clans by his double dealing and treachery, and now his territory was at their mercy, and they were not slow to wreak their vengeance upon their hereditary foe. From all sides the clans hastened to the banner of Montrose, thirsting for the blood of the hated Campbell. The MacDonalds of Clanranald, Keppoch, Glengarry, and Glencoe; the Stewarts of Appin ; Camerons from Loch Eil and Glen Nevis, in Lochaber; Farquharsons, MacLeans, and many others who had suffered from the rapacity of Argyll, now eagerly joined the royal forces, determined to carry fire and sword into the very heart of their enemy's country, and, if possible, surprise *Mac Cailean Mòr* in his stronghold of Inveraray, by the shores of Loch Fyne. Argyll, who was in Edinburgh when he heard of Montrose's meditated descent upon the Campbell country, hastened to Inveraray, and feeling assured that at this inclement season of the year, it being then the month of December, the mountain passes would be inaccessible, took no active steps to place himself in a state of defence, relying upon the great natural bulwarks with which his territory was surrounded to afford him all the protection that was necessary. He reckoned without his host : Montrose's hardy Highlanders, inured from their birth to all the rigours of the climate in which they had been reared, thought nothing of facing the biting blasts that howled through the desolate passes of Argyllshire. Like a mountain torrent in spate, they poured down from the hills, and with resistless force carried everything before them, burning and destroying all that came in their way; so that within the space of six weeks, from 13th December 1644 till the end of January 1645, the whole male population of Argyll and Lorn were either driven out or slain, and the country entirely devastated. On the first news of the near approach of Montrose, Argyll had, with a degree of cowardice which it is difficult to realise, incontinently fled to Dunbarton, leaving his country to the mercy of his foes. And now having, as he believed, thoroughly shattered the power of his old enemy, and taken his fill of vengeance upon the detested Campbell race, Montrose collects his straggling army, —who, flushed with victory, and laden with the spoils they have accumulated, are reluctant to leave the land they have conquered,—and anxious that the grass should not grow under his feet, marches rapidly through the wild pass of Glencoe and the braes of Lochaber with the intention of seizing the town of Inverness, which was at that time protected with only two regiments. Arriving at Kilcumin (or *Cille-Chuimein*), at the head of Loch Ness, he hears that the Earl of Seaforth is advancing to meet him at the head of a considerable force of men and horse. Montrose immediately determines to attack the earl, when other and more surprising intelligence is brought him, which entirely alters his plans. He now learns that his implacable foe, Argyll, has collected an army of three thousand men, and having reached Inverlochy, has taken up his headquarters at the old castle, from whence he is harrying Lochaber with fire and sword, and slaughtering its defenceless inhabitants in retaliation for the late raid on his own country.

The position of Montrose would now appear hopeless, hemmed in as he is on all sides by the enemies of the king. From the north, Seaforth is approaching with his army of five thousand men; from the east, a considerable body of Covenanting troops, under Major-General Baillie, are advancing across the Grampians, with instructions to fall upon Montrose as soon as he is engaged with Argyll, who now, having entrenched himself in the old fortress of Inverlochy, bars the road to the south with three thousand armed Campbells, sworn to revenge their slain kinsmen, and the great galley of *Mac*

glen, husbanding their strength for the coming conflict, which all knew would be a desperate one. The night is magnificent, the moon being nearly full, and illuminating the whole scene with picturesque grandeur. Above the sleeping Highlanders, who lie in groups all around wrapped in their plaids, towers the massive bulk of Ben Nevis, snow-crowned and majestic in the clear moonbeams; now and again upon the frosty air rings out the challenge of the Campbell sentries, as they stop some wayfarer or camp follower who tries to pass through their lines; the river Nevis, now almost frost-bound, runs babbling along chanting a lullaby to the slumbering warriors who line its banks; here and there the ghost-like figure of an officer clad in Highland garb moves noiselessly among the sleepers, as he goes with some important orders from one portion of the encampment to the other; and now, while the two armies sleep in peace under the starry firmament of heaven, waiting for the dawn that will herald in a day of mortal strife, let us consider for a few moments the component parts of the forces that are to so soon engage in deadly combat.

Argyll's army at Inverlochy consisted mainly of members of his own clan who had escaped from the hands of Montrose's men during the late raid in Argyllshire. The most important of his officers was his cousin, Duncan Campbell, the Laird of Auchenbreck (*Ach-na-breac*), who had been recalled by Argyll from Ireland, where he had been staying, to help in the military organisation of the clan, and was now, next to his chief, its principal leader. The other officers were Campbell of Lochnell, the eldest son of Lochnell, and his brother Colin. MacDougall of Rara was also a combatant on the side of Argyll. Turning now to the force under Montrose, we find it of a more complex nature, and composed of so many incongruous elements that nothing but the consummate tact and skilful generalship of the Great Marquis could have kept them harmoniously together. The chief command was given to Alasdair MacDonell of Antrim, who had proved himself a most able leader, and it may be said without exaggeration that many of Montrose's successes were

H

largely due to his Major-General's good advice and skilful
generalship. The Highland clans that formed the most
important part of the force were the MacDonalds of Keppoch,
under their chief, Donald Glas; the MacDonalds of Clan
Ranald, under the Captain of Clanranald; the MacDonalds of
Glengarry, under their chief, Æneas MacDonald[1] (IX. of
Glengarry), and his two sons, *Iain Mòr* (I. of Scotus) and
Iain Beag; the MacDonalds of Glencoe, and a large contingent
of MacLeans, MacPhersons, MacGregors, Robertsons (*Clann
Donnachaidh*), and Stewarts of Appin. Clan Cameron sent
three hundred men by command of their old chief, *Alein
Mac Iain Duibh*, who was too old and infirm to take any
active part in the combat. The acknowledged chief of the clan
was *Eobhan Dubh* ("Black Ewen," XVII. of Lochiel), grandson
of *Alein*, who at this time was a mere stripling of sixteen, and,
by the irony of fate, was now at Inveraray Castle, under the
guardianship of the very nobleman who was to shortly engage
in battle with his fellow-clansmen, almost within bowshot of
his ancestral home on the shores of Loch Arkaig. Of Sir Ewen
Cameron of Lochiel I shall have more to say in another
chapter.

There was one other personage among the followers of
Montrose who deserves notice here; this was the bard, Iain
" Lom " MacDonell, known locally as the " Bard of Keppoch."
It was he who had first carried the news of the occupation of
Inverlochy by the Campbells to the camp of Montrose, and
had afterwards guided the king's army through the trackless
wilds of Lochaber, the land of his birth, whose sublime scenery
of mountain, moor, and loch, abounding in legendary traditions
of Ossianic heroes, had inspired him with true poetic instinct,
and lent to his stanzas all the weird and picturesque charm that
is associated with Gaelic verse. Little is known of his history
prior to the wars of Montrose, except that he was descended
from Donald, who was a son of Iain "*Aluinn*," fourth chief of

[1] The old chief, *Domhnull MacAonghais mhic Alasdair*, grandfather of Æneas,
died on the day of the battle, over a hundred years old.

Keppoch. There is a story existing that Iain had been sent at an early age to Spain, to be educated for the priesthood, and that he had served his novitiate at the great ecclesiastical seminary of Valladolid.

Owing to some youthful indiscretion, he was expelled from the college and sent back to his native Lochaber, where he soon developed a taste for poetry, and employed his leisure time in composing some of the most powerful odes in the Gaelic language. He was a master of satire and pungent sarcasm, and in the expressive phraseology of his mother tongue he found ample scope for gratifying that love of caustic utterance which distinguished in a more or less degree all his compositions, and gained for him the respect of many of his superiors, who feared to offend the bard, lest some of the barbed arrows of his verses might be directed against them.

Montrose, with his usual insight into the character of those among whom his lot was cast, soon discovered that Iain Lom possessed a keenness of intellect, and was gifted with talents of a far higher order than were to be found among the majority of the Highlanders at that period, and he was not slow to hold out the hand of friendship to the bard, whose services he rightly concluded would be of great assistance to him in the enterprise he was now engaged upon. Iain readily responded to these friendly overtures, for he also saw that in Montrose he would possess a powerful ally, whose aid he might look for in helping him to inflict severe punishment upon his old enemies the Campbells; and so it came about that, between these two men of apparently diverse natures, the one a great and victorious soldier, the other a peaceful and studious poet, a strong friendship sprung up which lasted to the end. In a letter written by Montrose to Iain Lom from the camp near Kilsyth, we find him subscribing himself "Your very loving and true friend to command," thus showing the amicable feeling that existed between them. Some years after the events now related, the bard was appointed poet laureate to Charles II., for Scotland,

and I shall have occasion to refer to him later in connection
with the part he played in avenging the atrocious murder of
his young chieftain in the year 1663.

On the eve of the battle of Inverlochy, he was requested
by Alasdair MacDonell to arm himself with a claymore, and
fight for King Charles against his enemy Argyll, but Iain
prudently refused the proffered sword, remarking, "If I fall
in the field to-day, who is to sing your praises to-morrow?"
Such an argument was unanswerable, and so the bard, instead
of wielding the sword, took up the pen, which we know is
far mightier, and composed a triumphant ode descriptive of
the achievements of his clan in the great battle that was raging
all around him.[1] This poem, "*Latha Inbher-Lochaidh*," is a
masterpiece of word-painting, and is quite Homeric in some
of its descriptions, but as no translation (even if I were able
to give it) would adequately convey the sense of the idioms
and metaphors of the original Gaelic, I have taken the bold
course of describing the fight at Inverlochy in unpretentious
verse of my own, which I trust my readers will not criticise
too harshly.

THE BATTLE OF INVERLOCHY,

2ND FEBRUARY 1645.

THE winter's sun has sunk to rest behind the Morven hills,
The wintry blast blows keen and sharp o'er Lochy's murm'ring rills,
It stirs the pine trees quiv'ring leaves, by Loch Eil's rocky shore,
It fans the slumb'ring warrior's cheek, who dreams of far Lochawe.
Darker and darker grows the night, and deeper falls the gloom,
The air is filled with ghostly sounds, like voices of the tomb;
By Inverlochy's ivied keep, the night-hawks screaming fly,
Startling the hinds that in the depths of Mamore forest lie.
"Why sleep the sons of Diarmid, by the waters of Loch Eil?
Why come ye armed to Lochy's bank, with target and with steel?
Why leave your herds untended, by far Inveraray's shore?
Where dwells the chieftain of your race, the proud Mac Cailean Mòr."

[1] Iain Lom is said to have viewed the battle from one of the towers of Inverlochy
Castle, from whence he amused himself by hurling insulting epithets at the
vanquished Campbells.

While right athwart his pale, cold face, the morning's sunbeams gleam;
His galley bears him from the shore, far from the battle's din,
While from his foeman's ranks goes up a shout, " God save the King."
With flashing eye, and scornful lip, Montrose speaks to Glencoe,
" See how the traitor, like a hound, flees from his ancient foe,
But by the good sword in my hand, and by the Holy Rood,
This day shall many a Campbell bold provide the ravens food;
Do you Glengarry lead the right, and with your gallant band
Drive back the rebels, where they rest by Lochy's silver strand.
And you, brave Cameron, on the left, will rush upon the foe,
With all your trusty clansmen true, and deal them blow for blow;
Charge as ye love Lochaber and fair Ach-na-carry's towers,
While your war-pipes sound the onset, and the storm of battle lowers.
And you, my noble chieftains, Clanranald, Stewart, Hay,
Will share with me the honour of this great and glorious day;
You, Alasdair MacDonell, with your loyal Irish host,
Will wait my signal for the charge, whene'er I need ye most;
And now for God and country, for our honour and our king,
We'll fight this day that all your bards our valour oft shall sing."

　　*　　　　*　　　　*　　　　*　　　　*　　　　*

As when a foaming mountain stream, stemmed by some mighty rock,
Bursts its strong banks asunder, with a sound like thunder shock,
So with a shout that rends the air, and echoes thro' the glen,
The loyal clans, with headlong rush, charge on false Argyll's men;
The Campbell's make a gallant stand, with musket and claymore,
And many a Cameron bites the dust, beside his native shore;
The virgin whiteness of the snow is stained with heroes' blood;
It crimsons all the crystal tide of Lochy's rushing flood.
Fiercer and fiercer grows the strife, the clash of steel on steel
Rings out upon the frosty air, as back the Campbells reel;
Like leaves before an autumn blast, borne swiftly on the wind,
They turn and flee, in one mad rout, nor give one glance behind,
" Now on them, brave MacDonell," the noble Marquis cries,
And with a yell of mortal hate the Irish host replies—
Swift as an arrow from the bow, all eager for the fray,
They leave the cover of the rocks, and rush upon their prey;
The men of Keppoch, staunch and true, all mingle in the fight,
And strike for king and country, for their honour and the right.

　　*　　　　*　　　　*　　　　*　　　　*　　　　*

And now a shout of triumph loud resounds from hill to hill,
From mountain peak and granite crag it echoes loud and shrill;
It thunders down the Ardgour shore, to Cona's lonely glen,

It scares the eagles from their nests on mighty Nevis Ben ;
It floats upon the wintry breeze, and o'er the water glides,
Where on the bosom of Loch Eil Argyll's fair galley rides.
Full well he knows the meaning of those shouts that rend the skies,
He sees his clansmen backward reel, he hears their piercing cries ;
He sees them like a rabble rout rush downward to the shore,
He sees the chieftains of his clan slain 'mid the battle's roar.
Backward, and ever backward, to the banks of blue Loch Eil,
Borne down by the impetuous foe, they stumble and they reel ;
Hard on the flying Campbell host Montrose's horsemen ride,
Till hundreds find a watery grave 'neath Loch Eil's flowing tide.
Argyll stands on his vessel's prow, with glance of cruel hate ;
He sets his galleys to the breeze, nor heeds his kinsman's fate.
His fleet, impelled by sails and oars, flies swift before the wind,
As curses loud go up to heaven from those he leaves behind ;
False to his country and his king, his race and ancient name,
Saved from Montrose's vengeance, but to die a death of shame.

The words of Iain Lom's poem will be found in the
Appendix,[1] as written by him in the seventeenth century, and
will, I am sure, prove of interest to those of my Gaelic
readers who are unacquainted with his works.

CHAPTER VI.

YES, incredible as it may appear, the mighty chieftain of Clan
Campbell had fled from the vengeance of his victorious enemy,
leaving the wretched remnant of his army exposed to all the
fury of the relentless MacDonalds and Camerons, who had old
scores to pay off for many an act of cruelty and barbarous
treatment they had received at the hands of *Mac Cailean Mòr*.
The carnage was terrific, and claymore and dirk did their bloody
work only too well. Two hundred Campbells, with a desperate
rush, endeavoured to find a safe retreat within the walls of the
old castle; but the attempt was futile, and being observed by
Montrose, a body of horse was sent to intercept them, and they
were put to the sword, or, seeking to escape along the shores of

[1] Appendix XVI.

Loch Eil, were driven into the sea and drowned. A large number fled along the Achintore road to a spot near where Fort William now stands, followed closely by their hereditary enemies, the MacDonalds, and having reached a meadow at the base of the Cow Hill, made a last gallant effort to shake off their remorseless foes. Forming up in battle array, the miserable remnant of the great Campbell host awaited the arrival of their pursuers, and, with sword in hand, determined to sell their lives dearly. Flushed with the excitement of victory, the MacDonalds charged across the river Nevis, and with irresistible force threw themselves upon their enemies, who, quite unable to resist the vigour of the onset, were cut down where they stood. While the slaughter was proceeding, MacDonell of Antrim placed his banner on a small hill to encourage his men to action. The spot is still known as *Torran-na-brataich*, or the "Knoll of the Banner"; and the field where the fight took place is called to this day *Acha-a-chatha*, the "Field of Battle." Some few of the Campbells, more active than the rest, managed to escape from the scene of bloodshed, and were not observed by the MacDonalds until they had proceeded some distance. Enraged that any of the race of Diarmid should evade the fate that had been meted out to their fellows, MacDonell gave chase along what is now the upper Achintore road; but the Campbells having had a good start, he could not come up with them, and reluctantly had to give up the pursuit near Loch Lundavra. In accordance with the custom of the Highlanders, he placed a huge stone near the place at which he halted, which may yet be seen, and is known locally as *Clach nan Caimbeulach*, "The Campbell's Stone."

It is said that even now, when some enthusiastic member of the Clan Campbell passes along the road, he throws down the stone from its exalted position, and there it lies until a descendant of one of the loyal clans that fought under Montrose comes by the spot, and mentally consigning the whole of the race of Diarmid to the nether regions, he replaces the boulder in its old situation, and goes on his way rejoicing.

The Campbells are said to have lost no less than fifteen hundred men at Inverlochy, and among the most notable of the slain were Duncan Campbell of Auchenbreck, Campbell ot Lochnell, Colin MacDougall of Rara, and Major Menzies, brother to the laird of Ardchattan Barbreck.

Auchenbreck was made prisoner by Alasdair MacDonell, and given the choice of dying by the sword or the rope. His reply was characteristic, and has become proverbial, "*Dha dhiù gun aon roghainn*" ("Two evil alternatives that give no room for choice"). Scorning the degradation of death by hanging, he elected to meet a soldier's fate by the sword; and MacDonell, drawing his huge double-handed weapon, instantly beheaded him. Another remark which was made on this day has also passed into a proverb. One of the Robertsons, a smith or tinker by trade, had greatly distinguished himself in the battle, and MacDonell, who had watched his deeds of valour, complimented him by saying, "*Is truagh nach bu cheaird sinn gu leir an diugh*" ("'Tis a pity we were not all tinkers to-day").

The loss on the side of Montrose was trivial; the only officer of any note who was fatally wounded was Sir Thomas Ogilvie, son of the Earl of Airlie. He was badly injured in the leg, and died a few days after the battle, greatly regretted by his illustrious leader, who had lost in him a staunch friend and able officer.

The following remarkable dispatch was penned by Montrose on the field of battle, and sent by a special messenger to King Charles :—"Give me leave, after I have reduced this country, and conquered from Dan to Beersheba, to say to your Majesty, as David's general to his master, 'Come thou thyself, lest this country be called by my name.'" Possibly the scriptural phrases used by Montrose in this letter to his royal master were intended as covert sarcasms on the Covenanting slang of the period.

The victory was a brilliant one; the king's cause was triumphant, and his enemies had met the fate they merited as traitors to their rightful monarch. It is true the arch-traitor Argyll had escaped, but his punishment was yet to come, as all readers of history know; for the present, he was

I

safe in his castle of Inveraray, brooding over his disasters, and hatching fresh schemes of vengeance against Montrose.

The flight of Argyll from Inverlochy has never been satisfactorily explained, although many excuses have been offered for his extraordinary conduct in leaving his clan to face their hereditary foes without his presence at their head. There is a story that a few days previous to the battle he had sprained his right arm, and was thus prevented from using his sword. There may be some truth in this tradition, so far as the accident is concerned, but it is impossible to believe that such a cause as this would prevent a great Highland chieftain from leading his clan into action. Seen by the light of other events, Argyll's behaviour is, to say the least, suspicious, and certainly savours of cowardice, and it is easy to understand that his enemies made the most of what to them must have seemed a dastardly act. There is a quaint explanation of Argyll's flight given by the author of "Britanes Distemper" which is worth repeating. He says: "In this confusion, the commanders of there armie lightes wpon this resolution, not to hazart the marquiss owne persone; for it seemes not possible that Ardgylle himselfe, being a nobleman of such eminente qualitie, a man of so deepe and profund judgement, one that knew so weel what belongeth to the office of a generall, that any basse motion of feare, I say, could make him so wnsensible of the poynt of honour as is generally reported. Neither will I, for my owne pairt believe it; but I am confident that those barrones of his kinred, wha ware captanes and commanderes of the armie, feareing the euent of this battelle, for divers reasones; and one was, the Allan M'Collduie, ane old fox, and who was thought to be a seer, had told them that there should be a battell lost there, by them that came first to seike battell, this was one cause of there importunitie with him that he should not come to battell that day; for they sawe that of necessitie they must feght and would not hazart there chiefe persone, urgeing him by force to reteire to his galay, which lay hard by, and committe the tryall of the day to them, he, it is to be thought, with great difficultie yeelding to there request, leaves his cusine, the laird of Auchinbreike, a most walorous and braue gentleman, to the generall commande of the armie."

Whatever may have been the real cause of Argyll's precipitate flight, we cannot imagine that a man of his arrogant and overbearing disposition could have been coerced by his kinsman into such a questionable action at a time when his presence was of the greatest importance to his clansmen. The Highland chieftain of the fifteenth century was no mere figurehead, as some of his degenerate descendants are at the present day. He lived among his people, and acquainted himself with their wants and necessities, and exercised an almost paternal authority over them; in return for his protection, their lives and what little property they possessed were at the chief's absolute disposal in times of feudal war with neighbouring clans, or in the numerous *creachs* or forays that were of common occurrence among the Highlanders of that age. At such periods the chief was expected to take his place at the head of his clan, and share with them the dangers of the fight and the honours of the victory. The conduct of *Mac Cailean Mòr*, judged by this standard of Highland custom, must have seemed inexplicable to his followers, and it is certain that he lost considerable prestige among them after the events just related.

" *Palmam qui meruit ferat,*" the laurels of victory now crowned the brow of Montrose, who by sheer determination and pluck had overcome all obstacles, and shown himself worthy of the confidence his royal master had placed in him.

It is beyond my province to follow in detail the events of Montrose's campaign in the Highlands, or trace the fortunes of the brave chieftains and loyal gentlemen who were attached to the cause he represented. After Inverlochy came the engagements of Auldearn, Alford, and Kilsyth, in all of which the royal army was successful, and then the fickle goddess forsook her favourite, and the tide of war was changed. The disaster at Philiphaugh on 13th September 1645, in which, after a hardly fought battle, Montrose was defeated by the

Covenanting general Leslie, was followed by an order from
the king to disband the army.   Montrose reluctantly com-
plied with the royal command, and after saying farewell to
his devoted Highlanders, embarked on board ship for Norway.
The end was soon to come.   After the execution of Charles I.,
Montrose sailed for the north of Scotland, and having again
collected a small army, he came into collision with the enemy
(who were commanded by Lieutenant-Colonel Strachan) at
a place called Carbisdale, on the borders of Ross-shire.   Here,
on the morning of 27th April 1650, his force was completely
routed, and though Montrose escaped immediate capture, he
shortly after fell into the hands of the Covenanters, and was
conveyed to the castle of Edinburgh.   All students of history
know the details of the heroic end of James Graham, first
Marquis of Montrose, so tragically and pathetically described
by Aytoun in his " Lays of the Scottish Cavaliers"; he tells
us how—

> " He mounted up the scaffold,
>   And he turn'd him to the crowd ;
> But they dared not trust the people,
>   So he might not speak aloud ;
> But he looked upon the heavens,
>   And they were clear and blue,
> And in the liquid ether
>   The eye of God shone through ;"

and then, after having bent his knee to his Maker in humble
contrition for his shortcomings, while the black-robed Covenanting clergy stood scowling by,—

> " A beam of light fell o'er him,
>   Like a glory round the shriven,
> And he climb'd the lofty ladder
>   As it were the path to heaven.
> Then came a flash from out the cloud,
>   And a stunning thunder roll,
> And no man dared to look aloft,
>   For fear was on every soul ;
> There was another heavy sound,
>   A hush, and then a groan ;
> And darkness swept across the sky—
>   The work of death was done !"

An ending such as this was a worthy conclusion to a life of devotion to king and country, and Lochaber may well be proud of its associations with the Great Marquis, whose name will live in the memory of his fellow-countrymen as long as Scotland exists ; and if any apology is needed for my having devoted so much space to this subject, it will be found in the fact that even to this day the men of Lochaber cherish every tradition and legend that pertains to the gallant Montrose.

The old castle of Inverlochy still stands, a grim and silent witness of that terrible Sabbath morning, nearly two hundred and fifty years ago, when the might of the great Clan Campbell was broken, and the bodies of its slain chieftains left on the field for the eagles of Ben Nevis to quarrel over. Little now remains of this once great stronghold. A few crumbling fragments of masonry, held together by a thick growth of ivy, the vivid green of which serves to accentuate the gloomy recesses of the ruins. Yawning chasms, black as night, leading to fearful unexplored dungeons below, from whence at dusk issue weird bat-like creatures, easily transformed by the superstitious High-landers into the forms of *daoine sith* (literally, "men of peace," fairies), or other supernatural and uncanny beings peculiar to the district. The great Comyns Tower still remains almost intact, and part of the winding stone staircase can yet be seen within it, up which we may ascend and look forth from the opening in the massive walls (here ten feet thick), where a window has once been, over a glorious prospect of mountain and lake, moor and pasture, where the shaggy Highland cattle are contentedly grazing among the heathery knolls, in picturesque groups, worthy of the brush of a Landseer or Rosa Bonheur. The tinkle of the sheep-bell breaks harmoniously upon the silence, followed by the short, sharp bark of the collie, who we may see rushing wildly here and there intelligently driving his fleecy charges from one pasture to another, his black-and-tan, or sable and white coat, shining like silk in the sun, "his gaucie tail" wagging with the very exuberance of his

high spirits and the mere joy of existence. I love the Highland
collie, with his mild sad eyes that altogether belie the excitable
nature that lies beneath his glossy coat. Keen and of the
highest intelligence, he is almost human, and whole volumes
might be filled with anecdotes of his wonderful sagacity.

> " His honest, sonsie, baws'nt face,
> Aye gat him friends in ilka place,"

wrote Burns of one of the race, and all who have studied
the habits of the collie can appreciate the lines of the
ploughman poet.

Within a few feet of the western side of the castle, the river
Lochy (here of considerable width) flows swiftly by, and as we
rest in the cool shade of the great walls, we may hear the plash
of a salmon as it rises to take some passing insect, and catch a
glimpse of the silvery sheen of its flashing scales—

> " *Tha bradan tana-gheal 'sa choire gharbhlaich,*
> *Tha tig 'n o'n fhairge bu ghailbheach tonn* "[1]—

as for one moment a ray of sunshine transforms it into a
resplendent jewel ; or we can watch the never-ending flight of
the swallows, as with graceful twists and turns they glide over
the face of the water.

It is a place to come and while away an hour or so in
communion with our own thoughts, and muse over the great
historical events that happened in the neighbourhood of the old
fortress ; and as the glamour of the surroundings sinks into our
soul, we can repeople the ancient walls with the ghostly shapes
of the great warriors who fought and died under their shadow.
The shades of evening begin to close in around us, and the
sun, with all the glorious splendours of transcendent colouring,
slowly disappears behind the great peak of *Sgor-a-ghuisachain*,
that guards the head of Loch Eil, which, like a sea of molten
gold, blazes in the distance. With reluctant footsteps we turn
from the scene, and as we retrace our homeward way the stars
come out one by one in the pale green and amber of the autumn

[1] Duncan Bàn MacIntyre, "*Coire Cheathaich.*"

twilight, and one great planet scintillates brilliantly above the
dark outlines of the Ardgour hills "with mild benignant ray,"
shining bright and clear in the afterglow. Upon the summit of
old Ben Nevis[1] the sunbeams still lovingly linger, as though
loth to leave him to the mists and clouds that gather round his
hoary brow as the darkness of night approaches. "Soft falls
the eventide" in these northern latitudes, no rapid transition
from day to night, but a gradual and imperceptible fading away
of the daylight amidst such wonderful changes of colouring that
not even a Claude or Turner could depict ; delicate half tints of
pale rose, blending harmoniously with an indescribable hue that
is neither green nor yellow, forming a background for great bars
of purple and gold clouds, against which the mountain masses
stand out boldly, their every peak and ridge sharply defined in
the clear atmosphere. And so night comes on, stealing upon
us before we are aware of its presence ; the reds and greens of
the sky have changed into a curious luminous grey, and the
purple cloud shapes are now of inky blackness, and can hardly
be distinguished from the mountains they so nearly resemble.

Looking across Loch Eil, we can see the lights in the cottage
windows at Corpach; and the white obelisk at Kilmallie, erected
to the memory of noble John Cameron (who fell at Quatre Bras
at the head of his gallant Highlanders), stands out weird and
ghost-like against the hill of *Cnoc-nam-Faobh.* Far away down
Loch Linnhe the flash of the Corran lighthouse pierces the
gloom with intermittent brightness, and we may perchance
see the lights of the great steamer, and hear the throb of its

---

[1] There is considerable diversity of opinion among Lochaber folk as to the
derivation of the name of this famous mountain.   The most usually accepted theory is
that Ben Nevis is a phonetic contraction of the Gaelic *"Beinn-neàmh-bhathais," i.e.,*
"the mountain with its summit in the sky"; from *beinn,* "mountain"; *neàmh,* "heaven
or sky"; and *bhathais,* "forehead or summit."   The pronunciation of this compound
word is almost identical with the English "Ben Nevis."   The late Mrs MacKellar,
a competent local authority, gives it as her opinion that the name is derived from
"*Beinn-nimh-uisg,*" literally, "the mountain of the biting cold water," from the fact
that the torrents that continually pour down its granite sides have their source in the
snow-filled crevasses of the summit, and are in consequence intensely cold.   There
are probabilities of truth in both theories, but personally I lean to the one first stated.

paddles as it ploughs its way to its resting-place for the night at Corpach, bearing a freight of humanity from many climes, who have come here to see something of the "land of brown heath and shaggy wood," far from the noise and bustle of the great cities of the world, where nature is forgotten in the struggle for wealth and position. Surely the everlasting mountains, the glorious ocean, and the ever-changing landscape, with all its varied colouring and romantic associations, must have a soften-ing influence for good, even upon the most frivolous and cynical minds, and tend to raise them to a higher level.

CHAPTER VII.

AFTER this deviation from my narrative, for which I trust my readers will pardon me, I must return to the state of affairs in Lochaber after the battle of Inverlochy and the execution of Montrose. The realm of Scotland was now plunged in all the miseries of civil war, and again the Highlanders of Lochaber were called upon to take an active part in the strife. The young king, Charles II., who had fled to the Continent a short time previously to the execution of his father, had accepted the offer of the Scottish Parliament, and had given his kingly word that he would conform to the principles of the Presbyterian body, and accept the Solemn League and Covenant in its entirety, and further its tenets by every means in his power. On these terms he returned to Scotland, and received the crown from the hands of the Marquis of Argyll at the old palace of Scone. While these events were occurring, Cromwell had mustered a large army of sixteen thousand men for the invasion of Scotland, determined at all hazards to prevent a union between the Covenanters and the English Presbyterians, which he knew would prove disastrous to his own ambitions. Advancing rapidly by forced marches, and with that untiring energy which distinguished this great commander, he crossed the Border on 22nd July 1650, and in an almost incredible space of time had made himself master of the lowlands south of the Clyde and Forth, with the exception of Stirling, which held out for some time later, and only succumbed to the English after a terrible bombardment. Crossing the Forth at Queensferry, exactly at the spot where the Forth Bridge now stands, Cromwell reached Perth only to find the king had fled into England at the head of a considerable force of about fourteen thousand men, two thousand of whom were English, and had attached themselves to their royal leader at various points along the line of march. Leaving one of his most tried officers, Monk, behind, Cromwell hastily followed the king into England, and, overtaking him at Worcester, engaged him in battle, and after a desperate fight of five hours' duration, the king's army was entirely routed, and Charles had once again to seek safety in flight.

Meanwhile the Cromwellian general, Monk, was not idle in the north, and as his name is so closely associated with the civil war in Lochaber, I will give a short account of his history and antecedents.

He appears to have been of gentle birth and of good education, and was for some time an officer in the army of Charles I., but having been made prisoner by the Roundheads, he abjured his Royalist principles, and, having accepted a commission in the Parliamentary forces, soon raised himself to the position of general by his high courage and military accomplishments, and, at the time of which I write, was the most trusted of Cromwell's officers in Scotland. Placed in supreme command of the English troops in the north, he lost no time, during his leader's absence, in erecting forts and planting garrisons in all the disaffected districts, and his attentions were very soon directed to the Western Highlands, and Lochaber in particular, where dwelt, in the security of their native mountains, those troublesome Highlanders whom no amount of persuasion or bribery could bring to his side. Determined to punish their pride and insolence, he sent three separate detachments of soldiers into Lochaber, under General Dean and

K

Colonels Lilburn and Overton, in order to overawe the recalcitrant chieftains. The result was ludicrous, and is humorously described by Balfour in the following quaint language :—

"The Frassers came in to them and condiscendit to pay them cesse; bot Glengarey stood out, and in effecte the heighlandmen fooled them home again to the lowlandes; some with faire wordes, others stoode to the defence; and the Inglishe finding nothing amongst them save hunger and strokes, were glad (ther bisquet and cheesse being all spent, and ther clothes worne, with ther horsses out-tyred,) to returne, cursing the heighlandes, to ther winter quarters, . . . General Dean lost some few men and horsses in viewing of the heighlanders."

We also hear, on the same authority, that Colonel Overton had every reason to congratulate himself on his escape from the clutches of the "heighlanders," as we are told that "If my Lord Marquesse of Argyle had not protected him, he and all that wer with him had gottin ther throttes cutte. So, weill laughin at by the heighlanders, he wes forced to returne with penurey aneuche, werey glad all of them that ther lives were saved."

Not a very dignified retreat, certainly, and we may well imagine the amusement the appearance of these Sassenach intruders in full flight must have caused the kilted Highlanders.

The result of this expedition was anything but satisfactory to General Monk, who now came to the conclusion that a strong permanent garrison must be established in the heart of the rebellious district of Lochaber, and selected a projecting point of land at the confluence of the river Nevis and Loch Eil, about a mile from the old Castle of Inverlochy (now fast falling into decay), to erect his new fort. The position, from a strategic point of view, was, on the whole, a good one, and being of a triangular form, only one side was exposed to a land attack, the other two sides being unassailable except by water. Material for its construction was brought rapidly by sea, and in a very short space of time the fort was completed, and several hundred men were landed and installed under the command of Colonel Bryan.

The following account of the new garrison and its environs is given in the MS. "Memoirs of Sir Ewan Cameron of Locheill":—

"The scituation of this Garrison is so singular and currious, that it deserves to be described. . . . It stands upon the South syde of a small gulf of that arm of the sea called Locheill, when by the turn of the mountains, it forms itself into an angle, and receives the rush of the great and rapid river of Lochy, which from the North, or opposite side rushes into it with such force and violence, that it preserves its stream intire, without any mixture, for a long way. The fort is scituated upon a plain almost level with the sea. . . .

"Behind the fort there arises a huge mountain, of prodigeous hight, called Beniviss, at that time addorned with a variety of trees and bushes, and now with a beautiful green. Its ascent is prety steep, though smooth. The top or summit is plain, covered with perpetwall snow, and darkened with thick clouds. On the East, the prospect opens into a glen or valley betwixt two mountains, beawtified with diversity of trees, shrubs, and bushes, besides many lovely greens, with a river at the bottom; which after being brocken by a heap of misscheapen stones; glides away in a clear stream, and wandering through woods, vales, and rocks in many windings, looses itself in the sea.

"On the West the Lake or arm of the sea, called Locheill, extends itself five long miles, through two ridges of hills, riseing on both sides, with many woods, greens, mosses, and torrents, falling doun with great noise and force from the rocks and precipices; and terminates the view by another mountain, which appears like a vast cloud in a distant region." . . .

There is little doubt that Monk's primary object in planting a garrison on this spot was to keep in check the powerful Clan Cameron, whose chief, Sir Ewen Cameron of Lochiel, he had vainly tried to bribe or threaten into submission.

I have already had occasion to mention this chieftain in

a previous chapter, when, as a lad of sixteen, he was living at
Inveraray Castle under the guardianship of the Marquis of
Argyll, and I will now proceed to give a more detailed account
of this remarkable man, who is inseparably connected with
the history of Lochaber.

Born in February 1629 A.D., at Kilchurn Castle, Loch Awe,[1]
Ewen Cameron of Lochiel (or, as he was known among the
Highlanders, *Eobhan Dubh*) was, at the age of ten, sent to
Inveraray to receive his education as a ward of the Marquis
of Argyll, who, crafty and calculating as we know him to
have been, doubtlessly used all the influence he possessed to
persuade his youthful charge to embrace those views which he
himself had decided to adopt. He succeeded only partially,
as the high spirits of the boy chief could not tolerate the
gloomy and morose teaching of the Covenanting clergy. His
conversion to his guardian's political and religious creed was
in name only, and we have every reason to believe that young
Lochiel was always at heart a staunch Royalist. Sir Walter
Scott states that Lochiel was converted to the side of the
king by the exhortations of Sir Robert Spottiswood, who
was executed for his adherence to Montrose. Whether this
was the case or not, we find him at the age of eighteen
declaring for the king, and it was his intention to have joined
the army of Montrose, but by the time he had left Inveraray,
the brave Marquis was a prisoner in the hands of his enemies.
Burning with an ardent desire to draw his sword in the cause
of his royal master, he joined the Earl of Glencairn in 1652,
who, after the execution of Montrose, had endeavoured to
maintain the honour of King Charles in Scotland.

Shortly after, we hear of Lochiel fighting bravely at the
head of his clan in a skirmish with Colonel Lilburn at
Braemar. A mountain pass had to be held during the retreat
of the royal army, and Glencairn had offered the difficult and
dangerous post to Lochiel. Accepting it with alacrity, he took
up his position, and held it bravely against considerable odds

---

[1] His mother was a daughter of Breadalbane.

for some time, but by a strategic movement a party of Lilburn's men made a detour, and Lochiel found himself attacked in flank. The Camerons under their chief made a gallant stand, but finding themselves completely outnumbered by their assailants, they retreated slowly and in good order up the side of the hill, showing their front to the enemy. This exploit saved Glencairn's men from being cut to pieces, and added fresh laurels to the fame of Lochiel.

Having thus won his spurs in the king's service, he returned to Lochaber, and had the mortification of finding, on his arrival at Ach-na-carry, that Monk had forestalled him, and had built a fort in the very centre of his territory, with the evident intention of overawing his loyal clansmen. He also received the unwelcome tidings that all the other important Highland chiefs had submitted to Cromwell, and that he was now entirely isolated, and could hope for no support from the neighbouring clans. This news, of grave import to himself and his faithful Camerons, so far from inducing him to follow the example of his brother chiefs, only made him all the more determined to avenge this insult to his name and race, the mere thought of which made the blood of his ancestors boil in his veins. His undaunted spirit could not brook the idea of the presence of the Sassenach red-coats in Lochaber, and he resolved that they should find in him no pleasant neighbour.

CHAPTER VIII.

CROMWELL'S recent experiences in Ireland, where his troops had frequently come in contact with the natives among the woods and mountains of that wild, and, at that time, uncultivated country, had taught him a lesson of prudence, and he had while in Scotland impressed upon his officers the importance of cutting down the forests and underwood in the proximity of any fort or garrison, in order that the enemy should not take advantage of the natural cover they afforded. In pursuit of this policy, which he fully appreciated, Colonel Bryan, a few days after his arrival, decided to commence operations among the wooded shores of Loch Eil. Fearing an attack from the Camerons, he sent the major portion of his men (it is said about three hundred) to engage in the work of destruction, and having embarked them in two sloops of war, they sailed across the loch to a place called Achdalieu, where they landed; and while one vessel remained there to afford them a means of retreat in case the necessity should arise, the other anchored under the hills of Ardgour on the opposite side. While these movements were proceeding, Ewen Cameron, who had been informed by spies of all that was taking place, arrived on the scene, and leisurely watched the actions of the English soldiers from behind the shelter of a clump of trees on the hillside, accompanied by thirty-eight picked men of his clan armed with muskets and bows, and with their trusty claymores slung at their backs. In the hearing of his followers, Lochiel vowed that the red soldiers should pay dearly for every tree they destroyed, and for every bullock they carried off from the black soldier's property (alluding probably to his own swarthy complexion, which had gained for him the name of *Eobhan Dubh*, or "Black Ewen"). With calm deliberation he counted the English as they landed, and informed those around him that they numbered one hundred and fifty men, exclusive of workmen, who, armed with bill-hooks and axes, had begun the work of devastation.

Devoted as the Camerons were to their young chief, and enraged at the intrusion of the hated Cromwellian soldiers into Lochaber, they were nevertheless disinclined to attack the English on the present occasion, as, owing to their limited numbers, defeat was almost a certainty. Lochiel probably guessed their thoughts, and asked those among them who had fought with the clan under Montrose whether they recollected any occasion on which that great leader had encountered a force so disproportionate to his own. The reply was that at no time could they remember such an occurrence. This answer only fired the ambition of the intrepid Lochiel, who was burning to avenge his wrongs, and turning to the kilted warriors, who were anxiously awaiting his decision, he said: "We will fight nevertheless, and if each of us kill a man, which is no mighty matter, I will answer for the result."

This courageous speech was received with acclamations and enthusiasm, especially by the younger and more inexperienced of his followers, who could hardly be restrained from at once dashing among the foe. The older members of his little band were more prudent, and would at first only agree to attack the English on the condition that their chief and his younger brother, Alan Cameron, should absent themselves from the fight; for they feared that if both were killed the chieftainship would pass out of the direct line of succession. Such a condition as this was of course out of the question so far as Lochiel himself was concerned—his chivalric and fearless nature scorned to accept any stipulation which might possibly affect his honour; but with regard to his brother Alan, he was only too glad to avail himself of the opportunity the occasion offered, to forbid him to risk his life in such a mad enterprise. Knowing how nearly the lad's spirit was akin to his own, and feeling assured that he would disregard any commands he might give him to abstain from joining in the approaching conflict, he had him tied to a tree in a place of safety, and stationed a boy with him in case any of the enemy should come near the spot. This treatment did not at all suit the fiery temper of young Alan Cameron, and he soon found means, by persuasion or threats, to induce his youthful guardian to release him from his ignominious position. Shaking himself free from his severed bonds, he hastened to his brother's side, who, finding it useless to attempt his recapture at this critical moment, and doubtless feeling a just pride in Alan's intrepidity, he allowed him to take his part in the action which was now impending.

Lochiel, although only twenty-five years of age at the time

of which I write, had already received some instruction in the art of war at the hands of Glencairn, and having had some experience of English military tactics in the previous engagements already referred to, was assured that his only hope of success on the present occasion was by creeping on his foes unawares under the cover of the thick undergrowth of the dense forest that came down almost to the water's edge. Instructing his men to reserve their fire until they were close to the enemy, they advanced slowly among the trees until within a few feet of the English, who were totally unprepared for the attack, many of them having laid aside their weapons so that they might be the better able to capture the bullocks with which they intended to replenish their larder. At a signal from Lochiel, the Camerons discharged their muskets and let fly their arrows, with so deadly a result that no less than thirty Englishmen were placed *hors de combat*, and before the remainder could recover from the panic this unexpected attack had thrown them into, the Highlanders, with a terrific shout and with the war-pipes sounding the onset, charged into their midst, dealing death and destruction on every side, as with claymore and Lochaber axe in hand they clove their way through the ranks of the red soldiers, driving them with irresistible force, all wounded and bleeding, into the blue waters of Loch Eil, whose placid surface was soon lashed into fury and stained crimson with the blood of the combatants.

A considerable body of the English, under an officer of splendid physique and distinguished valour, had become detached from the others, and were retiring in good order towards their ships, which now stood close inshore to take the fugitives on board. Lochiel, observing this movement, determined to intercept their retreat, and sent a small party of his men, with a piper, to attack them in rear, with orders to make as much noise as possible, so that the English might think that another body of Highlanders had arrived to assist the Camerons. The plan answered as he had anticipated.

With fearful yells, and with the piper blowing his loudest the pibroch of the Clan Cameron (the words of which are addressed to the wolves and birds of prey—"*A chlanna nan con! a chlanna nan con! thigibh a' so 's gheibh sibh feoil!*" "Children of the dogs! come to me and I will give you flesh!"), the Highlanders rushed from the wood upon the retreating soldiers, who, imagining that escape was now hopeless, turned bravely round and faced their former assailants; but before they had time to rally, the Camerons were upon them, hacking and hewing with axe and claymore, until in sheer desperation they fled along the shore, closely pursued by the Highlanders, and plunged headlong into the sea. Reckless with excitement, the Camerons followed until both parties were chin deep in the water, and still the fight went on, amid the shrieks and groans of the wounded and drowning men, and the victorious shouts of the Highlanders, who saw their mortal enemies perishing before their faces. An incident now occurred which it is impossible to avoid mentioning, although it has been described over and over again by many abler pens than mine. While the fight was at its height, the English officer before mentioned, noticing that Lochiel had been separated from his companions, sprang forward and engaged him in single combat. The superior strength and stature of the Englishman gave him considerable advantage over the young Highland chief, and for a time it seemed that nothing but a miracle could save Lochiel from destruction. It was now that his early training among the hills of his native country stood him in good stead; with the keenness of sight and activity of limb engendered by many a day spent among the mountains in pursuit of the red deer, he watched his opportunity, and with a rapid and dexterous movement he suddenly disarmed his antagonist. In a moment the powerful Englishman closed with Lochiel, and after a desperate struggle both fell to the ground clasped in a deadly embrace. It chanced that the officer was uppermost, and seeing his sword lying within a few paces, he made a frenzied effort to obtain possession of it. While in the act of stretching his

L

arm in the direction of his weapon, he left his throat unprotected, and Lochiel, with the desperation of a man in mortal peril, immediately fastened his teeth in it, and, almost mad with passion, bit right through the windpipe, and did not let go until his enemy's hold loosened, and he died where he lay.

It is said by some historians, Sir Walter Scott among others, that Lochiel, so far from being ashamed of this episode, frequently boasted of it, and was even known to have said that the Englishman's flesh was the sweetest morsel he had ever tasted.

Having thus rid himself of his opponent, Lochiel hurried to the shore, where the fight was still raging, and joining his men, who were now fast obtaining the mastery over the redcoats, he sprang into the sea to their assistance; he had not proceeded far, when he noticed that a soldier on board one of the ships was in the act of levelling his piece at him; to duck his head was the work of an instant, and he narrowly escaped death, as the bullet grazed his head and carried away a lock of his dark hair. Surely Sir Ewen must have borne a charmed life that day, for his hairbreadth escapes were miraculous. A few moments after the first bullet had nearly ended his existence, another was fired at him, and would certainly have proved fatal had not his foster-brother observed the danger, and with heroic self-devotion flung himself in front of his chief, and received the missile in his own body.

In connection with the events of this day, Mrs MacKellar (who was a Cameron of the Camerons), in her very interesting guide to Fort William and neighbourhood, tells an amusing story of an incident that occurred during Sir Ewen Cameron's visit to London many years later. He had occasion to go into a barber's shop to get his beard and hair dressed. The garrulous barber having fixed him in position, and probably guessing from his accent that he was not born south of the Tweed, remarked: "You are from the north, sir, I believe?" "Yes," answered Lochiel, "I am; do you know people from the north?" "No," shouted the angry barber, "nor do I wish to; they are savages there. Would you believe it, one of them tore the throat out of my father with his teeth, and I only wish I had the fellow's throat as near me as I have yours just now." We may imagine that Lochiel's emotions at this juncture must have been the reverse of pleasant, and we may be sure he breathed more freely when the operation was over and he was again in the open air. We are told he never afterwards entered a barber's shop.

After the defeat of the English at Achdalieu, there were continued skirmishes between the Camerons and the soldiers of the new garrison; the Highlanders in nearly all instances coming off the victors. Thinking that the English would not again molest his territory, Lochiel attached himself to the small remnant of the loyal army in Scotland under General Middleton; but he was shortly afterwards recalled to Lochaber by the news that the garrison at Inverlochy were once more destroying his property, and harassing those of his clan who had not followed him to the field. Taking with him one hundred and fifty Camerons, and obtaining leave of absence from Middleton, he marched with great haste and secrecy, and upon his arrival in the neighbourhood of Inverlochy, he posted his men in the woods to which the English soldiers came every morning to cut fuel for the garrison. The day following his return to Lochaber, he was informed by spies that four hundred of his enemies intended making a great raid in the forest with a view to destroying a possible ambush. This was gratifying news to Lochiel, who now saw a swift means of revenging himself upon the detested Sassenachs, who were quite unaware of the trap laid for their destruction. Crouching among the thick growth of heather and bracken, the Camerons awaited in perfect silence the appearance of the foe. They had not long to wait, as in a few minutes the tramp, tramp of the English was heard, and they were seen approaching. Like famished wolves the enraged Highlanders sprang from their hiding-place, and the rapidity and vigour of the assault was so great, that at least a hundred Englishmen were killed within the first few minutes: the remainder fled and were pursued right up to the walls of the fort, and no further opposition was made except by the officers, who bravely made a last effort to retrieve their honour. It came too late, however; overpowered by Lochiel's men, they were slaughtered where they stood, and not one survived.

After this severe lesson the garrison became more cautious, and only ventured out when they knew the Camerons were engaged elsewhere. From time to time, however, Lochiel made his presence unpleasantly felt, and took every opportunity of harassing and annoying the Cromwellian soldiers, who began to find their existence in such a remote locality anything but an enjoyable one.

Occasionally the Highlanders would swoop down unexpectedly upon the detached hunting parties of Englishmen, who sought the pleasures of the chase as some relief to the monotony of their lives. In this guerilla warfare numbers were slain, till at last the garrison was almost depleted; and the authorities, seeing the futility of trying to coerce Lochiel into submission by the means they had up till now adopted, and not seeing their way at the present juncture to send a strong military force into Lochaber, decided to see what could be done by more peaceful and diplomatic measures, to make terms with the troublesome chieftain. The services of the astute Argyll were called into requisition, as it was concluded that he would have some influence with his late ward; and so it proved, as the politic marquis offered such honourable terms to Lochiel, in the name of the Commonwealth, that he found little difficulty in accepting them. The treaty was simple and concise, and very much in Lochiel's favour. He had merely to give his word of honour to live in peace with his neighbours, and on this condition he and his clansmen were not only allowed to retain their arms, but he was to receive an indemnity in money for all the losses he had sustained at the hands of the garrison.

The official acceptance of the treaty was made the occasion

of a dramatic spectacle, quite in keeping with the romantic
scenery which formed the background of the tableau. Mustering the whole of the Clan Cameron, in all the glory of their
picturesque attire of tartan kilt and plaid, Lochiel placed
himself at their head and marched them down to the level
ground at the rear of the fort. Armed with the terrible
Lochaber axe, and with claymore and dirk at their sides, the
Camerons formed up in military array, the bright sunlight of
a May morning flashing from their weapons as they stood on
the green sward, eyeing with glances of suspicion and curiosity
their late foes, while the pipers, with vigorous lungs, skirled
out the gathering tune of the clan. The English garrison,
headed by the commander of the fort, was drawn up in line,
facing the Highlanders at a few paces distant, their drums
beating the assembly, while over their heads the standard of
the Commonwealth floated in the breeze. After a brief
interval, Lochiel, with noble and dignified bearing, stepped
forward, and having saluted the English officer with a courtly
bow, laid his sword on the ground, stating, in the hearing of
the assembled forces, that he did so in the name of king
Charles, and at the same time motioning his followers to do
likewise. This order was carried out with some reluctance by
the Camerons, but they eventually followed the example of
their chief, and with many invectives in forcible Gaelic, which
were anything but complimentary to the English, they laid
their arms upon the grass and stood waiting to see what
would happen next. Lochiel now stooped down, and picking
up his trusty weapon, replaced it in its sheath in the name
of the Commonwealth, and again saluting the commander
rejoined his men, who had by this time recovered their own
arms.

Thus the honour of both sides was satisfied, and peace
secured to Lochaber for some time at least.[1]

[1] Appendix XVII.

CHAPTER IX.

FOR some years after the occurrences recorded in the preceding chapter, there is little of importance to relate in connection with the Western Highlands of Scotland, but in the great world without, events pregnant with the fate of the realm were occurring every day, and to follow the sequence of history it will be necessary to slightly touch upon them here.

On 29th May 1660, Charles II., after an enforced absence from his kingdom of nine years, entered the City of London amid the joyful acclamations of the populace, and once again sat upon the throne of his Stuart ancestors. The days of the Commonwealth were at an end; the same mob which had surged round the scaffold of the unfortunate Charles I. at Whitehall, on that bleak January morning eleven years before, and with their ribald jest and blasphemous religious cant had endeavoured to drown their dying monarch's last words, now shouted themselves hoarse, as they welcomed his son on his entry into the metropolis.

There was one nobleman in London at this time who could not but feel some misgivings as to the treatment he was likely to receive from the recently returned king; this was Argyll, who, upon hearing of the restoration of the monarchy, hastened to London to make the best terms he could with his sovereign, and hoping that in the general amnesty granted to political offenders, his own traitorous actions during the late civil war might be overlooked. However ready Charles might have been to forgive and forget past injuries, his cavalier advisers took care that Argyll should not benefit by any clemency their royal master might extend to those that had taken up arms against him. Almost immediately upon his arrival in London, Argyll was arrested and conveyed to the Tower, and shortly afterwards sent a prisoner to Scotland, where he was tried for high treason, and being found guilty, was beheaded at Edinburgh on 27th May 1661. It is only just to say that he met his fate with the greatest fortitude, as became the descendant of the race of Diarmid. By a curious coincidence, his head was placed after his execution on the same spike, on the Tolbooth, that had been occupied by the head of Montrose.

The years immediately following the Restoration were years of grave import to the realm of Scotland, sad, mournful years of trial and suffering to those staunch Covenanters who still held to the oath they or their fathers had sworn in the days of Montrose. The history of that terrible period is yet indelibly stamped upon the minds of the descendants of those brave men, who, however mistaken their ideas may have been, had the courage to suffer martyrdom for the faith they loved better than life itself. It would be quite impossible here to attempt the task of describing the many tragic events that followed upon the return of the Royalists into power, and happily the district of Lochaber, by its very inaccessibility, was spared the scenes of bloodshed that were now of common occurrence in the lowlands, engendered by the intense hatred with which the Royalists regarded the Covenanters, at whose hands they had suffered so much during the last few years, and whom they looked upon as morally responsible for the murder of their beloved monarch.

Charles II. died suddenly on 6th February 1685, his end being doubtless hastened by the habits of dissipation which he had indulged in since his restoration to the throne. Upon his death, his brother, the Duke of York, succeeded to the crown of the two kingdoms as James II. of England and James VII. of Scotland; but owing to his having embraced the Roman Catholic faith, he was regarded with suspicion by a very large number of his subjects, both in England and Scotland, who foresaw that the privileges and benefits conferred upon the realm at the time of the Reformation were now in danger of being withdrawn, a prospect which they could only look forward to with feelings of grave apprehension. The next in succession to the throne was the king's eldest daughter, Mary, who had espoused Prince William of Orange, the Statholder of the Dutch Provinces. This young prince was already distinguished for his courage

and military prowess, and his well-known staunch adherence
to the Protestant faith rendered him an object of considerable
interest to the supporters of that creed in England, who looked
upon him as a possible saviour of their country from the Popish
thraldom under which it was now beginning to suffer.

Having thus briefly explained the state of affairs in the
world beyond the Highland mountains, we will return to
Lochaber, and see what had been happening there.

Shortly after the restoration of Charles II., probably about
the year 1663, an event occurred in Lochaber of tragic interest,
known to history as " The Keppoch Murder." Allusion has
already been made to this incident in a previous chapter when
describing the career of " Iain Lom," the " Bard of Keppoch."
It is an old and well-worn story of a barbarous crime and
its well-merited punishment, but having been perpetrated in
Lochaber, it must find a place here.

Donald *Glas*, the eleventh chief of the MacDonalds of
Keppoch, who had fought on the side of king Charles at
Inverlochy, died a few years after that celebrated victory,
leaving two sons, Alexander and Ranald. At the time of
their father's decease the two boys were at school in France,
whither they had been sent to receive such education as
would befit them for the position they were to fill as heads of
a great and powerful clan. Immediately upon the death of
Keppoch, seven cousins of the absent heirs assumed the manage-
ment of the estates, and appropriated the revenues to their own
use, exercising at the same time all the privileges of chieftainship
over the clan, and enjoying with full zest the pleasures of their
newly acquired power and increased wealth. The arrival of the
young chiefs from France put an end to their short-lived
aggrandisement, and it was with feelings of bitter jealousy
rankling in their hearts that they welcomed the two brothers to
Keppoch. Taking counsel together, they determined to rid
themselves of their young kinsmen at the first opportunity that
presented itself. The evil day was not far off, as shortly after
the return of the two Keppoch chieftains to their ancestral

home, they invited their seven cousins to dine with them. At first all went well, but after dinner, when the wine began to flow freely, the catastrophe took place. Young Ranald of Keppoch, by way of a joke, presented one of his cousins with a French cap which he had brought with him from the Continent. Spurning the proffered gift, which he threw angrily from him, he drew his dirk and stabbed Ranald to the heart. In an instant all was confusion, chairs and tables were overturned, and Alexander, enraged at his brother's death, sprang at the murderer, and, young as he was, would probably have slain him had he not been overpowered by the others. Mortally wounded he fell to the ground, and breathed his last over the body of his dead brother.

Some presentiment of evil seems to have entered into the mind of the sister of the two lads, for at the conclusion of the repast she left the house in search of her old friend and kinsman, "Iain Lom." Taking him into her confidence, she told him her suspicions, and asked his counsel in the event of a quarrel taking place. Comforted by the sympathy and advice of the venerable bard, she returned home to find her brothers foully slain, and the wretches who had done the deed escaped.

When the news of the outrage reached "Iain Lom," he vowed a terrible oath of vengeance against the assassins, and swore never to rest until he had brought them to justice. Strange as it may appear, the clansmen of Keppoch seem to have had no great desire to punish the murderers of their chiefs. This was probably due to the fact of their long absence from the property, and doubtless the usurpers had taken every opportunity of ingratiating themselves with the people they had hoped to rule.

"Iain Lom," finding he could not arouse them from their apathy, applied to MacDonald of Glengarry, who, being allied by ties of blood to the murdered lads, he doubted not would assist him in his efforts to avenge their death. Glengarry, however, could not be persuaded to interfere with the affairs of another branch of the clan, notwithstanding the passionate entreaties of the bard. Indignant at his reception by Glengarry,

M

"Iain Lom" turned to another chieftain of Clan Donald, Sir Alexander MacDonald of Sleat, and composed some very fine verses in his praise which are still extant. The meeting with Sir James MacDonald of Sleat, the son of the chief, is thus described by a well-known writer on Highland affairs:[1] —

"Where are you come from?" asked Sir James.

"From Laodicea," replied the bard.

"Are they cold or hot, now, in that place?" asked Sir James.

"Abel is cold," cried the bard, "and his blood is in vain crying for vengeance. Cain is hot and red-handed, and the hundreds around are lukewarm as the black goat's milk."

The bard's importunities were at last crowned with success; MacDonald of Sleat promised he would send sufficient men into Lochaber to assist "Iain Lom" in fulfilling his vow. A message was at once sent to Archibald MacDonald of Uist[2] to proceed to Keppoch with fifty well-armed men, and place them at the disposal of the bard. Upon the arrival of this force "Iain Lom" proceeded to the house of the murderers at Inverlair, which he found strongly fortified and barricaded, and it was some time before an entrance could be effected. Resistance, however, was useless, and notwithstanding a gallant defence, the seven brothers were surrounded on all sides, and met their fate beside their own hearthstone.

The day of reckoning had arrived, the blood of the murdered lads no longer cried out for vengeance, but the wrath of "Iain Lom" was not yet appeased. The dirk with which Ranald of Keppoch had been stabbed had been carefully preserved by Iain, and he now found a use for it. Drawing it from its sheath, he cut off the heads of the seven brothers, and making a rope of heather, tied them to it by the hair. Slinging the ghastly burden over his shoulder, he departed from the scene of slaughter, and after washing the heads in a well close to the

---

[1] Mrs MacKellar.

[2] Archibald MacDonald, known among his people as "*Ciaran Mabach*," was an illegitimate son of Sir Alexander. Like his friend Iain Lom, he was a bard of some pretensions, and several of his compositions have come down to us, his "*Marbhrann do Shir Sheumas Mac Dhonuill*" being the best known.

side of Loch Oich, he presented them to Glengarry, and finally sent them to Sir Alexander MacDonald of Sleat as evidence that justice had been done. The well may still be seen, and is known locally by the Gaelic name of "*Tobar nan Ceann*" ("the Well of Heads"). A gruesome monument has been erected by the side of the well, representing seven human heads rudely carved in stone, with a long inscription in four languages, which will be found in the Appendix.[1] Some years ago the reputed grave of the murderers was opened, and the seven headless skeletons discovered, proving beyond doubt the truth of the story.

The "Bard of Keppoch" composed a mournful lament to commemorate the tragedy, entitled "*Mort-na-Ceapach*,"[2] and the sister of the murdered boys, who was also a gifted poetess, wrote some pathetic verses, known in Gaelic as "*Marbhrann ni'n Mhic Raonuill*." Of more interest to English readers will be the beautiful poem by Mrs Ogilvy, which will be found in her book on "Highland Minstrelsy," of which the following is an extract :—

> "All is completed,
> The wicked defeated,
>   Conquered and slain ;
> Gory heads seven,
> From traitor heads riven,
>   We bring o'er the main.

> "The murderers are quiet now,
> Calm is each lifeless brow
>   Tranquilly sleeping ;
> Over the graves at night
> Hovers no more the sprite,
>   Watching and weeping.

> "All is fulfilled now,
> Murmurs are stilled now,
> Once more the Bard sings,
> Once more the heart rings,
> Once more I'll look on thee,
> Child of the Sennachie,
> Marsali, Marsali !"

---

[1] Appendix XVIII.

[2] Another lament for the murdered chiefs, by Iain Lom, will be found in Appendix XIX.

CHAPTER X.

AFTER the Camerons, the two most important clans in the district of Lochaber were the MacDonalds of Keppoch[1] and the Mackintoshes; the latter clan, as I have before mentioned, occupying a leading position in that powerful Highland association, the Clan Chattan, which comprised among others the MacPhersons, the Davidsons, the Farquharsons, the Shaws, and the MacBeans.

A long standing feud had existed between the MacDonalds of Keppoch and the Mackintoshes respecting the possession of certain lands in Glenroy, which were now held by Coll MacDonald, the fifteenth chief of Keppoch, a man of fearless courage, and well able to maintain the honour and reputation of his name and clan against his hereditary foes. He was the grandson of *Alasdair Buidhe*, the thirteenth leader of the clan, who had succeeded to the chieftainship of Keppoch after the murder of his nephews, Alexander and Ranald, in 1663. Alasdair of Keppoch had married twice; his first wife, who was a daughter of MacDonald of Bohuntine, was accidentally drowned in the river Roy, on Christmas night, while she was returning from a visit to some friends at Loch Treig.[2] After the usual period of mourning had expired, he espoused a daughter of Glengarry, who bore him two sons, Allan and Archibald. In the usual course Allan would have become chief upon his father's death, but owing to a suspicion that he had taken part in the "Keppoch murder," he was not allowed by the clan to assume the eagle's feathers, and his brother was elected chief in his stead.

[1] The chiefs of the Keppoch branch of the Clan MacDonald have always spelt their name MacDonell or M'Donell, but as we so frequently find them associated with the MacDonalds of Glengarry, Clanranald, and Glencoe, I have throughout this work adopted the customary method of spelling.

[2] The spot where the fatal occurrence took place is still known as "*Linne na-h ighnean.*"

Archibald, who thus assumed the chieftainship of Keppoch as fourteenth in descent from Alasdair Carrach, was a man of considerable parts, and exhibited in a marked degree the talent for versification which seemed to be hereditary in the Keppoch family, and which is still possessed by one at least of the modern descendants of that famous Lochaber chief, as the introductory poem with which this volume commences amply proves. Archibald married a daughter of MacMartin of Letterfinlay, the representative of the oldest branch of the Clan Cameron; by this lady he had issue, Coll, Ronald (of Tirnadris), Alexander,

Signature of MacDonell of Keppoch to an Address to George I. on his Accession to the Throne, 1714; in the Museum at Edinburgh.

Angus, and nine daughters, the eldest of whom, Juliet (or Cicely), was a poetess of some repute in Lochaber.[1]

Coll of Keppoch, descended as he was from the MacDonalds on one side and the Camerons on the other, could scarcely fail to prove a formidable opponent to the claims of Mackintosh, to the lands that his ancestors had held with the strong hand for centuries.

It would appear that Mackintosh had undoubtedly a pre-scriptive right to the territory in question, it having been granted to one of the ancient chieftains of his clan by the Lord of the Isles, 1447 A.D., in return probably for some

[1] This lady is known in Gaelic as *Sile*, or *Silis Nighean Mhic Raonuill*.

military service. This charter had been more recently confirmed by the Crown; but as in the Highlands, more especially, "possession was nine points of the law," Mackintosh
found it no easy matter to assert his rights to the property
while it was actually occupied by Keppoch, who, when asked
by what authority he held it, boldly stated that his charter
was not a paltry sheepskin, but his trusty sword, and that if
Mackintosh wanted it, he must come and take it. This proud
boast so enraged Mackintosh, that he determined that now or
never he would chastise his presumptuous rival, and endeavour
by every means in his power to regain his lost possessions.
The fiery cross (*crois tara*) was sent round Badenoch,
and in a short time the Clan Mackintosh, to the number
of a thousand, gathered round the yellow banner of their
chief. This force was considerably augmented by a body
of Government troops, under the command of Captain Mac-
Kenzie of Suddy, sent by order of king James, and we
have no doubt the assistance was very welcome to Mackintosh,
whose resources were strained to the uttermost.[1] With the
most sanguine hopes of success they marched into Lochaber
through Glen Spean, with the idea of attacking MacDonald
in his house at Keppoch, never doubting that he would
make that place his principal point of resistance. They
were surprised on arrival there to find the place entirely
deserted,[2] and Mackintosh, concluding that the presence of
the Government soldiers had decided Keppoch to avoid
a collision with a force so considerably outnumbering
his own, fondly imagined that victory was his without a
struggle. For his better protection, however, he decided to
strengthen his position by the construction of a fort on the
side of a steep hill above the river Roy; and it was while
employed in this manner that news was brought him that
Keppoch with about five hundred MacDonalds, strengthened
by detachments of their kinsmen from Glengarry and Glencoe,
were lying in ambush within a short distance, with the purpose

[1] Appendix XX.   [2] Appendix XXI.

of surprising the Mackintoshes at daybreak. This purpose
he decided to anticipate, and hastily mustering his clan, marched
them over the intervening hills that lay between him and his
enemies.

Arriving just as the dawn was breaking in the eastern sky,
upon the slope of a hill known as Mulroy (*Meall Ruadh*),
which attains an elevation of about 800 feet, he discerned
among the mists which shrouded its summit a large body of
MacDonalds, with Keppoch[1] at their head. With shouts of
derision the rival clans descried each other, and with indescribable fury the battle commenced. From the heights above, the
MacDonalds swept down upon their foes like an avalanche of
destruction, shouting their war-cry, "*Dia 's Naomh Aindrea*"
with deafening clamour, to which the Mackintoshes replied with
"*Loch-na-Maoidh*," the slogan of the clan, and stood firmly
awaiting the onset.

Amid this terrific din the fight raged, the rocks and
mountains re-echoing the fearful sounds, as steel met steel,
and the great war-pipes (*Piob mor*) of the opposing clans
sounded the ancient pibrochs which had rung out on many
a field of slaughter such as this. Notwithstanding their dis-
advantageous position, the Mackintoshes stood the onset
without wavering, and it at first appeared that they would
come off the victors. The presence of the soldiers under
MacKenzie was a matter of considerable anxiety to Keppoch,
as he was well aware that if any important officer among
them was injured or slain, the Government would hold him
responsible, and make the circumstance an excuse for reprisals
of the greatest severity. Fully comprehending the importance
of avoiding a direct collision with MacKenzie's men, he gave
orders to his clansmen that, except they were in peril of their
lives, they were to refrain as much as possible from attacking
the redcoats, and to reserve their weapons for their feudal
enemies, the Mackintoshes. It was a difficult matter, in the

[1] This famous chieftain of the Keppoch MacDonalds was known throughout
Lochaber as "Coll of the Cows."

heat of the conflict, to carry out these instructions, as events soon proved.

Among the ranks of the MacDonalds was a young chieftain, a cadet of Keppoch, named MacDonald of Tulloch, who, by the chances of war, found himself opposed by the commander of the Government troops, MacKenzie of Suddy. MacKenzie came of a bold and fearless race, and was not the sort of man to shirk a personal encounter with a foe worthy of his steel; levelling his pistol at the head of Tulloch, he fired, but the bullet, instead of striking his antagonist, passed within an inch of his head, and killed one of Tulloch's brothers, who was by his side. The blood of his slain relative cried aloud for vengeance, but Tulloch, bearing in mind the direct orders of his chief, and knowing what disastrous consequences to his clan would follow the death of an officer of MacKenzie's rank, called out, "Avoid me, avoid me!"—and would have sought some other part of the field in which to avenge his brother's death; but MacKenzie, not understanding the meaning of the words addressed to him, and probably attributing them to cowardice, answered with a sneer, "The MacDonald was never born that I would shun," rushed at Tulloch with his pike. Stung by the implied insult, Tulloch threw a pistol which he had in his hand at his adversary's head, with such deadly effect that MacKenzie's skull was split open, and he died within a few hours.

Maddened by the sight of their wounded leader, the soldiers now joined the ranks of the Mackintoshes, and the combined strength of these two powerful bodies of men would probably have soon driven Keppoch from the field, had not a curious incident occurred, which entirely changed the course of events. While the fight was at its thickest, one of Keppoch's herdsmen, a half-witted fellow of great muscular strength, made his appearance among his brother clansmen, armed with a gigantic club. He had been left by Keppoch in charge of the cattle, which had been driven some distance from the scene of conflict—Keppoch being fully cognisant of the predatory instincts of his foes in the matter of live stock. Evidently the peaceful occupation of bullock-minding was not to the taste of "the red haired Bo-man" (as he was called), and hearing from afar the skirl of the pipes sounding the pibroch of the MacDonalds, he seized the first weapon that came to hand, and with his red hair and tattered plaid streaming in the wind, hurried to the hill of Mulroy, just in time to see his clan almost overwhelmed by the enemy. With the frenzied excitment of a madman, he leapt among the Mackintoshes, wielding his enormous club above his head, and shouting at the same time, "They fly, they fly! upon them, upon them!" dealt such awful blows with his improvised weapon, that he soon stood alone in a circle of dead or dying men. The Mackintoshes were quite paralysed by this sudden attack, and before they had time to fill up the gaps made in their ranks by this murderous onslaught, Keppoch and his MacDonalds were among them, slashing and hewing with axe and claymore, and driving them over the steep banks of the river Roy, to meet a terrible fate among the great boulders forty feet below.

During the stampede, a special effort was made by the MacDonalds to capture the standard of the Mackintosh, which was being borne from the field of battle by a *duine-uasal* ("gentleman") of the clan, to whose care it had been entrusted. Hotly pursued by his foes, he reached the precipitous banks of the Roy, at a spot where it seethes and foams like a boiling cauldron among the jagged rocks that here form its bed. Grasping his sacred charge firmly in his hands, and mentally measuring the distance to the opposite side, he made a running leap across the awful chasm, and landed safely upon the other bank, and thus escaped, as the MacDonalds, brave as many of them were, dared not follow him. The place is still known as "The Leap of Mackintosh."

A vivid description of the engagement has been handed down to us from the lips of a tobacco-spinner's apprentice of Inverness, who, apparently to escape the daily drudgery and monotony of his existence, enlisted in the force under

MacKenzie of Suddy, and was present on the hill of Mulroy on the occasion of which I write. He says: "The MacDonalds came down the hill upon us, without either shoe, stocking, or bonnet on their heads; they gave a shout, and then the fire began on both sides, and continued a hot dispute for an hour (which made me wish I had been spinning tobacco). Then they broke in upon us with sword and target, and Lochaber axes, which obliged us to give way. Seeing my captain severely wounded, and a great many men lying with heads cloven on every side, and having never witnessed the like before, I was sadly affrighted. At length a Highlandman attacked me with sword and target, and cut my wooden-handled bayonet out of the muzzle of my gun. I then clubbed my gun and gave him a stroke of it, which made the butt end to fly off, and seeing the Highlandman come fast down upon me, I took to my heels, and ran thirty miles before I looked behind me, taking every person whom I saw or met for my enemy."

Donald MacBane (this was the lad's name), having thus served his apprenticeship to war, and tasted blood for the first time, could no longer submit to the tame and uneventful existence that awaited him in Inverness at the shop of his worthy master. Enlisting in the army, he served with distinction in the wars in Flanders, under the great Duke of Marlborough, and upon his return to Scotland became one of the most expert swordsmen of his day. At the age of sixty-seven, a report reached him that an Irishman named O'Brien was in Edinburgh, boasting of his prowess with the sword, and assuming the title of champion of Great Britain. This was too much for MacBane, and he at once set out for Edinburgh, with the determination of punishing the braggart who had dared to set his countrymen at defiance. Upon arrival in that city he at once made his way to the house of Field-Marshal John, Duke of Argyll, in whose regiment he had served. The Duke gave him every encouragement, and promised to be present at the encounter.

When the day arrived, a platform was erected, and a large crowd of spectators were attracted to the unusual spectacle, among whom were large numbers of the Scottish nobility. The fight was long and severe, but in the end Donald came off victorious, amid the plaudits of the assembled multitudes; and thus having saved the honour of his country, he returned to the Highlands. He died some years later, and was buried in the Craigs Cemetery at Fort William, where a stone was erected to his memory, recording, among other things, that "he died in his bed at home, and was graced with a decent funeral by his surviving wife."

Keppoch was now entirely master of the situation, and Mackintosh was a prisoner in his hands. Sir Walter Scott states that "when the captive heard the MacDonalds greeting their chieftain with shouts of 'Lord of Keppoch! Lord of Keppoch!' he addressed them boldly, saying, 'You are as far from being lord of the lands of Keppoch at this moment as you have been all your life.' 'Never mind,' answered the victorious chieftain, with much good humour, 'we'll enjoy the good weather while it lasts.' Accordingly, the victory of his tribe is still recorded in the pipe-tune called 'MacDonald took the brae on them.'"

While this conversation was taking place, both chieftains were surprised to hear the sound of the pipes in the distance, heralding the approach of another body of Highlanders, but whether friends of Keppoch or Mackintosh, it was impossible for the moment to determine. All doubts were, however, set aside when shouts of "*Creig dubh Clann Chattan*" were heard, as the newcomers arrived within earshot. This was the war-cry of the MacPhersons, and it at once became evident that they had for the nonce decided to forget the long-standing disagreement that had existed between their chief, Cluny, and the Mackintosh, in connection with the disputed chieftainship of Clan Chattan, and were now come to offer him the assistance of their arms in his struggle with Keppoch.

Mackintosh watched the arrival of the MacPhersons with

mingled feelings of pride and humiliation—pride, because he
knew that the MacDonalds in their present weakened condition
could not hazard another engagement with a new and powerful
enemy, and he would have the satisfaction of seeing them beat
an undignified retreat ; and humiliation, for he was sure that
the MacPhersons would take advantage of his defenceless
position, and carry him before their chief, Cluny. He was
nearly right in his surmises, for as soon as Keppoch became
aware that he would now have to stand the brunt of a fresh
attack, he decided to retire. While he was in the act of giving
orders to the MacDonalds to this effect, a flag of truce was
sent to him from the MacPhersons, demanding that he should
give up his prisoner, or, in default of so doing, they would
immediately engage him in battle. Discretion being the better
part of valour, he reluctantly handed over Mackintosh to the
party of MacPhersons who had accompanied the flag of truce,
and, assembling his clan, marched back to his house at Keppoch,
secure for the present in the possession of the disputed estates.

The proud chief of Mackintosh experienced the bitterest
mortification upon finding himself a captive among his rivals
the MacPhersons, although he was treated by them with the
greatest respect, and received every attention at their hands.

The proposal that he should return with them to Cluny
Castle, to have an audience with their chief, was indignantly
rejected as a direct insult, and he threatened that if force were
used to conduct him thither, he would plunge his dirk into his
heart, rather than appear before Cluny MacPherson so ignomini-
ously. These noble sentiments were applauded by the brave
MacPhersons, who now declared that Mackintosh was a worthy
member of Clan Chattan, and with pipers playing and banners
flying, they escorted him to his castle at Moy. Such was the
last clan battle fought in Scotland, and it is well worthy of
being recorded, as showing that even in those warlike times the
Highlanders were imbued with the same noble and generous
instincts as will be found among their descendants at the
present day.

As some of my readers may like to know how the Highlanders of this date (1688 A.D.) were clothed and equipped, I will
give an extract from an account given by William Sacheverell,
Governor of the Isle of Man, who visited the Western Highlands
in 1688, with a view to recovering the treasure of one of the
galleons of the Spanish Armada that was sunk in the harbour
of Tobermory, in Mull. He writes: " The usual outward habit
of both sexes is the pladd ; the women's much finer, the colours
more lively, and the squares larger than the men's, and put me
in mind of the ancient Picts. This serves them for a veil, and
covers both head and body. The men wear theirs after another
manner, especially when designed for ornament : it is loose and
flowing, like the mantles our painters give their heroes. Their
thighs are bare, with brawney muscles. Nature has drawn all
her stroakes bold and masterly ; a thin brogue on the foot, a
short buskin of various colours on the legg, tied about the calf
with a striped pair of garters. What should be concealed is hid
with a large shot pouch (*sporan*), on each side of which hangs a
dagger and a pistol, as if they found it necessary to keep those
parts well guarded. A round target on their backs, a blew
bonnet on their heads, in one hand a broadsword and a musquet
in the other. Perhaps no nation goes better armed ; and I
assure you they will handle them with bravery and dexterity,
especially the sword and target."

A very graphic picture this of the Gael of the seventeenth
century, and interesting as proving conclusively that the tartan
plaid and kilt (*feilebeag*) was the universal dress of the Highlanders of that epoch ; a fact which is now often disputed by
English writers, who go so far as to maintain that the tartan is
of quite modern invention.

About the time that these hostilities were in progress in
Lochaber, alarming news from England reached the chiefs of
the Western Highlands, and they were soon called upon to
take their share in a struggle which was destined to produce
important and far-reaching results, not only in the Highlands of
Scotland, but throughout the length and breadth of the realm.

James II., by his ill-judged attempts to subvert the Protestant religion by every means in his power, had altogether alienated from himself the reverence and affection of his subjects. The crisis came when he endeavoured to re-establish the obnoxious Court of High Ecclesiastical Commission, by which he sought to punish the clergy for the independent spirit they had shown in the pulpit, where they had made frequent protests against the king's papistical tendencies, in powerful and scathing language.

The refusal of six of the most distinguished English bishops (among whom was Sancroft, Archbishop of Canterbury) to read the king's Declaration of Indulgence in their cathedrals, was immediately followed by their arrest and committal to the Tower. After a short interval they were brought before the Bar of Westminster Hall, and, after a trial famous in the annals of history, were acquitted amid the acclamations of the assembled multitude. The imprisonment of the bishops was the death-knell of the Stuart dynasty, for now all eyes were turned to Holland, and messengers were constantly passing between the heads of the Protestant party and William, Prince of Orange, with important despatches, urging him to cross the channel and accept the crown, which they promised to assist him in obtaining by every means at their disposal.

On 10th June 1688, the queen gave birth to a son, of whom we shall hear more hereafter; but such were the suspicions with which everything connected with the Court were regarded by the people, that it was believed on all sides that the infant was fraudulently thrust upon the nation by the Popish advisers of the king, with a view to establish an impediment to the claim of William of Orange, and that the queen had not been confined at all. All students of history, of course, are aware that there were no grounds for this belief, and the legitimacy of the young prince has been fully established. The immediate result of this event was the renewed effort on the part of the Protestants in England,

and Covenanters in Scotland, to induce the Prince of Orange to at once set sail for England, where he was assured that a hearty welcome awaited him. The birth of a son and heir to James decided him to take this step, and having had a fleet of five hundred ships and an army of fifteen thousand men placed at his disposal by the States of Holland, he put to sea, and, after some little delay caused by rough weather, landed at Torbay on 5th November 1688.

Upon the news of William's arrival reaching the army of king James, disaffection commenced with extraordinary rapidity, and one by one the officers and men went over to the invader, the most celebrated of the deserters being the great Duke of Marlborough, who had only recently been raised to the peerage.

To king James the tidings of his rival's bloodless successes were gall and wormwood, and feeling the utter impotence of his position, and also realising the personal danger he was exposed to from his rebellious subjects, he resolved to escape while there was yet time, lest the fate that befell his royal father might overtake him. His mental sufferings at this time were increased by the news that the Princess Anne had gone over to the enemy, and, under the cover of night, had left London for Nottingham. Deserted by all save a few faithful attendants, the unhappy monarch, dejected and forlorn, fled from the metropolis, and reaching a small seaport on the south coast of England, was just about to embark for France when he was captured and brought back to London, where the Prince of Orange was now installed in royal state. Fearing that public opinion might change in favour of the deposed sovereign if he remained in the capital, William decided that it would be more politic to remove James to some secluded provincial town, and having selected Rochester (Kent), he gave orders that the king should at once proceed there. James, who was not now in a position to refuse, obeyed the injunction, and after a few days residence in the old cathedral city of Rochester, found means of escaping on board a fishing boat, and landed at Ambleteuse, in France, on 23rd December 1688.

With the flight of king James from his kingdom, the glory of the Stuarts departed, to return at intervals in flashes of lurid brilliancy, burning deeply upon the open scroll of history, marks that the hand of time will never efface.

CHAPTER XI.

"BONNIE DUNDEE."

> " There are hills beyond Pentland, and lands beyond Forth,
>   If there's lords in the south, there are chiefs in the north ;
>   There are brave Duinnewassals three thousand times three,
>   Will cry ' Hey, for the bonnets of Bonnie Dundee !'"

THE accession of William, Prince of Orange, to the throne of Great Britain, although favourably regarded by a large portion of the Scottish people, headed by the Dukes of Hamilton and Argyll, was exceedingly distasteful to the majority of the Highland clans, and more especially to those of Lochaber, whose loyalty to the Stuarts was proverbial. They now only needed a bold and spirited leader, in whom they could place implicit confidence, and they were ready to follow him to the death in defence of the rights of their legitimate sovereign, king James. Such a leader was at hand in the person of John Graham, Viscount Dundee, in whose veins ran the heroic blood of his famous kinsman, Montrose. Proud of his descent from the Great Marquis, and never weary of listening to stories of his brilliant achievements, Dundee was rejoiced at the opportunity that now presented itself of gathering under his standard the loyal clans, by whose aid he trusted to be able to emulate the victories of Montrose. By the marriage of one of his ancestors, William, Lord Graham of Kincardine, with Mary, the second daughter of king Robert III., Dundee could trace descent from the royal line of Stuarts, and he doubtlessly felt a personal interest in supporting their cause against the usurper.

His father was Sir William Graham of Claverhouse, a nobleman of estimable qualities, but of no striking individuality, and famous only on account of the actions of his celebrated son.

Of the early years of Dundee we know but little. Born in 1643 A.D., he received the usual training and education that his rank in life demanded. At the age of twenty-three he entered the University of St Andrews, where he attained considerable proficiency in mathematics and other subjects, and after pursuing his studies there for about ten years, he left Scotland for France, where he attached himself to the army as a volunteer, but shortly afterwards quitted the service of the French king for that of the Prince of Orange. By the strange irony of fate, he was instrumental in saving the life of the Prince at the battle of Seneffe in 1674, and otherwise distinguished himself by his bravery in the field, and his skill in all matters connected with military affairs. Annoyed by the refusal of the Prince of Orange to grant him the coveted command of one of the Scottish regiments then serving in Holland, he returned to his native land in the year 1677.

Upon his arrival in Scotland, he received a captain's commission in one of the new regiments that Charles II. was raising to aid him in suppressing the Covenanting Whig party, and his zeal in carrying out his orders in that direction, and the relentless severity with which he treated all prisoners that fell into his hands, earned for him the sobriquet of "the bloody Clavers"; and he shared with General Dalziel the distinction of being credited with supernatural powers and the assistance of his satanic majesty, who was said to have made his body proof against leaden bullets, and as an additional mark of his favour, had presented him with a coal-black steed, possessed of magical powers. When mounted on this Pegasus, Claverhouse was popularly believed to perform prodigies of equestrianism, such as scaling inaccessible mountains or crossing fordless rivers; in fact, no story, however absurd or improbable, was called into question, if only Claverhouse was the hero of it.

On the death of Charles II. we find Claverhouse high in favour with king James, who advanced him rapidly by successive steps to the rank of major-general, and seven days after the arrival of William of Orange the title of Viscount Dundee was bestowed upon him by his grateful sovereign. Dundee, from his earliest youth, had always shown great partiality for the Highlanders, and everything connected with their past and present history. He had studied their language, and become acquainted with their ancient poetry and traditions, and by his proved loyalty to the royal house of Stuart had gained the entire confidence of their chieftains, as Montrose had done in the past; and they were equally ready, as their fathers had been in 1645, to follow one of the bold Grahams, and aid him with their claymores in re-establishing king James on his throne.

The long flowing wig of black ringlets worn by Dundee, and his brilliant military exploits, gained for him the Gaelic appellation of *"Iain Dubh nan Cath"* ("Black John of the Battles"), and it was by this name he was generally known among his Highland friends.

Such, in brief outline, was the career of Dundee up till the year 1689, when we find him supporting the cause of the exiled king against his rebellious subjects in Scotland, aided by a large number of the Highland clans of Lochaber and Badenoch, who, attracted by his persuasive eloquence and military ardour, had flocked to his standard. While Dundee was employed in the congenial task of organising the forces he had raised, and endeavouring to patch up, for a time at least, the many feuds that existed between the Highland chiefs, Coll of Keppoch had, after his victory over Mackintosh, advanced with a considerable body of his clan to the walls of Inverness, which he threatened to destroy unless a large sum of money was handed over to him.

At this period the town of Inverness consisted of a few hundred houses of the most primitive description, with thatched roofs and walls composed of stones and mud, few of them having any glass in the windows. There were two churches, and rows of booths where such luxuries as knives, horn spoons, tin kettles, etc., were to be had by those who had the money to pay for them. The arrival of a vessel of any size in the port was an event of the greatest rarity, and on such occasions the whole population would assemble on the shore to watch its progress. Fortifications there were none, unless a ruined castle and a tumble down wall could be termed such.

To the Highlanders, however, reared in the midst of mountain solitudes, Inverness was looked upon as an object of wonder and a prize worth the taking. For many years feelings of enmity had existed between the worthy burghers of Inverness and the MacDonalds, and it was only a few years previous to this date that the town had been similarly threatened with an assault by this powerful clan. So extraordinary were the terms offered by the MacDonalds on that occasion to grant the town an immunity from plunder, that they are worthy of record, as showing to what lengths the Highland chiefs could go in their total disregard of all authority but their own. We are told that the MacDonalds demanded the payment of a heavy indemnity, and that the magistrates should bind themselves by oath to hand over to the vengeance of the clan any citizen who should shed the blood of a MacDonald ; and further, that every inhabitant of Inverness, irrespective of rank or quality, meeting a Highlander clad in the MacDonald tartan, should ground arms in token of submission.

And now once again the burghers of Inverness were called upon to submit to the demands of the bold MacDonalds, who, under Keppoch, surrounded the town, which he threatened to destroy if the money he demanded was not instantly forthcoming.

Such was the state of affairs on Sunday, 28th April 1689, and we may imagine the worshippers in the churches did not pay much attention to the ministrations of their clergy while the Philistine, in the shape of Keppoch, was at their gates. The two following days passed without the expected attack being made, and on the third relief arrived from a most unexpected quarter, and in the person of the redoubtable Dundee.

To understand the reason of Dundee's appearance at Inverness, we must return to the progress of events beyond the Highlands, and in a few words explain the state of affairs in Scotland incident upon the change of monarchy. The Prince of Orange was now established on the throne of Britain under the title of William III., his regal state being equally shared by his wife Mary, who, as we know, was the eldest daughter of the exiled monarch. Soon after William's arrival in London, the Duke of Argyll, Sir James Montgomery, and Sir John Dalrymple were despatched to London to offer the crown of Scotland to the victorious Prince and his spouse, on the condition that he would support the Covenant and put down Episcopacy. William demurred at first, as he had no wish to commence his reign in the character of a religious persecutor; but as Argyll informed him that the oath was merely formal, he eventually consented, and the Scottish noblemen returned to Scotland, their task being accomplished, and immediately took upon themselves the vigorous enforcement of the royal oath, and marked out the Earl of Balcarras and Viscount Dundee for their first victims. Balcarras was at once arrested at his country house and conveyed to Edinburgh, where he was imprisoned. Dundee was, however, too quick for his enemies, and having heard that warrants had been issued against him, he fled across the river Dee to the friendly Gordons, where he was joined by the Earl of Dunfermline with fifty mounted men.

And here I must pause to introduce another important actor in the stirring events of the year 1689, to whose enterprise (although on the wrong side) Lochaber has some cause to be grateful, as I shall have occasion to show. This was General Hugh MacKay, who was now in command of William's troops in Scotland. He was the son of Colonel Hugh MacKay of Scourie, on the west coast of Sutherlandshire. The Scourie MacKays were descended from Donald MacKay of Scourie and Eriboll, elder son of Y. MacKay, third chief of the clan, by his first wife, who was a daughter of Hugh MacLeod of Assynt. General MacKay was born in 1640, and shortly after the Restoration he received an ensign's commission in the Royal Scots Regiment, and accompanied it to France. He then appears to have served in the Venetian army, and this not proving to his taste, he again went to France and fought under Marshall Turenne in the Netherlands. We next hear of him in Holland, as a major in a Scots regiment in the service of the Prince of Orange, but after attaining the rank of colonel, he transferred his allegiance to James II., who in 1685 made him major-general of the royal forces in Scotland, where he became a member of the Privy Council. The service of king James was evidently distasteful to MacKay, as it only lasted a year. After resigning his commission, he crossed the sea to Holland, and once more attached himself to the army of his old commander, William, Prince of Orange, who was now preparing to invade England. MacKay was at once made major-general, and was put in command of the British troops which were to assist the Prince in obtaining the throne. Upon William's arrival in London, he issued a warrant, dated 4th January 1689, in which MacKay was appointed "Major-General of all forces whatever, within our ancient kingdom of Scotland."

It was the rapid advance of this officer from Edinburgh that had induced Dundee to depart for Inverness, where he hoped to attach Keppoch and his clan to the cause of king James. Arriving in the camp of the MacDonalds on the morning of 1st May, he found them about to make a raid on the town, but by his offer to settle the dispute without recourse to arms, he prevented what would probably have developed into a desperate battle. The arbitration of Dundee appears to have been remarkably one-sided, as we learn that the town of Inverness had to hand over the sum of two thousand dollars before the peaceful inhabitants could get rid of their Highland neighbours.

This tangible result of Dundee's intervention raised him high in the estimation of the MacDonalds, and he found no difficulty in persuading them to join him, while the spoil was yet heavy in their sporans; he soon learnt, however, that it was quite another matter to reconcile Keppoch with his old feudal enemies, the Mackintoshes and MacPhersons. The rival clans could not assimilate, and both Mackintosh and MacPherson decided to remain neutral rather than fight by the side of Keppoch.

These clan feuds were a constant source of annoyance and irritation to Dundee, and he adopted every means he could think of to pour oil on the troubled waters, but without success: the wounds, caused by centuries of recrimination and bloodshed, could not be healed by a few soft words, and he found, to his great disappointment, that many of the Highland chiefs, who were among his greatest personal friends, could not be induced to join an army to which their old enemies were attached.

Meanwhile, MacKay had advanced as far as Forres, and the news of his proximity reaching Dundee, he decided to intercept him with all the force he could command; but here again his intentions were frustrated by his Highland allies. With the MacDonalds there were a considerable body of Camerons, who, hoping to share the plunder, had marched with them to Inverness, and having received their portion of the two thousand dollars, were anxious to return to their homes in Lochaber, to deposit it in a place of safety. When the order for the march to attack MacKay reached them, they informed Dundee that, much as they should like to assist him, it was against the custom of the Highlanders to engage in battle without their chief, and as Lochiel was at Ach-na-carry, Dundee had no alternative but to let them depart. To engage MacKay with the men that were left him, could only result in disaster, and after having arranged with Keppoch for a gathering of the loyal clans in Lochaber on 18th May, he marched for Perthshire, to raise the men of Athole.

It has been my endeavour in this work to centralise the interest of my narrative as far as possible around the district which is its *raison d'être*, but so closely is the history of Lochaber

interwoven with the history of Scotland, and even England, that
I have found it sometimes impossible to avoid introducing, what
to some of my readers may seem extraneous matter, in order
to elucidate the many ramifications which dynastic changes
necessarily produce in the government of a country.

CHAPTER XII.

THE Lochaber of 1689 differed little from the Lochaber of
1652. Monk's fort still stood, although in a dilapidated
condition, on the small point of land at the confluence of
the river Nevis, beneath the shadow of the great Ben. A
few huts had been built around it by the natives, who had
been attracted to the spot by the presence of the garrison,
with whom they sought to trade. Lochiel, now sixty years
of age, but strong and active as ever, had, since the
death of his old enemy Cromwell, remained in comparative
peace at Ach-na-carry, among his turbulent Camerons.

Shortly after the accession of James II., Lochiel paid a
visit to the Court, with the object of paying his devoirs to
his sovereign, and to obtain a pardon for one of his clan,
who had unwittingly caused the death of several Atholemen by
firing on them in mistake. The king received him graciously,
and with every mark of distinction, and at once granted the
boon he asked. The great services Lochiel had rendered to
the Stuart cause demanded some recognition at the royal
hands, and the king took the opportunity of Lochiel's visit
to offer him knighthood, and, as a special honour, asked Lochiel
for his own sword with which to perform the ceremony. Unfortunately, during the long ride from Scotland, the rain had
caused the sword to rust. Lochiel found it quite impossible
to withdraw it from its sheath. Mortified by this untoward
event, and annoyed beyond measure that the English courtiers
should think him unequal to the task of drawing his own
sword, he could scarcely refrain from tears.

The king, observing his confusion, said in a kindly voice: "Do not regard it, my faithful friend, your sword would have left the scabbard of itself had the royal cause required it." The sympathetic words of his beloved sovereign restored Lochiel to his wonted composure, and, kneeling at the king's feet, he received the honour of knighthood with the monarch's own jewelled rapier, which he afterwards received from the royal hands as a gift; and the staunch old chieftain returned to Lochaber a greater Jacobite than ever. It was shortly after Lochiel's return to his native land that an incident occurred which served to temporarily alienate his loyalty, and for a time, at least, produced in his mind a feeling of resentment against his sovereign.

Keenly sensitive to any interference with their ancient prerogatives, the Highland chieftains of that period could not, or would not, understand that the altered state of affairs in the realm demanded a severer discipline among their lawless clansmen, and that the bloody feuds and predatory expeditions of a previous and less enlightened age could no longer be countenanced by the government of a Christian monarch. King James had on more than one occasion expostulated with Lochiel on the disorderly condition of Lochaber, and the thieving propensities of the Highlanders, and had often chaffed him good humouredly on the subject, hoping by that means to bring the Cameron chieftain to a sense of the shortcomings of his unruly vassals. Once when Lochiel entered the royal presence at Whitehall, the king remarked jestingly to his attendant nobles, "Gentlemen, take care of your pockets; here comes the king of the thieves." We are not told Lochiel's reply to this sally, but it is evident from the following story, that the royal remonstrances had produced little effect.

Shortly after Lochiel's return to Ach-na-carry, he was informed that king James had commanded the sheriff of Inverness to proceed to the fort at Inverlochy, and hold a commission of inquiry into the state of the district, with full powers to inflict punishment upon any Highlanders found guilty of disturbing the peace, or who had in any other way offended the majesty of the law. This action on the part of his royal master was bitterly resented by the proud Lochiel, who saw in it a covert attempt to weaken his authority among his own people, and an insidious endeavour to wrest from him those prerogatives and rights that had been enjoyed by his ancestors for many centuries. Annoyed by the unwelcome news, he carefully planned a scheme to render the sheriff's visit as unpleasant as possible, while at the same time outwardly professing the greatest respect for that august representative of the law. The better to show his loyalty and reverence for the royal commission, he arrived at the fort attended by four hundred fully armed Camerons, whom he had previously taken into his confidence and instructed how to act.

The sheriff having taken his seat, was about to read the king's mandate, when a tremendous uproar commenced among the Highlanders, who, with well-counterfeited ferocity, proceeded to lay about them with their weapons, uttering at the same time the most unearthly yells, to which the discordant notes of the bagpipes gave terrible emphasis. Cries of murder were heard above the clash of steel, and bloody faces were uplifted among the tumultuous crowd, striking terror into the soul of the unhappy sheriff, who expected every minute would be his last. With face blanched white with terror, and trembling in every limb, he frantically appealed to Lochiel to quell the howling mob of bloodthirsty Camerons, who appeared ready to murder him outright. Assuming a voice of authority, Lochiel ordered his clansmen to desist from further strife, and in a few moments peace was restored, and the sheriff, thanking his lucky stars that he had escaped alive out of this den of wolves, hastily quitted Lochaber, under an escort provided by the thoughtful Lochiel, who thus gained for himself the credit of having done good service for the Crown.

Sir Ewen Cameron of Lochiel had married, in 1657, the sister of Sir James MacDonald of Sleat, and had been blessed by

P

Providence with a large family, mostly girls. In those days of almost constant warfare, a female child was regarded as somewhat in the light of an encumbrance, and a man whose quiver possessed more than one or two of them was regarded by his neighbours as unfortunate. Lochiel, however, with his usual gallantry, remarked to the nurse who had announced the advent of his twelfth daughter by saying that another " lady " had been presented to him, " Yes," said he, " a *real* lady, and every one of them will bring me a lad." Whether this prophecy came true or not, I am unable to discover; but most of Sir Ewen's daughters were married to the chiefs of neighbouring clans, and there is little doubt that he found himself plentifully supplied with grandsons as time went on.

The year 1689 was not far advanced when tidings of war reached Sir Ewen Cameron in the seclusion of his castle by the shores of Loch Arkaig, and aroused the old warrior to action. Both MacKay and Dundee were fully alive to the importance of securing the assistance of Lochiel and his clan. Overtures had been made early in the year by MacKay, who had attempted to open a correspondence with Sir Ewen, and by the suggestions of Viscount Tarbat, a nobleman of great tact and diplomatic ability, had offered, with the sanction of the English Government, to discharge all the claims which Argyll had upon the Cameron estates, provided he would support the cause of the Prince of Orange. To such an insulting epistle Lochiel vouchsafed no reply, and MacKay, irritated at finding that his generous (?) offers met with no response, swore that Lochiel should have cause to regret his decision. Similar bribes were offered to MacDonald of Glengarry and other Highland chiefs, but, to their honour be it recorded, one and all of the western clans indignantly refused to take up arms against their king.

The 18th May 1689 was a red-letter day in the annals of Lochaber, and worthy of the powerful language in which Lord Macaulay describes the mustering of the loyal clans on that occasion. He says, after giving an account of Dundee's actions after he left Inverness: " The fiery crosses had been wandering from hamlet to hamlet over all the heaths and mountains thirty miles round Ben Nevis; and when he (Dundee) reached the trysting-place [1] in Lochaber, he found that the gathering had begun. The headquarters were fixed close to Lochiel's house, a large pile built entirely of fir wood,[2] and considered in the Highlands as a superb palace. Lochiel, surrounded by more than six hundred broadswords, was there to receive his guests. MacNaughten of MacNaughten and Stewart of Appin were at the muster with their little clans. MacDonald of Keppoch led the warriors who had, a few months before, under his command put to flight the musketeers of king James. MacDonald of Clanronald was of tender years, but he was brought to the camp by his uncle, who acted as regent during the minority. The youth was attended by a picked body-guard, composed of his own cousins, all comely in appearance, and good men of their hands. MacDonald of Glengarry, conspicuous by his dark brow and his lofty stature, came from that great valley where a chain of lakes, then unknown to fame, and scarcely set down in maps, is now the daily highway of steam vessels passing and repassing between the Atlantic and the German Ocean. None of the rulers of the mountains had a higher sense of his personal dignity, or was more frequently engaged in disputes with other chiefs. He generally affected in his manners and in his housekeeping a rudeness beyond that of his rude neighbours . . . . but on this occasion he chose to imitate the splendour of the Saxon warriors, and rode on horseback before his four hundred plaided clansmen, in a steel cuirass and a coat embroidered with gold lace. Another MacDonald, destined to a lamentable and horrible end, led a band of hardy free-booters from the dreary pass of Glencoe. Somewhat later came the great Hebridean potentates. MacDonald of Sleat,

---

[1] The place fixed for the rendezvous was Moy, on the west bank of the river Lochy.

[2] This is an error; the old castle of Ach-na-carry, of which some slight vestige yet remains, was built of granite and stone, and was of great antiquity even at this period.

the most opulent and powerful of all the grandees who had laid claim to the lofty title of Lord of the Isles, arrived at the head of seven hundred fighting men from Skye. A fleet of long boats brought five hundred MacLeans from Mull, under the command of their chief, Sir John of Duart. A far more formidable array had in old times followed his forefathers to battle; but the spirit of the clan had been broken by the arts and arms of the Campbells. Another band of MacLeans arrived under a valiant leader, who took his title from Lochbuy."

Such a gallant array must have filled the soul of Dundee with pleasurable emotions, as, mounted on his black steed, he watched the gradually increasing strength of his Highland army. He had long looked forward to the day when, like his noble kinsman Montrose, he should find himself at the head of a large body of these hardy mountaineers; and now, within a few miles of the spot where the Great Marquis gained his famous victory over *Mac Cailean Mòr*, the wish of his heart was accomplished; and as clan after clan arrived at the rendezvous with pipers playing and banners flying, he felt the satisfaction that a brave general must always experience who knows that he possesses the confidence of those who serve under him.

Dundee had, however, yet to learn that it was no easy matter to curb the fiery spirits that were assembled under his banner. To these independent Highland chieftains restraint of any kind was irksome and unbearable, and to impose any rigid military discipline on their followers Dundee soon found to be impossible. Each clan looked to its own chief for orders, and would acknowledge no superior command. Much as they admired Dundee for his courage and audacity, traits of character which went straight to their bold Highland hearts, they nevertheless would not submit to his authority, unless his instructions reached them through their own chiefs. As an officer who had served in some of the finest and most disciplined armies of the Continent, Dundee could not but deplore the laxity and insubordination which he saw all around him, and which he felt himself powerless to prevent. Chafing under his inability to instil the rudiments of military organisation into the minds of his unruly Highlanders, he took counsel with Lochiel, and urged upon him the necessity of instructing his men in the art of war as practised among the armies of Europe. In this proposal he was supported by the lowland officers who had attached themselves to the Jacobite cause. James Seton, Earl of Dunfermline, Lord Dunkeld, and several others spoke strongly in favour of Dundee's suggestion, but their eloquence was wasted on Lochiel, who, while admitting that the Highland mode of warfare might not be the best, explained to the assembled officers that it would be unwise, at the eleventh hour, to introduce a new system which it would take years to make his men proficient in. Better to let them fight as their ancestors had done, with all the mad impetuosity that from the time of Fingal and his mythical battles, down to the great fight at Inverlochy, had so often struck terror into the hearts of their enemies.

This line of argument, coming from the lips of the veteran warrior, and borne out as it was by indisputable historic facts, carried conviction to the minds of Dundee and his officers, and so the matter dropped.

CHAPTER XIII.

THE enforced idleness of their life in the Lochaber camp was demoralising to the Highlanders, as they now had ample time to brood over real or imaginary insults. Quarrels, more or less serious, were of everyday occurrence, and it required all the tact of Dundee to prevent a serious outbreak, the result of which it would be impossible to foresee. Hardly a day passed without some raid being made upon the territories of the neutral clans. Keppoch, who had not forgotten the hard blows he had received at Mulroy, now took the opportunity of burning and destroying the property of his enemy, Mackintosh, in the neighbouring district of Badenoch. The Camerons, who had old scores to pay off with the Grants, invaded their country, and carried off large numbers of cattle. This foray was like to have had disastrous results, as we are told that in the defence of their homes some of the Grants were killed. It so happened that among the slain there was a MacDonald of Glengarry, who had probably married a Grant and taken up his abode with that clan. When the news of his clansman's death reached the ears of Glengarry, he flew into a desperate passion, and seeking the presence of Dundee, demanded instant vengeance on the Clan Cameron.

Dundee attempted to pacify the raging chieftain by explaining that the man who had been slain was a traitor both to his king and clan, and was not worthy of commiseration. The Grants were in arms against king James, and the MacDonald had fallen in fair fight at the hands of a body of the royal forces. These remarks, sensible as they were, only served to still further inflame the wrath of Glengarry, who threatened that if Dundee did not inflict condign punishment upon the slayer of his clansman, he would take the law into his own hands, and fall upon the Camerons with the whole strength of his clan at his back. Dundee pointed out that such a rash action could only result in defeat, as the Camerons under Lochiel were more than double the strength of the MacDonalds. "That is no matter," replied Glengarry; "one MacDonald is worth two Camerons." It was fortunate for Dundee that Lochiel did not take Glengarry at his word, and submit the dispute to the ordeal of battle; had he done so, Glengarry would have had cause to regret his idle boast, and Dundee's army would have been minus some hundreds of claymores. As it was, the anger of Glengarry was at length appeased, and for a short time at least harmony reigned in the camp.

The time slipped quickly away, without any incident of importance beyond a few skirmishes with MacKay's troops, in which Dundee's men were victorious. This desultory mountain warfare was little to the taste of General MacKay, and finding it impracticable to attack Dundee in his stronghold in Lochaber with any chance of success, he marched to Inverness. While there he despatched an urgent letter to the Duke of Hamilton, who was now Lord High Commissioner, impressing upon him the importance of establishing a strong garrison at Inverlochy, from whence he could control the troublesome Highlanders, who now set William's authority at defiance.

No heed appears to have been taken of this appeal, and MacKay, disappointed at receiving no reply to his letter, made up his mind to lay his scheme for the erection of the fort before the Government in person, and with that intention set out for Edinburgh, where he arrived early in July. Immediately upon reaching the capital he had an audience of Hamilton, to whom he explained in detail the suggestions he had to make regarding the proposed garrison. Hamilton listened with apparent interest to the unfolding of the scheme, which was to levy a body of fifteen hundred men from the northern counties, and arm them with spades and pickaxes, and provide them with sufficient food for a month's rations. To carry these supplies a large number of horses would be necessary, and for protection while work was going on four hundred soldiers would have to be attached to the expedition. Whether Hamilton was convinced of the necessity of doing as MacKay suggested or not, we are not told ; but nothing came of the interview, and MacKay had the mortification of finding that his vigorous arguments had fallen upon deaf ears, and for the time, at least, the fort at Inverlochy was " a castle in the air."

Dundee still remained at his camp at Moy,[1] in Lochaber. This place, beautifully situated near the banks of the river Lochy, among the most romantic scenery, was associated with weird stories and gruesome traditions of a noted witch named " *Gormshuill* " ("Blue-eyed "), who had taken up her abode there in the sixteenth century, and had rendered the spot notorious

---

[1] Our old friend Iain Lom was greatly concerned at the long delay in commencing hostilities, and composed a song to rouse the chiefs to action.

by her sorceries and incantations.[1]   When, in the year 1588,
the battered and storm-tossed remnants of the great Spanish
Armada, driven by the tempest round Cape Wrath, were dashed
to pieces among the rocky islands of the Hebrides, it is said
that "*Gormshuill*," joined by others of her devilish sisterhood
from the island of Mull, rode upon the wings of the storm,
and aided by their spells the work of destruction.   One great
galleon, "The Florida," detached from the rest, reached the
bay of Tobermory in Mull, and tradition states that "*Gormshuill*" and her uncanny crew, by dint of unholy rites, sank
the vessel with all on board.   Many attempts were made to
recover the lost treasure that went down with "The Florida,"
but I am unable to say whether they were successful or not.

The inactivity of camp life palled upon Dundee, and he
longed to be up and doing.   Had it not been for the delay
in the arrival of his expected Irish reinforcements, he would
probably have moved out of Lochaber and precipitated an
action with MacKay before this.   His force, during his prolonged stay at Moy, had gradually diminished, many of the
chiefs having with their clans returned to their homes when
they learnt that MacKay had left the Highlands, and Dundee
feared that some of them might fail to put in an appearance
when the critical time arrived.

We find him, on 23rd June 1689, inditing a letter to
MacLeod of MacLeod, in which he says: "I shall only tell
yow, that if you heasten not to land your men, I am of opinion
yow will have little occasion to do the king great service;
for if he land in the west of Scotland, you will come too
late, as I believe yow will thinck yourself by the news I have
to tell yow."   He then goes on to explain the probable chances
of success if king James were to land on the west coast, as
it was expected at that time he would do, and concludes

---

[1] Tradition states that it was *Gormshuill* who cautioned Sir Ewen Cameron of
Lochiel against meeting the Earl of Athole unattended, when proceeding to *Lochan a
Chlaidheamh* ("Loch of the Sword"), on the moor of Rannoch, to discuss a question
regarding the boundaries of the Cameron lands.   Taking the witch's advice, Lochiel
saved himself from falling into a treacherous ambuscade prepared for him by the earl.

by giving the names of those chiefs who were either still with him at Moy or in close proximity. "Captain of Glenrannald is near us these severall days; the laird of Barro is there with his men. I am persuaded Sir Donald is there by this. M'Clean lands in Morven to-morrow certainly. Apen, Glenco, Lochell, Glengaire, Keppoch[1] are all raidy. Sir Alexander and Largo have been here with there men all this while with me, so that I hope we will go out of Lochaber about thre thousand. . . . My L——— Seaforth will be in a few dayes from Irland to rais his men for the King's service. Now I have layd the whole business before yow, you will easily know what is fitt for yow to do. All I shall say further is, to repeat and renew the desyre of my former letter, and assure yow that I am, Sir, your most humble servant, DUNDIE."

"You will receave the king's letter to yow."

The Irish troops mentioned in the letter were being raised by the Earl of Melfort on behalf of king James, and Dundee fully anticipated that at least five thousand men would be sent over to his assistance. He had written to Melfort recommending Inverlochy as the safest and most convenient place for disembarkation, and he now impatiently awaited tidings of their approach.

MacKay still remained in Edinburgh, where he lost no opportunity of laying before the Council his favourite project of garrisoning Lochaber, but finding his importunities of no avail, and disgusted at the apathetic and off-handed manner in which the Government treated his proposals, he decided to reassemble his army and again take the field against his formidable opponent. The circumstances that led up to the famous battle of Killiecrankie are of too complex a nature to explain here, and are irrelevant to the purpose of this work, which concerns Lochaber only; but for those of my readers who are

[1] From papers in the possession of Mrs MacDonell of Keppoch, I find that Dundee had previously held a meeting of loyal chiefs at Keppoch, and it was then that the whole plan of the campaign was arranged.

Q

interested in the career of this gallant soldier of king James, the pages of Scott and Macaulay are open for their perusal.

The memory of "*Ian Dubh nan Cath*" will ever remain associated with the traditions of Lochaber, among whose mountains he learnt to know and admire the noble qualities of his Highland friends and allies. His chivalrous and dignified bearing, his frank and generous behaviour to those with whom he was brought in contact, endeared him to the Highlanders who served under his command. Devoted to the Stuart cause with all the ardour of his impulsive and passionate nature, he infused the same loyal spirit into the breasts of his companions in arms, by his irresistible energy and indomitable will, and there is little to be wondered at in the fact that such men as Lochiel and Glengarry should have been attracted to one who was so much *en rapport* with their own daring and courageous natures. The character of Dundee has been much maligned by his enemies, and an unjust stigma attached to his name by the inveterate hatred of the Covenanters, who firmly believed that he was in league with the powers of evil. Doubtless they had some cause for fearing the man who regarded all traitors to his royal master as worthy of death.

It was no part of Dundee's duty as a military officer to inquire into the religious tenets of the king's enemies; it was sufficient evidence of guilt in his eyes to find them disobeying the direct orders of their sovereign, and, orthodox or unorthodox, it was his business to punish them. It is impossible to believe that this accomplished nobleman should have taken delight in inflicting suffering and torture on the poor defenceless wretches who fell into his hands. Severe examples had doubtless to be made in order to prevent the spread of the rebellion, and it must not be forgotten that the brutal murder of the venerable Archbishop Sharp of St Andrews by a band of Covenanting assassins, and the barbarous treatment of the Royalist prisoners after the battle of Philiphaugh in the time of Montrose, had exasperated the soldiery to such a pitch, that when the means of vengeance were placed within their reach, they were only too eager to take advantage of them. To brand Dundee as a bloodthirsty tyrant because he did his duty as a loyal and honourable soldier, is to perpetrate an injustice that is altogether inexcusable. Faults he had without doubt, but they are altogether overshadowed by his life of noble devotion to the waning fortunes of the Stuart dynasty. Faithful unto the end, he died like a knight of old with sword in hand, fighting against the enemies of his king and country. It is time that Scotsmen of all denominations and creeds should realise that in Dundee they have a hero worthy of a pedestal in the national Pantheon side by side with Bruce, Wallace, and Montrose.

The following tribute to his memory, written by one of his contemporaries, should be sufficient refutation to the arguments of those who, only ready to exaggerate his faults, fail to applaud his virtues. The writer describes him as "one who was stainless in his honour, pure in his faith, wise in council, resolute in action, and utterly free from that selfishness which disgraced many of the Scottish statesmen of the time."

Killiecrankie might justly be called the Thermopylæ of Scotland, for never was ancient battle fought with so much heroism as was displayed by the victorious Highlanders on that terrible 27th June 1689. The sublime scenery of the magnificent Pass served as a fitting background for deeds of valour, such as Homer might have described in the "Iliad" with glowing colours, or the Celtic bard, Ossian, in sonorous Gaelic verse.

> " The foes met by Turthor's stream;
> They heaved like ridgy waves.
> Their echoing strokes are mixed.
> Shadowy death flies over the hosts.
> They were clouds of hail, with squally winds in their skirts.
> Their showers are roaring together.
> Below them swells the dark rolling deep."
>
> —*Cath. Loda*, Duan ii.

With the shouts of victory ringing in his ears, the soul of Dundee fled; struck by a bullet in the early part of the action, he fell to the ground mortally wounded. An officer named Johnstone attempted to staunch the blood that was flowing from the wound, and while engaged in this merciful task, Dundee, with eyes fast glazing in death, murmured, "How goes the day?" "Well for king James, but I am sorry for your Lordship," replied Johnstone, "If it is well for him," answered Dundee, "it matters less for me." Loyal to the last, he had the satisfaction of knowing that the Highlanders he loved so well had faithfully fulfilled their promise, and with their good broadswords had won the day for the king.

The men of Lochaber played their part in the great fight with the same heroism that their fathers had shown at Inverlochy in 1645. Camerons and MacDonalds[1] vied with each other in personal acts of bravery, and many a traitor Sassenach and renegade Scot fell by their hands as they charged down the steep hillside, driving the foe before them into the river Garry, which foams and tumbles among the boulders through the whole length of the Pass. It was due to Lochiel's advice that the battle was fought on this day, as the majority of Dundee's lowland officers were opposed to the idea of attacking MacKay in the defile of Killiecrankie. Lochiel, however, confident of success, and knowing that his men were all eager for the fray, addressed Dundee in energetic language: "Fight, my Lord, fight immediately; fight, if you have only one to three. Our men are in heart. Their only fear is that the enemy should escape. Give them their way: and be assured that they will either perish or gain a complete victory. But if you restrain them, if you force them to remain on the defensive, I answer for nothing. If we do not fight, we had better break up and retire to our mountains."

---

[1] James II. wrote a letter to Keppoch upon receipt of the news of the victory at Killiecrankie, thanking him for his loyal adhesion to the cause of the Stuarts. *Vide* Appendix XXII.

The old chieftain was seconded by MacDonald of Glengarry, who spoke in the same strain, and so contagious was the intrepid spirit displayed by these two Highlanders, that Dundee at once determined to hazard a battle. Previous to going into action, Lochiel had mingled freely among his men, encouraging them with his presence, and addressing a few inspiriting words to each. The Camerons idolised their chief, and one and all promised to maintain the honour of the clan in the approaching conflict, and we know how well they kept their word.

It is said that Lochiel was the only member of the Clan Cameron who possessed the luxury of shoes, and that upon the order being given to charge, he threw them away, and led his men to the attack barefooted. During the battle, Lochiel was attended by a son of his foster brother, and as at the skirmish at Inverlochy, so again at Killiecrankie, his life was saved by an act of unselfish heroism on the part of a devoted clansman. Missing his attendant at an early part of the battle, Lochiel turned round, and discovered to his intense grief that the poor fellow had been pierced with an arrow, and was now lying on the ground wounded unto death. Gazing into the tearful eyes of his beloved chief, the lad told Lochiel how he had seen one of MacKay's Highlanders taking aim at him with his bow and arrow from behind, and that he had only just time to interpose his body between Lochiel and his assailant, when the arrow flew from the bow and struck him to the heart.

Such was the love that Lochiel inspired in the breasts of his fellow-clansmen. Brave and generous himself, and possessed of all the many noble and distinguished qualities that characterised the true Highland gentleman, he was always ready to share the perils and hardships to which his men were exposed during the constant skirmishes in which they were engaged.

He had a dignified contempt for luxury or effeminacy, as became one who had been born and bred among the bleak mountains of Lochaber, and hunted the few remaining wolves among the dense forest that covered the shores of Loch Arkaig and Loch Eil. On one of these hunting expeditions during the winter months, Lochiel was accompanied by one of his sons, and being overtaken by night some distance from home, the party had to sleep in the snow, wrapped in their plaids. Noticing that his son had rolled a large ball of snow under his head for greater comfort, he exclaimed: "Are you become so luxurious that you cannot sleep without a pillow!"

Highland Weapons in the possession of the Author's friend,
W. Jex Long, Esq., Moffat.

MacKay's disastrous retreat after Killiecrankie was, as all readers of history are aware, followed by the successes of William's army at Dunkeld and Cromdale, and for the moment king James's prospects in Scotland were not of the most flourishing description. Finding themselves powerless in the face of the large and well-trained army that was now opposed to them, the Highlanders returned to their homes to await further developments, and it was while in this disorganised condition that the news of MacKay's approaching expedition reached them.

On the 3rd July 1690, MacKay, with a force of about three thousand men and horse, arrived at Inverlochy after a tedious march through the wilds of Badenoch and the desolate mountains of Glen Spean. It was forty-five years since such an imposing army had camped beside the shores of Loch Eil, and awakened with their martial music the echoes of Ben Nevis. The memory of the Great Marquis was still green in Lochaber : many of the older inhabitants remembered the great fight at Inverlochy, and some had probably taken their share in the gallant deeds of that day. Old Iain Lom, the "Bard of Keppoch," still lived among his people, and had only recently invoked his muse to lend him her aid in the composition of a biting satirical ode on the usurper William and his wife. The poem is still extant in the original Gaelic, and expresses in the most scathing language the detestation in which the bard held the unfilial conduct of Mary in allowing her unhappy father to be expelled from his throne and kingdom. The presence of the Sassenach in Lochaber was a bitter pill for the old bard to swallow, but, like his brother Highlanders, he recognised the utter futility of any open attempt being made to drive out the intruders. They would bide their time, and use every means at their disposal to harass the garrison.[1] Lochiel, remembering how he had punished the red-soldiers in the time of Monk, deplored his inability to

[1] It is common belief in Lochaber that Iain Lom was present at the battle of Killiecrankie ; his poem descriptive of that event certainly bears evidence of having been composed by a spectator of that famous Highland victory.

adopt the same tactics now that old age was creeping upon him, sapping his energies and rendering him physically incapable of taking an active part in any hostile demonstration against MacKay and his expeditionary force. To render his position even more helpless, he was now confined to his bed, suffering from the effects of a severe and dangerous wound which he had accidentally received whilst acting the part of peacemaker between the fiery Glengarry and a lowland gentleman who had the temerity to speak disparagingly of his Jacobite sympathies.

Glengarry was not the man to brook a real or implied insult, especially from a lowlander, and in an instant weapons were drawn, and had not Lochiel, who happened to be present, interfered between the contending swordsmen, a fatal result would probably have ended the struggle. As often occurs, the mediator got no thanks for his interference, and Lochiel not only received the abuse of the thwarted duellists, but an inadvertent sword cut as well, which nearly ended his days.

MacKay's most inveterate enemy was thus placed *hors de combat*, and while the old chief lay fretting at his enforced idleness at Ach-na-carry, no time was lost in erecting the fort, and by the time Lochiel had regained his strength it was a *fait accompli*. The old fortification built by Monk was still in existence, but, as I have before mentioned, in a ruinous condition. Its position did not commend itself to the keen eye of MacKay, whose military experience taught him that a battery constructed by a possible enemy on the heights of the Cow Hill (which immediately overlooked the garrison at the rear) would render it quite untenable. As, however, the other suggested sites had even greater disadvantages, MacKay decided to demolish all that was left of the old structure, and erect a thoroughly substantial fort, with all the most recent improvements. The actual date of the commencement of this work was the 5th July, and in about eleven days the principal part of the building was accomplished, and the walls raised to their full height of twenty feet. A fosse or moat was dug, into which the waters of Loch Eil could be made to flow by an arrangement

R

of sluices; strong palisades were fixed; and the defences strengthened by a glacis and ravelin.[1] A battery of twelve twelve-pounders was mounted on the parapets, taken from one of the warships that had accompanied the expedition; and for greater security a bomb-proof magazine was constructed for the storage of gunpowder and arms. For creature comforts the garrison was well provided, as we are told that among other articles of diet "there was no lack of oatmeal, red herrings, and beef, and rather a superabundance of brandy." Barracks were built with accommodation for 2 field officers, 2 captains, 4 sub-alterns, and 96 privates, the whole being placed under the command of an officer named Hill. Upon the completion of the work the standard of William of Orange was hoisted from the battlements, and it received the name of Fort William, a name which has stuck to it until the present day.[2]

With the erection of Fort William a new era was to commence in Lochaber, and, anomalous as it may appear, it is nevertheless certain that the day the usurper's standard first floated on the breeze from the walls of the newly built fortress, is a day to be remembered with satisfaction by the present inhabitants of the thriving and populous town which has gradually grown around the frowning walls of MacKay's fort, and which, now the railway has been brought to it by the perseverance and skill of the engineers entrusted with the construction of the West Highland Railway, bids fair to become a rival to Oban as a tourist centre. Yes, had it not been for General MacKay and his pet scheme, Inverlochy and its neighbourhood would probably have remained as little known to this day as some of the remote places on the west coast. The presence of a considerable body of soldiers in their midst (MacKay having left a garrison of at least one thousand men behind him when he departed) encouraged the inhabitants to bring their farm produce from the surrounding districts several times a week, and a steadily increasing trade was

[1] The original plans of the fort are to be found in the British Museum Library.
[2] Appendix XXIII.

the result. It became quite a common expression among
the Lochaber folk, when asked where they were going with
poultry, eggs, or milk, as the case might be, to say "*An
gearasdan*"—"the garrison"—and to this day the name is
frequently used by the Gaelic-speaking population.

Houses of turf and wattles began to spring up like mush-
rooms around the fort, and extended along the sea-shore for
some distance, and thus the nucleus of the present town was
formed. The piece of level ground at the rear was used by
the garrison as a parade ground, and it was here that the
troops went through their military evolutions, to the amusement of the Highlanders, who regarded the precise system of
English drill and discipline with feelings of undisguised
contempt. Though more than two hundred years have elapsed
since Fort William was built, the ground on which these
exercises were performed is still known as "The Parade."

A more melancholy memento of the existence of the
English garrison in Lochaber is the "Craigs" burial-ground,
in which many a Sassenach soldier lies buried, far from his
home and kindred. It is probable that, previous to the erection
of the fort, no cemetery existed here; and it may be assumed
that the first graves dug were to receive the bodies of those
English soldiers who died while in the performance of their
duties at Fort William. Some of the graves are very old,
and the inscriptions cannot be deciphered, owing to the
ravages of time and the destructive action of the sea air.
There is one, dated 1708, which has so far escaped obliteration
that the letters can still be seen and read, although with some
difficulty. The lines are as follows: "Here lies Ludovick
Muirhead, who spent the most of his life from his youth in
military service, with honour and bravery. He was descended
from the ancient family of British-holm. He died on
23rd February 1708, aged 49 years."

Situated on the slope of a grassy hill through which great
masses of rock protrude in picturesque confusion, the Craigs
burying-ground is one of the most beautiful spots in the

vicinity of Fort William. Seated here, the eye may wander at will over a wide prospect of magnificent Highland scenery, and take in at one glance one of the most charming and interesting views in Lochaber. The peaceful dead sleep beneath the daisy-spangled turf, heedless alike of the soft summer breezes and the howling blasts of winter. The murmuring river flowing swiftly by, chants a requiem to the silent ones who rest from their labours beside its verdant banks. Gael and Sassenach, antagonistic in life, mingle their dust in God's Acre, and await together the last great muster before the mighty Chieftain of the universe.

The year following the erection of Fort William was an *année terrible*, and the inhabitants of Lochaber were to stand appalled before such an act of fiendish cruelty and horrible barbarity, that the mind shrinks from the mere recital of its ghastly details. Perpetrated beyond the limits of Lochaber, I shall only refer to the massacre of Glencoe in so far as it affected the district of which I write.

When MacKay departed from the new garrison that he had at last succeeded in planting in the Western Highlands, he left the military command of the district to Colonel Hill, who became the first governor of Fort William. Hill appears to have exercised his powers with discretion, as we hear of no collision between the Highlanders and the garrison during his *régime*, and had it not been for the part he had to play in the terrible tragedy of Glencoe, history would probably have had little to say of him.

When the English Government, for the better pacification of the Highlands, decided to entrust the immense sum of fifteen thousand pounds to John Campbell, Earl of Breadalbane, for distribution among the disaffected chiefs of the Western Highlands, they could not have found an agent less likely to succeed in conciliating those bold and independent supporters of king James. "Cunning as a fox, wise as a serpent, but as slippery as an eel," Breadalbane had everything to gain and nothing to lose in the event of the chiefs refusing the offer of the Government, and thus necessitating harsh measures being taken against them. The result of his negotiations is a matter of history, and need not be recorded here.

Lochiel was one of the last to give in, and narrowly escaped the same fate as Glencoe; as we find Sir John Dalrymple writing to Breadalbane on 2nd December 1691 : "The Clan Donald must be rooted out, *and Lochiel.*" The old chieftain, even at this most trying moment in his career, maintained the honour and dignity of his name and clan. "I will not," said he, "break the ice. That is a point of honour with me. But my tacksmen and people may use their freedom."

MacIain of Glencoe, with even greater obduracy, defied the orders of the British Government till the last possible moment, and as we know it cost him dear. Finding that all his brother chiefs had submitted, the staunch old Jacobite found himself completely isolated, and feeling assured that nothing could be gained by holding out any longer, he decided to make the best of his way over the snow-clad mountains to Fort William, there to tender his oath of allegiance to Colonel Hill, the governor of the district. Unfortunately for Glencoe and his clan, his tardy submission came too late; the time at which the terms of the proclamation expired was 1st January 1692, and it was not until 31st December 1691 that MacIain of Glencoe arrived at Fort William. Hastily seeking out Colonel Hill, he requested him to administer the oath, which he was now prepared to take, but a difficulty arose that MacIain had not foreseen. The proclamation distinctly stated that the oath was to be taken before a civil magistrate; Colonel Hill was a military officer, and was consequently not empowered to receive it, but being a man possessed of humane feelings, and sympathising with MacIain in his embarrassment, good-naturedly advised him to proceed with all speed to the Sheriff of Argyllshire at Inveraray. To assist him in making his peace with the Government, Hill gave MacIain a letter addressed to Sir Colin Campbell of Ardkinglass, who was at that time Sheriff of Argyllshire, requesting him to receive the "lost sheep."

As considerable obloquy has been heaped upon the head of Colonel Hill on account of the order he issued on 12th February 1692, to Lieutenant-Colonel James Hamilton, which resulted in the awful massacre, it is only fair to say that he did what he could to assist MacIain in his desire to submit himself to the Government; and there is no valid reason for believing that he shared the vindictive spirit of his superiors. He was a soldier, and it was not for him "to reason why"; the orders given to him were clear and precise, and it was his duty to obey them, however distasteful they may have been. Let the onus of the whole disgraceful business fall upon the shoulders of the dastardly wretches who planned the murderous outrage in the security of their luxurious homes—Stair, Breadalbane, Dalrymple—these were the real butchers of Glencoe. Branded for ever with the mark of Cain, execrated by their fellow-countrymen, their names will go down to posterity linked with such a crime as even the brutal Nero in all the excesses of his bloodthirsty reign could not have surpassed.

The miserable tools of these unnatural assassins, Campbell of Glenlyon, Duncanson, Hamilton, and Lindsay, have deserved all the odium and infamy with which their names will ever be associated; but let it not be forgotten that they were mere soldiers carrying out the orders of the Government in whose service they were enlisted, and whose pay they were receiving. Criminal as they doubtless were, the real responsibility of the awful deeds of that sanguinary 13th February must rest to all eternity with the Judas trio by whose instructions they were carried out to the bitter end.

It was fortunate for the MacDonalds of Glencoe that, owing to the storm of wind and snow which prevailed at the time, Major Hamilton, who had left Fort William early in the morning with a force of four hundred men, was unable to cross the ferry, which affords the only means of access to the glen from Lochaber. This delay afforded an opportunity for many MacDonalds to escape from the scene of carnage, and hide themselves among the stupendous mountains that block in Glencoe on all sides, and which, at that inclement season of the year, were impassable by any but those to whom every glen and corrie were known from childhood. Alas! many a poor creature only escaped the sword of the assassin, to perish with cold and hunger amid the blinding snow-drifts that impeded the progress of the fugitives. Exposed to the full force of the icy blast, without food, and with only a few rags to cover their nakedness, delicate women, some with newly born babes at their breasts, young children, and the aged and infirm of both sexes, suffered all the rigours of the pitiless storm, and many sunk exhausted in the snow, and perished where they lay; others crept into holes and clefts in the rocks, and died of exposure and starvation, their bleached skeletons being discovered from time to time many years afterwards, ghastly mementoes of that direful tragedy.

Scotsmen of the present day are too ready to throw the *whole* blame of the massacre of Glencoe upon the English Government; that they should do this is evidence that they have not made themselves acquainted with the real facts of that diabolical outrage. The Government of William of Orange has much to answer for in this connection, but the fact stares us in the face, that with very few exceptions the whole of the actors associated with the awful tragedy were Scottish to the backbone.

History must be just and impartial, and however distasteful it may be to make such an admission, it is certain that had it not been for the counsel and advice of his Scottish ministers — who had their own wicked ends in view — William's reign would not have been disgraced by one of the foulest crimes that the world has ever seen.

The day of the massacre was an exciting one for Fort William, and the inhabitants of the small town [1] that had grown up around it.

<hr>

[1] This small assemblage of houses was originally called Gordonsburgh, from their having been erected on the estates of the Duke of Gordon, but about this time it was renamed Maryburgh, in honour of the consort of the Prince of Orange.

Early in the morning the bugle call to arms had awakened them from their slumbers. Ignorant of the terrible import of these warlike sounds, but suspicious of evil, they had looked from the doors and windows of their huts, and peering through the showers of thick falling snow-flakes, had seen the troops of the garrison assembling, to the number of four hundred, on the parade ground, under the command of Lieutenant-Colonel Hamilton. The lurid light of the flickering torches lit up the scene with a weird and uncanny effect; it flashed upon the arms and accoutrements of the soldiers as they fell into their places in the ranks, and steeped them in a blood-red glare. As the intermittent and tremulous radiance fell upon the men's faces, it transformed and distorted their features, and rendered them hideously grotesque, and cast their gigantic, spectre like shadows upon the walls of the fort, where they reeled and danced like demons at a witches' sabbath. It was a fitting prelude to a day of fiendish cruelty, and surely some of the Highlanders whom alarm and curiosity had drawn to the spot, must, with that gift of second-sight (*Taibhsearachd*) for which the Celtic race is famous, have seen something in the ominous surroundings to have aroused their suspicions that some dire calamity was portending.

In the darkness of that February morning, amid blinding showers of snow and hail, and pierced to the very marrow by the freezing blast that howled down upon them from the heights of Ben Nevis, the troops departed on their merciless errand, the very elements conspiring to prevent a crime at which hell itself might stand aghast. Later in the day tidings of the massacre reached Fort William, as one by one stragglers arrived from the scene of blood, and horrified the inhabitants with descriptions of the awful scenes they had witnessed in Glencoe.

Incredible at first, they received the news with hesitation, as beyond belief; but when night fell confirmatory evidence was forthcoming in the approach of great droves of cattle, sheep, and goats along the Achintore road, and the village was soon filled with a great crowd of animals that had been driven from Glencoe by the soldiers, and which were now destined for the use of the garrison. Nine hundred cows, two hundred horses, and immense numbers of sheep and goats were the spoil of the murderers, and these, we are told, were divided among the officers at Fort William as their share of the plunder.

CHAPTER XV.

FOR some years after the massacre of Glencoe peace reigned in the Highlands, and Lochaber shared in this happy state of things. The presence of the strong garrison at Fort William restrained the fiery chieftains of the Camerons and MacDonalds from making any open attempt to take up arms for the king over the water, whose chances of regaining his kingdom must now have appeared to them almost hopeless. Still their hearts and sympathies were with the exiled monarch, and found voice in many a spirited ballad, such as the one written by Lady Mary Drummond, daughter of the Earl of Perth:—

> "I may sit in my wee croo house,
>   At the rock and the reel to toil fu' dreary;
> I may think of the day that's gane,
>   And sigh and sab till I grow weary.
> I ne'er could brook, I ne'er could brook,
>   A foreign loon to own or flatter;
> But I will sing a ranting sang,
>   The day our king comes o'er the water.
>
> "O gin I live to see the day
>   That I ha'e begged, and begged frae heaven,
> I'll fling my rock and reel away,
>   And dance and sing frae morn till even;
> For there is ane I winna name
>   That comes the reigning bike to scatter;
> And I'll put on my bridal gown
>   That day our king comes o'er the water."

That happy day now seemed farther off than ever, and there was little prospect of Lady Mary donning bridal array in honour

S

of king James for the present. About this period we first hear of a proposal being made to William of Orange, by Breadalbane, to make use of the military strength of the Highlanders "in case of any insurrection at home or invasion from abroad," and a list of the chieftains and the estimated strength of their clans were laid before him. Breadalbane credits himself with 250 men, Lochiel's clan is represented by 150, MacDonald of Keppoch's with 50, Glengarry's with 100, Clanranald's with 100, and Mackintosh's with 100; the strength of the other clans not connected with Lochaber bring up the total to 4000 men. It was suggested that this force should be commanded by some important Highland gentleman, who should receive the rank and pay of a general officer. There is little doubt that Breadalbane intended this position for himself, as he proposed that Lochiel should be the second in rank, and falsely stated that he (Lochiel) was favourably disposed to the existing Government, and was anxious to prove his loyalty by taking up arms in its service. Although nothing came of Breadalbane's scheme, it is worthy to be placed on record as being probably the first time that any intentions of utilising the Highlanders for the military service of the State had been taken into serious consideration by the Government.

The time was not yet ripe for any such project as this to commend itself to the minds of such men as Lochiel or Keppoch, imbued as they were with strong Jacobite sympathies, and eager for the time which they hoped would not be long in coming, when, by the aid of their good claymores, the king should enjoy his own again.

"*L'homme propose, mais Dieu dispose.*" James II. (VII. of Scotland) was never again to set foot on British soil. While worshipping in his chapel at St Germains on Good Friday 1701, and listening to the solemn words of the anthem ("Remember, O Lord, what is come upon us; consider and behold our reproach. Our inheritance is turned to strangers, our houses to aliens; the crown is fallen from our head. Wherefore dost Thou forget us for ever?"), which produced, as they well might, a visible effect upon the fallen sovereign, he was attacked with a paralytic stroke, from which he never thoroughly recovered. This was followed on 13th September of the same year by a second stroke, which proved fatal.

Shortly before the end came, the French king, Louis XIV., arrived at St Germains, and hastening to the bed-chamber of the dying monarch, informed him that he had important news to communicate. The courtiers, assuming that their presence would not be required, were about to leave the apartment, when Louis, who had observed the movement, said in commanding tones, "Let nobody withdraw. I come to tell your Majesty that, whenever it shall please God to take you from us, I will be to your son what I have been to you, and will acknowledge him as king of England, Scotland, and Ireland."

It is doubtful whether these words of comfort reached the ears of king James, as, beyond a murmur, he gave no sign of comprehending their purport. He died on 16th September 1701, and was buried in the Chapel of the English Benedictines at Paris.

The French king kept his promise, and proclaimed and recognised the son of the deceased monarch as James III. (VIII. of Scotland), king of Great Britain and Ireland, and received him in audience with royal honours.

The death of Mary, the consort of William of Orange, on 28th December 1694, was followed in the year 1700 by the death of the Duke of Gloucester, the only surviving child of Anne. This catastrophe raised the hopes of the Jacobite party to the highest pitch, and, notwithstanding the death of James II. in the following year, they were still sanguine that success would attend their efforts to restore the Stuart dynasty. Four months later, on 8th March 1702, William of Orange paid the penalty of nature, and followed his father-in-law to the grave, and was succeeded on the throne of Great Britain by Anne, the second daughter of James II. Thus chance played into the hands of the loyal Jacobites, and they hailed the accession of Anne with feelings of the greatest satisfaction and delight—first, because she was a Stuart; and secondly, because they fully anticipated she would use all her power and influence to obtain a repeal of the Act of Succession, in favour of her brother James, and thus secure the crown for the Stuarts in the direct line. This contingency had of course been foreseen by the Whig ministers of William of Orange, and as there was little probability that Anne would bear any more children, they had to provide a successor who would satisfy the requirements of their party, and uphold the Protestant faith. Passing over the claims of the whole of the direct descendants of James II., of whom at that time there were fifty-three in existence, they selected the Princess Sophia, Electress and Dowager Duchess of Hanover, granddaughter of James I. (VI. of Scotland), and passed an Act of Parliament in June 1701, settling the crown upon her and her descendants.

This most arbitrary and unjust proceeding gave great offence to the Jacobites, who thus saw the hopes of their party ruthlessly dashed to the ground in one fell swoop. It was for this reason that they regarded the accession of Anne with undisguised pleasure, feeling assured that they would shortly be able to turn the tables on their enemies the Whigs. Had Anne remained true to her race, all might have gone well; but she succumbed to the machinations and intrigues of the celebrated Sarah, Duchess of Marlborough, and threw in her lot with the enemies of her own kindred, to the disgust and indignation of her Scottish subjects.

> " Let us think with what blood and what care
>   Our ancestors kept themselves free;
> What Bruce, and what Wallace could dare !
>   If they did so much, why not we?

> " Let Montrose and Dundee be brought in,
>   As later examples before you ;
> And hold out but as you begin,
>   Like them, the next age will adore you."

These were the sentiments expressed in an old ballad of the period, entitled, "On the Act of Succession," and fairly reflect the feeling in Scotland at that time. The only real advantage that the Jacobites had derived from the change of monarchy had been an act of indemnity, which had been granted by Anne to such of the exiled supporters of king James II. as chose to return by a certain stipulated time, and take the oath of allegiance. Many of the Highland chieftains availed themselves of this opportunity to return to their native land, among them being Simon Fraser, Lord Lovat, Sir John MacLean, Robertson of Struan, Captain John Murray, and Captain James Murray.

The arrival of these notorious Jacobites created something like alarm among the more timid of the Whigs, and they now began to regret that they had not more strenuously opposed an Act, the consequences of which, they feared, would lead to another outbreak of civil war. The following letter, written by Captain Hamilton from Inverness, and addressed to Brigadier-General Maitland, who was then governor of Fort William, did not help to allay their fears. The letter commences by informing Maitland that an important hunting-match was about to take place in the Highlands, and a large attendance of the clans and their chiefs was anticipated.

"The Duke of Hamilton is to be there, the Marquis of Athol; and our neighbour the Laird of Grant who has ordered 600 of his men in arms, in good order, with tartane coats all of one colour and fashion. This is his order to his people in Strathspey. If it be a match of hunting only I know not, but I think it my duty to acquaint you, whatever may fall out of any such body of men in arms, particulary in our northern parts."

Maitland, on receipt of this despatch, took steps to strengthen his position, in case the "suspicious hunting match" should develop into an eighteenth-century "Chevy Chase." Whatever may have been the outcome of that early

Inverness meeting, it did not result in any attempt being made to surprise the garrison at Fort William, and for the present they were left undisturbed.

It may interest some of my English readers to learn that even at this period there was a good school at Fort William, towards the maintenance of which the Government gave an annual grant of £30 sterling. This sum was paid over to Maitland, who was "to be accountable for the right using and applying of the said sum for the use aforesaid." This grant was believed to have been made as some sort of compensation for the massacre of Glencoe. Whether this was so or not, it is satisfactory to know that education, even in the year 1700, was thus placed within the reach of the Highlanders of Lochaber, who, we are told, were not slow to take advantage of it. Fort William has always been celebrated for its good schools, and many a child of humble parentage has gone forth from them to make his mark in the world of literature or science.

Nothing of interest occurred in Lochaber during the reign of Anne, save the death of our old friend "Iain Lom." After the avengement of his kinsman's death, the bard employed his time in the congenial employment of versification, and many beautiful compositions were the result of his leisure. His death took place in the year 1709, when, honoured and respected by all who knew him, "he was gathered to his fathers." He sleeps among his native hills of Brae Lochaber, on an eminence named *Dun Aingeal* ("Angel Hill") in *Kill a Choireil* ("Church of St Cyril"); and it has been left to a modern Highlander, Dr Fraser Mackintosh of Drummond, to raise a cairn to the memory of the old Lochaber bard. It is in the form of one of the ancient Celtic monumental stones, and has the following inscription engraved upon it in Gaelic:—

"An so'n Dun-Aingeal a'm Braigh-Lochabar,
Tha Bárd na Ceapaich gu trom na chadal;
Se Iain Lom Mac Dhomhnuill b'ainm dha,
Iain Lom! ach theireadh cuid Iain Manntach;"

translated into English as follows by the Rev. Dr Alexander
Stewart ("Nether Lochaber"):—

> "Here in Dun-Aingeal, in the Braes of Lochaber,
> The Bard of Keppoch is very sound asleep;
> His name was John MacDonald, John the Bare—
> John the *Bare* and *Biting*! but by some called
> John the Stammerer."

Before closing my brief account of this remarkable man, I will
recount one incident in his career which is often passed over
by his biographers.

After the battle of Inverlochy in 1645, the vanquished
Marquis of Argyll, stung by the ridicule to which he and his
clan were subjected owing to the scornful verses of Iain Lom,
offered a large reward to anyone who would bring him the head
of the offender. So far from being frightened by this threatened danger, Iain looked upon Argyll's anger merely as another
tribute to his skill as a poet, and in a spirit of sheer bravado,
he determined to beard the lion in his den, and set out for
Inveraray on a visit to the outraged *Mac Cailean Mòr*. At first
blush this action on the part of the bard appears nothing short
of madness; but no one knew better than the cautious Iain,
that among the Highlanders the office of bard was considered
sacred, and he was perfectly well aware that though Argyll
might storm and threaten, he dared not injure one hair of his
head. Having arrived at Inveraray, he made his way to the
castle of the Campbell chieftain and demanded an audience.
Argyll must have been heartily surprised to see his implacable
foe within his gates; but he dissembled his anger, and with
studied courtesy conducted his unexpected, and, without doubt,
unwelcome visitor through the various places of interest in
the castle. At length they came to a room in which was
hung a trophy of the chase, consisting of an immense number
of black-cock heads. Turning to Iain, the marquis asked him
if he had ever seen so many black-cocks together.

"Yes," answered the bard.

"Where did you see them?" inquired Argyll.

"At Inverlochy," replied Iain, unable, even when in the stronghold of his inveterate enemy, to refrain from giving vent to his stings of satire.

"Ah, John," said the marquis, concealing his annoyance, "will you never leave off gnawing the Campbells?"

"I only regret," returned the undaunted Iain, "that I could not swallow them."

A characteristic and probably true account of what really took place, and interesting as showing to what length the bards of that era could presume without fear of punishment.

While Anne was on the throne Lochaber was at peace, and Lochiel and Keppoch could only bide their time and await the day, which they foresaw must soon come, when their clans would have to take up arms in the cause of James III. (and VIII.), the title by which the son of James II. was commonly known. Lochiel, now too old to exercise the duties of chieftainship, had after the battle of Killiecrankie placed the entire control of the clan into the hands of his son John, who was a most ardent and zealous Jacobite, and deeply implicated in every scheme to restore the exiled family.[1]

On the 1st August 1714, Anne succumbed to a lethargic disorder, and thus "the crown that came with a lass, went with a lass," for never again was a Stuart to sit on the throne of Great Britain, though much blood was yet to be shed in the endeavour to restore that unfortunate dynasty to its old exalted position in the realm. While Anne lived there was always a possible chance that she might repeal the unjust Act of Succession, and so, at least, atone for her unfilial conduct in respect to her father, and place the crown within reach of her royal brother; but with her death the last hopes of the Jacobites vanished, and they now saw that only by the sword could they hope to restore their rightful sovereign to his throne and dignities.

On 5th August, "the High and Mighty Prince George, Elector of Brunswick, Luneburg," was proclaimed king of

[1] "Memoirs of Sir Ewen Cameron."

Great Britain, France, and Ireland at the cross of Edinburgh, and on 18th September the "wee, wee German lairdie" set foot for the first time on the shores of his newly acquired kingdom.

> "And he's clappit doun in our gudeman's chair,
> The wee, wee German lairdie!
> And he's brought fouth o' foreign trash,
> And dibbled them in his yardie;
> He's pu'd the rose o' English loons,
> And brake the harp o' Irish clowns,
> But our Scot's thristle will jag his thumbs,
> The wee, wee German Lairdie!"

Such were the sentiments awakened in the breasts of Geordie's Scotch subjects upon his arrival in Britain, and he was soon to discover that the national emblem was a most appropriate one, and that though it might be possible to find a rose without thorns, a thistle without prickles was a botanical impossibility.

"Coot peoples, vy do you wrong us? Ve be come for all your goots," was the remark addressed to the English mob by the Countess of Darlington, one of Geordie's Hanoverian female importations, as they crowded round the royal carriage. "Yes, d——n ye!" shouted one of the crowd, "and for all our chattels, too, I think."

Truer words were never spoken. Luxurious as the courts of the last Stuart monarchs had undoubtedly been, the people had not suffered to any appreciable extent; in fact, the very prodigality of Charles II. had given an impetus to trade, owing to the increased demand for articles of luxury, that employed thousands of hands in their manufacture. But with the advent of the Hanoverian usurpers all was changed. The refined sybaritism of the Stuarts, with its accompanying lavish expenditure of money, was exchanged for the repulsive debauchery and sordid greed of a race of boorish Teutonic adventurers, who, to supply the funds necessary for their drunken orgies, reduced the nation to beggary, and besmirched her fair fame with the ineffaceable stains of their shameless immorality.

T

The Stuarts, with all their faults—and they were many—
were at least kingly and dignified, and maintained their royal
office with courtly munificence and becoming state. But what
good word can be said for the German intruders who displaced
them — vulgar, mean, avaricious, without a single redeeming
quality, their sole aim being to gratify their sensual natures and
to enrich themselves at the expense of their starving subjects.
So contemptible a spectacle do they present, that we can
only stand amazed at the forbearance of our ancestors, who
suffered them to rule the destinies of our country.

CHAPTER XVI.

IT is refreshing to turn from the contemplation of such unpleasant
topics, and get back to our Highland mountains. The news of
the Hanoverian accession caused some consternation among our
Lochaber friends, who had been waiting the turn of Fortune's
wheel that would put king James on his throne again. Sir
Ewen Cameron of Lochiel received the tidings of the proclamation of George I. with apparent unconcern, but at heart the
staunch old Jacobite looked forward wistfully to the day
when he might see his king, and sing his "Nunc dimittis"
before leaving the scenes of his earthly prowess. John
Cameron shared his father's loyal spirit, and saw that his
gallant Camerons were kept in a state of preparation for the
service of king James. His brother Alan was in close attendance upon his sovereign in France, and sent all the latest news
from St Germains to his kinsmen in Lochaber, who were
thus closely posted up in the course of events.

It is not my purpose to give a detailed account of the
rebellion of 1715; but as it certainly concerned Lochaber to a considerable extent, I must necessarily record the main outlines of
that heroic but unfortunate attempt to restore the fallen dynasty.

The leader of this forlorn hope was John, Lord Erskine,
eleventh Earl of Mar, who, during the reign of Anne, had filled

the office of Secretary of State. His knowledge of Highland affairs had led to his being selected by the Privy Council as the most suitable person to distribute the considerable sums of money that had been voted by Oxford's Administration as peace offerings to the Highland clans.

Although a Jacobite at heart, Mar had, for political reasons, supported the Treaty of Union, and had in consequence lost popularity in Scotland, where he was regarded with suspicion. Upon the arrival of the Elector of Hanover, Mar was one of the first to seek an interview, with the intention, no doubt, of securing his position as Secretary of State for Scotland, and the income of £5000 per annum which went with the office. Probably Mar's professed loyalty to the Elector was only part of a deep-laid Jacobite scheme to place a spy in the very heart of the enemy's camp, who could warn them of any intended hostile movement, and advise them of the most propitious moment for a rising in favour of the royal exile. This theory is borne out by the fact that Mar was in possession of an address from the principal Highland chieftains, expressing their readiness to follow the direction of the Earl of Mar in faithfully serving " king" George. The chiefs who subscribed their names to this document were Cameron of Lochiel, MacDonell of Keppoch, MacDonell of Glengarry, Mackintosh of Mackintosh, MacLean of MacLean, MacKenzie of Fraserdale, MacLeod of Contulick, MacPherson of Cluny, Grant of Glenmoriston, Chisholm of Comar, and Sir Donald MacDonald.

It is quite impossible to believe that all these staunch supporters of James III. (VIII. of Scotland) could have been sincere in their protestations of loyalty to the enemy of their cause, and we can only imagine that the whole thing was a plot to throw the Whigs off the scent. Whether this was so or not, George declined to receive either Mar or his address, and that nobleman, instead of receiving the welcome he had anticipated, found himself not only dismissed from Court, but also from his office of Secretary of State.

Vowing vengeance against the house of Hanover, and the

Elector in particular, he departed secretly for the north to raise the standard of rebellion against the usurper. Upon his arrival in Scotland he proceeded to his estates of Braemar, in Deeside, where he collected a considerable number of the adherents of the exiled Stuarts.

On 6th September 1715 the standard was raised in the presence of about two thousand men, and the Chevalier de St George proclaimed as king James VIII. of Scotland and James III. of England and Ireland. The spirited song, so well known to all Scotsmen, "The Standard on the Braes of Mar," gives a nearly complete muster roll of the loyal Jacobites who were either present on this occasion or joined the force under Mar shortly afterwards.

> " Wha wadna join our noble chief,
>   The Drummond and Glengarry :
> MacGregor, Murray, Rollo, Keith,
>   Panmure and gallant Murray ;
>   MacDonald's men,
>   Clanranald's men,
>   MacKenzie's men,
>   MacGilvray's men,
>   Strathallan's men,
>   The Lowland men
>   Of Callander and Airlie."

Although the words of this song are modern, having first seen the light of day in Smith's " Scottish Minstrel," published in 1824, the air to which the martial words are wedded is said to have been the gathering tune of the clans to which they marched on the morning of the battle of Sheriffmuir, 13th November 1715.

The invitation to join Mar's army was not immediately responded to by the clans of Lochaber and the adjoining district. Cameron of Lochiel and Stewart of Appin, both loyal to the core, made no movement, and the Campbells of Breadalbane, whose chief had promised Mar his support, were still waiting among the hills of Argyllshire, apparently disinclined to take an active part in the coming strife.

This seeming indifference on the part of such enthusiastic
Jacobites as Lochiel and Appin, was due either to some
lingering suspicion of Mar's sincerity, or more probably to
the fact that their close proximity to the territory of the
powerful Duke of Argyll, whose Whig propensities were fully
known and understood, rendered an open outbreak of rebellion
on their part both foolish and impolitic. Circumstances, however, which they were unable to foresee or control, forced
them into activity. To Lochaber and its brave Highlanders
belongs the honour of opening the campaign of 1715 on
behalf of king James VIII., for now a desperate effort was
to be made to surprise the garrison of Fort William, and
drive out the Sassenach redcoats, whose hated presence had
been a standing insult to Lochiel and his brother chieftains.

Mar had, shortly after unfurling the standard in Braemar,
despatched one of his principal officers, General Gordon, with
instructions to raise the western clans, and march with them
upon Glasgow. Gordon was an officer of considerable experience, and possessed of great personal courage. The mission
was a congenial one to this gallant soldier, and the difficulties
he encountered only served to increase his ardour for the cause
in which he had embarked. Having secured the assistance
and support of Glengarry, the other chiefs came in one by
one. Clanranald brought with him the MacDonalds of Moidart
and Arisaig, and Sir John MacLean arrived with a strong
following of his clan from Mull. Gordon's force now amounted
to between four thousand and five thousand men, consisting
of the above-mentioned clans and a small body of Camerons,
who had taken the field with the acquiescence of their chief.

With this body of men under his command, Gordon
attempted a bold attack on Fort William, with only partial
success; for though he managed by sheer impetuosity to carry
some of the outworks and take several prisoners, the main
body of the garrison made such a stubborn defence, and
were so well protected by the fortifications which MacKay
had erected, that he had reluctantly to withdraw his men, and

retire towards Argyllshire, where he took up a position close to Inveraray, with a view to overawing the Campbells, and giving an opportunity for any of the Jacobite clans in the neighbourhood to join his army.

After this incident the tide of battle flowed away from Lochaber, and although many of her brave sons followed the fortunes of Mar in the field, and paid the penalty of their loyalty with their lives on the field of Sheriffmuir, it would be inconsistent with the purport of this work to follow step by step the events of the rebellion of 1715, interesting though they are to all who love to hear of the noble deeds of their fellow-countrymen.

Shortly after the attack on Fort William, John Cameron of Lochiel, with the consent of his venerable father Sir Ewen, mustered the Clan Cameron, and placing himself at their head, hastened to join the army under Mar. The other neighbouring chieftains, Glengarry, Clanranald, Keppoch, Glencoe, and Appin, had already attached themselves to the Jacobite force, and now only waited the command of their leader to precipitate an action with the Hanoverian army commanded by the Duke of Argyll, who, like his ancestors, was to be found on the side of his country's enemies.

The battle of Sheriffmuir was fought on 13th November 1715, and though many were slain on both sides, and great prodigies of valour performed, victory hung in the balance, and neither side gained any material advantage, and, as the old ballad says,—

> " There's some say that we wan,
> And some say that they wan,
> And some say that nane wan at a', man;
> But one thing I'm sure,
> That at Shirra-muir,
> A battle there was, that I saw, man;
> And we ran, and they ran,
> And they ran, and we ran,
> But Florence [1] ran fastest of a' man."

---

[1] Florence was the name of the Marquis of Huntly's horse.

Among the slain was the young and gallant Ailein Moidartach, captain of Clanranald, chief of the MacDonalds of that ilk, who fell in the commencement of the action, stricken to the heart by a bullet.[1] His kinsman Glengarry, observing that the sad end of their chief had so depressed the clansmen of Clanranald that they stood disconsolate around his dead body, instead of joining in the charge, ran in among the mournful group, excitedly waving his bonnet above his head, and shouting, " Revenge, revenge ! To-day for revenge, and to-morrow for mourning !" with so great an effect that, aroused from the absorption of their grief, they hurled themselves upon the enemy with such impetuosity and fury that Argyll's left gave way under the terrible blows of the claymores and axes of the enraged Highlanders, and incontinently fled.

The sad death of Clanranald was a severe loss to the Stuart cause. Young, brave, and generous, he had endeared himself to all, and was adored by his clan. His military experience was considerable, he having served for some years in the French Guards, and while in their ranks had applied himself with all the ardour of youth to the study of the profession of arms, and had at the same time taken the opportunity his residence in France offered of making himself personally acquainted with his sovereign at St Germains. His reply to Mar's letter of invitation to take up arms and assemble his clan in the king's service was worthy of the stock from whence he had sprung. " My family," he wrote, " have been on such occasions ever wont to be the first on the field, and the last to leave it."

Another gallant Highlander was Sir John MacLean, who had come with his clan from Mull to help forward the cause. Forming his men in line previous to the commencement of the battle, he addressed them in the following forcible and characteristic language : " Gentlemen, this is a day we have long wished to see. Yonder stands Mac Cailean Mòr

[1] The well-known Gaelic song, " *Tha tighinn fodham eirich*," was composed in honour of this popular young chief.

for king George. Here stands MacLean for king James.—
God bless MacLean and king James!—Charge, gentlemen!"

The celebrated Rob Roy was also present at Sheriffmuir
with a following of his clan, but from some unexplainable
cause held aloof from actual conflict, and coolly surveyed the
battle from a slight eminence in the neighbourhood.

> " Rob Roy then stood watch
>   On a hill for to catch
>   The booty, for aught that I saw, man ;
> For he ne'er advanced,
>   From the place he was stanced,
>   Till no more was to do there at a', man."

Possibly the explanation of Rob Roy's behaviour on this
occasion will be found in the above lines. Had he allowed
his MacGregors to have lent their assistance to the almost
victorious army of Mar, the day might have been won for
king James. Unfortunately, the ruling passion for plunder
was too strong in the heart of the old *cearnach*, and he could
not let slip such a splendid opportunity of enriching himself
and his clan ; and we are told that after the battle was over
friends and foes were alike despoiled by his rapacious followers
without distinction.

Although Rob Roy had little or no connection with
Lochaber, there is one incident in his adventurous career that
caused his appearance at Fort William under extraordinary
circumstances, which may interest those of my readers who
have not heard the story.

When Mar unfurled the banner of his king at Braemar, in
the presence of a large number of noblemen and chiefs of
proved fidelity to the exiled Stuarts, a bond was signed by
those present on that memorable occasion, by which they bound
themselves to support their rightful sovereign, king James VIII.,
and also to give mutual assistance to each other should necessity
arise. Among the signatories to this dangerous document was
the redoubtable Rob Roy, whom Mar, with a view of securing
his powerful aid, had invited to the hunting match (?). By

some mischance this important paper had fallen into the hands of a zealous Whig officer, Captain Campbell, who was then at Fort William, and it was feared that he would at once take steps to place it in the hands of the Government. The consequences of such an action would have been disastrous to Mar and his Jacobite friends, and it was determined at any cost to obtain possession of the document before it could reach the hands of the Privy Council. The question was, who was to beard the lion in his den, and make him deliver up the precious bond?

Rob, with his usual intrepidity, threw himself into the breach, and promised by hook or by crook to recover what had been so carelessly lost. Disguising himself so cleverly that his own followers could not recognise him, he set out for Fort William, and upon reaching the garrison, boldly asked to speak with Captain Campbell. This request being granted, he made himself known to him, and being related to the Captain by ties of blood, gained the desired information as to the whereabouts of the document.

It appears that, upon coming into possession of the paper, Campbell had at once been convinced of its importance, and, after perusing it, had handed it over to Governor Hill of Fort William, who decided to forward it to the Privy Council without a moment's delay. Fortunately Rob had not taken long on his journey, and he now had the satisfaction of learning that he had not arrived too late, for the bond was still in Hill's keeping, and was to be despatched in the course of a few days to the Government, under an escort from the garrison.

Finding out the probable strength of the escort and the route they proposed to take, Rob returned to his home, and collecting about fifty of his clan, awaited in Glendochart the arrival of the soldiers with their valuable charge. As soon as the troops came in sight, Rob and his MacGregors sprang from their hiding-place and barred the way, and shouted to the officer in command to halt and deliver up his despatches. The officer at first refused, but Rob was not the sort of man to take no for an answer, and told the officer, in language more forcible

U

than polite, that he meant having their lives and despatches together, or their despatches alone.

Surrounded on all sides by these ferocious Highlanders, armed at all points, the officer came to the conclusion that in this instance discretion was the better part of valour, and without further parley handed over the despatches to Rob Roy, who quietly undid the bundle, and after abstracting the document he had taken so much trouble to obtain, gave back the remaining papers to the astonished officer, and apologising for having delayed his journey in so unceremonious a fashion, took his departure in triumph. It is probable that but for this bold act on the part of Rob Roy many lives would have been forfeited and many estates confiscated.

Of the deeds of the Camerons at Sheriffmuir history says but little, but we may be sure they sustained the honour of the clan as their ancestors had done of yore, although their leader was personally deficient in military skill. Previous to taking up arms for king James, John Cameron of Lochiel had prudently made over the estates to his son Donald, who was thus placed in possession of his patrimony while his grandfather and father were still alive. John Cameron was for some reason or another unpopular with his clan, and had in addition given serious offence to his father Sir Ewen, who had forbidden him to return to his estates. Shortly after the period of which I am now writing, he retired to France, and died at Boulogne in 1747.

The utter incapacity for military generalship shown by Mar at Sheriffmuir lost him the confidence of the Highland chiefs; and those of their number who had fought under the banner of Dundee at Killiecrankie, gave vent to their vain regrets that he was not now alive to lead them to victory. Tradition says that during the battle, an old Highlander, impatient at Mar's delay in giving the order to charge, cried out, "Oh for one hour of Dundee!" and doubtless his sentiments were shared by many of those present.

CHAPTER XVII.

AFTER Sheriffmuir, many of the Highlanders returned to their homes to await a more auspicious occasion, and the advent of a more competent leader, before again risking their lives in the service of the king. James VIII., commonly known as the Chevalier de St George, landed at Peterhead on 22nd December 1715, with the hope that his presence in Scotland would assist in keeping alive the waning energies of his loyal adherents, and provoke them to fresh action on his behalf. A curious incident in connection with the arrival of the king on Scottish ground occurred at Ach-na-carry, where old Sir Ewen Cameron of Lochiel was lying on a bed of sickness, to which age, with its consequent infirmities, had brought him.

On the morning of the 22nd December, Sir Ewen, who had been sleeping soundly, awoke with a start, and calling loudly to his wife, who slept in an adjoining apartment, told her the king had landed, and commanded a bonfire to be made and the best liquors in the house to be brought out for his lads to drink the king's health. Lady Cameron at first imagined that her husband was in a delirium, and took no notice of his instructions ; but he was so persistent that they were eventually carried out, and feasting and mirth reigned supreme among the Camerons of Lochiel.[1]

This strange gift of second-sight has been attributed to the Celtic race from time immemorial, and many are the weird stories and legends of celebrated seers that still linger among the inhabitants of Lochaber and the western islands. Dr Johnson, in his " Journey to the Hebrides," devotes considerable space to an account of this mysterious faculty, and remarks, in his usual sapient and dictatorial manner, that second-sight "seems to mean a mode of seeing, superadded to that which nature generally bestows," and consists of "an impression made either by the mind

[1] " Memoirs of Sir Ewen Cameron.'

upon the eye, or by the eye upon the mind, by which things distant or future are perceived, and seen as if they were present."

The wish of the old chieftain's heart was now fulfilled; his loved sovereign had come to claim his own, and although his aged eyes had not seen him in the flesh, it had been vouchsafed to him to perceive as it were in a vision the features of his king; and his old heart must have rejoiced with exceeding gladness when the tidings reached Lochaber that his second son, Alan Cameron, had been accorded the honour of accompanying king James on the voyage to Scotland, and had been selected as one of that monarch's personal attendants during his hazardous enterprise to recover his lost kingdom.

An account of Sir Ewen's appearance at this period has been copied from the Balhadie MS. by a Miss Cameron of Lochiel, and runs thus:—

"His eyes retained their former vivacity, and his sight was so good in his ninetieth year that he could discern the most minute object, and read the smallest print; nor did he so much as want a tooth, which to me seemed as white and close as one would have imagined they were in the twentieth year of his age. In the state when I had the good fortune to see him in 1716, and so great was his strength at that time that he wrung some blood from the point of my fingers, with a grasp of his hand; his bones big, his countenance fresh and smooth, and he had a certain air of greatness about him, which struck the beholder with awe and respect."

Although the Camerons fought with their wonted bravery at Sheriffmuir, they were unfortunately placed on the Earl of Mar's left wing, and thus sustained the whole brunt of the onset, and, overpowered by numbers, had to give way and beat a retreat. It is possible that the estrangement that existed between John Cameron and his father had its origin in this circumstance, as we know the old chief was keenly sensitive to anything that affected in the slightest degree the honour of his clan, and he may have thought that had he been physically capable of leading them himself on the day of the battle, that the result might have been a victory for king James.

There is a footnote in Sir Walter's Scott's "Tales of a Grandfather" bearing on the subject, which may be read with interest. Referring to Sir Ewen's state of health at this period, it runs as follows :—" He (Sir Ewen) was in perfect possession of his faculties during the year 1715, and expressed great regret that his clan, the Camerons, being in the Earl of Mar's left wing, had been compelled to fly on that occasion." "The Camerons," he said, "were more numerous than they were in his day, but they were become less warlike."

The same authority goes on to narrate the following anecdote, viz. :—" An English officer, who came from Fort William on a visit, having made use of some words which the old chief took amiss, he looked on him sternly, and said, 'Had you used that expression but a few months since, you would not have lived to repeat it.'" Consistent to the last, the old Highland warrior, who had fought at Achdalieu and Killiecrankie, resented the slightest reflection upon the behaviour of his clan from Sassenach lips, although, on the occasion referred to, his position as host debarred him from doing more than make a dignified protest.

The news of the arrival of king James in Scotland was hailed with satisfaction by his brave subjects in Lochaber, for they now anticipated that a determined effort would be made by the Jacobites throughout the three kingdoms to oust the "wee, wee German lairdie" from the throne he filled with so little credit to himself and so little honour to the nation. Unfortunately the ill-fortune that, like a black cloud, hung over the destinies of the Stuarts, once more asserted itself, and the representative of that fated race found himself quite unable to assemble a force of sufficient proportions to warrant a serious campaign against the large and well-disciplined army of the Elector. Had he arrived in Scotland earlier, when the enthusiasm of his party was at its highest, and before the incompetency of Mar had disgusted many of his principal supporters, James's presence at the head of what was then a considerable army might have been productive of some good result, and would at least have encouraged his devoted followers to persist in their endeavours to win back the crown for his family. But now his presence in Scotland was embarrassing, as, after Sheriffmuir, his army had melted away, and it would be a task of great difficulty to remuster it.

His personal appearance, too, was not calculated to inspire confidence in the minds of his Highland friends, who regarded physical strength and manly vigour as two important charac-teristics in their *beau ideal* of the chief who was to lead them in the field. It cannot be said with truth that king James VIII. possessed either of these qualifications, for we are told that "his person was tall and thin, seeming to incline to be lean rather than to fill as he grows in years. His countenance was pale, but perhaps looked more so than usual by reason he had three fits of ague, which took him two days after his coming on shore. Yet he seems to be sanguine in his constitution, and there is something of a vivacity in his eye that perhaps would have been more visible if he had not been under dejected circumstances. . . . His speech was grave, and not very expressive of his thoughts nor over much to the purpose; but his words were few, and his behaviour and temper seemed always composed."

Such was the appearance of the king whose coming had been so long looked for, and it can hardly be said that it was of such a nature as to favourably impress the impartial beholder; certain it is that the Highland chiefs, who, by the king's special request, were brought before him during his stay in Perth, were not unnaturally disappointed on discovering that their hero had not one single quality to render him, in their estimation, a fit person to command them in an enterprise which could not but prove a difficult and dangerous one. Their idol proved but clay after all; and although it would be unjust to the memory of the throneless monarch to impute to him any want of courage, or lack of interest in the preparations for war which were being made on his behalf, it is nevertheless true that his apparent indifference, whether due to the weak state of his health or to a natural antipathy to military displays of any kind, produced a feeling of apprehension and suspicion among the loyal clans, who had already suffered considerably owing to the bad generalship of Mar.

These fears were not allayed by the news that shortly after spread like wildfire through the camp, that the king intended to desert them in the hour of need, without striking a blow or risking an engagement with Argyll, who was advancing rapidly on their position at Perth. To the Highlanders such faintheartedness was incomprehensible, and at first they utterly refused to credit the rumours that came to their ears. Bold and fearless themselves, and altogether reckless of the consequences of a collision with such a force as Argyll had under his command, they could not bring themselves to believe that their king was less brave than their own chiefs. Accustomed as they had always been to fight against overwhelming odds, they had learned to disregard mere numbers, and trusted to their own good broadswords to hew a path to the throne for the son of James VII. Bitter, indeed, was their chagrin when, on the 4th February 1716, they learnt that the king, accompanied by the Earl of Mar, Lord Drummond, Alan Cameron of Lochiel, and a few other gentlemen, had embarked on board a small French vessel at Montrose, and set sail for France.

In justice to Mar, it should be said that he had strongly objected to seek safety in flight, and had requested the king that he might be allowed to remain behind with the remnants of the army he had raised; but he could not refuse to obey the direct command of his sovereign, and reluctantly consented to accompany him to the Continent, where for the next few years he acted as the principal minister in attendance upon the royal exile, and took an active part in the many intrigues of the Court at St Germains. In 1725, being suspected by his party of having entered into communication with the Government of the Elector of Hanover, he was dismissed from his office, and died in retirement in 1752.

CHAPTER XVIII.

WITH the departure of the Chevalier from Scotland, the rebellion of 1715 came to an inglorious end, and the Jacobite clans, indignant at the timidity of their leaders, threw down their arms in disgust and retreated to their native hills. The effect of the flight of the Chevalier and his officers was soon felt in Lochaber by the renewed activity of the garrisons at Fort William and Ruthven in Badenoch. Orders had been issued by the Government that the Highlanders who had fought under the standard of Mar were to surrender their arms to officers appointed to receive them at various places throughout the Highlands and Isles. Upon the condition that this was done by a certain date, a free pardon was promised to all. General Cadogan was selected for the duty of receiving the submission of the Lochaber chieftains and their clans, a task that he found of considerable difficulty. Lochiel had decided to resist to the utmost, and, if necessary, resort to force in opposing the obnoxious order to disarm. In this bold resolve he was supported by Keppoch and Clanranald. On hearing of the obstinate refusal of these chiefs to deliver up their arms, General Cadogan, who was then at Inverness, where he had just received the submission of MacDonald of Glengarry, sent instructions to Colonel Clayton at Fort William, to take a strong detachment of soldiers and march to Lochiel's house at Ach-na-carry, and disarm the refractory Camerons, who, as usual, treated the orders of the English Government with contempt.

The news of the meditated assault on Ach-na-carry having reached Lochiel, he was induced to alter his determination, out of regard for his devoted clansmen, whom he knew would be the sufferers in the event of an engagement with the well-armed troops under Colonel Clayton. Weakened by their losses at Sheriff-muir, and by the hardships they had encountered in the long and demoralising campaign of 1715, the Clan Cameron was in no fit condition to withstand an attack from such a well-organised force as the garrison at Fort William could now send against it. None knew better than Lochiel the reckless valour of his followers, and he was fully aware that there was not one of them, from the young *gillie* of fourteen to the veteran *duine-ùasal* of eighty, who would not have defended his property with their lives had he but spoken the word.

As no real advantage could be gained by refusing to obey the orders of the Government, Lochiel resorted to strategy, and leaving instructions to his clan to deliver up their arms peaceably, he retired from the district until the general had departed. Keppoch and Clanranald followed his example with little delay, and the Camerons and MacDonalds, collecting all the old and useless weapons they could lay their hands upon, laid them, with many a grim smile and emphatic utterance in guttural Gaelic, at the feet of the English officers ; while safe within their dwellings, in many a nook and corner, lay hidden the trusty claymore, the dirk and *sgian dubh*, that were destined to play havoc with the Sassenach redcoats at Prestonpans and Culloden.

The majority of the arms collected from the West High-landers were deposited at Fort William, while those of the lowland clans were sent to Edinburgh Castle. The apparent submission of the disaffected clans having been thus effected, they were left in comparative peace, and for the next few years the historian of Lochaber has little to record.

An event of melancholy interest occurred in 1719, which cannot be passed over without comment. In the month of February of that year the old chief, Sir Ewen Cameron of Lochiel, then in his ninetieth year, was taken suddenly ill of a high fever, which rapidly proved fatal, and, amid the lamentations of his sorrowful people, the war-worn spirit of the aged warrior passed peacefully away.

"*Exegi monumentum ære perennius.*" The deeds of Sir Ewen Cameron needed no sculptured memorial to record them. Engraved deeply upon the tablets of the history of his country, and enshrined in the hearts of his compatriots, they

X

will ever be remembered with a glow of pride. For nearly a century the striking personality of this remarkable man had been before the world, and successive Governments had wondered what this *terra incognita* of Lochaber could be like, that could produce such gallant sons. Its very remoteness invested it with a halo of mystery; and as from time to time the tidings of some more than ordinary deed of heroism reached the ears of the English ministers, they must have thought that the Arthurian age still existed among the mountains of *Ultima Thule*, and that the Sir Lancelots and Sir Galahads of the Round Table had left their favourite hunting-grounds in extinct Lyonesse, only to reappear in the unknown glens of the distant north, in quest of further adventures.

There is something peculiarly romantic in the career of Sir Ewen Cameron, his interesting surroundings, his many hairbreadth escapes, his knightly valour, his bold and dignified bearing in times of danger and difficulty, his staunch and devoted adherence to a fallen dynasty, and, above all, his unblemished honour, which remained untarnished to the end, notwithstanding the many attempts that had been made by his enemies to subvert it—all these traits in his character merit for him the title of the "Bayard" of the seventeenth century, *sans peur et sans reproche*.[1]

I cannot here refrain from quoting the sublime language of Ossian, whose description of the death of the Irish chieftain Cathmor, is so applicable to the event I have just recorded.

" I hear the call of years; they take my spear as they pass along. . . .
My fathers, Ossian, trace my steps; my deeds are pleasant to their eyes.
Wherever I come forth to battle, on my field, are their columns of mist.
But mine arm rescued the feeble; the haughty found my rage was fire.
Never over the fallen did mine eye rejoice.
For this, my fathers shall meet me, at the gates of their airy halls, tall,
    with robes of light, with mildly kindled eyes.
But, to the proud in arms, they are darkened moons in heaven, which
    send the fire of night, red-wandering over their face."

---

[1] The old chieftain sleeps in the burying-ground of Kilmallie, surrounded by the mortal remains of his distinguished descendants.

The mantle of the departed chief fell upon the shoulders of his grandson Donald, who, it will be remembered, had been left in charge of the estates upon the departure of his father to join the army of Mar in 1715. John Cameron had never been popular with his kinsmen, and although, upon the death of Sir Ewen, he became the titular head of the clan, he did not attempt to assert his position, and remained in France while his son Donald took upon himself all the duties and responsibilities in connection with the property, and was looked upon by the Camerons as their chief in everything but name.

To avoid confusion in the description of the events that are to follow, in which the Camerons took an active share, I will give a brief account of the various members of Lochiel's family who were living at this period (1719).

Sir Ewen left three sons—John, Alan, and Ludovick. John Cameron, the titular chief, was in exile, and of his after career we know but little. He had five sons:—(1) Donald, who now commanded the clan, and was known as the Young Lochiel, and later by the title of the "Gentle" Lochiel, on account of his lovable disposition; (2) John of Fassfern, who, although taking no active part in the '45, suffered great injustice at the hands of the Government, and being exiled, became a merchant and settled in the West Indies, but returned to Lochaber and died at Fassfern; (3) Archibald Cameron, who was educated for the medical profession, and known to history as Doctor Archibald Cameron; (4) Alexander, who became a priest; and (5) Ewen, who emigrated to Jamaica, and died a sugar-planter.

Of the two other sons of Sir Ewen, Alan Cameron had embarked for France with the Chevalier, and was now in close attendance upon him at St Germains; and Ludovick Cameron of Torcastle was living on his estate of that name in Lochaber, watching the interests of his nephew Donald, and assisting him in the military organisation of the clan.

In Donald Cameron of Lochiel, the Camerons had found a

worthy successor to their departed chieftain. Although his disposition was gentle, and without the brusqueness of manner that distinguished his grandfather, his notions of honour and justice were in every way as keen, and he was quite as ready to resent an insult or injury to his name or clan. Having been born in a more enlightened age than his celebrated grandsire, and having received the advantages of a more liberal education, he endeavoured, upon his accession to the chieftainship, to discourage as much as possible the periodical *creachs*, or forays, which the Camerons, in common with most of the other Highland clans, had been wont to indulge in from time immemorial. General Wade, of whom we shall hear more anon, in making his report on the state of the Highlands in 1724, says: "The clans, in the Highlands, the most addicted to rapine and plunder, are the Camerons, on the west of the shire of Inverness; the Mackenzies and others in the shire of Ross, who were vassals to the late Earl of Seaforth; the M'Donalds of Keppoch; the Broadalbin men, and the M'Gregors on the borders of Argileshire." Thus we find that two of the principal Lochaber clans, the Camerons and the MacDonalds of Keppoch, were specially pointed out as being the worst offenders in this respect.

The *creach*, or foray, was peculiarly a Highland institution of questionable morality, and the cause of innumerable feuds and quarrels. If a chief thought himself insulted by a neighbour, he mustered his clan in secrecy, and placing himself at their head, raided the offender's territory, carrying off all the cattle he could lay hands upon, and seeing nothing derogatory to his honour in what was then considered a justifiable act of reprisal. As a general rule, few lives were lost in these predatory excursions, as orders were usually given by the chiefs engaged in them to avoid personal encounters as much as possible. So great was the secrecy with which these expeditions were planned and carried out, that the unfortunate owner of the stolen cattle was often quite ignorant of his loss until some days after the *creach* had taken place. In some cases a reward was offered for the restitution of the stolen beasts. This was called *tasgal* money, and although it was sometimes accepted and the cattle returned to their rightful owner, it was more often indignantly refused; and we are told that the Camerons especially had bound themselves by oath never to receive it, as they considered the acceptance of such money so dishonourable an action that their chiefs had made it a capital offence, and any of the clan who were known to have done so were put to death.

The cultivated mind of Young Lochiel revolted at this barbarous custom, which he could not distinguish from mere vulgar robbery, and although quite a lad he took active steps to put a stop to these cattle-lifting forays among his people, and inflicted the most severe punishment upon any member of his clan who was found guilty of taking part in them.

There is a tradition, the truth of which I cannot vouch for, that the last execution in Scotland under the old feudal laws took place during the time that Young Lochiel was in command of the Clan Cameron, as a punishment for this very crime. The story runs that one of the clan having *lifted* a bull from the property of a *duine-ùasal* of the name of Ewen Cameron, he was promptly followed, and having been secured, was brought before the chief at Ach-na-carry. Determined to stamp out the offence which brought so much discredit on his clan, and justly enraged that one of his vassals should have dared to disobey his direct orders, Lochiel, after having heard the evidence on both sides, and being fully assured of the man's guilt, condemned him to death. Some writers say that the unfortunate victim of feudal justice was hanged immediately after the sentence was pronounced on the chief's "gallows tree" at Ach-na-carry; but a more authentic account states that the prisoner was removed to the jail at Fort William. While the thief was lying there under sentence of death, a petition to stay the execution was sent to Lochiel, and great pressure was brought to bear upon him to remit the punishment, but without avail, as he considered it necessary that a terrible example should be made in order that other unruly members of the clan should be deterred from a similar crime by the fate of their comrade. The execution was carried out at a spot known as *Tom-na-faire* ("The Watch Hill"), close to the ruins of Inverlochy Castle, in the presence of the wife and family of the unfortunate man. Previous to his execution, the condemned man composed a Gaelic song of several verses, in which he describes himself as being bound with ropes, and having no food save a bottle of beer and a piece of cake, and calling upon his kinsmen to avenge his death.

Shortly after this tragic incident, we are told that one of the Camerons, named "*Domhnull donn a bhrollaich*" ("Brown-haired Donald of the beautiful breast"), went to the chief and persuaded him to swear on his dirk that in future no Cameron should suffer capital punishment without a full trial.

This narrative is of great interest, as proving that as late as the eighteenth century the old feudal privileges of "pit and gallows" were still in force in the Highlands, and that, notwithstanding all the changes that had taken place in the government of the country, the despotic power of the Highland chiefs over the lives and property of their vassals was in no wise diminished; and, strange as it may appear, it is nevertheless true that they possessed more absolute control and authority in their little kingdoms among the mountains than the *de facto* monarch of the realm could boast of.

Young Lochiel found it no easy matter to wean his followers from a custom which they had come to look upon as a perfectly legitimate way of enriching their pockets at the expense of their enemies, and it was long before they could be persuaded to devote their energies to agricultural pursuits and other kindred industries as a means of earning a livelihood. It may be truly said of young Donald Cameron of Lochiel, that he was the pioneer of civilisation in Lochaber, and that, while maintaining all the dignity and authority that his position entitled him to, he brought the influence of a well-educated and refined mind to bear upon his actions, thus setting a noble example before his clansmen, who could not but follow in the footsteps of their chief.

The other Lochaber chiefs did what they could to assist Lochiel in his endeavours to improve the morale of the clans;[1] but such radical changes were not to be effected all at once, and for a time the old *creachs* went on as merrily as ever.

CHAPTER XIX.

BY the year 1724 the state of affairs in the Highlands was so bad, that the Government was importuned to take active steps to enforce order among the troublesome clans of the north and west; who, now that the army had been disbanded, formed themselves into gangs and went about the country committing all sorts of depredations without interference. Roused to action by these repeated representations, the Government of the Elector of Hanover issued a warrant under the sign manual, authorising Field-Marshall Wade, an engineer officer of considerable skill and experience, to thoroughly investigate and report upon the condition of the Highlands; and after having made himself acquainted with the country, he was to offer suggestions as to the best methods for remedying the lawless state into which it had fallen, and gain any other information that might prove useful in bringing about the submission of the Jacobite chieftains. He was also instructed to devise means for the better opening up of the country by roads or other modes of communication, in order to make it more accessible for the passage of troops in the event of another rising on behalf of the House of Stuart.

Marshall Wade departed on his errand with ample authority,

[1] Appendix XXIV.

and it may here be said that he executed his commission with the greatest humanity and tact; and although, in the discharge of his duty, he was necessarily brought into contact with many whose politics differed widely from his own, he made few enemies, and was regarded with sentiments of respect even by those who held in detestation the Government by whom he was employed.

Wade reached Inverness in the month of August 1725, and shortly after forwarded a long and intelligent report to the Government, recommending, among other necessary reforms, the nomination of suitable persons for the office of sheriffs, the establishment of justices of the peace and constables with small salaries, and the periodical holding of quarter sessions at Killyhuimen (Fort Augustus), Ruthven, and Fort William. He also suggested, "That companies of such Highlanders as are well affected to His Majesty's Government be established under proper regulations, and commanded by officers speaking the language of the country, subject to martial law, and under the inspection of the governors of Fort William, Inverness, and the officer commanding different garrisons and castles in North Britain."

The immediate result of Wade's activity in the Highlands was the cessation of lawlessness and disorder in the neighbourhood of Inverness; the bands of Highland marauders who had infested the districts of Lochaber and Badenoch, carrying terror into the hearts of the more peaceful members of the community, now refrained from open depredations, and contented themselves with an occasional night raid upon the cattle of an unpopular chief, or the more portable property of some lowland laird, as Sir Walter describes in his humorous ballad :—

> " Donald Caird finds orra things
>   Where Allan Gregor fand the tings;
>   Dunts of kebbuck, taits o' woo,
>   Whiles a hen and whiles a sow,
>   Webs or duds frae hedge or yard—
>   'Ware the wuddie Donald Caird."

The "wuddie" was, alas! to claim many a victim from among the brave Highland hearts of Lochaber before many years were over, for more serious crimes in the eyes of the Government than the abstraction of *webs* and *duds* from the auld wives' drying-grounds, or the surreptitious removal of *dunts o' kebbuck* from the farmer's aumrie.

The proposal of Wade to raise a force of armed Highlanders for the service of the State was carried into effect about 1729, when six strong companies were formed, and, after having been instructed in their military duties by the regular officers, were despatched to their respective stations under the command of Highland gentlemen of Whig proclivities, who were in receipt of commissions from George I. These were Lord Lovat, Sir Duncan Campbell of Lochnell, Colonel Grant of Ballindalloch, John Campbell of Carrick, Colonel Alexander Campbell of Fonab, and George Munro of Culcairn. Their companies were stationed at various strategic points among the mountain passes from the Isle of Skye in the west to Dunkeld in the east, with a view to suppress any attempt that might be made at armed rebellion by the Jacobite chieftains, who were known to be in correspondence with the Court at St Germains.

Lochiel was a notorious suspect, and the fact that his father and uncle had both distinguished themselves on the side of the Chevalier in the recent campaign, caused his every movement to be closely watched. Lochiel's uncle, Alan Cameron, was at this time in the Highlands, whither he had been sent by his royal master to gain what information he could as to the prospects of another rising on his behalf, and he was instructed to open up a correspondence with the loyal chiefs in order to learn what force they could place in the field in the event of a landing being effected. The arrival of Alan Cameron was known to Wade, and, as an additional precaution against surprise, one of the new companies was despatched to Fort William, under the command of Campbell of Fonab, with instructions to keep a sharp look-out for any movement among the Camerons, who, it was feared, were planning mischief.

Y

To the Lochabrians the appearance in their midst of a body of well-disciplined Highlanders, wearing a semi-military uniform, and charged with the enforcement of the obnoxious orders of a foreign government, must have come as a surprise. They could not associate the wearing of the national garb with a want of sympathy for the national sentiment. The "heart that beat beneath the tartan plaid" could not, they thought, be untrue to the traditions of the race that had worn it since the days when their great ancestors ruled the land, now desecrated by the presence of the Sassenach soldiery. And they were right: the hearts that throbbed in the breasts of the Government soldiers were Highland hearts after all—brave, noble hearts, that in the years to come were to inspire heroic actions on many a well-fought field, and earn for their regiment the laurels of an imperishable fame. Gallant "*Freiceadan Dubh*"! ("Black Watch.") Your country may well be proud of you and your achievements. The colours that float so bravely over your nodding plumes, as you march with stately stride through old Dunedin's crowded streets, or across the scorching sands of the Egyptian desert, bear upon their silken folds such a record of splendid victories that cannot fail to kindle a glow of pride and enthusiasm in the soul of even the most unemotional observer. Corunna, Peninsula, Waterloo, Alma, Sebastopol, Lucknow, the links in a chain of soul-stirring associations; what memories of noble deeds are called up by the sight of these glorious names, as, in all the splendour of golden embroidery, they flash upon our vision. More than a century of the history of our nation is written there, a century of honourable warfare in defence of the rights and liberties of a free and unconquered people. Tyrants have trembled before the irresistible onset of your kilted heroes, and the skirl of your pibrochs have sounded in their ears as the funeral dirges of their vanished armies. "*Clanna nan Gaidheil ri guaillibh ó cheile*"[1] has been your war-cry in the past; let it

---

[1] "Highlanders, shoulder to shoulder!"

be your watchword in the future. Whether in peace or war, at home or abroad, show the world the reality of Highland clanship by your fidelity to your name and race!

Sanguine as Marshal Wade was with regard to the newly formed Highland companies, and the effect they would have in overawing the disaffected clans, it is doubtful whether the Government derived any material advantage from their employment for this purpose. *Quis custodiat ipsos custodes?* The guards were in this instance of the same flesh and blood, the same race and sympathies, as those over whom they were to keep strict watch and ward; and in many instances the privates were closely related by ties of kinship to the suspected *cearnachs* and freebooters whose depredations they had been sent to prevent and punish. Blood is proverbially thicker than water, and Private Angus MacDonald, of the *Freiceadan Dubh*, was very often to be found conveniently looking in another direction while cousin Donald Cameron was engaged in a little harmless cattle-driving in a neighbouring glen. However, Wade was satisfied, and that was the main point; for we find him writing a long congratulatory letter to his employers, in which he says that "robberies and depredations formerly complained of, are less frequently attempted than has been known for many years past, there having been but one single instance where cattle have been stolen without being recovered and returned to their owners."

Having thus, as he thought, tamed the Highland wolves, the energetic marshal turned his attention to the much-needed work of road-making, and it is principally owing to his efforts in this direction that his name is even to this day respectfully regarded by the Highlanders of Lochaber, in whose district some of his greatest engineering feats were carried out. The splendid road from Fort William that crosses the river Spean at High Bridge, and follows the shores of Loch Lochy, Loch Oich, and Loch Ness to Fort George, traversing the entire length of the Great Glen (*Gleann Mòr nan Albin*), is in itself a lasting memorial of his skill and perseverance.

Another of Wade's roads proceeds from the rear of Fort
William, and runs nearly due south over the hills to Glencoe,
and from thence to Inveraray, where it communicates with
the main road from Callander.

In the work of constructing these great highways Wade
employed large numbers of the soldiery, and both Highlanders
and Englishmen might have been seen working side by side in
this peaceful occupation. To render the labour popular, Wade
granted extra pay to all the soldiers who were engaged in the
laborious task; and though the difficulties to be surmounted
must have seemed almost insuperable, the prospect of additional
pay infused a spirit of cheerful determination in the minds of
the troops to overcome all obstacles, and so the work went
merrily on, and by the year 1737 the roads were completed.
At first these new highways were regarded with anything but
favour by those who were eventually to derive great benefit
from their construction. Pennant, writing some years later,
says: "These public works were at first very disagreeable to
the old Chieftains and lessened their influence greatly; for by
admitting strangers among them their clans were taught that
the Lairds were not the first of men."

It was, of course, only natural that this should be so. The
Highlanders who were loyal to their exiled king could not but
see that these roads were specially designed for the more rapid
movements of the Hanoverian troops, and they feared what
might be the result of the opening up of their hitherto
impregnable strongholds among the mountains should they
be again called upon to take the field in the cause of the
Stuarts.

Associated with Marshal Wade in his various undertakings
was an officer named Burt, a captain of engineers, who, while
serving in his official capacity at Inverness, found time to study
the manners and customs of the people among whom his lot
was cast. The result of his self-imposed task was a series of
very interesting letters, descriptive of various incidents that
occurred during his residence in the Highlands, and written in

FORT WILLIAM   173

a quaint, humorous style that is highly amusing to the modern reader. These letters were eventually published in London in book form, under the title of "Letters from a Gentleman in the North of Scotland to His Friend in London."

Containing as they do much valuable information as to the state of the Highlands in the years 1725-1727, they have been repeatedly quoted by various writers on the subject. The majority of the letters refer to Inverness and its immediate surroundings, but there are several in which the gallant captain recounts his adventures among the wilds of Lochaber, which I think should find a place here.

He writes with reference to Fort William: "The Fort is situate in Lochaber, a country, which, though bordering upon the Western Ocean, yet is within the shire of Inverness. Oliver Cromwell made there a settlement, as I have said before, but the present Citadel was built in the reign of King William and Queen Mary and called after the name of the King. It was in great measure originally designed as a check upon the chief of the Camerons, a clan which in those days was greatly addicted to plunder, and strongly inclined to rebellion. It stands in a most barren, rocky country, and is washed on one of the faces of the fortification by a navigable arm of the sea. It is almost surrounded on the land sides, with rivers not far distant from it, which though but small, are often impassible from their depth and rapidity. And lastly, it is near the foot of an exceeding high mountain, called Benevis, of which I may have occasion to say something in some future letter, relating particularly to the High Country. The Toun was erected into a Barony in favour of the governor of the Fort, for the time being, and into a Borough bearing the name of Queen Mary. It was originally designed as a Sutlery to the garrison in so barren a country, where little can be had for the support of the troops.

"The houses were neither to be built with stone or brick, and are to this day composed of timber, boards, and turf. This was ordained to the end they might the more suddenly be burnt, or otherwise destroyed, by order of the governor, to prevent any lodgment of an enemy that might annoy the Fort, in case of rebellion, or invasion."

In a further letter we find a very diverting account of an attempted ascent of Ben Nevis by a party of brother officers; and it is evident that the expedition was looked upon as a daring feat of plucky endurance by those in the garrison, who had probably never ascended any eminence of greater altitude than Richmond Hill. Captain Burt did not himself take part in this hazardous enterprise, but contented himself with playing the part of an eighteenth-century reporter, and chronicled the event in the following words:—

"As a specimen of the height of these mountains I shall here take notice of one in Lochaber called Benevis; which from the level below to that part of the summit only, which appears to view has been several times measured by different artists and found to be three quarters of a mile of perpendicular height. It is reckoned seven Scots miles to that part where it begins to be inaccesible. Some English officers took it in their fancy to go to the top, but could not attain it for bogs, and huge perpendicular rocks; and when they got as high as they could go, they found a vast change on the quality of the air, saw nothing but the tops of other mountains, and altogether a prospect of one tremendous heath, with here and there, spots of craggs and snow. This wild expedition in ascending round and round the hills; in finding inaccesible places, helping one another up the rocks, in disappointments, and then returning to the foot of the mountain, took 'em up a whole Summer day from five in the morning."

This "wild expedition" occurred during the summer months, when the track is in fairly good condition, and was undertaken by a party of presumably athletic young men. What would Captain Burt have thought had he been told that in another century the ascent of the great mountain would be made in the coldest month of the year by three Highland lasses, in spite of the intense frost that prevailed at the time. The *Oban Times*, under date 14th January 1893, records the successful attempt of three ladies of Fort William to reach the summit of Ben Nevis on the second of the month to "*first foot*" the benighted beings who sacrifice the comforts of home and the company of their fellow-mortals to the cause of science, at an elevation of 4400 feet above the sea-level. The advent of the lasses, laden with creature comforts in the shape of cake and *uisge-beatha* (a well-known Highland temperance beverage), must have gladdened the hearts of the hermits of the mountain, and they were doubtless reluctant to let their fair visitors depart; but as the summit of Ben Nevis on a January night is hardly the place for even Highland young ladies, the *deoch-an-doruis* was drunk, and the plucky mountaineers departed on their perilous descent, and arrived safely in Fort William, after an absence of nine hours.

"Comparisons are odious," and Burt's graphic account of the Sassenach officers floundering about among the bogs that surround the lower levels of the mountain, and eventually returning tired and discomforted to their quarters, makes but a sorry picture when placed side by side with the one just described.

When in Fort William, Burt was told a pathetic story by the governor's wife of an incident that had happened a short time before his visit, during a temporary dearth of food, owing to the provision ships having been delayed by stress of weather. Food of all kinds was so scarce, that many of the poorer people were in a state of starvation, and they had to beg the governor to let them buy meal from the stores in the garrison. At length these supplies began to run short, and orders were given that no more meal was to be sold. A poor Highland woman, who had a large family of children, had managed to scrape together a shilling (a large sum in those days), with which she hoped to keep the wolf from her door. Finding the granary of the garrison closed against her, she sought out the governor's wife, and entreated her to persuade the governor to sell a measure of meal for the shilling she had saved; but being informed that it was impossible to do this, the woman vehemently flung the coin on the table, saying, " My children cannot eat *this!*" and burst into a flood of passionate tears. It is satisfactory to learn that the sympathies of the governor's wife were aroused at the grief of the poor creature, who could not realise that her treasured money was useless, and she humanely provided food for the hungry children, until the famine was put an end to by the arrival of the vessels.

PART III.—THE "FORTY-FIVE."

CHAPTER XX.

See 25

IT will now be necessary to retrace our steps a few years, in order that we may the better understand the circumstances that led up to those remarkable events which were to form one of the most romantic and stirring chapters of Scottish history, and called forth, in the highest degree, all that was chivalrous, all that was noble and self-sacrificing, in the Celtic nature, and directed the attention of the whole of Europe to the struggle for right against might, of undisciplined courage against brutal strength, which was to be fought out to the bitter end on Culloden's fatal field.

The Chevalier (James VIII.) had married in the year 1720 the wealthy and accomplished Princess Clementina Sobieski, granddaughter of the famous John Sobieski, king of Poland, whose brilliant victory over the Turks in Austria had made his name celebrated throughout the length and breadth of Europe.

On 31st December of the same year the princess presented her royal husband with a son and heir to his crown and kingdom, a crown which, unhappily, he was never to wear, and a kingdom he was destined never to rule. Born in exile, and surrounded by the unwholesome atmosphere of Court intrigue, Prince Charles Edward became imbued with an exaggerated sense of his position, an idea which was continually being fostered by the unwise flattery of his father's courtiers, who saw in the young prince an object worthy of their affection and

Z

loyal enthusiasm, both on account of his lovable disposition and as the future hope of their party. This adulatory environment was not the best school for the education of a prince who was to suffer all the disappointments and indignities that his father's dependent position rendered likely, if not inevitable. Fortunately nature had endowed Prince Charles with a sanguine temperament and a strong physical constitution, gifts which were to stand him in good stead during the adventurous career that fate had in store for him. As he grew in years he developed many pleasing traits of character, which endeared him to all those in whose society he was thrown. Courteous and affable in manner, and possessed of an amiable and generous disposition, he completely won the hearts of the Highland gentlemen who had followed the exiled family to France after the affair of 1715, and they swore to assist him in the recovery of his father's kingdom when he should attain a sufficient age to make the attempt. The blood of two heroic families mingled in the veins of the young prince, and filled him with a desire to emulate the great example of his progenitors.

Consecrating his life to the task of restoring the ancient dignities of his royal house, he infused into his dispirited party something of the animation of his youthful and impetuous spirit, and raised the most sanguine hopes in their minds as to the speedy prospect of a successful invasion of Scotland. During the Prince of Wales's childhood, Alan Cameron, the nephew of young Lochiel, had, as we are aware, been employed by king James in the dangerous mission of visiting the loyal Highland chieftains, and endeavouring to obtain from them some definite promise of support in the event of a favourable opportunity for an invasion occurring. Beyond a general protestation of devoted loyalty to their king across the water, the chiefs were unable to enter into any engagements, as their clans had scarcely recovered from the effects of the last abortive rising, and were, besides, assured that the times were not propitious for such a rash enterprise. Finding it useless to remain longer in Scotland, Cameron returned to his sovereign with the intelligence that the country was not at present ripe for any such desperate undertaking as had been premeditated. This news, though disappointing to the Chevalier, was rendered less unwelcome by the many messages of devoted loyalty that Cameron had brought with him from the Jacobite chiefs, who, while deploring their inability to take the field at the present juncture, promised to use their utmost endeavours to put their respective clans on a sound military footing, so that when the struggle came they should not be found unprepared. Alan Cameron appears to have directed the Chevalier's special attention to the exertions that his nephew Lochiel was making on his behalf, for we find James writing a letter to that chief on 11th April 1727, which runs as follows :—

"I am glad of this occasion to let you know how well pleased I am to hear of the care you take to follow your father's and uncle's example in their loyalty to me, and I doubt not of your endeavours to maintain the true spirit of the clan. Alan is now with me, and I am always glad to have some of my brave Highlanders about me, whom I value as they deserve. You will deliver the enclosed to its address, and doubt not of my particular regard for you, which I am persuaded you will always deserve.

(Signed)   "JAMES R."

"You will tell Mr MacLachlan that I am very sensible of his zeal in my service."

This gracious letter was enclosed in a long epistle from Alan Cameron, who, fearing that Lochiel would be unable to read the king's writing, explained its contents, and impressed upon his nephew the very great honour that had been rendered to the house of Cameron by such friendly sentiments as were expressed in the royal missive.

A few months later, on 11th June 1727, the Elector of Hanover was called to his account, and his son was proclaimed king of Great Britain and Ireland, under the title of George II. This news reached king James at Bologna, and once again his hopes of recovering his lost kingdom were raised to the highest pitch. His first impulse was to at once set sail for England, and trust to Providence and ·the exertions of his supporters to effect a *coup d'état*, which, in the confusion attending a change of rulers, he fondly hoped might place him upon his throne. Had such a rash project been carried out, it could only have resulted in utter disaster, as the great mass of the people of England and Scotland were utterly indifferent to the claims of the Stuarts, whom they had long been taught to regard as Popish monsters, and subverters of the Protestant religion, and whose only aim was to introduce into Britain all the horrors of the stake, and the tortures of the Inquisition.

It was fortunate that the king possessed friends who saw that any such reckless attempt to win back the crown would have been fatal to the cause for which they had suffered so much, and who were sufficiently bold to dissuade their royal master from risking his life in such a fruitless adventure.

A letter written to Lockhart of Carnwath—one of his most staunch supporters—about this time, shows the bent of his thoughts, and how strongly his mind was set upon a visit to England. The letter is too long to insert here, but the last few sentences will show its purport. He says, " I desire, therefore, you may think seriously on this matter, and let me have your opinion as soon as possible ; and if my going into England be not advisable, whether my going to the Highlands of Scotland might not be found proper."

The trusty Alan Cameron was the bearer of this important dispatch to Lockhart, who was then residing at Liége, whither he had fled on learning that a warrant for his arrest had been issued by the English Government.

After mastering the contents of the letter, he took Cameron into his confidence, and together they discussed the situation, and resolved to frame such a reply that would deter the king from carrying out his bold scheme.

Upon receipt of the sensible advice contained in Lockhart's

diplomatic reply, king James decided to give up the idea of visiting his rebellious subjects for the present, and withdrew to Avignon, to take counsel of the Pope.

Among the chiefs who had followed the king to France after the abortive rising in 1715, was Coll of Keppoch, who, after the disarmament of his clan, rightly thought that he could be of more service to his sovereign by personally attending his Court, and being ready to offer sound practical advice in connection with the meditated plan for a further attempt to overthrow the House of Hanover. His thorough acquaintance with the Highlands, and his well-tried courage in the field, gave force to his counsel, and he became a valued friend to the exiled monarch, who found in the old hero of Mulroy, Killiecrankie, and Sheriffmuir, an object worthy of his affectionate regard.

Coll of Keppoch was, however, not destined to take part in the final struggle for supremacy that he had helped to plan. Sometime during the year 1730, the cold hand of death was laid upon his brow, and the spirit of the brave MacDonald chieftain passed quietly away, amid the gathering clouds of approaching battle.

He had married Barbara, a daughter of Sir Donald MacDonald of Sleat, by whom he had three sons, viz., Alexander, Donald, and Archibald; and a daughter, who afterwards married Cameron of Errachd. Alexander, who succeeded his father as the sixteenth chief of Keppoch, had been educated in France, and at the time of his father's death was an officer in the French army. Between the young prince and Keppoch a strong friendship existed, fostered by the close relations into which they were continually thrown. There were few secrets between them, and when the expedition to the Highlands was finally decided upon, Keppoch received early intimation of it. I am unable to give the exact date that Alexander of Keppoch returned to Lochaber, but he was certainly there at the time of the prince's landing, as he was one of the first to take up arms for his sovereign.

It would be out of place in such a work as this to follow the chain of circumstances that brought about the rising of 1745, and I shall endeavour to confine myself as much as possible to those incidents that occurred in Lochaber and its immediate neighbourhood during that eventful period. It may be truly said of this romantic and beautiful district, that it was the cradle of the '45. Ever staunch to the royal house of Stuart, the brave Highlanders of Lochaber were now to prove that their loyalty was no empty name, but a real and self-sacrificing devotion to a cause they loved as life itself. These noble sentiments had been fostered by their gallant chieftains, Lochiel, Keppoch, Clanranald, and Glengarry, all of whom had set such an example of unselfish fidelity to their unfortunate sovereign, that they had imbued their clansmen with the same spirit, and it was now to bear fruit in the approaching struggle, and afford the world a spectacle of true heroism such as it had rarely seen. Young Lochiel, ever ready to further the cause in which his ancestors had fought and suffered, had in 1740 formed one of the seven associates, who, at Edinburgh, had entered into an engagement to risk life and fortune in another attempt to restore the Stuart monarchy, provided the French king would lend them the support of a portion of his army; and he had despatched his nephew, Drummond of Balhadie, to the Chevalier at Rome, with full particulars of the efforts that were being made on his behalf. Drummond afterwards went to Paris to advocate the cause there, but the French ministers were too much engaged at that time, owing to the death of the emperor, Charles VI., to listen to his importunities.

Meanwhile, the Lochaber men remained expectant, and waited patiently for the day that was to bring their prince to their shores. Tidings reached them from time to time that he was busily engaged in fitting out an expedition in one of the French ports, and everything was held in readiness for his arrival; but as year after year passed, and no sign came of the ships that were to bear their hero across the main, they began to lose interest, and their intrepid spirits commenced to droop at "hope deferred that maketh the heart sick." The chiefs themselves, better acquainted with the tortuous course of foreign politics than their followers, regarded the delay as providential, for they were able to see that the landing of Prince Charles in Scotland, unless at the head of a powerful army, would only precipitate a war of extermination, in which they and their clans would be the principal sufferers.

CHAPTER XXI.

ABOUT the month of June 1745, it was whispered from mouth to mouth that at last the prince was coming, but nothing certain was known of his movements, until shortly after the 25th of July, when a messenger arrived at Ach-na-carry with the long expected tidings that at last the heir of the Stuarts had set foot on British soil. Devoted as Lochiel was to his beloved prince, the news, though partly anticipated, was embarrassing; and for some time after the receipt of the royal summons his breast was wrung with the conflicting emotions of loyalty to his king, and compassion for his brave Camerons, who, he knew, would follow where he led, were it into the jaws of death. He was fully convinced of the madness of the enterprise, and foresaw that only disaster could attend an attempt to commence hostilities without either men, arms, or money.

Determined to use all his powers of persuasion to prevent Prince Charles from risking his life and those of his followers in so reckless a manner, Lochiel set out for Borodale, a wild, desolate region on the shores of Loch-nan-uamh, where he had been told he would find the prince. To reach Borodale, Lochiel had to pass the house of his brother, John Cameron of Fassfern, which was situated on the slope of a hill, within a short distance of the beautiful Loch Eil, and surrounded by some of the most magnificent and picturesque scenery in the Highlands. Here Lochiel paused to consult his brother as to the best method of dissuading the rash prince from proceeding further with his ill-advised undertaking. Fassfern, aware of his brother's sensitive and impressionable nature, saw at once that if he was allowed to come within the sphere of the powerful influence, and listen to the passionate eloquence of the prince, all his resolutions would be abandoned, and he would be utterly unable to refuse acquiescence. "Brother," said Fassfern, "I know you better than you know yourself; if this prince once sets his eyes upon you, he will make you do whatever he pleases."

Fassfern strongly advised Lochiel to put his objections into writing and forward the letter by special messenger to the prince, but this suggestion did not meet with Lochiel's approval, as he considered it his duty to wait upon the royal visitor in person. The result of that historic interview, fraught with the gravest consequences to Scotland, is well known; the respectful arguments of Lochiel, the dignified pleading and firm determination of Prince Charles to persist in trying his fortune by the sword, and the ultimate yielding of the Cameron chieftain, need no recapitulation here. The die was cast, the one man whose yea or nay contained in their single syllable the destiny of a royal race, had uttered the noble words that will ever linger in the traditions of his country: "I will share the fate of my prince, and so shall every man over whom name or fortune has given me any power." Fassfern had spoken truly, the fascinating presence and chivalrous bearing of Prince Charles Stuart had overcome all the scruples of Lochiel, who, having put his hand to the plough, would not look backwards.

Taking leave of the prince, Lochiel hastened back to Ach-na-carry to raise the Camerons, and send the fiery cross through the mountains and glens of Lochaber, with instructions that all able-bodied men of the clan were to arm themselves with all possible speed, and be ready to march with him to Glenfinnan on 19th August, the day that Prince Charles had fixed for raising the royal standard. The other

Lochaber chieftains followed the example of Lochiel, and proceeded to prepare their men for the service of their prince. Clanranald had been one of the first to tender his allegiance to his royal highness on board the "Doutelle" (the vessel that had brought the prince from France), and was now engaged in collecting a body of MacDonalds to join the forces of his brother chiefs, Glengarry and Keppoch. The Lochaber MacDonalds, like their kinsmen of the Isles and Glencoe, had always been devoted to the House of Stuart, and had proved their loyalty on many a hard fought field. Above the din of battle their war cries of *"Craig an Fitheach"* and *"Fraoch Eilean"* had rung out with terrible clamour, where the fight was the thickest, and the strife the most bloody. Their good claymores had done excellent service for the Stuarts in the glorious times of Montrose and Dundee, and were now to be unsheathed in the same good cause. From all quarters they came to assist their gallant prince to claim his own, and drive out the Hanoverian usurpers.

> " Gather, gather, gather,
> Gather from Lochaber glens ;
> Mac-ic-Rannail calls you ;
> Come from Taroph, Roy, and Spean,
> Gather, brave Clan-Donuil,
> Many sons of might you know,
> Lenochan's your brother,
> Auchterechtan and Glencoe."

The honour of opening the campaign, and of striking the first blow on behalf of king James, was reserved for MacDonald of Keppoch[1] and his brave men, who, by the force of circumstances, were brought into collision with the English troops

---

[1] After this portion of my work was completed, Miss MacDonell of Keppoch placed in my hands some MS. notes relating to the '45 which had been taken down during the lifetime of Prince Charles by John MacDonell, the grandson of the hero of Culloden. These notes, which I believe have never been published before, are of considerable historic value, and from them we gather that the chief of Keppoch played a more prominent part in the preliminary events of that stirring period than he has been usually credited with. Those of my readers who are interested in the subject will find a copy of the MS. in Appendix XXV.

before any official declaration of war had been made by the prince, who was then lying concealed at the house of MacDonald of Kinlochmoidart. The unusual activity of the Highlanders in the neighbourhood of Fort Augustus had aroused the suspicions of the governor, and having learnt that large bodies of Camerons and MacDonalds had been observed marching in the direction of Fort William, he determined to despatch two companies of the Scots Royals to strengthen the garrison there, and gain information as to the meaning of this apparently hostile movement on the part of the clans. The command of the detachment was given to Captain John Scott, an officer of undoubted courage, but, as the event proved, quite ignorant of the military tactics of the Highlanders.

Leaving Fort Augustus at an early hour on the morning of August 16th, in order that his men might traverse the twenty-eight miles that lay between that place and Fort William before night came on, Captain Scott marched his detachment along the great military road that General Wade had completed some eight or nine years previously, and which has been described in a former chapter. After about twenty miles had been covered without incident, and just as the soldiers were approaching the bridge that crosses the river Spean, which at this spot rushes tumultuously through a narrow gorge of precipitous rocks, the wild notes of a pibroch were heard, and to the surprise and alarm of the captain a body of well-armed and powerful Highlanders was observed in possession of the bridge, while others were to be seen moving about among the rocks and trees on either side of the road they would have to pass. A halt was called, and Captain Scott held a brief consultation with his brother officers as to the best course to be adopted. Scott himself was strongly in favour of carrying the bridge by force; but this opinion was not shared by his colleagues, who pointed out the foolhardiness of engaging an enemy of whose strength they were entirely ignorant, and who were protected from attack by the cover the rocks and shrubs afforded. To lend force to these arguments the Highlanders commenced a series of energetic movements, leaping from crag to crag, and uttering unearthly cries, and as the English soldiers watched them with some trepidation, they could see the glint of steel weapons among the trees, and imagined that a considerable force was mustering to overwhelm them. Captain Scott was in a dilemma, and knew not whether to advance or retreat. The counsel his friends gave certainly appeared prudent, but it was repugnant to his feelings as an officer to flee from the face of the foe without firing a shot, and he decided to send out a couple of scouts to reconnoitre, and if possible learn the strength and position of the enemy. A sergeant and one man (the captain's own servant) were thereupon ordered to cross the bridge and gain, if possible, the desired information, but before they had proceeded far, a couple of Highlanders dashed out from behind some rocks and made them prisoners before their comrades had time to protect them.

Believing it useless to attempt a rescue, Captain Scott gave the word to retreat, and in a few moments the soldiers turned their backs to the invisible foe, and commenced their homeward march. Ridiculous as it may seem, the formidable enemy that had thus caused two companies of the Scots Royals to fly from before them consisted of ten or twelve Keppoch MacDonalds, commanded by a cousin of Keppoch, Donald MacDonald of Tirnadris, who, by a clever display of strategy, had led Captain Scott and his officers to believe that they were opposed by a numerous body of Highlanders. By placing the men at intervals among the trees and boulders that line the banks of the Spean, and by constantly changing their position so that they were continually on the move, Tirnadris created an illusory army, which, to the eyes of the English soldiers, assumed immense proportions, on the principle that " *Omne ignotum pro magnifico.*"

The result of this manoeuvre raised the spirits of the High-landers, and they could hardly be restrained from dashing from their ambuscade upon the retreating Sassenachs; but as such an action would have at once betrayed their strength, Tirnadris bade them wait until they were joined by the reinforcements that he anticipated would arrive from Keppoch and Lochiel, he having despatched messengers to both chieftains, upon first catching sight of the redcoats, with a request for assistance.

Allowing Captain Scott and his party to proceed about two miles, and feeling assured that his friends could not be far off, Tirnadris cautiously followed in pursuit, keeping his men as much out of sight as possible, and avoiding every means of attracting the attention of the fugitives. By the time the soldiers had reached the road that runs along the north-eastern end of Loch Lochy, near Laggan-ach-drum, where it is over-hung by a steep wooded acclivity, the Highlanders had caught. up with them, and having left the road, had gained the heights above, some distance in front of the line of march, and waited, muskets in hand, for the detachment to approach. Immediately Captain Scott and his men came within range of their weapons, the MacDonalds opened a destructive fire from behind the shelter of the rocks, which, besides doing considerable execution among the unfortunate soldiers, alarmed the whole country, and brought numbers of armed Highlanders to the scene of conflict.

The retreat now became a disordered rout, *sauve qui peut!* was the cry, and breaking into a run, the whole body of troops fled in the direction of Loch Oich, amid the fierce yells of the pursuing Highlanders and the discordant notes of the war pipes. Rapidly crossing the neck of land that divides Loch Lochy from Loch Oich, Captain Scott found himself confronted by another body of hardy mountaineers, who appeared determined to bar his progress. This fresh enemy proved to be a band of about fifty Glengarry MacDonalds, who had been hastily summoned to arms, and were now about to join hands with their kins-men of Keppoch. This further accession of strength to the ranks of his enemy did not deter Captain Scott from making a bold effort to proceed. Forming his men into square, he marched steadily on ; but at this juncture MacDonald of Kep-poch arrived on the scene with a further contingent of his clan, and taking in the position of affairs at a glance, he advanced alone in front of the now exhausted and dispirited soldiers, and called upon Captain Scott to surrender or take the consequences of his refusal, which could only mean the signal for a general massacre.

"Of two evil alternatives it is always best to choose the least," and Captain Scott, now convinced that any further resistance on his part would be useless, ordered his men to lay down their arms, which, in their present fatigued condition, they were not loth to do. While the terms of surrender were being discussed, Lochiel, who had received intelligence of the skirmish, arrived from Ach-na-carry with a large body of Camerons. The prisoners were placed in his charge, and shortly afterwards conveyed under an escort of Highlanders to his house on the shores of Loch Arkaig, where they were treated with the greatest kindness and humanity.

In this affair two soldiers were killed and five or six wounded, among the latter being Captain Scott, who, upon reaching Ach-na-carry, was permitted by Lochiel to send to Fort Augustus for a surgeon to dress his wounds. As, however, the governor of the fort would not allow the doctor to leave the garrison, Lochiel humanely gave the captain permission to proceed there on parole, in order that he might receive the attention he required.

CHAPTER XXII.

THE news of this victory over the Elector's soldiers soon reached Prince Charles in his retreat at Glenaladale, on Loch Shiel, whither he had removed after leaving Kinlochmoidart, and filled his mind with the most sanguine hopes of ultimate success, and he set out for the rendezvous at Glenfinnan, on the morning of August 19th, in the highest spirits, surrounded by a little band of devoted followers, whose paucity of numbers he anticipated would be largely augmented when he reached the spot fixed for the muster of the loyal clans.

It would have been impossible to have selected a more suitable place for the assembly than the sequestered vale of Glenfinnan. Shut off from the outer world by stupendous mountains that rise almost perpendicularly from the level of the blue surface of Loch Shiel, it forms a natural amphitheatre of soft green turf, intermixed with great masses of heather, which at that season of the year would be clothed in all the glory of purple raiment, and afford a carpet of nature's own weaving worthy of being trodden by the feet of the gallant young prince, whose name, from that August morning in 1745, will always be associated with the peaceful solitudes of this lovely glen.

It was about eleven o'clock when Prince Charles and his party disembarked from the boat that had brought them from Glenaladale, and, to his surprise and chagrin, he found on arrival at Glenfinnan that the vast concourse of armed Highlanders he had expected would have been there to receive him with their acclamations were conspicuous by their absence; and save for a few shepherds, who wished him "God speed" in Gaelic as he passed, not a human being was to be seen throughout the whole length and breadth of the glen. The disappointment of Prince Charles upon finding himself thus isolated was intense, and he suffered all the revulsion of feeling that his sanguine temperament rendered possible. Not all the reassuring utterances of his friends could cheer his despondency, and he retired into one of the small shielings to brood over his misfortunes, and endeavour to think of some excuse for the absence of those who had promised to support him.

Thus he waited two long, weary hours until about the hour of noon, when, borne upon the summer breeze, at first faint and scarcely audible, and then gradually swelling in volume as it approached nearer, came the welcome sound of the pipes, and those who were near informed the prince that the tune he could not recognise was the war pibroch of Clan Cameron "Sounding, sounding, deep over mountain and glen;" and as every eye scanned the distant hills, they were soon able to see the brave

Camerons descending the slope of a mountain in all the pride of military array, with pipes playing and banners flying, to the number of about eight hundred. This sight brought the colour to the cheeks of Prince Charles, and he at once resumed his wonted cheerfulness, as with proud and dignified mien he took up his position to receive his loyal Highlanders.

With the Camerons came a body of about three hundred MacDonalds of Keppoch, commanded by their celebrated chieftain,[1] bringing with them as proof of their valour the prisoners they had taken a few days previously in the skirmish at Loch Lochy ; and they also brought the horse recently ridden by Captain Scott, which they concluded would prove an acceptable present for their prince.

Advancing in two long lines, each of three men deep, with the disarmed prisoners in their midst, the Camerons and MacDonalds made a brave display as they approached the spot where Prince Charles stood, surrounded by the chiefs who had come with him from Glenaladale, and we may be sure that the sight of these kilted warriors, of whose gallant deeds he had so often heard, must have kindled his enthusiasm and filled his soul with delight.

There was another person present on this historical occasion whose future career has given rise to much speculation and controversy, and I must admit that after taking considerable trouble to sift the truth from the falsehood, and having consulted every available authority on the subject, I have to acknowledge that there still remains considerable doubt in my own mind as to the truth of the story I am going to relate ; but as almost every writer on the subject of the '45 has referred to it, and as it is intimately connected with Lochaber, I feel it is due to my readers that it should not be omitted in a work specially treating of that district.

[1] Most historians of the '45 erroneously state that Keppoch did not arrive until late in the evening, but I am informed by his descendant, Mrs MacDonell of Keppoch, that the above version is correct, and I have had the privilege of perusing documents in proof of the assertion that Keppoch arrived in Glenfinnan at the same time as the Camerons.

The story runs that among those summoned by Lochiel to assist the prince with men was Allan Cameron of Glendessary, at the head of Loch Arkaig, a cadet of the clan, but who at the time was a minor, and had little or no experience as a military leader, and when the news of the prince's arrival reached him, he was quite incapable of performing the duty of organising and arming his followers for the service required of them. This task was willingly undertaken by his aunt, Miss Jenny Cameron of Glendessary, a woman of considerable spirit and courage, and who was determined that whoever else might fail in their duty to the brave youth who had come so far to regain his royal father's throne, it should never be said that any Cameron was left behind when the clan was to the fore. Throwing herself vigorously into the work of raising the Glendessary Camerons, she was soon able to muster a very presentable force of two hundred and fifty well-armed Highlanders. On the morning of August 19th she mounted a bay gelding, gorgeously arrayed in trappings of green and gold, and placing herself at the head of her men, and holding a drawn sword in her hand, she started for the rendezvous at Glenfinnan. Dressed in a green riding-habit, with scarlet lappets and gold trimming, and with a velvet cap and scarlet feathers on her head, from beneath which her hair escaped in loose curls, she presented a very extraordinary spectacle; and upon arriving in the prince's camp all eyes were turned upon this remarkable woman, who, like a second Joan of Arc, had come to fight for her king, sword in hand.

The prince's attention being directed to this fair Amazon, he went out to meet her, and offer his thanks in person for this unexpected addition to his forces. Saluting Prince Charles without the least embarrassment, Miss Cameron informed him that the youth of her nephew having prevented him from being present, she had thought it her duty to raise the men and bring them to his royal highness, feeling assured that there was not one among them who would not be ready to hazard his life in his behalf; and that though they were now commanded by a woman, it would be found that they had nothing womanly about them, for so noble was the cause that had brought her there, that it had filled her breast with such manly thoughts and aspirations as to quite exclude the more tender feminine emotions usually attributed to her sex. "If that is so with me, what an effect then must it have on those who have no womanly fear to combat, and are free from the encumbrance of female dress? These men, sir, are yours; they have devoted themselves to your service; they bring you hearts as well as hands. I can follow them no farther, but I shall pray for your success."

These gallant words impressed the prince greatly, and after having inspected the men and complimenting them upon their appearance, he conducted their fair commander to his tent, and treated her with the courtesy that so well became him.

Some accounts state that she remained with the prince's army until it marched into England, and that she rejoined it at Annandale, and being present at the battle of Falkirk Muir, was taken prisoner and confined in the castle of Edinburgh.

That there was a lady of this name attached to the prince's army is certain, as we find a Miss Jeannie Cameron frequently mentioned in the papers of the period. It was only natural that the English writers of the years 1745 and 1746 should seize upon this incident as a means of reviling the character of the noble lad, whose only crime was that he had come to claim his father's rights, and thrust out the rapacious Hanoverian horde who defiled with their drunken revelry the palaces of his ancestors.

I find in "James Ray's Compleate History of the Rebellion," published in 1754, the following passage referring to the retreat of the Highland army from Stirling in February 1746:—
"From thence the Mock Prince fled with so much precipitation that he neglected to carry off his Female Colonel *Cameron*, who was taken and, some time after, sent to Edinburgh Castle;"

2 B

and in the *Scots Magazine* for November 1746 we read : " Miss Jeannie Cameron was admitted to bail on the 15th, the Duchess of Perth on the 17th, the Viscountess Strathallan on the 22nd November. They had lain in the castle of Edinburgh (whither Miss Jeannie Cameron was brought from Stirling) since the beginning of February."

It is therefore evident that a person styling herself Jeannie Cameron was with the prince's army, but there is absolutely nothing to prove that she and Miss Cameron of Glendessary were one and the same individual.

In Chambers's " History of the Rebellion of 1745," an extract is given from " The Lyon in Mourning," MS., with reference to this matter :—" It has been already stated, on the authority of Mr Æneas MacDonald, that Mrs Jean Cameron witnessed the setting up of the standard at Glenfinnan. The whole passage respecting her in Mr MacDonald's narrative is as follows :— ' Here a considerable number of both *gentlemen* and *ladies* met to see the ceremony ; among the rest the famous Miss Jeany Cameron, as she is commonly, but very improperly called, for she is a widow, nearer fifty than forty years of age. She is a genteel, well-looked, handsome woman, with a pair of pretty eyes, and hair as black as jet. She is of a very sprightly genius, and is very agreeable in conversation. She was so far from accompanying the prince's army, that she went off with the rest of the spectators as soon as the army had marched. Neither did she ever follow the camp, nor was ever with the prince but in public, when he had his Court in Edinburgh.' "

This account is probably the correct one, although Sir Ewen Cameron of Fassfern (nephew of Lochiel of the '45) is stated to have said that although the lady in question sent the prince a present of cattle on the occasion of the muster of the clans at Glenfinnan, she never saw him herself. These various state-ments are certainly very conflicting, and the identity of the lady taken prisoner at Stirling, and imprisoned in Edinburgh Castle, still remains a mystery for the curious to solve. The portrait shown here is from an old print in my possession, but whether authentic or not I have been unable to discover.[1]

CHAPTER XXIII.

UPON the arrival of Lochiel and Keppoch, with their respective clans, the prince at once proceeded to raise his standard, and declare war against the Elector of Hanover and his adherents, with all the ceremony that the time and place would allow.

> "Then raise the banner, raise it high,
> For Charles we'll conquer or we'll die :
> The clans a' leal and true men be,
> And shaw me wha will daunton thee !
> Our gude King James shall soon come hame,
> And traitors a' be put to shame ;
> Auld Scotland shall again be free :
> O that's the thing wad wanton me ! "

The honour of unfurling the banner was allotted to the Marquis of Tullibardine, who had accompanied Prince Charles in his voyage from France on board the "Doutelle." Selecting a slight eminence in the centre of the glen on which to stand, the marquis raised aloft the standard of his king ;[2] and as its silken folds of red, white, and blue slowly spread out upon the summer breeze that was wafted from the mountain tops, the

---

[1] An extraordinary work, purporting to be a faithful biography of Jeannie Cameron, was published in the year 1746, entitled "Memoirs of the Remarkable Life and surprising Adventures of Miss Jenny Cameron, A Lady who, by her Attachment to the Person and Cause of the Young Pretender, has render'd herself famous by her Exploits in his Service, and for whose Sake she underwent all the Severities of a Winter's Campaign," by the Rev. Archibald Arbuthnot, one of the Society for Propagating the Christian Knowledge, and Minister of Kiltarlity, in the Presbytery of Inverness. Although written by a minister of the gospel, the contents of this book are of so gross and obscene a nature that extracts would be impossible. From beginning to end it is a purely imaginary account of the amours and adventures of a loose woman, dubbed by the name of Jeannie Cameron by its author, for the purpose apparently of giving it an air of probability, as the arrest of a person of that name at Stirling would have been fresh in the mind of the public at the time of publication. The book is extremely curious and of great rarity.

[2] The MS. notes of John MacDonell, already referred to, give a somewhat different account of this event. *Vide* Appendix XXV.

whole assembled multitude sent up to heaven a deafening shout of welcome, that was echoed and re-echoed from hill to hill and resounded from glen to glen, startling the deer in the seclusion of the dense thickets of Drumsallie, where, cowering among the bracken, they lay trembling at this unwonted disturbance of their peaceful retreat. Loud and long were the acclamations of the Highlanders, as they now realised for the first time that the prince they had long hoped for was at last to take his place at their head and lead them on to victory. Every extravagant form of enthusiastic devotion was exhibited on this occasion. Bonnets were hurled into the air in clouds; claymores were unsheathed and held aloft by brawny arms, where they flashed and scintillated in the rays of the noontide sun; pipers, clad in all the glory of tartan bravery, and with the great drones of their pipes over their shoulders, strutted proudly over the heather, vying with each other in the execution of the pibrochs of their respective clans. The whole scene was one of bustle and animation, and full of vivid interest to Prince Charles. Then, if ever, he must have felt the blood of his great ancestor, Robert Bruce, stir in his veins and prompt him to action; then, if ever, he must have felt the pride of royal descent kindle within his breast, and fire him with a fervent desire to regain all the lost honours which were his by right of birth. Pretender, forsooth! by what fallacy of reasoning could such an opprobrious and lying epithet be bestowed upon the legitimate heir to the throne of Britain. Here was no vulgar impostor, no Lambert Simnel or Perkin Warbeck, over whose well-merited fate sympathy would be wasted; but a gallant, noble, and chivalrous prince, possessed of all the qualities that should have gained for him the love and devotion of his countrymen. Descended in the direct line from the Stuart kings, without a flaw in his pedigree or the slightest taint of illegitimacy in his blood, the great-grandson of the martyred Charles I. was to be dubbed *Pretender*, and by whom? Surely the servile and sycophantic parasites who battened in the corrupt atmosphere of the Court of St James, and basked in the oleaginous smiles of Teutonic *demi-mondaines*, picking up the crumbs that fell from the rich man's table, and wallowing in the noxious slough of Hanoverian debauchery; surely such as these had no right to cast the stone of bastardy at the inoffensive head of a prince, whose shoe latchet they were unworthy to unloose.

There was no bar-sinister in his escutcheon, no stain on his honour; like Theseus of old he went forth on his adventurous quest to slay the Minotaur, and rid the fair land of Britain of its voracious progeny. Let those who sneer at modern Jacobitism read and study the true history of the Georgian period as told by that master of satire, William Makepeace Thackeray, and they will no longer wonder that, notwithstanding the hundred and fifty-three years that have passed since that August afternoon when Bonnie Prince Charlie raised his royal father's standard in Glenfinnan, there are still some among us who fondly cherish the memory of the gallant lad, and treasure as sacred every relic, every song, and every place with which his name is associated.

All honour to that staunch Jacobite, the late Alexander MacDonald of Glenaladale, for erecting a lasting memorial of the historic event on the spot where it occurred, and thus preserving for future generations an imperishable testimony to "the generous zeal, the undaunted bravery, and the inviolable fidelity of his forefathers, and the rest of those who fought and bled in that arduous and unfortunate enterprise."[1]

At the conclusion of the ceremony, and after king James's manifesto had been duly read, the Marquis of Tullibardine, with a guard of fifty Camerons, escorted the standard to the prince's quarters in the glen. Later in the day a body of MacLeods arrived in the camp, and offered their apologies to Prince Charles for the absence of their chief, whom they could not persuade to come with them. Lochiel, upon hearing of MacLeod's reluctance to join the Highland army, wrote him a persuasive letter, but instead of producing the desired result, it only served to widen the breach, as the proud spirit of MacLeod

[1] Transcribed from the inscription on the monument. *Vide* Appendix XXVI.

resented the impeachment of his honour, and he refused to be coerced.

Notwithstanding the defection of MacLeod and his neighbour, Sir Alexander MacDonald of Sleat, Prince Charles found himself, on the evening of August 19th, at the head of an army of about twelve hundred devoted followers. From Glenfinnan he removed, a day or two later, to Kinlocheil, and on the 22nd August issued the celebrated proclamation offering a "reward of thirty thousand pounds sterling to him, or those, who shall seize and secure till our further orders the person of the Elector of Hanover."

From Kinlocheil the prince went to the house of Lochiel's brother, John Cameron of Fassfern, and slept there on the night of the 23rd; but he did not prolong his stay at Fassfern, as shortly after his arrival tidings reached him that a sloop of war had been observed cruising off Fort William, and that the garrison of that place was on the alert. The proximity of Fort William was a source of danger, and it was thought advisable by the prince's officers to remove the camp to Moy, a small clachan on the banks of the river Lochy, which I have described in a former chapter as having been the place fixed by Viscount Dundee for his camp during the civil war of 1689. The baggage and other impedimenta was given in charge of a force of two hundred Camerons, and leaving Fassfern on the morning of the 24th, they proceeded along the road that skirts the shores of Loch Eil, passing within sight of Fort William. The prince, however, for greater safety, took the road over the hills, and reached Moy on the 25th August.

The news of his arrival had now spread far and wide throughout Lochaber, and every day brought a fresh accession of strength to the resolute band of Highlanders who rallied round the royal standard. From dark Glencoe came MacDonald of that ilk, bringing with him one hundred and fifty men of his clan. Keppoch, not satisfied with the force he had led to Glenfinnan, had collected a further body of MacDonalds, and brought them to his prince; but an unfortunate dispute having arisen between him and his clan on a question of religion, a large number of his men refused to come out. The Keppoch MacDonalds were Catholics, and wished a priest to accompany them on the march, but this their chief, who was a Protestant, would not allow. The refusal produced considerable friction and ill-feeling among the members of the clan, and many absented themselves from the muster on this account.

Leaving Moy on the 26th August, Prince Charles crossed the river Lochy, and upon arriving at Low Bridge his army was further augmented by the welcome addition of two hundred and sixty Stewarts of Appin, commanded by Ardshiel. The march was then continued along the shores of Loch Lochy to Letterfinlay, where it was decided to bivouac for the night, but before the men were settled down, news reached the prince that caused him to alter his plans. A messenger had come into the camp with tidings that General Sir John Cope, with a large body of troops, had appeared in Badenoch, and intended to cross the great hill of Corrieyairack by Wade's military road, and attack the Highland army on the following morning. Upon receipt of this piece of intelligence, Prince Charles struck his camp at Letterfinlay, and in the darkness of night, and amid a hurricane of wind and rain, proceeded to Invergarry Castle, the stronghold of MacDonald of Glengarry, on the shores of Loch Oich, where he stayed the night.

Before setting out for Invergarry, a strong party of Highlanders had been ordered to make a forced march to Corrieyairack and secure the pass before Cope and his Sassenach redcoats could reach it. Before daybreak on the morning of the 27th, Prince Charles left Invergarry at the head of his brave mountaineers, rejoicing in the hope of a speedy encounter with the English general. At Aberchalder he was joined by a large body of Glengarry MacDonalds, about six hundred strong, under the leadership of Lochgarry, and by a numerous party of Grants from Glenmoriston. This further increase of strength raised the spirits of the whole army, which now numbered about two thousand, and so exultant was Prince

Charles, and so confident of success, that he observed while putting on a new pair of Highland brogues, "that he would be up with Mr Cope before they were unloosed."

Upon arrival at the foot of the mountain, Lochgarry and Murray (the prince's secretary) were ordered to ascend the northern side, and report the position and strength of the enemy, but on reaching the summit they could see no sign of Cope or his army. This astonishing information was soon conveyed to the prince, and no explanation was forthcoming, until, shortly afterwards, a Cameron who had been pressed into Cope's service arrived in the camp with the news that the dauntless general had considered "discretion the better part of valour," and was now fleeing, as fast as his legs would carry him, along the main road to Inverness, leaving the road to the south open to the prince's army.

Shouts of derision greeted this intelligence. That an English general, with a well-armed force at his back, should fly from their approach without so much as firing a shot, seemed to the brave Highlanders almost incredible, and contrary to all their preconceived notions of honourable warfare. The fact is, as Home says, "Cope was one of those men who are fitter for anything than the chief command in war, especially when opposed, as he was, to a new and uncommon enemy," and, as the prince was afterwards to discover on the memorable field of Prestonpans, he was quite incapable of withstanding the impetuous military tactics adopted by the tartan-clad Highlanders, the mere sight of whose peculiar costume and weapons terrified him into an ignominious retreat.

> " But when he saw the Highland lads
> Wi' tartan trews and white cockades,
> Wi' swords and guns, and rungs and gauds,
> O Johnnie he took wing in the morning; "

and, as another version of the same old song runs,

> " ' I' faith,' quo' Johnnie, ' I got sic a fleg
> Wi' their claymores and philabegs;
> If I face them again, deil break my legs!
> So I wish you a very gude morning.' "

Elated at the joyful tidings of the flight of the English troops, Prince Charles called for a glass of brandy, and drank " To the health of good Mr Cope, and may every general in the usurper's service prove himself as much our friend as he has done ; " a sentiment which was heartily endorsed by every one present. Bumpers of usquebaugh were served out to the men by the express wishes of the prince, and merriment became the order of the day.

Two courses were now open to Prince Charles. The one was to follow the fugitive army and hazard an engagement with Cope before he could reach Inverness, and the other was to march with all speed into the lowlands while the road was clear of Government troops. The first idea was the one that commended itself to the exultant Highlanders and their courageous leader, but the advantages of an un-opposed descent upon the lowlands so far outweighed the more hazardous scheme of pursuit, that it was unanimously agreed by the assembled chiefs that Cope should be left free to march to John o' Groats if he pleased, while they took the opportunity he had so kindly afforded them of making a diversion in a contrary direction.

This council of war was held at Garvamore, a few miles from the foot of Corrieyairack, and as soon as the prince had signified his approval of the decision of his officers, he despatched Dr Cameron (the brother of Lochiel), Lochgarry, and O'Sullivan to surprise, and, if possible, destroy the fort at Ruthven in Badenoch. The garrison offered a stubborn resistance, and as neither side was possessed of artillery, the storming party had to retire without having effected an entrance, and with the loss of one man. From Ruthven they proceeded to Cluny Castle, the seat of Cluny MacPherson, the chief of the powerful clan of that name. For politic reasons, Cluny had recently accepted the command of an independent company in the service of the Government, but his sympathies were with the Stuarts, and he only waited a favourable opportunity to attach himself to the side of his youthful prince. This opportunity was now within his

2 C

reach, but, with shrewd good sense, he did not seize it too readily.
Feigning reluctance to accompany Dr Cameron to the prince's
presence, he allowed himself to be conveyed to the Highland
camp as a prisoner on parole, and, as we know, he shortly afterwards avowed his allegiance to king James VIII., and raised
the whole of his clan for the service of his royal master.

The prince was at Dalwhinnie when Cluny was brought
in, and being assured of the fidelity of this famous chieftain,
he determined to lose no time in pressing on to Edinburgh.
To follow the adventurous march of the Highland army in
their journey southwards is no part of my intention. I have
already strayed beyond the confines of Lochaber and must
now return thither, leaving to my readers the pleasant task of
referring to one or other of the many histories of the '45 for
further information as to the progress of Bonnie Prince Charlie
in his bold attempt to wrest the throne of his forefathers
from the brow of the usurper.

CHAPTER XXIV.

LOCHABER was deserted, from clachan and shieling, from strath
and glen, her brave sons had gone forth to fight under the
standard of their prince, and do battle in the cause for which their
ancestors had wielded the claymore in the days of old Sir Ewen.
Right gallantly had the men of Lochaber responded to the call of
duty. Foremost in the van were the chiefs of Clan Cameron and
MacDonald. Young Lochiel, with his uncle, Cameron of Torcastle, and his brother, Dr Archibald Cameron, worthily supported
the honour of their name; and side by side were their neighbours
and kinsmen MacDonald of Keppoch,[1] and his relatives Tirnadris,
Clanranald, Lochgarry, and Æneas MacDonell of Glengarry.

Cameron of Fassfern, wise in his generation, had refused
to come out, but while taking no active part in the campaign,

---

[1] Keppoch's younger brother Donald and his son Angus were also with the
prince's army.

he looked after his brother's estates and kept him supplied with money. Angus Mackintosh, who had succeeded his brother William in 1741 as chief of the clan, professed loyalty to the Elector of Hanover, and had been appointed to a command in the newly raised regiment of Lord Loudoun's Highlanders; his wife, however, who was a daughter of Farquharson of Invercauld, was strongly attached to the House of Stuart, and scorned allegiance to the usurper. Being a woman of considerable spirit, and of somewhat masculine disposition, she so far overcame the scruples of her husband, that he placed no obstacle in her way when she proceeded to raise the clan for the prince's service. Her military ardour and energetic action were so far successful, that she not only brought out her husband's clan, but added to it over three hundred Farquharsons, and placed the whole under the command of MacGillivray of Dunmaglass. Her zeal in the cause gained for her the title of "Colonel Anne," an appellation by which she will always be remembered in Lochaber.

Prince Charles had thus attracted to his side the whole of the important clans of Lochaber. Camerons, MacDonalds, Mackintoshes, and MacPhersons[1] had all flocked to his standard, leaving their flocks and herds to the charge of their women folk, who, with tearful eyes and saddened hearts, tended the sheep on the mountain sides, anxiously awaiting tidings of their dear ones in the unknown south. News came at last of valorous deeds, in which their Donalds and Duncans had rendered a good account of themselves, and worthily upheld the old traditions of their ancestors. Perth and Dundee had been captured for king James, and later in the month of September all Lochaber rang with the joyful intelligence that Dunedin, the impregnable, had succumbed to the victorious arms of the Highlanders, and that Bonnie Prince Charles held his father's Court in the old palace of

---

[1] The MacPhersons, although, strictly speaking, not a Lochaber clan, are so intimately connected with that district, that they may fairly be mentioned in that category.

Holyrood, surrounded by a brilliant crowd of loyal chieftains and noble ladies, eager to do him homage and swear fealty to James VIII. Then messengers arrived bringing tidings of the glorious victory of the Highland army at Prestonpans, and the almost ludicrous retreat of Johnnie Cope. There, as at Killiecrankie and Sheriffmuir, the Lochaber men, by their desperate valour and fearless courage, proved that they were more than a match for the disciplined troops of the Elector, who flew from before the vigorous strokes of their broadswords and axes like chaff before the wind.

> " The brave Lochiel, as I heard tell,
> Led Camerons on in clouds, man ;
> The morning fair, and clear the air,
> They loosed with devilish thuds, man ;
> Down guns they threw, and swords they drew,
> And soon did chase them off, man ;
> On Seaton's crafts they buff'd their chafts,
> And gart them rin like daft, man."

The fight had been brief but bloody ; out of a force of two thousand five hundred men whom Cope had led into action, only two thousand escaped death or wounds. Among the slain was the gallant Colonel Gardiner, whose conspicuous bravery on this occasion offered a striking contrast to the poltroonery of his commanding officer. While making a last desperate effort to rally his panic-stricken men, he received a terrible blow from a Lochaber axe wielded by one of the Clan Cameron,[1] from the effects of which he shortly afterwards died.

Although victorious, the Highland army suffered considerable loss, thirty-four of their number being killed and seventy-six wounded. The Lochaber men had, as usual, borne the full brunt of the fighting, and the proportion of their slain was in consequence very heavy. Three out of the four officers who had met their death at Prestonpans were from Lochaber. They were Captain Alan Cameron of Lundavra, Captain Archibald MacDonald, of Keppoch's, and Ensign James Cameron, of

---

[1] The slayer of Colonel Gardiner was Samuel Cameron, a native of Kilmallie, in Lochaber. His grandson was in 1835 an elder of Kilmallie church, and always said that his grandfather killed the colonel in self-defence.

Lochiel's; the other unfortunate gentleman being a near neighbour, Captain Robert Stewart, of Ardshiel's clan.

Thus, amid the pibrochs of victory that resounded through the
glens of Lochaber, was heard the wild and mournful wailings of the
coronach, as some poor stricken Highlander was committed to
the earth among his native hills, which he had left only a few
short months before in all the pride and strength of manhood.

Week followed week, and news of the prince's movements
reached Lochaber only at long intervals. It was known that
Carlisle had fallen, and that at the head of his bold Highlanders
he was marching rapidly on London; but the distance was too
remote for accurate details, and those who were left behind
could only wait patiently for information of their kinsmen who
had given up all to follow Prince Charlie. Sometime during
December the incredible intelligence arrived that the Highland
army, having proceeded as far south as Derby without a check,
was now retreating before the English troops under the Duke
of Cumberland; and as time wore on the news was confirmed
by stragglers who, believing all hopes of the prince's success
gone for ever, returned to their homes among the mountains
while there was yet time to escape the vengeance they knew
would be meted out to all who had supported the Stuart cause.
Fort William was at this time under the command of General
Campbell, and as he anticipated that an attack would be made
upon the garrison by the Highland forces, he took active steps
to strengthen his position and provide for emergencies. Three
hundred Argyllshire men, with a good engineer, were drafted
into the fort, and two sloops of war, "The Serpent" and "The
Baltimore," were ordered to cruise in the waters of Loch Linnhe
and Loch Eil. Fifty men of Guise's regiment, who had been
gathered together at Edinburgh under the command of the
captain-lieutenant, and some other troops, were also sent thither,
and, as we shall see, these precautions came to be of use.
Retreating rapidly by the way they had come, the prince's
army, after a skirmish with the Duke of Cumberland's troops
at Clifton, in which Cluny and his MacPhersons distinguished

themselves by their gallant behaviour, passed through Carlisle, and thence into Scotland *via* Annan and Ecclefechan.

On the day following Christmas day 1745, Prince Charles arrived in Glasgow, and immediately set about the task of providing clothing and stores for his troops at the expense of the worthy citizens of that flourishing town, and, in addition, demanded payment of a levy of £10,000, which the magistrates had to supply under military compulsion. From Glasgow the prince retired to Bannockburn, and shortly afterwards, on 17th January 1746, he engaged the English army under General Hawley at Falkirk Muir, and gained a complete victory over that officer, who shared the fate of his colleague Sir John Cope, of Prestonpans fame. Owing to the confusion into which the conflicting forces were thrown, it was at first impossible to ascertain which side had the advantage, and a storm of wind and rain that prevailed at the time added to the difficulty; but when it was seen that large bodies of English cavalry were fleeing in wild disorder towards the town of Falkirk, there was no longer any doubt as to the side on which victory rested. An old Jacobite song of the period thus describes Hawley's discomfiture :—

> " Gae dight your face, and turn the chase,
> For fierce the wind does blaw, Hawley,
> And Highland Geordie's at your tail,
> Wi' Drummond, Perth, and a', Hawley.
> Had ye but staid wi' lady's maid
> An hour, or may be twa, Hawley,
> Your bacon bouk, and bastard snout,
> You might have saved them a', Hawley.
>> Up and rin awa', Hawley,
>> Up and scour awa', Hawley;
>> The Highland dirk is at your doup,
>> And that's the Highland law, Hawley.

> " Says brave Lochiel, ' Pray, have we won ?
> I see no troops, I hear no gun :'
> Says Drummond, ' Faith, the battle's done :
> I know not how or why, man;
> But my good lads, this thing I crave,
> Have we defeat these heroes brave ?'
> Says Murray, ' I believe we have,
> If not, we're here to try, man,' "

The allusion in the first verse of this song to the "lady's maid" is in reference to the fact that on the morning of the battle Hawley had accepted the invitation of the Countess of Kilmarnock to breakfast with her at Callander House; an artful ruse on the part of the loyal Jacobite lady which was entirely successful, as Hawley was so infatuated by her beauty and fascinating manner, that he spent the whole of the forenoon in her society.

The losses of the English were very heavy, over two hundred and eighty being officially returned as killed, wounded, or missing, a large proportion of officers being among the slain. Prince Charles lost thirty-two men, and one hundred and twenty wounded. MacDonald of Tirnadris, the cousin of Keppoch, who, it will be remembered, had been the first Highlander to open the campaign in Lochaber, when he attacked and defeated the two companies of Scots Royals at Loch Lochy, fell into the hands of General Hawley by a curious accident. In the dusk of the evening he had perceived a body of men standing under arms, apparently indifferent to the flight of the English troops. Their apathy did not at all commend itself to the excited Tirnadris, and he ran towards them shouting at the top of his voice, "Gentlemen, why do you stand here? Why don't you pursue the dogs?" He soon realised the fatal error he had made; the soldiers he had taken to be a portion of Lord Drummond's regiment proved to be the right flank of Hawley's army, who had kept the field. Immediately upon observing Tirnadris, they raised a cry of "Here is a rebel! here is a rebel!" and in a few moments the unhappy MacDonald was a prisoner. He was afterwards taken to Edinburgh, and eventually executed at Carlisle. Lochiel and his brother, Dr Archibald Cameron, were both slightly wounded in this action, but their wounds did not deter them from following the prince in his march northwards.

After the battle the Highland army occupied Falkirk, and here a most unfortunate accident happened, which resulted in the desertion of a considerable number of the prince's followers. One of the MacDonalds of Clanranald, having appropriated a musket from the battlefield, was amusing himself in his quarters by removing the charge with which it was loaded. Having extracted the bullet, he placed the weapon to his shoulder, and fired from the window into the street. As ill-luck would have it, the piece had been loaded with a double charge, and the remaining ball struck Æneas MacDonell of Glengarry;[1] who was standing in the street with some brother officers discussing the events of the late engagement. Pierced to the heart, he fell into the arms of his friends, and died in a few minutes, requesting with his last breath that the unhappy man who had unwittingly caused his death should not be punished.

So exasperated were the clansmen of Glengarry at the sad fate of their leader, that, notwithstanding his last commands, they proceeded to take summary vengeance against the unlucky man whose carelessness had produced such a dire result. He was conducted by the enraged MacDonalds to a wall outside the town and shot. Having lost their leader, the Glengarry men ceased to take interest in the prince's cause, and the majority of them returned to their homes, where they spread abroad the alarming intelligence of the failure of the Highland army to reach London, and the probable approach of a powerful force under the Elector's son, the Duke of Cumberland.

Meanwhile Prince Charles, after wasting three weeks in an attempt to reduce the fortress of Stirling, reluctantly consented to adopt the advice tendered by the chiefs and officers of his army, and retreat northwards upon Inverness, and not hazard another engagement with the English troops until the spring months, when it was hoped an army of at least ten thousand effective Highlanders could be brought together for his service. Proceeding through Doune, Dunblane, and Crieff, Prince Charles and his dispirited followers marched rapidly in the direction of the northern capital. On 4th February he reached

[1] Second son of John MacDonell, XII. of Glengarry.

Blair in Athole, and from there went to Ruthven in Badenoch, where he destroyed the fort and made prisoners of the garrison.

By the 16th he had arrived at Moy Castle,[1] the ancestral home of the chiefs of the Clan Mackintosh, and the abode of his fair adherent, Lady Anne Mackintosh, who was delighted at the honour of having the prince under her hospitable roof. In these comfortable quarters, which must have seemed doubly pleasant after the hardships and disappointments he had encountered on his arduous march, Prince Charles decided to remain until he could muster a sufficient force to enable him to attack the Earl of Loudoun, who was then at Inverness at the head of an army of two thousand men. Lady Mackintosh, fearing that Lord Loudoun would hear of the prince's arrival at Moy, endeavoured by every means in her power to keep his visit a secret, but all her exertions were futile, and the news leaked out. Someone played the unenviable part of traitor, and the tidings of the prince's proximity to Inverness was whispered into the ears of Lord Loudoun, who immediately conceived a plan to surround Moy and arrest him. Fortunately for the prince's safety, the Dowager Lady Mackintosh, who resided in Inverness, got wind of Loudoun's scheme, and at once took steps to communicate the intelligence to her daughter-in-law; but as Loudoun had given strict orders that no one should be allowed to leave Inverness on the night in question without a pass, she found some difficulty in carrying out her intentions. However, by the aid of a daring lad named Lachlan Mackintosh, she succeeded in informing the prince of the danger that threatened him. Young Lachlan, finding he could not pass the sentries without risk of arrest,

---

[1] The night before the prince's arrival at Moy Hall he had stayed at Keppoch, and while there the wife of the chief gave birth to a daughter, who was named Charlotte, in honour of the royal guest. It was during this visit that Mrs MacDonell presented the prince with a tartan plaid that she had spun and dyed with her own hands. This plaid was left at Moy, and for many years afterwards was laid over the bed in which the prince had slept. This interesting relic was given by Sir Æneas Mackintosh to Miss Jane Abernethy in 1817, and is now in the possession of Miss Boyle, by whom it was lent to the Stuart Exhibition. Portions of the plaid are also held by the Farquharsons of Invercauld.

2 D

hid himself in a ditch until the soldiers who were on their way
to capture the prince had passed. He then ran off at the top
of his speed by a road across the hills, and reached Moy in a
fainting and breathless condition about five o'clock on the morning of 17th February. Scarcely able to speak, he panted out
the alarming news to the Highland guard who kept watch over
the sleeping prince, that Loudoun's men were close at hand.

In a few moments the prince was unceremoniously awakened
from his slumbers, and realising the importance of haste, he
instantly dressed and joined his men in the courtyard below.
Lady Mackintosh, who had also been aroused by her maids,
did not allow herself time to don her ordinary attire, but hastily
descended the stairs *en déshabillé*, to take her place by the
prince's side and direct his course to a place of security. Had
she known what had meanwhile happened to the expeditionary
force, she would have laughed outright, and, instead of distress-
ing herself with anxious fears for her hero's safety, would have
drained a bumper to the gallant fellows who had, by a ludicrous
and clever ruse, thrown the enemy into confusion, and rendered
Loudoun's carefully matured plan of no avail. Although this
incident, known as the " rout of Moy," can hardly be considered
as relating to Lochaber, it is of interest as showing the inherent
shrewdness of character possessed by the Highlanders, who
were thereby often enabled to gain material advantage over
their English opponents, even when outnumbered, as on this
occasion, to the extent of over two hundred to one.

The Dowager Lady Mackintosh, having despatched the
messenger to Moy, took the double precaution of mustering a
small party of five staunch Highlanders headed by a blacksmith
named Fraser, known as the "smith of Moy." Having explained
the object she had in view, Lady Mackintosh sent them forth
on their errand, with instructions to proceed along the road from
Inverness and lie in wait for the Government troops, who,
they were informed, numbered about fifteen hundred men.
At first blush the enterprise in which they had embarked
seemed a mad one ; but so confident were they in that native

wit with which Dame Nature had endowed her hardy sons
of the North, that the desperate nature of the undertaking
rendered it all the more attractive to their resolute hearts.
Upon arriving at a spot where they could await, under the
cover of the bushes, the approach of Loudoun's men, Fraser,
with all the skill of a general, placed his men at intervals
along the roadside among the trees, and had hardly finished
this operation when the sound of the advancing soldiers
reached his ears. As soon as they came within gunshot, he
raised his musket and shot the chief of MacLeod's piper,[1] who
was in front, through the heart. At the same time the
others opened fire from behind the bushes and shrubs upon
the startled troops, who, finding themselves shot at from all
sides, imagined they had a large force to deal with. To add
to this impression, the clever blacksmith shouted out the war-
cries of the Camerons and MacDonalds, and called loudly
upon those clans to advance. This artful manœuvre produced
the desired effect, and in a few moments the terror-stricken
soldiers, thinking they had the whole of the prince's army
lying in ambush for them, took to their heels and fled to
Inverness in the wildest confusion. The occurrence afforded
considerable amusement to Prince Charles, when the news of the
blacksmith's exploit reached him in the security of his retreat
by Loch Moy; and being assured that all immediate danger was
over, he returned to the house of his hospitable hostess.

On the 18th February the prince entered Inverness without
any resistance being offered by the citizens; the regiment
commanded by Lord Loudoun having retired into Ross-shire.
Early in March a strong force of Irish, under Brigadier
Stapleton, was despatched from Inverness by Prince Charles
to besiege Fort Augustus, which was garrisoned by three

[1] This was Donald Bàn MacCrimmon, one of the most celebrated of the hereditary
pipers of the MacLeods of Dunvegan, who composed the celebrated pibroch, "*Cha
till mi tuille,*" on the occasion of his leaving Skye with his chief to join Lord Loudoun's
force. His sympathies were said to have been with Prince Charles, and his presentiment that he would never return was expressed in the lament, now so well known
through Sir Walter Scott's verses.

companies of Guise's regiment. Owing to a heavy fall of snow, Stapleton could not bring up his artillery in time for the attack, but nevertheless succeeded in driving the defenders from the barracks into the fort. On the 5th of March the powder-magazine blew up and forced the garrison to surrender.

General Campbell, who commanded at Fort William, having received intelligence of the fall of Fort Augustus, became alarmed for his own safety, and instructed one of his officers to despatch a letter to the Duke of Cumberland, informing him of the desperate strait they were in. Accordingly the following letter was penned and sent off by special messenger to the duke, who was then at Aberdeen :—"We have advice here, that a party of the rebels amounting to one thousand men is at Glennevis, within two miles of us, and that their train of artillery is to be to-morrow at Highbridge, which is six miles from the Fort. We have heard of the taking of Fort Augustus, and expect to be attacked ; but General Campbell is determined to defend the place to the utmost of his power. For some days past there have been some small parties of rebels posted on each side of the narrows of Carron (Corran), in which on Sunday last they took one of the boats belonging to the 'Baltimore' sloop, as she was coming from Scallestall (probably Inverscaddle) Bay, and sent the crew prisoners to their headquarters. . . . In consequence thereof, Captain Askew of the 'Serpent' sloop sent his boat with twenty-seven men in it, another boat of the 'Baltimore's' with twenty-four men, and a boat belonging to Fort William with twenty men, down to the narrows, where they all arrived by daylight. Captain Askew's men were landed first, and were immediately attacked by a party of eighty rebels who fired upon them, but without doing any damage, and upon the rest of the men belonging to the boats coming up the rebels fled. Our people pursued them, burnt the ferry-houses on both sides of the water, and a little town (? Onich) with about twelve houses in it, a quarter of a mile distant from the ferry-house, and destroyed or brought off all the boats. Two of the rebels were killed in this affair and several wounded."

General Campbell's next step, after sending off this despatch to the commander-in-chief, was to barbarously destroy the adjacent village of Maryburgh by fire, a wanton act of cruelty, which called forth the wrath of the "gentle" Lochiel, and caused him to pen, in conjunction with Keppoch, a remarkable and characteristic letter, dated 20th March 1746, from Glen Nevis House, where he was then staying, he having been ordered by Prince Charles to take command of the detachment that had been sent from Inverness to lay siege to Fort William, and which was to act in conjunction with the force of Irish under Brigadier Stapleton, who, having reduced Fort Augustus, had marched *via* High Bridge, and were now engaged in prosecuting the siege of Fort William. The letter referred to above will be found in the Appendix,[1] and should be read by all who wish to learn something of the chivalrous and noble nature of the much maligned Highlander of the '45. This humane epistle will be found to afford a striking contrast to the cruel orders of "the butcher" Cumberland and the brutal Hawley.

CHAPTER XXV.

BEFORE proceeding to describe the siege of Fort William, I will ask my readers' permission to make a slight digression, in order to give some account of the lovely spot that Lochiel had selected for his headquarters.

Glen Nevis may fairly lay claim to share with its rivals Glencoe, Glenorchy, and Glenogle the honour of being one of the most magnificent in Scotland. Throughout its whole length of about seven miles, every variety of Highland scenery may be observed; at each turn of the road new scenes of surpassing beauty unfold themselves before the gaze of the

[1] Appendix XXVII.

pedestrian who is fortunate enough to have penetrated into
this unfrequented wonderland. The mighty Ben Nevis,
monarch of British mountains, dominates the landscape with
regal splendour, its stupendous bulk occupying almost the
entire length of the glen on the north-east side, and forming
an immense natural barrier to the bitter winds that blow from
that quarter, and affording shelter to the numerous flocks of
sheep that from time immemorial have grazed on the grassy
lower slopes that form its base. The entrance to the glen is
unsurpassed for sylvan beauty; great spruce firs and sycamores
spread their boughs above the road, and form a glorious canopy
of green, through which the hottest rays of a June sun can
hardly penetrate. The music of murmuring water falls upon
the ear with gentle cadence, and we catch a glimpse of the
crystal Nevis rushing over its bed of pebbles, that glisten white
and sparkling as a stray sunbeam, piercing through the interlaced branches of the rowan trees, falls upon the water and
reveals the mysteries of its translucent depths, where the
speckled trout, hardly distinguishable from the stones, may
be seen by the keen observer lazily basking in the warm
sunshine. Here, "when Phœbus 'gins to rise," we may hear
"the mavis singing his love song to the morn," or we may
watch the amusing antics of the little brown squirrels, leaping
from bough to bough as if unconscious of our presence, but
all the while regarding us with their bright eyes, as we
shall discover if we make the slightest movement in their
direction, when, with a whisk of their bushy tails, they will
vanish among the trees overhead. As we penetrate farther
down the glen the character of the landscape changes, the
avenue of trees comes to an end, and we emerge into a more
open stretch of country, with the heather-covered slopes of the
Cow Hill on our right, and the great green eminence of Meall-
an-t-Suidhe towering 2300 feet above us on the left.

At this part of the glen is the remarkable moss-covered
boulder known as the "*Clach Shomhairle*," or "stone of
Somerled." Local tradition states that in the days of old a

chieftain of the "*Sliochd Shomhairle Ruaidh*" ("the children of Somerled the Red"), the patronymic of the Camerons of Glen Nevis, gained a victory over a rival clan on this spot, and placed the stone there as an imperishable memorial of the event. Another reading makes the name to be "*Clach Chomhairle*" ("the stone of advice or counsel"), and this has some countenance in two stories still current. On one occasion a party of enemies, stated variously to be Camerons of Lochiel (who were often at feud with their kinsmen of Glen Nevis), MacDonalds, or Campbells, were on their way to make an attack on Glen Nevis, and stopped a little to the west of the stone to consider the plan of attack. For some reason or other (one story being that it was due to the second-sight of their seanachie) a precipitate flight was determined upon, and next morning the Camerons of the glen, on coming out, found the traces and most of the belongings of the invaders, but no sign of the foes themselves. Yet another story has it that, with the ostensible purpose of cementing a truce, some members of either the Lochiel or Glengarry families were invited to dine with the Glen Nevis men, and were to come without a following, as the errand was of so peaceful a nature. This stipulation sufficed to arouse the suspicions of the guests, and before proceeding to the house of MacSorlie, they stopped at the big stone to review matters, and came to the wise decision that it would be better to return the way they had come than accept the questionable hospitality of the chief of Glen Nevis. Whether this resolution was due to the influence of the magic stone or to the wisdom of their leaders, it is impossible to say; but certain it is that had they entered the door of MacSorlie they would never have returned alive, for it was afterwards discovered that their murder had been cunningly planned, and the invitation was merely a lure to destruction.

The auld wives say that on a certain night of the year (the exact date they keep to themselves, for obvious reasons) the boulder turns round three times, and that any one fortunate enough to find it on the move will get answers to any three questions he may put before it finally settles to rest again. I am sorry I am unable to vouch for the truth of this legend from personal experience. Many a time and oft, by day and by night, have I passed this venerable relic, and have even had the reckless audacity to knock out my pipe ashes on its moss-covered surface; but it has never honoured me with so much as a tremor, and I have come to the conclusion that it reserves its gymnastic exhibition only for the Highland lasses who may wish to have proof of its oracular powers, and will not be stirred into action by mere male creatures like myself. There is a tradition that the *Clach Shomhairle* marks the last place of sepulture of Somerled himself, while another says that it was his putting-stone.

After passing the boulder, the glen opens out considerably, and the ground becomes of a swampy nature, and is covered with a rank growth of bog-myrtle (*Roid*), which, when trodden under foot, exhales a strong aromatic perfume. This plant, which is common throughout the Highlands, was the chosen badge of Clan Campbell, and in the days of the old feuds was regarded with detestation by those clans who had been subjected to the tyrannies of *Mac Cailean Mòr*. Among the great clumps of heather, rushes, and myrtle, the curious cotton-like tufts of the *canach* grass attract attention as they flutter in the breeze. The ancient bards frequently introduced the *canach* into their poems as a metaphor when describing the charms of their heroines. Ossian, in his beautiful poem of " Cath-Loda," makes use of the simile—

"If on the heath she moved, her breast was whiter than the down of
    Cana ; . . .
  Her eyes were two stars of light ; her face was heaven's bow in showers ;
    her dark hair flowed round it like streaming clouds,—
  Thou wert the dweller of souls, white-handed Strina-dona !"

Following the road a short distance farther, we come to the cultivated land belonging to the farm of Glen Nevis, and may observe the house itself nestling among the trees immediately in front. A few paces from the path on our right is a noticeable tree-covered eminence, rising abruptly from the level ground at the foot of the Cow Hill. This grassy mound is called in descriptive Gaelic phraseology *Tom-eas-an-t-slinnein* ("knoll of the waterfall of the shoulder"), and possesses a pathetic interest as being the last resting-place of the now (I believe) extinct branch of Clan Cameron, the Camerons of Glen Nevis.

To sit here, as I have often done, on a calm summer afternoon, when all nature seems hushed in slumberous repose, and nought disturbs the ear but the faint rustling of the leaves and the distant murmur of the rippling Nevis, is to experience something of that "peace which passeth all understanding"; the noisy, bustling, crowded world, where vice is rampant and virtue can scarce raise its head, is shut out from us by the everlasting hills. Here, indeed, is rest, a haven of sweet repose, where we may commune with Nature amid her most glorious handiwork, and with the peaceful dead sleeping beneath our feet. A few lines composed on the spot may not be out of place here, and may perhaps assist the reader to imagine the scene I have tried to depict.

TOM-EAS-AN-T-SLINNEIN.
GLEN NEVIS.

Upon a fir-crown'd knoll, sun kissed at morn,
  And where at eve the length'ning shadows creep,
God's Acre lies, of weary souls the bourne,
  Who, tired of life's brief fever, calmly sleep.

No sound disturbs their peaceful slumbers deep,
  Save when an eagle from its rocky height
Sweeps screaming down upon the tremb'ling sheep,
  Making the glen resound with their affright.

The foxgloves nod upon their slender stems,
  The pine trees whisper in the noontide breeze;
From flower to flower, like ever-flashing gems,
  All honey-laden, flit the humming bees.

A vanished race lie here, an ancient clan,
  Sprung from the loins of Somerled the Red;
Who in Glen Nevis, so the legend ran,
  Ruled long and wisely, of his foes the dread.

2 E

Cradled among the hills that saw their birth,
  Where giant Ben Nevis lifts his cloud-crown'd head;
They rest in peace beneath the kindly earth,
  While o'er their graves the verdant branches spread.

Forgotten of the world, unwept, uncared,
  The gallant soldier, the fair Highland maid,
The tender infant death might well have spared,
  Lie here together, 'neath the larches' shade.

Strew scented wild flowers o'er the silent dead,
  As soft your footsteps tread the hallow'd sod;
Far from our ken th' immortal spirit's fled,
  Their day on earth is done, they rest with God.

The history of the "vanished race" is shrouded in fable and doubt, and the various writers who have touched upon the subject do not all agree as to the origin of the *Sliochd Shomhairle Ruaidh*. Skene, whose researches in the interesting field of Celtic history have done so much to throw a light upon the genealogy of the Highland clans, gives in his valuable work on the Highlanders a succinct account of the various branches of Clan Cameron, among which he mentions the Camerons of Glen Nevis. "Originally," he writes, "the Clan Cameron consisted of three septs—the Clan ic Mhartin, or MacMartins of Letterfinlay; the Clan ic Ilonobhy, or Camerons of Strone; and Sliochd Shoirle Ruaidh, or Camerons of Glen Nevis." He gives it as his opinion that the MacMartins were the oldest chiefs of the clan, and the family of Lochiel the oldest cadets. He accounts for the chieftainship falling into the hands of the Lochiel branch by the reasonable hypothesis that the MacMartin Camerons, having adhered to the successful faction in the dispute between the Mackintoshes and the MacPhersons in 1396 respecting the right to the chieftainship of the Clan Chattan, became absorbed into that great confederacy, and the Camerons of Lochiel having declared themselves independent, remained neutral, and thus gained the position they have held ever since.

According to MacKenzie, the progenitor of the Glen Nevis

sept was John de Cambrun, who appears as witness to a deed
in the year 1230 A.D., but admits that this is open to doubt,
and states that it has been maintained the Glen Nevis men
were not Camerons originally, but MacDonalds ; and, as supporting this view, Dr Fraser Mackintosh cites (*Transactions
of the Gaelic Society of Inverness*, vol. xvii. p. 34) a charter
of 20th April 1466, in which John, Lord of the Isles, grants
to Somerled a davoch of Glen Nevis, and considers this refers
to the Somerled known as Shoirle " Ruaidh." Certainly there
were many feuds between the Glen Nevis and the Lochiel
families. In 1577 Lochiel grants a deed of assurance of safety
to Mackintosh of Dunachton on behalf of the Clan Soirle ;
and again, towards the beginning of the seventeenth century,
Alastair Cameron of Glen Nevis was killed while assisting
the Earl of Huntly's son against Lochiel in an attempt to
oust the latter from the lands taken by him under a charter
from the king to the Argyll family in 1608.[1]

MacKenzie says that a new charter was granted to Glen
Nevis and others in 1618 by Huntly, but this is doubted by
Fraser Mackintosh, who states (*Trans. Gael. Soc. of Inverness*)
that the lands passed from Somerled to John, his son, and
Donald, his grandson, and that on 15th September 1522 Donald
resigned Glen Nevis into the queen's hands as superior, to
hold afterwards of the Earl of Huntly, who had got a crown
grant of the greater part of Lochaber. Donald was infeft in
1553, during the reign of the unfortunate Mary, and no further
title was made up till 1712, when Alan Cameron is entered
by the superior as great-great-great-grandson of Donald.

Such are the meagre details that have been handed down
to us of the history of this now extinct clan. Their name will
ever be associated with the traditions of the beautiful glen
which was their home in the days that are gone, and in which
their mortal remains now find rest.

Regaining the road and following the course of the river,
we now approach Glen Nevis House, a small but substantial

[1] MacKenzie's "History of the Clan Cameron."

dwelling of considerable antiquity, built of stone, partly covered with cement to keep out the winter storms. The house is almost surrounded by trees, and on one side is a splendid avenue of fine beeches, which is associated with several curious legends. Local authorities assert that this building is not the ancient home of the chieftains of the MacSorlies, which they say stood on a small knoll called *Dun Dige*, three or four hundred yards farther up the glen. Certainly this knoll bears very distinct traces of having been surrounded by a ditch or moat, and the mould contains a large quantity of burned wood. There is a remarkable story extant connecting this now demolished dwelling-place with the capture of the last of the seven MacDonalds who were concerned in the Keppoch murder, which has been described fully in an earlier chapter. The presence of the assassin in Glen Nevis is accounted for by the fact that a marriage connection of some sort existed between Glen Nevis and the chief of the murderers. In the Gaelic Society's *Transactions* (p. 40) there is a paper by Dr Fraser Mackintosh which seems to substantiate this tradition.

I can get no definite information as to when the present house was built, but it was certainly anterior to 1745, and was without doubt the headquarters of the Highland force commanded by Lochiel, who, to the number of fifteen hundred, invested Fort William, and caused General Campbell some alarm, and, as we shall afterwards learn, considerable trouble. Lochiel and Keppoch were both residing here in March 1746, during the time the siege was in progress, and it was from this place that the letter I have referred to was dated. Like many other old houses in the Highlands, it possesses its familiar spirit, the ghost in this instance taking the form of a little old woman clothed in grey, whose *raison d'être* I have been unable to discover.

It has been my privilege on many a well-remembered occasion to receive a hearty Highland welcome and pass many a pleasant hour under the hospitable roof of the old house of Glen Nevis, in the genial society of its worthy tenants and their friends. By its cosy ingle I have sat, after the fatigues of a long day's fishing excursion "doon the glen," and listened to weird stories of water kelpies, urisks, and other supernatural monsters peculiar to the Highlands, told by a famous *raconteur* and jolly fellow, whose mind is a very storehouse of Highland anecdote. *Air'ur slàinte* Tom MacKay in a bumper of *flor dhrùchd nam bèann;* I hope to have many a good day's fishing with you yet, and listen to a few more of your inimitable yarns under the old roof-tree.

CHAPTER XXVI.

MAIS "*revenons à nos moutons*" and proceed to explore the further beauties of the glen. Noticing as we pass along the famous "*Clach-an-turramain*" or rocking stone, which we may see in a meadow a short distance beyond the house. The ravages of time, or an act of vandalism on the part of some brainless tourist, has altered the poise of the upper boulder, and it no longer rocks. The hill immediately at the rear of the stone is called in the vernacular "*Cnocan-na-mi-chomhairle*," or "the hill of evil counsel," from the following circumstances. Sometime after the great fight at Invernahavon in 1386, the then chief of the Glen Nevis Camerons was desirous of making peace with his old enemies, the powerful Clan Chattan, and in order that some mutual agreement should be arrived at, he invited them to a friendly conference in Glen Nevis, to discuss the terms of the proposed treaty. These peaceful overtures on the part of their chief did not please the more warlike spirits among the Camerons, and although they attended the meeting at the bidding of MacSorlie, they did so with the greatest reluctance, and with the spark of hatred smouldering within their breasts. In this inflammable condition it is not to be wondered at that a quarrel should arise, as arise it did, with terrible consequences to the race of Somerled the Red. At first all went well, the assembled

Glen Nevis House.   Headquarters of the Highlanders during the siege of Fort William,
March 1746.

River Nevis at Poll Dubh.

that the insult had been specially directed against them, decided to remain where they were until nightfall, and then fall upon their sleeping foes sword in hand and utterly destroy them. Thus the hill upon which this fearful vengeance was planned is called until this day "the hill of evil counsel." The threat was, alas! no idle one. At midnight, when the inhabitants of the peaceful glen were wrapped in slumber, the murderous band swept down upon them like an avalanche of destruction, sparing neither man, woman, or child who came within reach of their swords. MacSorlie and most of his household were slain in cold blood by the pitiless assassins, but a special providence watched over his infant son, who miraculously escaped the fate of the rest of his kindred. The child was asleep in his cradle when the murderers entered, and was apparently unnoticed by them while the bloody work went on. In the midst of the deadly struggle that ensued upon the entrance of the MacPhersons, one of the Camerons, named "Iain Mac Dhon 'ic Raoil," disengaging himself from the clutches of his antagonist, seized the sleeping infant, and fled with it into the darkness of the night. With rapid steps he sped along the glen, clasping his precious burden in his arms, until he came to a great cavern, probably formed by volcanic agency, in the rocky bank of the river Nevis. Here he hid his young chieftain for some weeks, keeping the secret even from his wife, who lived a short distance off at Achriabhach.

At length the hiding-place was discovered by the aid of Iain's dog, who, having shared the privations of his master, was reduced to a state of semi-starvation. The natural instinct of self-preservation prompted the faithful animal to seek food in the place where it was most likely to be found, and one day, much to the surprise of Iain's wife, the dog made his appearance at Achriabhach, and having satisfied the pangs of hunger, departed to rejoin his master. The suspicions of the good woman being aroused by the strange behaviour of the dog, she determined to follow him, and learn, if possible, the fate of her husband, whom she had given up all hopes of

seeing again. When Iain discovered the dog's absence, he
feared that his secret would be discovered, and he took up
his position at the mouth of the cave, ready to defend his
young charge in the event of an enemy approaching. The
enemy proved to be his own wife, who, upon catching sight
of her husband, rushed forward to embrace him in the first
impulse of her joy at seeing him alive. Stern in the discharge
of his duty as guardian of the heir of MacSorlie, Iain forbade
his wife to come nearer, feeling assured that the secret would
be a secret no longer if it was confided to female ears, and
upon her attempt to disregard his injunction, he threatened to
kill her if she made another step in the direction of the cave.
His wild, unkempt appearance and ferocious gestures had the
desired effect upon the wretched woman, who, thinking her
husband bereft of his senses, fled from the painful scene.

This occurrence produced a feeling of insecurity in the
mind of Iain, and he began to think that the cave was no
longer a safe hiding-place, as he knew his wife would inform
her friends of what had taken place. He therefore took young
Somerled in his arms, and set out for a distant part of the
Highlands where the story was unknown. Here they dwelt
in peace for some years, until it became necessary that the
youthful chief should receive the education that his rank
required. Before leaving Glen Nevis House, on the night of
the massacre, Iain had prudently possessed himself of certain
documents that proved the lad's title to the estates of his
murdered father, and had also brought with him a silver
spoon, which was an heirloom of the chief of the Glen Nevis
Camerons. These precious articles he had carefully preserved
during his wanderings, and they were now to be of service in
restoring the exile to his position as head of the clan.

Returning to Lochaber with the young heir, Iain presented
himself in the guise of a beggar at the house of Inverlair, where
the sister of the unfortunate MacSorlie resided, and demanded
some food for the boy. This request having been granted by
the charitable lady, some porridge was brought out by the

servant, who was startled to see the seeming beggar produce a
silver spoon from his sporan, and proceed to feed the hungry
lad. So strange did this circumstance appear, that she went
to inform her mistress, who immediately came out to see the
unwonted sight of a beggar child being fed with a silver spoon.
As soon as she saw young Somerled, she perceived the remarkable resemblance he bore to her dead brother, and at the same
time catching sight of the family heirloom, began to suspect
the truth. A few inquiries cautiously made, satisfied her that
her suspicions were well founded, and she no longer doubted
that the beggar child was her own nephew; but as enemies
might be lurking in the neighbourhood, it was decided between
her and Iain that the secret of the lad's birth should for the
present be withheld from him. Under his aunt's care he
received all those limited educational advantages which the age
and place could offer; and he was trained in all manly pursuits
and athletic exercises by the faithful Iain, whom he regarded
as his father. Under this kindly tuition the young chief
developed all the noble characteristics of his ancestors, and
at the age of seventeen, being thought by his guardians fitted
in every way to take his rightful place at the head of his clan,
they disclosed to him the story of his adventurous career, and
bade him attend the gathering of the Camerons which was
shortly to take place at Mucomer, by command of Lochiel.
When the day arrived, young Somerled set out for the spot
attended by his devoted friend, and upon arrival proceeded
to take his place among the assembled chieftains. This bold
behaviour on the part of an entire stranger excited the surprise of all present, and Lochiel, turning to his clansmen, said,
" Whence comes this forward lad ? " With ready wit the young
chief replied in Gaelic verse, which may be Anglicised
thus—

> " I am not a stranger in the land;
> My ancestors oft followed the ' *toir* ' (chase).
> Nor did an arrow ever wound my step
> When taking cattle off *Tor-nan-cor*."

2 F

The allusion to the hill of *Tor-nan-cor*, which was close to the home of the chieftain of Glen Nevis, was at once comprehended by Lochiel and those who stood round him: the recollection of the terrible massacre was still fresh in their minds, although more than fifteen years had passed since that awful event. The lad's noble presence and resolute bearing gave some force to his pretensions, and caused Lochiel to regard him with favour; and he listened patiently, and with considerable interest, to the long story that Iain Mac Dhon 'ic Raoil unfolded. The production of the title-deeds removed any remaining doubts in Lochiel's mind as to the validity of the claim of young MacSorlie to his father's estates in Glen Nevis, and before the close of that auspicious day the chief of the ancient race of *Sliochd Shomhairle Ruaidh* found himself in full possession of his patrimony.

MacKenzie, in his " History of the Clan Cameron," refers to two other branches, or rather families, of Camerons, whose place of abode was far removed from their ancestral district of Lochaber, and whose connection with the parent clan it is difficult to discover. One of these families was to be found in Strathspey and the other in Cowal, the latter calling themselves "*Mac an Taillear*," or " sons of the tailor," and who were probably descended from the famous Donald " *Taillear dubh na tuaighe*" (whose history has already been given in an earlier chapter), who shares with Iain Mac Dhon 'ic Raoil the honour of having been the saviour of the young heir of MacSorlie from the hands of the assassins.

The story runs that the foster-brother of the chief was called Sorlie or Samuel, and during the assault on the house managed to break his way through the attacking party, carrying with him the infant son of his chief, the sole surviving member of the family. He hid for some time in Samuel's Cave, and then made his way to the Earl of Huntly, in whose charge the child was left. To avoid suspicion, he then travelled down to Cowal, where he supported himself by working as a tailor and from this circumstance his descendants were known as "the sons of the tailor."

It is evident that this story is merely another version of the former one; but from the fact that the Earl of Huntly is named as being the guardian of MacSorlie's heir, it would make the massacre of the Glen Nevis Camerons occur at a later date than the story of Iain Mac Dhon 'ic Raoil, as it was not until the early part of the sixteenth century that the Earls of·Huntly had any influence in Lochaber.

A short distance from "the hill of evil counsel," on the same side of the glen, is a remarkable green hill, rising about a thousand feet above the road, and·crowned with the remains of one of those peculiar relics of a prehistoric age known as vitrified forts, of which several may yet be found in the northern and western Highlands. The one in Glen Nevis forms a link in the chain of these structures which extends from Strathpeffer to Oban, and is especially interesting on account of its association with the name of the unfortunate Irish princess "Deirdre," the wife of Naisi or Nathos, son of Uisnach. The sad story of the untimely fate of this unhappy pair is to be found in an ancient Gaelic MS., dated 1238, and known as "Dàn Chloinn Uisneachain," and may be told briefly as follows :—

CHAPTER XXVII.

IN the days of old, when Conor was king of Ulster in Erin, he came to the dwelling of Felim, the Seanachie, to take counsel with him. And it fell out that after the king had entered into the house, in the time of lateness, the wife of the Seanachie was delivered of a daughter of whom Cathbad, the Druid, prophesied evil, saying that disaster should fall upon the land of Ulster because of the child who was born. And the stream of years flowed on, and the maid grew in beauty and comeliness, and the name that was upon her was Deirdre. Her

eyes were as the stars of heaven, her arms were white as the
foam of streams, like the shades of dusky night her dark hair
fell upon her heaving breasts, her teeth were as a river of
pearl between banks of rowan, like the rose her cheeks, and
her soul was a beam of light. Who among the maids of
Erin was as fair as she?

And the fame of her beauty was spread abroad through
all the land of Ulster, so that knowledge of it was at the
king; and he took a thought that he would make Deirdre his
wife when she had attained to womanhood.

Now when Conor had determined thus, fear was upon him
lest others should be tempted by the maid's exceeding loveliness to steal her from him, so he called Lavarcam, one of his
maidservants, and laid his commands upon her. Said the
king, "On the morning of the morrow's day, go to the house
of Felim, the Seanachie, and give him my blessing, and say
that it is his daughter that I would have for wife. Use thy
cunning and speak soft, flowing peaceful words of wisdom so that
he will give his daughter into thy hands. Do this and I will
set it to thy gain, for great will be the reward thou shalt get."

And on the morning of the morrow's day, Lavarcam went
to the house of the Seanachie, and spoke to him in the *fisniche
faisniche*,[1] soft, flowing, peaceful words of wisdom, and laid the
king's commands upon him, so that he delivered his daughter
Deirdre into her hands. At the mouth of night Lavarcam
brought Deirdre to Conor, and great joy was on the king when
he saw the white-bosomed maid trembling like a young fawn
by the side of his servant; but her years were yet tender, so
he commanded Lavarcam to take Deirdre to a place without
the city, where he had built a dun of great strength, and
dwell with her there for a space of two years in secret, and
at the end of that time he would take her to wife. So
Lavarcam hasted herself and went away with Deirdre to the
dun, and the black clouds of night were going and the white

---

[1] Obsolete Gaelic expression often used in old Highland stories, probably meaning
"soothsaying."

clouds of day were coming when they got there. And
Deirdre dwelt with Lavarcam in the king's dun, and saw no
one, save only those women whom Conor had sent to wait upon
her; and her life was blacksome and desolate, for love was not
with her for the king.

It happened that Naisi, the son of Uisnach, chief of Etha
in Albyn, dwelt with his brothers Ainli and Ardan, in the
land of Ulster, and the fame of Deirdre's beauty having
reached his ears, he became enamoured of her, and took a
thought how he could behold her loveliness, which was as the
silver moon in the blue firmament of heaven.

Now Naisi was comely and well favoured, his steps were
like the bounding roe, his stature like the fir trees of his
native hills, soft were his cheeks and ruddy, and from his eyes
of blue looked out his fearless soul.

From her window in the dun Deirdre had marked the
youth as with stately stride he passed to hunt the boar.
The great white-breasted dogs leaped at his side, his mighty
spear gleamed like a beam of light in his grasp; upon his
back, broad as the young oak, hung the bossy shield of car-
borne Cuchullin, hero of a hundred fights. And the soul of
the maid went out to Naisi, son of Uisnach, and she stretched
out her arms to him, and he saw her, and it was gladness that
was in his heart, for he knew that love was with her for him.

But the heart of Deirdre was sad, and fear was on her for
the anger of the king. So she called Lavarcam and took
counsel with her, for Lavarcam was friendly, and hate was
with her for the king her master.

Now Deirdre had a winning tongue, and the words dropped
from her lips as honey from the honeycomb, so that she prevailed with Lavarcam to bring Naisi to her, for her soul was
desolate. Said Lavarcam, "The kindness that thou gavest
thyself to me I will give it to thee; morsel I will not eat,
draught I will not drink, sleep there will not come on my
eyes until I have brought the youth to thee." And in the
night and lateness Lavarcam went secretly to Naisi, the son

of Uisnach, chief of Etha, and said, "*Failte!* (Hail!) Naisi of Albyn, fortunate indeed art thou among thy fellows, thrice happy shalt thou be, son of Uisnach, for the love of my mistress, the dark-eyed daughter of Felim, is with thee; so take haste to thyself, gird thyself quickly and follow me, for Deirdre desireth to have speech with thee, and not a cloud of sleep shall go on mine eye this night until I have brought thee to her."

So Naisi arose and hasted himself, for great joy was on him at the tidings that Lavarcam had brought; and he clothed himself in rich apparel and girded on his sword, and went forth with Lavarcam, and they came to the dun that the king had built without the city.

Thus came the young chief of Etha to the daughter of Felim, the Seanachie, as a bridegroom came he unto her, speaking soft, flowing words of love such as delighted her heart, so that she desired nothing better than to dwell with him wheresoever he would take her. And Naisi gave a kiss to her mouth and a caress to her flowing locks, and called her his belovèd, so that sorrow was no longer in her breast, for the desire of her heart was accomplished.

But fear was on Naisi lest the anger of Conor should be kindled against him and against Deirdre his belovèd, so on a night of nights he fled secretly with her to the land of his fathers, Albyn of the lakes, and made her his wife, and dwelt with her in the dun he had built for her in the vale of Etha; and Naisi with his brothers Ainli and Ardan, sons of Uisnach, became famous in the land of Albyn, and lifted the spear and struck the echoing shield, so that the enemies of the king of Albyn fled from before the nephews of car-borne Cuchullin, Tura's mighty chief. And Naisi built many duns of strength throughout the land of Albyn, and the name that was on them was the name of Deirdre his belovèd.

If it was happiness with Deirdre, it was rage and anger on Conor, king of Ulster, when knowledge came to him of what Naisi had done. "Adversity and calamities be upon thee, Naisi of Albyn," said the king; "bad is the thing that thou

hast done, and it is thyself that will be ill off; for I will
take thy head out of thy neck, and thy body shalt be riven
on the deadly points ere the space of a day and a year be
passed." Thus spake the king in his wrath, and at the mouth
of night he went to the house of Cathbad the Druid, the same
who had prophesied evil of the daughter that was born to
Felim the Seanachie, and took counsel with him how he
should compass the death of Naisi.

And the wisdom of the serpent and the cunning of the fox
were on Cathbad, and he let out his speech to the king, and
said: "Hearken, O king, to the words of thy Druid, and the
thing thou wisheth shall befall. Send to Naisi, the bold hero,
son of Etha's chief, a message of peace; and say that sadness is
upon thee because of his absence; for he was ever as a brother
to thee, and Deirdre ever as a daughter whom thou lovest;
promise great things to him: that he shall be a valiant high
champion among thy warriors of the Red Branch[1] (*Craobh
Ruadh*); that he shall rule in thy council; that honours and
riches shall be showered upon him; and that he and his wife
shall dwell in a house that thou hast prepared for them. It is
thus thou shalt persuade him to leave the land of Albyn
and take up his abode in Erin; so that thou can do with
him that which is in thine heart." So the king departed
from the house of Cathbad, and sent Fergus MacRoy, with his
sons Illan and Buine, across the sea to the land of Albyn of
the lakes, where Naisi dwelt in peace with his wife Deirdre.

And Fergus sought out Naisi; and when he found him, told
him the words of Conor, and how he had promised him great
honours in the land of Ulster, and that he should be a valiant
high champion among the warriors of the Red Branch, and
should dwell with his wife in the house that the king had
built. Thus Fergus reasoned with Naisi and prevailed with
him, so that he consented to do what Conor wished, for
belief was on him that the words of the king were true.

---

[1] The Red Branch was an Irish order of chivalry, founded by Conor, king of
Ulster, somewhat akin to king Arthur's Knights of the Round Table in Britain.

And Naisi gave a great feast to Fergus MacRoy, and to his sons Illan the Fair and Buine the Ruthless Red, by the shores of Loch Eitche (Loch Etive); and meat was set in the place for eating, drink in the place for drinking; music was raised and lament laid down; and they were at eating and drinking, and at singing and the telling of tales, until the white day should come.

But Deirdre suspected evil, and belief was not on her that the promises Conor had made to Naisi her husband, or the words Fergus had spoken, were true, and would have persuaded him to remain in the dun he had raised for her in Etha's lovely vale. With tears and entreaties spake she to him, but hardness was on his heart, and he would not listen to her pleadings, having promised Fergus that he would return with him to Ulster. So, on a day of days, Naisi and his wife Deirdre, with his brothers Ainli and Ardan, departed from Albyn and from the home that they loved. And the soul of Deirdre was sad, and she wept bitterly; and as she wept she sang,—

> " Beloved land, that eastern land,
>   Albyn, with its wonders.
>   O that I might not depart from it,
>   But that I go with Naisi.
>
> " Beloved is Dunfidhga and Dun Finn;
>   Beloved is the dun above them;
>   Beloved is Innisdraighende,[1]
>   And beloved Dun Suibhne.[2]
>
> "Coillchuan ! O Coillchuan !
>   Where Ainli would, alas ! resort;
>   Too short, I deem, was then my stay
>   With Ainli in Oirir Albyn.
>
> " Glenlaidhe ! O Glenlaidhe ![3]
>   I used to sleep by its soothing murmur;
>   Fish, and flesh of wild boar and badger,
>   Was my repast in Glenlaidhe.

[1] Inistryinch, Loch Awe.   [2] Castle Sween.   [3] Glenlochy.

" Glenmasan ! O Glenmasan ![1]
  High its herbs, fair its boughs.
  Solitary was the place of our repose
  On grassy Invermasan.

" Glen Eitche ! O Glen Eitche ![2]
  There was raised my earliest home.
  Beautiful its woods on rising,
  When the sun struck on Glen Eitche.

" Glen Urchain ! O Glen Urchain ![3]
  It was the straight glen of smooth ridges.
  Not more joyful was a man of his age
  Than Naisi in Glen Urchain.

" Glendaruadh ! O Glendaruadh ![4]
  My love each man of its inheritance.
  Sweet the voice of the cuckoo on bending bough,
  On the hill above Glendaruadh.

" Beloved is Draighen [5] and its sounding shore ;
  Beloved the water o'er pure sand.
  O that I might not depart from the east,
  But that I go with my beloved ! " [6]

Thus sang Deirdre as she crossed the sea with Naisi, her husband; and those that stood by marvelled at her voice, which was as the murmuring waters of love, sounding through Selma's echoing halls; and Naisi was silent, and looked out upon the faint gleaming deep. The sky grew dark, the moon, like a dim shield, rolled through the grey-bosomed mists, the form of ghosts were in their dusky skirts, they gathered on every side borne on the winds of heaven. Naisi saw them as they beckoned unto him, and the darkness of night closed round about him, and his soul grew sad, for he knew that he had done unwisely in hearkening not to the words of his wife.

So they came to the land of Ulster; and the king dissembled his wrath and received them with kindness, and put honours upon Naisi and his brothers Ainli and Ardan, so that they

---

[1] Glen Masan (Head of the Holy Loch).   [2] Glen Etive.   [3] Glen Orchy.
[4] Glendaruel (Cowal).   [5] Rudha nan Draighnean, near Bunawe, Loch Etive.
[6] Skene's translation from the "Dean of Lismore's Book," Introduction, p. lxxxvii.

thought they had done well in coming thither. But Deirdre, the wife of Naisi, suspected evil of the king, and her heart was troubled because her husband would take no heed to her words. And in dreams by night, and in visions by day, the spirits of her fathers spake unto her, and warned her that the hour of her husband's death was at hand. The pale forms of ghosts overshadowed her, and on the eddying winds arose the voice of death. High above the storm Deirdre heard the dreadful sound of the echoing shield, and from the hill of Mora came the song of woe. "Who comes through the night to the dwelling of Naisi in the season of his repose? Bring'st thou tidings of war that thou wakest him so rudely? Who art thou, son of the dusky night?"

And Naisi awoke from his sleep, and he heard the clanging shields and the death song of the bards, and the spirit of his uncle Cuchullin arose within him. Dark was his brow, and anger raged in his heart. He girded on his terrible sword, and in his hand gleamed the spear of his father Uisnach. Tall strode he in his wrath, and he called unto his brothers Ainli and Ardan, and told them the treachery of the king. And the sons of Uisnach laughed aloud, for they delighted in the strife of battle, and dear unto their hearts was the music of the clashing spears.

Like the bursting of a torrent rushed forth the sons of Etha's chief; forth went they in their strength to meet the foe at their gates. Thrice along the vale rolled the song of death; thrice hath the king struck with his spear the sounding shield. The sons of Ullin answer with shouts of war, and press onward like the foaming waves on Morven's rock-girt shore. Above the rushing throng towers the eagle crest of Naisi. Ainli and Ardan are by his side, tall as young fir trees; in their hands are gleaming swords. Mighty are the blows of the sons of Uisnach; death is in each stroke of their strong arms. Dreadful is the strife and bloody; the ghosts of heroes flee on every side; the clash of broken steel rises on the blasts of night.

The sons of Ullin fall in heaps before the swords of the

brothers; red are their feet in the blood of the slain, and the groans of the wounded are in their ears. Unequal grows the fight, and the arm of Naisi is weary of slaughter. Ainli falls by Ardan, and the waters of death close round about them. Naisi is pierced by the spear of Conor; his clustering locks are wet with blood; stricken he falls to the earth; the noise of battle is no longer sweet in his ears; no more shall his fearless soul look out from his eyes of blue; no longer shall he go forth to the chase with the white-breasted dogs bounding at his side; never again shall his voice be heard in Etha's lovely vale.

Deirdre saw her belovèd fall, and the blackness of death compassed her round about. "Where dwellest thou, O my belovèd? the light of my soul has departed, O Naisi, my husband! I hear thy voice calling me from the shadowy mist. Look forth from thy cloud upon me, for I am lonely in the midst of woe. Call me, and I will come unto thee; through the darkness of the valley of ghosts will I come unto thee, O my belovèd!" And the spirit of Deirdre went out from her, and the land of Erin knew her no more; but her fame, and the fame of her husband Naisi, spread through all the land of Erin and the country of Albyn of the lakes, and the words of the song that she sang are with us unto this day.

The name of this unhappy lady is still preserved in the curious structures which her husband Naisi is said to have built, and which are known as Dundearduils.[1] The one in Glen Nevis has suffered much from the hand of time, and only a few stones are left to mark the place where it once stood erect. There is, however, a much better preserved specimen on a hill overhanging Loch Ness, to which peculiar interest attaches from the fact that the loch itself is said to derive its name from Deirdre's husband. If this is so, it of course follows that the town of Inverness takes its name from the same mythical personage.

---

[1] Philologists are of opinion that the name is a corruption of *Dun-dearrsach*, "Shining Hill," or *Dun-dearg-shuil*, "Hill of the Red Eye," from the fact that these structures were undoubtedly used as beacons.

CHAPTER XXVIII.

AFTER passing the hill of Dundearduil (as it is called locally), the road becomes rough and uneven, and covered with loose stones washed down from the mountain sides. The scenery, like the road, also changes its character, and in place of the pastoral beauty of the first few miles, it becomes grand and awe-inspiring in its rugged magnificence. We are here some distance above the river Nevis, which may be seen winding like a thread of silver through the glen. Immediately in front rises the extraordinary peaked mountain of *Sgòr a' Mhàim*, 3600 feet high, its bleached summit glistening white against the blue sky, and appearing as if covered with snow. From this point we may also obtain a fine view of the hoary head of the great Ben, which rises 4400 odd feet from the sea-level. Its massive proportions dwarf the surrounding hills into insignificance, high though they be, and the great fir trees which clothe its lower slopes look like whin bushes or bracken. Enormous fissures or corries appear on its granite sides, due, probably, to the great volcanic upheaval which took place at the birth of the mountain, or to the shrinkage that must have occurred when the molten granite began to cool. From these dark recesses issue forth streams of water which rush down the scarred sides of the mountain with ceaseless murmur, and help to swell the crystal Nevis in the vale beneath.

At the foot of the great corrie, which almost cleaves in twain the stupendous *Carn Dearg* (" Red Cairn "), is another of those peaceful resting-places of the forgotten dead. It is known as "*Acha-nan-con*" (" the field of dogs "), and if the local tradition is to be believed, it was here that the Pictish kings kept their celebrated deer-hounds and trained them for the chase. A short distance farther, and we come to the small farm-house of Achriabhach, which I have mentioned before as having been the dwelling-place of Iain Mac Dhon 'ic Raoil, the faithful preserver of the heir of MacSorlie. The roar of water tells of the proximity of a fall, and as we cross the wooden bridge which here spans the river, we may see the tumultuous Nevis rushing between its rocky banks, and falling in two foaming streams among the boulders some forty feet below, throwing into the air clouds of glistening silver spray, in which miniature rainbows gleam with resplendent colours.

A little above the fall is pointed out the spot where one of the chiefs was murdered. He had gone to see his cattle, and was in the act of drinking from a large cog, when an arrow, shot by a man concealed in a bundle of heather or hay according to one account, behind a large stone according to another, nailed cog and head together. Before help could be summoned the murderer escaped. Tradition gives his name as "*Iain beag MacAindrea*" ("little John MacAndrew"), a very cunning and malevolent dwarf, and many tales are recorded of how he baffled his pursuers. On one occasion a party of the murdered chief's friends came to his house as he was sitting at the fire: his wife bade him rise and tell his father he was wanted. Iain departed to seek the non-existent father, and, possessing himself of his bow, climbed a tree commanding the house, called out that Iain was waiting outside, and as each man appeared at the door, an arrow from Iain's bow laid him low. At another time he was cutting peats, and, not suspecting attack, had laid his sword and dirk on the ground, when two men came up, saying they had got him this time. He affected to be fairly caught, but suddenly he stopped, gazed earnestly in another direction, and said, as if to himself, " Who in the world can that be coming?" His captors, taken off their guard by this remark, turned to see what the dwarf was looking at, when he instantly secured his weapons, and two more Camerons went to their account.

In the " New Statistical Account of Elginshire," *Iain beag MacAindrea* is said to have been a tacksman of Dalnahatnich, near Carr Bridge, and the story as to his killing the men from the tree is referred to another incident. The son of

Achluacharach, in the Braes of Lochaber, had made a foray
on the lands of Rose of Kilravock, and was on his way home
by way of Strathdearn, when he was overtaken by a large
party of Rose's friends, including *Iain beag*, who surprised the
reivers feasting on part of the booty, and protected, as they
fondly imagined, by a sentinel, who had, however, fallen asleep
at his post. The hut they occupied was surrounded, and all
the Lochaber men slain, save the sentinel. Achluacharach
himself was leaning on a beam of the house, and *Iain beag*,
who had singled him out, pinned him to the beam with an
arrow, killing him on the spot. The wife of the unfortunate
chief composed a very beautiful lament on his death.

Another version of the same story is, that the man who
escaped with his life had looked through the shoulder-blade[1]
of one of the beasts that had been eaten, and repeatedly
pointed out to his friends the steadily lessening number of
burns that intervened between them and their pursuers; and
at last, finding that no heed was taken of his warning, and
observing that only one burn now separated his party from
the avenging Roses, he left them and hid himself in a clump
of heather, and so avoided the terrible fate that overtook the
others. I have been unable to ascertain what became of the
redoubtable *Iain beag*.

After leaving Achriabhach, the glen becomes one vast
solitude, and the feeling of absolute isolation produced in the
mind is almost painful in its intensity and impressiveness.
Immense masses of misshapen rocks are strewn around in all
directions, suggesting the débris of some awful Cyclopean
combat, in which they had been used as missiles. Towering
high above our heads, the mountains rise in lofty grandeur,
like walls of granite, and shut us in on every side, their serrated
summits silhouetted against the intense blue of the sky.
Seamed with torrents, and shattered into all kinds of fantastic
shapes by centuries of storms, they present an awe-inspiring

---

[1] The shoulder-blade of animals was a favourite means of divination among
the ancient Highlanders.

spectacle calculated to fill the soul with wonder, and cause the most unreflective to ponder on the works of the Creator.

The river Nevis at this part of the glen is lost to view, but its music may be heard as it flows madly on in the rocky channel it has worn for itself many feet below the level of the road. Here is the "*Uamh Shomhairle*," or "cave of Somerled," to which the infant chief of the Camerons of Glen Nevis was brought by his devoted clansman on the night of the massacre at Glen Nevis House. Although the entrance is very narrow, and it is necessary to crawl in on hands and knees, the interior is of considerable dimensions, being in some places nearly fourteen feet high and eleven wide. The author, on his last attempt to explore its mysteries, unfortunately left his lantern behind at Fort William, and finding that the air currents blew out the wax-vestas as soon as lighted, thought it advisable to postpone the adventure until a more favourable occasion. Many of the inhabitants of the district firmly believe that one of the passages of this extraordinary cave extends five miles or so in the direction of Kinlochleven, at which place there is an exit. And to prove the truth of this theory, they say that many years ago a body of Camerons, who had been surprised in a cattle-lifting expedition, found themselves surrounded and their retreat cut off; but the piper who, as usual, accompanied them on these predatory excursions, marched the Camerons into the cave, and was heard playing in the remote distance by the pursuers, who were unable to come up with him, and therefore came to the conclusion that the reivers had found an exit which they were unaware of.

There is another tradition told by Mrs MacKellar, of a piper who, with some friends, had taken refuge in the cavern; but after they had been there some time a she-wolf of ferocious aspect entered, and, taking up its position at the cave's mouth, prevented their escape in that direction. Having heard that "music hath charms to soothe the savage breast," the piper struck up his most stirring pibroch, which had the effect he desired. The wild notes of the *piob mhòr* rendered the wolf docile, and,

under the influence of the music, it lost all its fierce animal
instincts, and made no attempt to carry out its original
intentions. Taking advantage of the beast's dazed condition,
the fugitives proceeded along the underground passage, the
piper slowly following, with his pipes in full blast, composing as he went words describing his position, to the music
he was playing—

> " A choin a righ's mi gun tri lamhan,
>   Da lamh's a piob's lamh's a chlaidheamh,"

—that is to say, that his only regret was that he had not two
hands for the pipes and one for the sword.

In this story the party who had taken refuge in the cave
were not so fortunate as the Camerons, for we are told that
they perished in the bowels of the earth, and were never seen
again ; but it is said that the wailing of that last pibroch is
sometimes heard by the chance wayfarer who passes the
entrance to the cave after nightfall.

The scenery here is indescribably magnificent, and the
verdure with which the bases of the mountains are covered
affords some relief to the eye, although it also serves to
emphasise the barrenness of their summits. All is wild confusion, as if Dame Nature had been disturbed in her operations
and left her work unfinished. Trees, shrubs, bracken, and
heather mingle in a tangled luxuriant growth, which the moist
atmosphere engenders, and afford a splendid cover for the red
deer, descendants of the primeval herds for which the great
forest of Mamore has always been celebrated, and from
which the ancient kings of Scotland drew their supplies of
venison.

Penetrating a few miles farther, our progress is barred by a
tremendous precipice, rising perpendicularly some thousands
of feet into the clouds, which usually veil its awful height.
From the summit of this wall of granite issues a rill of water,
which, after running a tortuous course among the crevices of
the rocks, falls in a continuous stream five hundred feet into

the valley beneath, affording a spectacle of great beauty, and well worth the trouble of a visit. This waterfall is called in Gaelic "*An Steall*," but is usually known as "The Upper Falls of Nevis."

Here our pleasant excursion comes to an end; and after this flight into the realms of tradition and romance, the author must rein in his Pegasus, and descend to the equally romantic province of authentic history, of which no page contains more incidents of engrossing interest than that on which is inscribed the story of the " Forty-Five."

CHAPTER XXIX.

THE force commanded by Lochiel, which had been despatched from Inverness to prosecute the siege of Fort William, consisted mostly of men of his own clan; but, in addition to these, he had with him a large body of the Stewarts of Appin and the MacDonalds of Keppoch and Glencoe. As early as 24th February, the Lochaber men, who were not with the prince's army at Inverness, had commenced hostilities in an intermittent and desultory manner, and, as we learn from General Campbell's despatch, had given the garrison a considerable amount of trouble; but it was not until Brigadier Stapleton came up with his Irish piquets, which was about 14th March, that the siege began in real earnest. On that day the garrison began to heighten the parapet of the fort, and raised the two faces of the bastions seven feet. The following day the governor took the offensive, and gave orders for the men of the " Baltimore" sloop to proceed to sea in armed boats and attack a detachment of Highlanders who had entrenched themselves at Kilmallie (or Corpach), on the opposite shore of Loch Eil. Captain Richard of the "Baltimore" was in command of the attacking party, and commenced operations by firing several shots from the swivel guns with which his boats were provided; but the attempt to land was abortive, as

2 H

the tide failed and the scheme miscarried. In this skirmish one sailor was killed and three wounded.

A more determined attack was made by Captain Richard on 18th March. The "Baltimore" was run as close inshore as the tide would allow, and her 44-pounders were brought to bear upon the Jacobite position, and opened fire with shot and shell while an attempt was being made to land the troops. The Highlanders, secure behind the stone walls of the byres and crofts of Kilmallie, could afford to laugh at the desperate efforts made by the enemy to dislodge them. Having loopholed the walls, they were enabled to pour a deadly fire upon the landing party, who soon found the reception too warm for them, and hastily retreated to their boats. The casualties in this instance were on the side of the defenders of Kilmallie, for we are told they lost four men killed and several wounded, among the latter being their engineer-in-chief.

After this second failure, General Campbell gave up the idea of effecting a landing on the Argyllshire shore, and concentrated his attention upon the besieging force which was now hemming him in on the land side.

By 20th March Stapleton had, after great difficulty, brought up his train of artillery, and having constructed a battery on the Sugar-Loaf Hill, a conical eminence about eight hundred yards in rear of the fort, commenced a vigorous bombardment; but, finding the distance too great, he threw up a new battery at the foot of the Cow Hill, and from this advantageous position opened a heavy fire, which did considerable damage to the fortifications, and demolished the roofs of the houses in the enclosure. On the 22nd Stapleton sent a French drummer with a message to Captain Scott (who was then in command of the garrison) demanding a surrender; but this he indignantly refused, stating that he "would make no terms with rebels." The natural consequence of this bold reply was the immediate reopening of hostilities, and a further destructive cannonade from the Cow Hill battery, which lasted for some hours. The guns in the fort replied to the fire of the Highland force, and in the end succeeded in rendering Brigadier Stapleton's battery untenable; but, nothing daunted, he set to work and erected a fresh one about three hundred yards off, from which he pounded away with renewed energy all Sunday morning, the 23rd, until three o'clock in the afternoon, when some ships arrived in Loch Linnhe with supplies and reinforcements for the besieged garrison.

Taking in the position of affairs at a glance, the captains of the newly arrived vessels weighed anchor in front of the Cow Hill, and discharged a broadside against Stapleton's new redoubt with disastrous results, many of his men being killed, and the battery itself beaten down. This reverse necessitated the withdrawal of the artillery from the exposed position it occupied on the Cow Hill (where it offered a splendid mark for the ship's guns) to the natural shelter afforded by the peculiar geological formation which has been before described, and which is known as the Craigs. Here the cannon were placed behind the cover of the projecting rocks, from which the place takes its name, and once again the roar of artillery echoed from hill to hill, and reverberated through the quiet Lochaber glens, where the cattle lay in peaceful repose, causing them to tremble at the unwonted sound, which they were unable to comprehend.

So the long days of the siege wore on, and the fort which General MacKay had built stood bravely against the storm of shot and shell which the guns of Brigadier Stapleton rained upon it. The garrison gave no signs of yielding, and, since the arrival of the ships of war, there had been no dearth of food. These vessels were employed in taking foraging parties to various places on the shores of Loch Linnhe, Loch Eil, and Loch Leven, and many head of cattle were forcibly taken from the unoffending peasantry by the voracious soldiery of Hanoverian George, who, not satisfied with robbing them of their possessions, murdered them in cold blood, and destroyed their habitations by fire.

On 25th March a party of soldiers was sent to a place five or six miles off to bring in cattle, and in the afternoon they returned with twenty-nine bullocks and cows. Another band of "forty thieves," of equal ferocity to their eastern namesakes of Arabian Nights' fame, was despatched to raid the estates of the Stewarts of Appin, in the country of Ardshiel, during their owner's absence with the Highland army. In this expedition two villages were burnt, and several inoffensive herdsmen were killed while defending the property of their chief. Four of their number were taken prisoners, and brought with the cattle and sheep to Fort William.

At length, on 31st March, the beleaguered garrison determined to make a desperate attempt to shake off the enemy, who had harassed them for nearly a month. The sally and its consequences are thus described in the *Scots Magazine* of 1746:—

"The men who sallied out on the 31st were in two parties, one commanded by Captains Foster and MacLachlan, the other by Captains Paton and Whitway; that the former attacked and took the battery at the back of the Craigs; that in another attack, made upon a four-gun battery at the foot of the hill, the king's troops were repulsed, with the loss of two men killed and a few wounded; that their retreat was made in good order under the guns of the fort; that they carried in two prisoners, one an Englishman, the other a Frenchman, or rather Spaniard; that this last gave an account that the besiegers were half-starving, and beginning to run short of ammunition; that the rebels lost a considerable number of men, not only in their flight from the Craigs, but in the second attack; that the governor was wounded, but not dangerously; that the town of Maryburgh and garden walls was levelled to the ground; that the garrison were 600 in number, all in good spirits, and were reinforced on the 1st April by 70 of Johnson's regiment; that the roofs of the fort were exceedingly damaged; and the old pile of barracks almost quite beat down, both roof and walls; that there were not six panes of glass remaining in the windows; and that Captain Scott had been indefatigable, both by night and day, in erecting new works."

The loss of his artillery, the increasing scarcity of provisions, and the knowledge that the prince required his services at Inverness, decided Stapleton to raise the siege of Fort William, and retire northward with his Irish contingent, the Highlanders being left behind, with orders to join the camp at Inverness as soon as possible. On 3rd April (some authorities say the 4th) the investing army dispersed, the Highlanders to their homes to prepare themselves afresh for the coming struggle, while Brigadier Stapleton and his brave Irishmen hastened to Inverness to help swell the force that Prince Charles was assembling to oppose the advance of the Duke of Cumberland.

With reference to this siege, a contemporary Whig writer, Ray ("Complete History of the Rebellion," p. 305), says :—
"The Siege of Fort William by the Rebels (of all their Undertakings) was the most regularly carried on from the 14th of March to the 3rd of April with 1500 Men, 8 Pieces of Cannon, and 7 Mortars under the command of Brigadier Stapleton, and under him Cameron of Lochiel, and Clanronald, with three or four more Chiefs of the Mackdonalds, Stewarts and Camerons: The Garrison being bravely defended by Capt. Scott, having several Reinforcements sent him and it being not in the Power of the Rebels to cut off the Communications by Sea, on the 14th (evidently an error, should be the 4th) they raised the Siege and left the Garrison in Possession of all their Artillery."

Having had occasion to mention the village of Kilmallie, I will take this opportunity of giving a short account of its history and traditions. The origin of the name is evidently derived from the Gaelic words "*Kil*" or "*Cill*," meaning "chapel" or "burying-ground," and "*Mallie*," the diminutive form of Mary. Kilmallie therefore means the chapel of

St Mary, and was doubtless the spot selected by one of the followers of St Columba, to whom the mission of converting the inhabitants of Lochaber to Christianity had been entrusted. The period of the erection of the first ecclesiastical edifice would therefore be sometime during the sixth century. However this may be, we get no authentic information until a later period, when one "*An gille dubh MacGille Chnamhaich*" ("the black son of the bones"), so called from a curious legend respecting his mysterious origin, erected a church on this spot and dedicated it to Saint Mary, and from that period the place has been known as Kilmallie (or Kilmalie; and sometimes, as in John Speed's map of Scotland dated 1630, Culmally).

The extraordinary story of the parentage of MacGille Chnamhaich is known to all readers of Sir Walter Scott's "Lady of the Lake," and will be found as a note to the fifth stanza of Canto III., which, to save the trouble of reference, I have included in the Appendix.[1] It will be noted that mention is made in this tradition of a place called Unnatt; it should be Annat, and still exists under that name, and is remarkable as being one of several villages in the Highlands with a similar appellation, which they all derive in common from the heathen goddess of victory, Andat or Andate; and it is probable that in Druidical times stones were erected at these places, where the worship of this deity was performed. In the Isle of Skye there still exists one of these stones known as the "*Clach na h-Annait*," clearly showing the origin of the name. The second church of Kilmallie was built by the famous *Ailein MacDhomhnuill Duibh*, XII. chief of Lochiel, commonly known as "*Ailein nan Creach*," to whom reference has been made in a previous chapter. He lived during the fifteenth century, and had in the years 1492 and 1495 procured various charters from the Crown as rewards for "good and faithful service," to unite the whole of his estates into a free barony to be called the "Barony of

[1] Appendix XXVIII.

Lochiell." The village of Banavie is declared the principal messuage. He is said to have formerly possessed the lands of Knoydart in Argyllshire, and the ten merk land of Gleneveiss (Glen Nevis) in Lochaber, with the estate of Mamore in the same country.

Alan was a bold and reckless man, fearing neither God, man, or devil, and so rapacious was he, and so desirous of extending his already immense estates, that he made seven great forays upon the territories of his weaker neighbours, and put all that opposed him to the sword without mercy. Terrible tales are told of his cruelty and oppression, and by many of his victims he was thought to have had dealings with the evil one. For years he was the scourge of the district, but at last advancing age caused him to desist from his wickedness, and he began to experience some feelings of remorse for his sins; and with a view to making his peace with his soul, he decided, by the advice of the witch Gormshuil, to consult the oracle of the "*Tau Ghairm*"[1] ("the Invocation of *Tau*"), and undergo the uncanny ordeal that the ceremony demanded. His first proceeding was to build a small hut on the Corpach Moss, near the river Lochy, to which, accompanied by one faithful follower, he retired to carry out the unholy rites according to the instructions he had received from Gormshuil. Having procured a cat (this animal, so tradition states, was selected for some obscure reason in connection with the Clan Chattan, or "children of the cats"), he ran a spit through the wretched creature, and handed it to his servant to roast alive before a huge fire he had made, while he took up his position before the door of the hut, with sword in hand, to keep off intruders. The cries of the suffering animal, which resounded far and wide, attracted all the cats in the neighbourhood. Cats of all colours, black, white, and grey, poured into the hut,

---

[1] This remarkable superstition was undoubtedly of Eastern origin, a fact which is of considerable interest when we remember that the Scottish Gaels have ever traced their descent from the East, through Gomer, eldest son of Japheth. The *Tau Ghairm* was performed by one of the MacLeans of Mull as late as the beginning of the seventeenth century.

regardless of the vain attempts of Alan to keep them out, and added their voices to the shrieks of their tortured relation. Each cat as it entered exclaimed, " *S' olc an carabh cait sin !* " ("This is bad treatment of a cat!") and Alan replied, "It will not be better just now," and told his servant to keep on turning the spit whatever happened.[1]

All the feline race of Lochaber seemed gathered together under the roof of the hut Alan had erected, and so fierce was their appearance that even the bold spirit of the reckless Cameron chieftain quailed before the angry flashing green eyes that gazed upon him from every side. The din was appalling, and to the frightened servant it seemed as if hell itself had broken lose, and that Satan and all his imps had taken the form of cats. While the noise was at its height, and Alan was expecting every minute to be torn to pieces by the infuriated animals, a gigantic black cat with one eye (*Camdubh*) entered, and after silencing his noisy brethren, turned upon Alan and remonstrated with him for his cruelty, and told him that unless he desisted at once from his present amusement, he would call his brother, "*Cluasan leabhra mo bhrathair*" ("long ears, my brother"), who would tear him limb from limb, and he would never see his Maker's face in mercy. Alan promised he would at once order his servant to cease his cruel employment, if *Camdubh* would tell him how he could obtain forgiveness for his past misdeeds. This *Camdubh* proceeded to do, by informing him that his only chance of securing the salvation of his soul was to build seven churches without delay. Upon this Alan told his follower to loose the cat from the spit, when, with a fearful yell, the whole crowd of cats, headed by their king *Camdubh*, fled helter-

---

[1] The command given by Alan to his attendant took the form of the following couplet, which is still used by Lochaber folk, who are probably quite unaware of its origin, viz.,—

" *Ciod air bith a chi, no' chual thu,*
Cuir mu 'n cuairt an cat."

" Hear you this, or see you that,
Round the spit, and turn the cat."

skelter from the hut and disappeared in the waters of the river Lochy, and the place where this occurred is known to this day as the Cats' Pool.

The result of this night's work was, that Alan erected the seven churches required of him, viz., Kilmallie, Kildonan, Kilcoral (*Kill a Choireil*, near Achluacharach); three dedicated to St Choan, viz., Kilchoan in Knoydart, Arisaig, and Morven; and one called Kilkillen, Loch Laggan.

Some authorities say that Kilmun (the chapel of St Mungo) on Loch Leven was one of the seven.

In the "Memoirs of Sir Ewen Cameron of Lochiel," a more likely story is given, "that *Ailein nan Creach* performed a penance for his crimes, and started on a pilgrimage to Rome; but arriving in Holland, he found himself unable to bear up against the fatigue of so long a journey, and therefore sent one M'Phail, a priest, who was his chaplain and confessor, to doe that job for him with the Pope." This account bears the stamp of truth, and is, besides, strongly characteristic of the man.[1] In addition to the seven churches, Alan Cameron built, or rebuilt, the castle of Tor by the shores of the river Lochy. I say rebuilt, because there is a tradition that a castle stood on the same spot at a much earlier period, and was the residence of Banquo, thane of Lochaber. In proof of this assertion it is only necessary to note the names of the places in the immediate vicinity. "*Meall Bhainbhe*" ("the hill of Banquo") is the hill with the gently rounded summit that rises a short distance away on the west side of the Lochy; "*Dail Bhainbhe*" ("the field of Banquo") is the local name of a field near the castle; and there can be little doubt that the village of Banavie derives its appellation from the same source.

---

[1] Still another tradition is, that *Ailein nan Creach* was presented with a small silver shoe, which was to be put on the left foot of every son born to the chief. This magic shoe fitted all but John Cameron, eldest son of Sir Ewen, whose conduct at Sheriffmuir was not in accordance with the traditions of the clan, a fact which the superstitious did not fail to note. It is said this shoe was lost when Ach-na-carry was burnt by the English soldiers in 1746.

Of the old church of Kilmallie, built by "*Ailein nan Creach*," there is no vestige remaining ; but it may interest some of my readers to know that it stood in the ancient burying-ground, and the site is marked by a low wall which was erected a few years ago. Of the sleeping occupants of this most beautiful God's acre I shall have something to say in a later chapter.

The parish of Kilmallie is of considerable extent, and contains within its boundaries the burgh of Fort William, and the hamlets of North Ballachulish and Onich, Ardgour, Banavie, Blaich, Clovullin, Corpach, Duisky, and Garvan, and, with the sister parish of Kilmonivaig, which comprises the villages of Spean Bridge, Bunroy, and Invergarry, may be said to include the whole of Lochaber.

Adjoining Kilmallie is the small hamlet of Corpach, delightfully situated on the shores of Loch Eil, and immediately facing Ben Nevis, whose majestic outline is nowhere seen to better advantage than from this place. The whole range of enormous mountains, stretching from Glencoe to Ben Nevis, offers a magnificent *coup d'œil* such as Switzerland may equal but can hardly beat. It is strange that this lovely spot should be associated with death, but so it is, the name Corpach meaning literally " the dead," or rather the " field of the dead." The reason for this lugubrious title is due to the fact that, in remote times, the whole of the great forest that covered both shores of Loch Eil was the lair of a ferocious breed of wolves, who, like the tigers of India at the present day, took an annual toll of human life from among the inhabitants of the locality. The dead were interred in the adjoining islands, and hence the place received the name by which it is still known.

A celebrated smith is said to have lived here, and became famous throughout the Highlands for the weapons he forged. Corpach broadswords were among the most cherished treasures of the warlike chieftains of Lochaber, and they were as much coveted as had been the swords of Luno of Lochlin in the days of Fingal. It was at a smithy in Corpach that "*Domhnull nan Ord*" ("Donald of the Hammer"), the son of Stewart of Invernahyle, forged the claymore with which he took a terrible vengeance upon "*Cailein Uaine*" ("Green Colin"), the chief of Dunstaffnage on Loch Etive, the murderer of his father. A long account of this tradition will be found in Sir Walter Scott's "Tales of a Grandfather."

Directly in front of Corpach, on the opposite shore of Loch Eil, is the bay of "*Camus nan Gall*" ("Bay of the Strangers"), backed by the wooded hills of Ardgour. Here the fleet of Argyll anchored during the battle of Inverlochy in 1645, while that wary nobleman watched, from the prow of his great galley, the progress of the fight which proved so disastrous to his clan.

CHAPTER XXX.

THE month of April 1746 was destined to prove a disastrous and fatal month in the annals of the unfortunate House of Stuart. From the time of the ill-advised retreat from Derby, when the great metropolis of London was almost within his grasp, Prince Charles had lost all heart in the great project he had undertaken, at so much personal risk to himself, and which up to that period he had pushed forward with so much vigour and ability. What the consequences of his nearer approach to London would have been it is, of course, impossible to say; but it is not outside the bounds of probability to imagine that the presence of the rightful heir to the crown of Britain among his royal father's subjects, at the head of a small but loyal army, might have induced them to throw off the oppressive yoke of Hanoverian tyranny, and declare their allegiance to king James VIII. (III. of England). Fate, however, decreed otherwise; the die was cast; the golden opportunity had been suffered to pass, and now, cooped up in a remote northern town, the gallant prince awaited with comparative indifference the approach of his inveterate foe, the Duke of Cumberland, who, having vacated his headquarters at Aberdeen on 8th April, was now advancing as rapidly as the nature of the force under his command, and the roads he had to traverse, would allow.

The 14th of the month saw the Elector's army at Nairn, a small town on the Moray Firth, about sixteen miles from Inverness, which they occupied after a slight skirmish with a body of Highlanders under Lord John Drummond. On the evening of the same day Prince Charles marched from Inverness at the head of about six thousand men, and having proceeded as far as Culloden House, four miles from the town, called a halt, and prepared to encamp in the wooded park that surrounded the mansion. Late at night Lochiel arrived from Lochaber with his clan; but Keppoch and his MacDonalds had been detained, and it was feared they would not be in time for the battle which was now hourly expected.

The Keppoch MacDonalds were not the only clan that had failed to put in an appearance. The Frasers, the MacPhersons, the MacGregors, and several other important bodies of Highlanders were among the absentees; but it was known they were mostly, if not all, on the march to join the prince's standard, and it could only be a question of a few hours before they arrived in camp.

The excitement of the warlike preparations that were going on all around him awakened in the mind of Prince Charles something of the enthusiasm he had felt on the memorable 20th August, when his father's banner had been unfurled in Glenfinnan; but he could not forget all that had happened in the eight months that had passed since that eventful day. The zeal he displayed then in the organisation of his small army he exhibited now with the larger force under his command; but repeated disappointments, and the continual anxiety and mental worry caused by the daily quarrels among his officers, produced a feeling of bitter resentment in his heart, and he became at times listless and dejected, as if the presentiment of coming disaster was present in his mind. It is much to the prince's credit that, notwithstanding his own troubles, he did not forget the poor half-starved Highlanders who had left all to follow him, and who now, far from their own homes, were almost perishing with hunger and fatigue. He did what he could to relieve their necessities, and before partaking of his own frugal meal of bread and a little whisky at Culloden House, he gave orders that foraging parties should be sent out, and food collected for the use of his loyal men. The provisions thus procured were sent to Inverness to be cooked, but, before they could be returned to the camp, the great battle had been fought and lost, and the grim hand of death had assuaged the pangs of hunger for ever.

Although " Culloden's fatal day " was productive of terrible consequences to Lochaber and its people, it was not fought within its bounds, and consequently does not come within the compass of this work. I shall therefore merely give an account, as far as I am able, of the individual part played in this last heroic struggle against the might of the disciplined and well-fed English army by those clans who had their abode in that historic district.

As every Scotsman knows, the battle of Culloden, or Drummossie Muir, was fought on 16th April 1746. The action commenced about one o'clock, in the midst of a torrent of rain and sleet, which, unfortunately for the Highland army, blew right in their faces, numbing their limbs and obscuring their vision, so that their leaders could hardly discern the movements of the enemy. By far the greater portion of the prince's force were Lochaber men, Lochiel having 600 men of his clan present, Keppoch 300, the clan Mackintosh, under Alexander MacGillivray of Dunmaglass (*Alasdair Ruadh na Feile*), about 200, and, if the clans of the MacDonalds of Glengarry and Clanranald may be included in this category, another 750 men should be added to the list.

For the first time in the history of Highland warfare, the Camerons found themselves placed on the right of the line, the extreme flank being occupied by the men of Athole. This circumstance, as every reader of the history of the " Forty-Five " is aware, was due to the fatal error of judgment on the part of Lord George Murray, who, regardless of all the military traditions of the Highlanders, insisted that the MacDonalds should waive their pretensions to fight on the right flank, an honourable position the clan had always filled since Robert Bruce had conferred it upon Angus MacDonald, Lord of the Isles, at Bannockburn. Prince Charles, to whom the matter was referred, pleaded ignorance of the question in dispute, and refused to offer an opinion as to its merits ; but as time was precious, he persuaded the several MacDonald chieftains to allow the controversy to stand over for the present, and he would make it his business to adjust the difficulty later. Although the chiefs unwillingly acquiesced in this arrangement, their clansmen were far from satisfied. Their ancestors had always maintained the honour of their clan in every engagement, why were they now to be relegated to a secondary position, when the fate of their king was at stake? The imagined insult rankled in their breasts, and loud and bitter were their protestations of indignation at the unmerited slight. Apart from these natural feelings of wounded pride, the latent superstition in their Celtic nature was awakened by this breaking through of an established custom, and they regarded their altered positions as ill-omened and full of dire possibilities, and, as we know, these prognostications of evil were fully verified. Thus it came about that Lochiel with his Camerons shared the position of honour with the Athole men, and his neighbours the Stewarts of Appin, who were placed on his immediate left, in the front rank of the prince's army.

For some time they stood the galling fire of the English artillery unmoved, although many of their number were wounded and lay in the agonies of death on the heather. The

sight of their dying kinsmen was too much for the fiery
spirits of the Camerons, and before the order to charge
reached them, they fixed their bonnets firmly on their heads,
and giving one terrific shout of vengeance, left their position
in the ranks, and threw themselves with desperate impetuosity
upon the serried ranks of the duke's left flank, which consisted of the two strong regiments of Barrel and Munroe.
With the Camerons came the Athole men, and such was
the force of their onset that the front line of the English
army gave way after a stout resistance, which cost them
about two hundred men killed and wounded. Simultaneously
with the advance of the Camerons (some historians say before),
the Mackintoshes, with MacGillivray of Dunmaglass at their
head, engaged the centre of the duke's position with reckless
courage, regardless of the awful hail of bullets and grape-shot
which mowed them down in scores; madly they rushed on
through smoke and fire, until they joined their comrades in
front of the second line of the English troops. A barrier of
steel, from behind which murderous volleys of musketry fire
were poured incessantly, barred their further progress, and they
fell in heaps in front of the bayonets of Bligh's and Sempil's
regiments. One of the MacGillivrays performed prodigies of
valour, and killed at least twelve of the enemy with his own
claymore. In sheer disregard of danger he advanced a gunshot past the English cannon, but was then surrounded and
cut down. This remarkable man was known as *Iain Mòr
MacGilvra* ("big John MacGillivray") by the Mackintoshes, and
the fame of his intrepidity having reached the ears of the Duke
of Cumberland, he is said to have remarked that he would
have given a large sum of money to have saved his life.[1]
While the right and centre of the Highland army were thus
engaged in mortal combat with their Sassenach foes, the
MacDonalds on the left flank refused to stir from their
position, and remained in apparent indifference to all that
was going on. Neither the fire of the enemy nor the repeated

[1] Letter of Bishop Mackintosh, 1810.

entreaties of the Duke of Perth could induce them to join
in the general onset. One volley they fired into the regiments
immediately in front of them, and then, seeing that the clans
on the other flank were retreating, they turned about and fled
from the pursuing cavalry, without having struck a single blow
on behalf of their prince. With impassioned gestures and voice
broken with emotion, Alexander, chief of Keppoch, besought his
followers to make one last effort to retrieve their honour by a
bold stand against the advancing enemy. His earnest words
were, alas! unheeded, and the retreat became general all along
the line. The brave spirit of the MacDonald chief groaned within
him at the sight of his retreating kinsmen, and in the bitterness of his soul he exclaimed, "My God, have the children of
my tribe forsaken me!" For himself he preferred death to
dishonour, and advanced alone to meet the English soldiers
with his trusty claymore in one hand and a pistol in the other,
determined to strike at least one blow for king and country.
A clansman, Donald Roy MacDonald,[1] moved by the despair-
ing cry of his chief, followed him at a short distance, but he
had not proceeded far when a bullet struck Keppoch, and he
fell to the ground badly wounded, though not mortally.
Running up to the fallen chieftain, Donald entreated him
not to risk his life further, but Keppoch refused to listen,
and staggering to his feet rushed on to certain death. He
had only time to advance a few yards, when he received
another shot which ended his mortal career. Thus, with his
face to the foe, died one of Lochaber's bravest sons, and it is
sad to think that his last moments were embittered by the
knowledge that those upon whom he had relied to support
the honour of his race had deserted him in the hour of
peril.

There are many traditions in Lochaber concerning the
Keppoch chieftains, who occupy, with the Camerons, a prominent place in the history of that country. Some of my

---

[1] Mrs MacDonell of Keppoch thinks this must have been the chieftain's brother
already referred to.

readers may have come across a very curious book, entitled
" A Keppoch Song," by John Paul MacDonald, private teacher
in Stonehaven, and published in the year 1815 at Montrose.
It was written with the object of bringing the claims of one
of the family to the forfeited estates in Lochaber before
George III., with a view to their restoration. It contains a
metrical history of the Keppoch MacDonalds from the
earliest times. The verse is execrable but quaint, and there
are many notes of considerable value to the historian and
antiquarian. It is here we find the story of "Keppoch's
Candlesticks."

Keppoch,[1] having occasion to visit England, was invited to
the mansion of a nobleman of great wealth, who was possessed
of a magnificent service of plate, which was somewhat ostentatiously displayed on the dinner-table. Among the various
articles was a fine pair of silver candlesticks, which attracted
the attention of the guests and evoked their enthusiastic
admiration. Keppoch, somewhat annoyed at certain whispered
remarks as to the proverbial poverty of the Scots which met
his ears, affected utter indifference to the lavish praise that
was bestowed on the candlesticks from all sides, and hinted
that he could produce a better pair in his Highland home.
This was too much for the equanimity of the assembled
Englishmen, who regarded the Highlanders as poor half-
savage creatures, who dwelt in hovels and lived on porridge,
in a land as little known as Kamtschatka is now. Bets for
large amounts were freely offered that he could not do as he
said, and, to the surprise of all, Keppoch accepted the wager,
which amounted to a large sum of money; and not only did
this, but invited two of the gentlemen present to his house in
Lochaber to decide who should be the winner.

After a few weeks had elapsed, the two Englishmen set out
for Lochaber, and upon arrival proceeded to the house of the

---

[1] The chieftain of whom this story is told was probably Alexander, tenth chief
of Keppoch, known as "*Alasdair nan Cleas*," on account of his sleight-of-hand
tricks. He ruled the clan from about 1591 to 1640 A.D.

MacDonald chieftain.   Instead of the castle they had expected
to find, they saw only a large, barn-like structure, where they
were told Keppoch dwelt.   Upon entering this rude dwelling
they were met by Keppoch himself, who received his guests
with all the warmth of Highland hospitality, and having welcomed them to his table, set before them a profusion of the
most delicate food that the country could produce.   Immense
salmon fresh from the Lochy or Spean, great haunches of
venison from the forests of Glen Roy, grouse, blackcock, caper-
cailzie, ptarmigan, and joints of the delicious Highland mutton,
graced the rough deal board which served for a table.   Nor
was good wine and usquebaugh wanting to cheer the hearts
of the Sassenach strangers.   Provisions of all kinds covered
the table; but the vaunted candlesticks were conspicuous by
their absence.   Keppoch, noting the unspoken inquiry of his
guests, informed them that the subject of the wager would
shortly appear; and, on a given signal, two gigantic Highlanders, clad in their picturesque garb of kilt and plaid,
entered, bearing enormous torches of resinous pine wood, and
marching with stately pace round the table, placed themselves
one on each side of their chief.   The Englishmen admitted
that their host had fairly won the bet; but Keppoch, with
that free-handed generosity which distinguished him, refused
to accept the money he was entitled to, and explained that
the amusement he had derived from the success of the ruse
he had planned, and the pleasure he had experienced from
their visit, more than recompensed him.   His guests stayed
some days longer, and returned to their homes in the south
delighted at the hospitality they had received among the
mountains of Lochaber.   This story has been immortalised
by the splendid painting of the late John Pettie, R.A.

The author of "A Keppoch Song" mentions a strange
tradition in connection with the Mackintosh family, which is
worth recording as an instance of the superstition of the
Highlanders.

The successor of the Mackintosh who fought against

Keppoch at Mulroy renewed that chieftain's grant to the estates. This overture of peace was satisfactory to Keppoch, and he offered, in order that the friendly feeling might be strengthened, to wed his son to one of the near female relatives of Mackintosh. This proposal was rejected with scorn by Mackintosh in insulting terms; and the wrath of Keppoch being aroused, he prophesied that neither the chief who had insulted him, or any future one, should beget an heir,—a prophecy which, the writer remarks, " remained correct until the present time"; and he invokes his muse with the following result :—

> " Keppoch th' peace with Toshach (Mackintosh) to keep,
> That discord may for ever sleep,
> Craves Toshach t' give his son a wife,
> And begin a new scene of life ;
> But he th' offer treats with disdain,
> Hence sterility with him doth remain." [1]

Keppoch's barn, which has been mentioned as the place to which the English guests were invited, was the largest in the Western Highlands, and upon all extraordinary occasions was used as a place of assembly and feasting, " the humble representative of the once great Lord of the Isles having no castle in which to receive his numerous descendants and vassals."

The Camerons and the Mackintoshes having, with the Frasers, the Athole men, the MacLeans, and the Stewarts of Appin, borne the brunt of the fighting, suffered severe losses in consequence, nearly the whole of their leaders and front-rank men being slain. Lochiel narrowly escaped the fate of Keppoch, for, while charging the enemy at the head of his

---

[1] This curious story is partially confirmed in the MS. history of the chief of Keppoch, kindly lent me by Miss MacDonell of Keppoch. The circumstances and date of the prophecy are, however, referred to the sixteenth century, when Raonuill Mòr was chief of the clan. He had married a sister of Mackintosh, but when she learnt, after her husband's execution at Elgin in 1547, that his capture, and consequently his death, was due to her brother's treachery, she uttered the curse which tradition states has remained with the Mackintosh family ever since.

clan, he was struck in both ankles by a discharge of grape-shot from the English cannon while in the act of drawing his sword. Fortunately his brother, Dr Archibald Cameron, and his uncle, Ludovick Cameron of Torcastle, who acted as his major, were close at hand. Raising the fallen chief in their arms, they carried him from the field, and, placing him on horseback, conveyed him to Ach-na-carry :—

> " Lochiel, Lochiel, my brave Lochiel,
>   Beware o' Cumberland, my dearie !
>   Culloden field this day will seal
>   The fate o' Scotland's ain Prince Charlie.

> " The Highland clans nae mair are seen
>   To fight for him wha ne'er was eerie,
>   They fallen are on yon red field,
>   An' trampled doun for liking Charlie."

So ran an old ballad of the period ; and true indeed it was that Culloden's field sealed the fate, not only of the gallant prince himself, but of the royal house of Stuart, of which he was so worthy a scion. From that disastrous April day the historic family, that for centuries had ruled the destinies of Scotland, and later of the whole of Britain, ceased to exist as a power in the land, and the prince, from whom so much had been expected by the loyal Jacobites, became, like Ishmael of old, a wanderer and outcast in the land of his fathers.

CHAPTER XXXI.

I WILL spare my readers a description of the awful carnage that ensued after the battle by the victorious English soldiery, who were encouraged in their murderous task by the brutal duke and the ferocious Hawley. Suffice it to say, that the deeds that were done that day branded for ever the brow of Cumberland with disgrace and infamy. There can be no excuse, no palliation for the savage butchery of the poor defenceless wretches, who, sorely wounded and without arms, fled along the road to Inverness, or who had fallen on the field of battle, and crawled into places of fancied security among the bushes. The mind recoils from the enormities committed by civilised (?) men on this occasion; and while reading the details given by historians of these barbarous atrocities, it is hard to realise that we are not perusing an account of some frightful orgie of bloodthirsty savages. For his share in the slaughter the duke received a vote of thanks from parliament, and blood-money to the extent of £25,000 per annum, in addition to his already large income; but all this enormous wealth could not prevent the infamy which will ever be attached to his name. As "the Butcher" he will always be known while the history of that terrible day remains in the traditions of our people.

Among the prisoners of note taken after Culloden was the brave Lady ("Colonel") Anne Mackintosh, who was in Inverness when the victorious army entered it. Ray says: "The Ladies, after Tea, were preparing to dress for a Ball in the Evening, expecting the Rebels had gain'd a Victory; but the King's Red-Coats were so rude as to interrupt them, and lead them up a Dance they did not expect"; a vulgarly expressed, but probably correct account of what happened. Lady Mackintosh was conveyed to London, where she was afterwards released; and there is a story that while in that city Cumberland gave a ball to which she was invited. During the evening he requested her to dance with him to the tune of "Up and waur them a', Willie." Accepting his offered hand, she trod the measure with some reluctance, and upon its conclusion said, that having danced to his tune, would he favour her by dancing to one she should select? This request, coming from so fair a dame, he could not refuse, and the ill-assorted couple were soon gyrating to the strains of "The auld Stuarts back agen," a tune hateful to Whig ears.

Prince Charles witnessed the defeat of his army from a small eminence in rear of the position he had selected for withstanding the attack of the duke's forces, and it required all the powers of persuasion possessed by his officers to prevent him risking his life by a reckless attempt to rally the retreating Highlanders. Better perhaps had he been allowed to do so, for had he died sword in hand at the head of his army, his admirers would have been spared the painful history of his maturer years, when a long life of disappointments and blighted hopes had rendered him morose and melancholy, and, what was far worse, had produced in him habits of intemperance which were degrading in their ultimate consequences.

He was led from the field by General O'Sullivan, who, seeing the day was hopelessly lost, seized the bridle of the prince's horse and hurried him away in the direction of Loch Ness. About sunset the party arrived at Gortuleg, the residence of Thomas Fraser, Lord Lovat's steward. His lordship was himself present on this occasion, and is said to have received the prince with expressions of sincere loyalty and affection, and urged him not to abandon his enterprise, reminding him of his "great ancestor Robert Bruce, who lost eleven battles and won Scotland by the twelfth." Not deeming it safe to remain at Gortuleg for the night, Prince Charles merely partook of a hasty meal, and, after changing his habiliments, rode rapidly on with a small party of his officers past Fort Augustus, which was then in ruins, to Invergarry, the castle of MacDonald of Glengarry, on the shores of Loch Oich, arriving there about four o'clock in the morning of 17th April.

Thus, after a campaign of eight months' duration, the prince found himself once more in loyal Lochaber; but how different were his circumstances now to what they had been on 27th August 1745, when he last visited Invergarry at the head of an army of eighteen hundred men, and been received by Glengarry with the lavish hospitality common to the Highlands. Where were all the devoted men who had followed him from the Lochaber glens, from the green hills of Appin, from the wilds of Badenoch, from dark Glencoe,

and the fir-clad braes of Athole? Ay! where were they now?
Lying stark and bloody on Drummossie's fatal moor, hacked
and mutilated by Sassenach butchers; torn limb from limb
by English grape-shot; their ghastly features distorted beyond
all recognition, with staring eyes fixed upon the sky above,
as if invoking heaven itself to avenge their brutal murder.
These were the dead, where were the living? Hiding in
caves among their native glens, into which they had crawled,
dragging their wounded limbs mile after mile over rough mountain paths, and suffering uncomplainingly the most intense
agony; skulking in the trackless wilds of the great forests of
Mamore or Loch Eil, with only the red-deer as companions, or
among the ruins of some disused stronghold of a dead and
gone chieftain, where the owl and the night-hawk made the
night hideous with their screams. Many poor stricken
creatures had toiled painfully up steep mountains, and died
from their wounds among the boulders, where years afterwards a few bleached bones told to a future, and, thank
God, a more humane generation, the mute story of their
sufferings.

And now Prince Charles himself was to drain the bitter
cup of misfortune to the dregs, and endure in silence all the
agony of mind and fatigue of body that his naturally buoyant
and sanguine temperament rendered all the more poignant.
"*Aujourd'hui roi, demain rien,*" the bold scheme had failed,
the crown of his ancestors had slipped phantom-like from his
grasp, and the prince of yesterday, the hero of a thousand
gallant Highland hearts, was now a fugitive fleeing for his life
before his merciless antagonist.

> "On hills that are by right his ain,
>   He roams a lonely stranger,
> On ilka hand he's pressed by want,
>   On ilka side by danger.
> Yestreen I met him in a glen,
>   My heart near bursted fairly,
> For sadly changed indeed was he—
>   Oh! wae's me for Prince Charlie!"

The bare walls of Invergarry, deserted by its owner, its rooms destitute of furniture, its aumrie empty of provisions, afforded but a poor shelter for a king's son; but had he known what was to come later, its tenantless chambers and draughty corridors would have been deemed magnificent. Tired and worn out with hunger and the physical exertion of the forty-mile ride from Culloden, Prince Charles and his party, upon entering the castle, threw themselves upon the uncarpeted floor in their travel-stained garments, and slept soundly until mid-day. It was fortunate for the famished wayfarers that the river Garry, famous then as it is now as being the earliest salmon river in Scotland, flowed in close proximity to their place of refuge, and yielded them a substantial meal, in the shape of two fine fish, which were providentially captured by the Highland guide, Edward Burke, who had conducted the fugitives from the battle-field. Having finished their much-needed repast, it was decided that the prince, with O'Sullivan, O'Neil, and Burke, should seek the shelter of the dense forest that clothed the shores of Loch Arkaig, while the remainder of the party fled in a contrary direction. Before setting out, Prince Charles disguised himself as well as he could by donning some of the clothing of his guide, a wise precaution, when it is considered that they were likely to be intercepted by some of the Fort William garrison, who were now probably cognisant of the result of the battle, and would be on the look-out for fugitives. Avoiding the main roads, the prince and his attendants pursued their course by the most unfrequented paths of the beautiful Glen Garry, and striking across country, arrived about nine o'clock at night at the house of Donald Cameron of Glen Pean, near the head of Loch Arkaig, in the territory of Lochiel. Here they spent the night of the 17th, and on the following morning proceeded farther westward to a small farmhouse at Meoble, where comfortable quarters and good food were obtained.

To follow the wanderings of this unhappy prince and his devoted companions among the islands of the west coast would be to undertake a congenial, but altogether superfluous task in connection with a work professing to deal only with Lochaber.

The work of recording this romantic chapter in the career of Prince Charles has been ably and intelligently done by Robert Chambers in his "History of the Rebellion of 1745-46," a most exhaustive history of that eventful period, and, on the whole, written with a just impartiality which renders it all the more valuable. While the hope of the Jacobite party was suffering all the hardships which an unkind fate had meted out to him, the scattered remnants of the Highland army were gradually making their way into Lochaber, whither most of their leaders had fled. Lochiel, notwithstanding his crippled condition, was far from being subdued: no one knew better than he the desperate state they were in, and that it was only a question of a few weeks, possibly only a few days, before the Duke of Cumberland would follow up his victory by a determined effort to dislodge the remaining supporters of the fallen dynasty from their ancestral strongholds among the mountains of Lochaber. No mercy could be expected at the hands of the "butcher of Culloden"; intoxicated with blood, he would fall upon the now helpless Highlanders and commence a *bellum intercinum* which would render the land desolate. The only way of preventing such a disaster was by making a united stand against the invading force.

Lochiel was greatly encouraged by the welcome arrival of £38,000 sterling in louis d'ors, which had been brought to Borrodale on the west coast by two French ships of war. This considerable sum of money had been placed in charge of Dr Cameron and Sir Thomas Sheridan, and was conveyed by them to Callich, on the north side of Loch Arkaig, where it appears to have been handed over to Secretary Murray. The sinews of war having thus been provided, Lochiel invited all the proscribed chiefs that were within hail to meet him at Callich (or Murlaggan) on 8th May, to discuss plans for a continuance of the war, which he was sanguine enough to think could now be carried on successfully. On the day appointed for the gathering, several important chieftains put in an appearance. Lochiel and his brother, Dr Archibald Cameron, were of course present. Young Clanranald, Mac-Donald of Barrisdale, MacDonald of Lochgarry, MacDonald, nephew of Keppoch, John Roy Stewart, Glenbucket, the Laird of MacKinnon, Alexander MacLeod of Neuck, Major Kennedy, Captain MacNab, and last, but not least, the crafty Lord Lovat, who, by some accidental circumstances, found himself one of the party.

Having reviewed the position of affairs, the whole of those assembled signed an agreement by which they bound them-selves to afford each other mutual support; and the chiefs promised to proceed at once to their respective estates and raise every available man for the prince's service, and assemble them at Ach-na-carry on the 15th of the month.

The clans who had not sent representatives to the meeting were to be immediately informed of the resolution that had been made, so that they might not fail to join the others on the day fixed for the general muster. Secretary Murray, assisted by one of his clerks, Charles Stewart, then distributed some of the money among the chiefs to assist them in raising their men, and the party dispersed to their various hiding-places.

While the leaders of the prince's army were thus engaged in concerting measures for carrying on the campaign, Lord Loudoun, who was in command of the newly formed High-land militia at Inverness,[1] received orders from the Duke of Cumberland to march into Lochaber with seventeen hundred men and take up his quarters at Fort Augustus, in order to stamp out the dying embers of the rebellion, and, if possible, secure the person of Prince Charles, who was believed to be lurking among the fastnesses of that district. This action on

[1] Lord Loudoun was in the Isle of Skye, with an army of thirteen hundred men, when he received the duke's orders to proceed to Lochaber.

the part of Lord Loudoun effectually prevented the premeditated rising on the part of the Jacobite clans, and nearly
resulted in the capture of Lochiel, who, mistaking a party of
the militia for Barrisdale's men, advanced to welcome them,
but being informed of his error by one of his clan, had just
time to jump into a boat and row to the other side of Loch
Arkaig and so escape.

Lochaber being now invested with the troops of the
English Government, it was thought advisable to place the
French gold in a place of security, and Secretary Murray,
assisted by Dr Cameron, Alexander MacLeod of Neuck, Sir
Stewart Threipland, and Major Kennedy, having placed
15,000 louis d'ors in three parcels, proceeded to the head of
Loch Arkaig, and at a spot opposite Callich, where a small
burn runs down the hillside, they deposited one of the
precious parcels under a boulder in the stream ; the other two
being buried in holes a short distance off. A further sum of
£12,000 was taken from Ach-na-carry a few days later, upon
receipt of intelligence that an attack upon the place was
meditated by a detachment from Fort Augustus, and deposited,
under cover of night, in a hole that was dug by Dr Cameron
and MacLeod of Neuck, near the foot of the loch. The hiding-
place of this treasure still remains an unsolved mystery.

Here is a story worthy the attention of our writers of fiction.
"The Mystery of the Prince's Gold" would make a good title
for a tale of thrilling interest, and would, moreover, possess the
advantage of being founded on actual fact. Lochaber folk still
have a saying which has a distinct reference to the buried
money, and which seems to imply that some of their ancestors
knew more about the matter than they cared to tell. When
a man acquires wealth by means which are unknown to his
neighbours, he is said to have discovered "*Sporrain ghobhlach
do dh'or a Phrionnsa*," i.e., "forked purses of the prince's gold."

Having accomplished the task of hiding the treasure, Dr
Cameron and MacLeod of Neuck returned to Ach-na-carry,
and early on the following morning the whole party, headed

by Lochiel on horseback, quitted the shores of Loch Arkaig, and proceeded by a circuitous route into Appin, and from thence into Badenoch, where Lochiel took up his abode in a small hut at Mellaneuir, near Loch Ericht, with his kinsman Cluny MacPherson, young MacPherson of Breakachie, and two or three clansmen, who acted as servants and kept a faithful watch over their chiefs.

CHAPTER XXXII.

WHILE Lochiel was thus making good his escape, the Duke of Cumberland, annoyed at the reluctance on the part of the Highlanders to deliver up their arms and submit their persons to his clemency, resolved to march with his army into Lochaber, and put the inhabitants who had dared to resist his authority to the sword. Leaving Inverness on the 23rd of May, he reached Fort Augustus on the following day, and pitched his camp near the ruins of that once important place. And now commenced a reign of terror such as would have disgraced a Nero. Hell itself was let loose among the beautiful glens and fir-clad hills of this land of heroes. The smoke of hundreds of burning dwellings ascended into the blue vault of heaven, so that the sun itself was obscured, and darkness, like a pall, hung over the fair country of Lochaber. The ancient dwellings of the proscribed chiefs were the first to feed the flames kindled by the English incendiaries. Ach-na-carry, the home of the gentle Lochiel; Invergarry Castle, the ancestral seat of the MacDonalds of Glengarry; the houses of gallant Keppoch, Cluny, Kinlochmoidart, Glengyle, and Ardshiel were destroyed, after being plundered of their contents by the rapacious soldiery.[1]

---

[1] Among the houses plundered by the English soldiery after Culloden was the old house of Glen Nevis, but by the timely flight of Mrs Cameron of Glen Nevis, with all the portable property she could lay hands upon, the robbers did not get much for their pains. The more bulky valuables which could not be conveniently carried away, including all the silver-plate and china, were buried deep outside the

Not content with this holocaust, the invaders next turned their malign attentions to the humble shielings of the poor Highlanders, many of whom had not even been present at Culloden, and had taken no active part in the campaign. With brutal disregard of the commonest feelings of humanity, the soldiers set fire to the huts and barns, and murdered the inmates with every species of fiendish ingenuity. One instance is recorded of a whole family being shut up in a barn and burnt to death, for no apparent reason other than the wanton cruelty of their inhuman enemies. Other inoffensive men, who had offered no resistance and who carried no arms, were shot down upon the hillsides or in their native glens, and their wives and children subjected to all kinds of nameless outrages by the licentious troops.

So far from endeavouring to put a stop to these excesses, the duke and his officers openly encouraged them, and the vicinity of the English camp became a veritable pandemonium. Revolting scenes of gross indecency were of daily occurrence, and formed the chief amusement of libertine officers and vicious men. Races of a disgusting character were instituted, in which semi-nude women took part, riding like men on bare-backed horses, and exposed to the coarse jokes and filthy gestures of the drunken soldiery. These disgraceful doings are thus described by Ray, who attempts to excuse them on the ground that the troops were suffering from melancholia and needed entertainment :—" This sad state of things," he says, " might have been still worse, had it not been for the Duke's Presence, which afforded Pleasure to every Soldier as often

garden wall. Mrs Cameron, with her infant son, remained hidden in "*Uamh Shomhairle*" ("Samuel's Cave") for some days, but were at last discovered by a body of soldiers, who had been amusing themselves by burning and destroying the houses in the glen. One of these ruffians, noticing that she had something hidden under her plaid, which was fastened by a silver brooch, attempted to grasp it, and upon the lady resisting, he drew his weapon and cut open the plaid, disclosing the baby nestling by its mother's breast. Finding no treasure, the soldiers departed with the brooch and plaid, and left Mrs Cameron to make her way back to her ruined dwelling. The child had been wounded in the neck by the sword thrust, and bore the scar of the wound until he died. He became the father of Mrs MacDonald of Achtriachtan, in whose family the silver-plate is still preserved.

as they beheld him; and to divert their Melancholy, his Royal Highness and Officers frequently gave Money to be run for by Highland Horses sometimes without Saddles or Bridles; both Men and Women riding: Here were also many Foot Races, perform'd by both Sexes, which afforded many Droll Scenes. It was necessary to entertain Life in this Manner, otherwise the People were in Danger of being affected with hypocondrical Melancholy."

The fulsome flattery of this writer is nauseating in the extreme, and I only quote from his writings to give my readers some idea of the lengths to which the duke's obsequious parasites could go. Some interest attaches to Ray's " History " from the fact that he was present as a volunteer throughout the whole campaign, and gives an account of those historical events which came under his own observation; the work is, however, on the whole, unreliable and full of flagrant errors.

While at Fort Augustus, the Duke of Cumberland expressed a wish to visit the neighbouring garrison at Fort William, and compliment the officers and men for their defence of the place during the recent siege. On 30th May the wish was carried into effect, and at three o'clock in the morning of that day the duke left Fort Augustus, with an escort of one hundred men of Kingston's horse, and reached Fort William a little before nine. Having partaken of some refreshment, the duke held an informal levee, at which the officers of the garrison were presented. As a reward for their services during the investment of the fort by the force under Brigadier Stapleton, they received the honour of kissing the ducal hand ; and after listening to the congratulations of the commander-in-chief, they were ordered to acquaint the private men that he gave them thanks for their good behaviour on that occasion. After a close inspection of the barracks and fortifications, the duke departed for his camp at Fort Augustus, where he arrived before nightfall. On the following day Houghton's battalion marched into Fort William to relieve the defenders, who were mostly composed of men of Guise's regiment.

Shortly after the new garrison had settled down in their quarters, a tragic incident occurred at the fort, through the criminal carelessness of the officer in command. In the absence of the governor, the control of the garrison was vested in a major of Houghton's regiment, who, like most army men of his time, indulged freely in the bottle. A free pardon having been offered by the English Government to all those of the lower classes who would deliver up their arms, many poor hunted Highlanders availed themselves of the opportunity to make their peace with the enemy, and Fort William, being in the centre of the disaffected district, it was selected by large numbers of the fugitives as the most convenient place for tendering their submission. Late one night, while the major and his brother officers were engaged in a drinking bout, the sergeant on duty entered the room and informed the major that three men were brought in with their arms—what should be done with them? "Why, hang them!" shouted the intoxicated officer, enraged at the interruption. The sergeant immediately retired to carry out the barbarous order, and, before an hour had elapsed, the unfortunate Highlanders suffered an ignominious death. Fuddled with the fumes of the wine he had drunk, the major thought no more of the matter, and retired to rest without so much as a pang of remorse for the men he had doomed to die. In the morning he rose from his bed, and, looking out of the window as was his wont, saw with some surprise the bodies of three men dangling from one of the beams of a mill a short distance off. Calling his servant, he demanded an explanation of the ghastly sight, and was horrified to find, when the details of the tragedy had been explained to him, that he, and he alone, was responsible for the awful crime which had hurried three fellow-men into the presence of their Maker. It is said that this intelligence threw him into a profound and lasting melancholy.

This story is culled from the very interesting " Letters from the Mountains," written by Mrs Grant of Laggan about the year 1773. She was the wife of the chaplain to the forces at Fort Augustus, and during her residence in the Highlands collected a vast amount of information relating to Celtic tradition, and having mastered the Gaelic, wrote many beautiful poems in that expressive language. Referring to the story just related, she says: "My father, though of all Whigs the bluest, speaks with horror of the transaction, and says he saw a very pretty young widow, whose father, brother, and husband had been the sufferers." It was some such bereaved woman as this that Cunningham had in mind when he wrote—

"O dreary laneliness is now
'Mang ruined hamlets smoking !
Yet the new-made widow sits and sings,
While her sweet babe she's rocking.

"On Darien think, on dowie Glencoe,
On Murray, traitor ! coward !
On Cumberland's blood-blushing hands,
And think on Charlie Stuart."

Sad indeed was the lot of that unhappy prince, as, with his few devoted followers, he fled before his merciless pursuers like a hunted deer, hiding in wretched hovels that would have been despised by the poorest wayfarer ; skulking in caves by the sea-shore or amid the desolate recesses of some uninhabited glen ; exposed to the inclemency of the weather on bleak hillsides, with scarce sufficient clothing to cover his tired limbs and shelter his delicately-nurtured body from the biting easterly winds which prevail during the spring months in the regions of the north ; enduring the pangs of hunger with uncomplaining stoicism and unselfish consideration for those who suffered with him, and offering, through all his misfortunes, an example of princely heroism that gained for him the regard of all those with whom he was brought in contact.

The old adage that "Adversity makes strange bedfellows" was never more truly exemplified than in the case of Prince Charles during this period of his life, and might be varied with equal truth to "Adversity makes unexpected friends."

Certain it is, that during the whole of his wanderings among the Highlands and Isles, notwithstanding the immense reward (£30,000) offered for his capture, the royal fugitive discovered that, beneath the rough and uncouth exterior of the poor uncultivated mountaineers with whom his lot was cast, there beat hearts true as steel, that no reward could tempt from the path of duty, that no bribe could turn from loyal allegiance to the prince they loved. Think what one tithe of such a sum of money would have meant to these poor Highlanders, who hardly knew what golden guineas were like. With it they could have purchased land, cattle, boats, and become great men in the land of their fathers; no more toil, no more privations; a comfortable croft, or well-stocked farm, full byres, and sufficiency of meal and usquebaugh to comfort the inner man during the long months of winter. These and many more things dear to the Highland heart would come to the man who spoke the word that betrayed his prince. Thank God! for the lasting honour of the Highlanders of the '45, that word was never uttered. There was no Judas among these hardy sons of the north to accept the blood-money of the usurper of Britain's throne, no false-hearted traitor to disgrace his name and race by divulging the secret of the prince's hiding-place to the "butcher" of Culloden.[1]

Among these devoted adherents of Prince Charles, who attended to his wants and shared his hardships and dangers, the name of Edward Burke, the Edinburgh sedan-carrier, who guided him from the fatal field of Culloden, and of the faithful old Donald MacLeod of Gualtergill, who piloted him across the dangerous current of the Sound of Sleat and the

[1] Since these words were written, Mr Andrew Lang, raking among the musty Stuart papers, has discovered "Pickle the Spy," and with his characteristic, but quite unaccountable eagerness to fasten any charge of treachery upon the Jacobite chiefs of the '45, has endeavoured to identify Alasdair MacDonell, eldest son of John MacDonell, XII. of Glengarry, as the traitor. I have had no time to examine the evidence carefully, but whether Mr Lang's assumption is true or not, the accuracy of my statement is not affected; for the historical fact remains, that notwithstanding the immense reward offered for the prince's capture, no one could be found to betray the secret of his hiding-place.

tempestuous Minch to the island of Benbecula, and afterwards
assisted the prince to escape the clutches of the English
man-of-war off the coast of Harris, should not be forgotten.
These men were real heroes, although the part they played
in securing their prince's safety has been somewhat obscured
by the romantic and self-sacrificing devotion of the brave
girl whose name will always be associated with the history
of Bonnie Prince Charlie. There is little doubt that had it
not been for the cool presence of mind displayed by Flora
MacDonald during the time the prince was hiding in Skye,
and the clever stratagem by which she transformed a king's
son into an Irish serving-maid, his capture would have been
effected by the blood-hounds of Cumberland, and one more
victim would have been sent to the shambles of Tower Hill
or Kennington Common.

CHAPTER XXXIII.

AFTER many hairbreadth escapes and thrilling adventures by
land and sea, the gallant prince once again sought a sanctuary
among those beautiful Lochaber glens where, less than twelve
months before, he had been received with shouts of welcome
from lips now silent beneath the blood-stained heather of
Drummossie. On July the 23rd, Prince Charles, attended by
Glenaladale, Lieutenant John MacDonald, and John MacDonald
of Borodale, arrived in Lochiel's country, and having despatched
Lieutenant MacDonald with instructions to ascend the mountain of Sgòr-nan-Coireachan, which overlooked the head of
Loch Arkaig, and gain, if possible, some information as to
the movements of the English troops, the prince with the
other chiefs climbed to the summit of a hill near Glenfinnan,
known as Fraoch Bheinn, with the same purpose. From this
elevation the surrounding country was clearly visible, and
Glenaladale noticed with some surprise a large drove of
cattle moving rapidly along the road at the base of the

mountain, while a number of men were running in the same direction, as if fleeing from an enemy. On inquiring the reason of the commotion, he received the alarming intelligence that the redcoats were at Kinlocharkaig, a few miles off, whither they had come to intercept the prince.

This news caused an alteration in the plans of the fugitive party, and Glenaladale immediately sent word to apprise Lieutenant MacDonald of the danger he was in, and asked him to return at once. He also sent a messenger to Donald Cameron of Glen Pean to inform him of the prince's arrival in Lochaber, and requested his good offices to guide him to a place of security.

During the time they were awaiting the return of the messengers with anxious hearts and empty stomachs, the wife of one of Glenaladale's tenants, having by some chance discovered that her landlord was near at hand and lacked food, set out for Fraoch Bheinn, where she had been told he would be found, with a pail of new milk, which her kind heart told her would be welcome to the tired chief. Prince Charles, seeing the woman approach, became somewhat alarmed, as he feared recognition. Hastily taking a handkerchief from his pocket, he tied it round his head, to convey the idea that he was suffering from headache. This ruse, and the tattered condition of his garments, gave him the appearance of a servant, and no suspicion of his rank was aroused in the mind of the charitable dame. The assumed character of the prince prevented Glenaladale from offering him some milk before he partook of it himself, and he endeavoured to persuade his garrulous friend to leave the pail in his possession, which at last she reluctantly did, and Prince Charles was then able to indulge in his humble meal without fear of detection.[1]

In the course of the day the man who had been despatched to the house of Glenpean returned with the alarming news that a large body of the Argyll militia, about a hundred strong, were advancing along the road at the foot of the hill upon

[1] Appendix XXIX.

which they now stood, with the evident intention of ascending it. To have waited for the arrival of Glenpean would have been to risk almost certain capture, and it was therefore decided by the prince and his attendants to make good their retreat while there was yet time. Hastily descending the hill, they proceeded cautiously through the trackless wilds of the braes of Loch Arkaig, where, by a stroke of good fortune, they fell in with Donald Cameron of Glen Pean, who was on his way to meet the prince. He had thoughtfully provided himself with all the food he could lay hands upon, and although it amounted altogether only to a few measures of oatmeal and a small quantity of butter, it was nevertheless of great service to the famished travellers, to whom even such meagre fare as this was a rarity.

Glenpean was a valuable addition to the party, as, from his intimate acquaintance with the district, he was able to take them by the most unfrequented tracks, that to anyone but himself would have been found impassable. A native of Lochaber, he knew every hill, every mountain, every glen, and almost every sheep-track in the land of his birth, and he was now able to put his knowledge to some advantage. Constituting himself as guide, he conducted his unlucky prince and his devoted friends by a safe but circuitous route, which took them all night to traverse, to the summit of a mountain known as Mam-nan-Callum, near Loch Arkaig, from whence they were able to discern the camp of the militia, which was about a mile off. As this place had been searched the day previously, a circumstance which had influenced Glenpean in selecting it as a safe retreat, it was not thought likely that any further attempt would be made to explore it, and the foot-sore and fatigued wanderers were able to take the rest they so much needed without fear of disturbance. Here the prince and his followers remained until the morning of 25th July, when, having eaten their slender stock of provisions, they were compelled to retire in the direction of the west coast, where it was hoped they might fall in with some of the Highlanders who had fled with their cattle from their farms on the approach of the redcoats.

It is remarkable that, notwithstanding the inhuman atrocities that were perpetrated by the English troops in Lochaber after Culloden, there is only one[1] authenticated instance of personal revenge being taken by the injured peasantry upon their brutal oppressors. The local account, which I believe is the true one, differs slightly from the usually received version, and is as follows:—When the order had gone out from the duke's camp at Fort Augustus that any Highlander found carrying arms would be condemned to instant death, many of those against whom this severe and cruel edict was directed went with their weapons to one or other of the detached garrisons to deliver them up to the officer in charge. Among those who decided to accept the arbitrary terms offered by Cumberland was Dugald Roy Cameron, one of Lochiel's tenants, who, not feeling disposed to abase himself before the jeering Sassenachs, sent his son, a lad of sixteen years of age, to give up his musket to the officer in command of the troops, who were stationed near Ach-na-carry. The poor lad, on reaching the camp, was received with every species of insult from the soldiers, and upon proceeding to lay down his weapon, he was instantly seized by the blood-thirsty wretches, bound to a tree, and shot dead by the commanding officer's own hand.[2] When the news of his son's cruel murder reached the ears of Dugald Cameron, he vowed never to rest until he had slain the inhuman monster

[1] Since writing the above, I am reminded of a second instance of retaliation which took place at Appin, mentioned by Dr Alexander Stewart ("Nether Lochaber"). It was the act of a young Highland woman, whose cow had been wantonly shot by an English sergeant and herself abused. Whilst trying to escape from her persecutor she picked up a stone, and throwing it with considerable force, struck the soldier on the head, and he died from the effects of the blow the same night. His body was buried at Airds, but it was afterwards exhumed by the exasperated Highlanders and thrown into the sea. The brother of *Silas Nic-Cholla* (this was the girl's name) flayed the skin from the arm of the corpse, and, after subjecting it to a tanning process, made a dirk sheath with it. This has been seen and handled by Dr Stewart.

[2] The officer who perpetrated this dastardly outrage was Captain Grant of Cnoc-ceanach.

who had committed the atrocious crime; and having heard that
he always rode a white horse, and could thus be distinguished
from the other officers, Cameron procured another musket, and
lay in ambush for the murderer among the dense thickets
that line the roadsides near Ach-na-carry.   For some weeks
the bereaved father waited for his victim, till at length a day
arrived when, being in the vicinity of the "*Mile Dubh*" ("Dark
Mile"), an avenue of magnificent trees on the north side of
Loch Arkaig, opposite the mansion of Lochiel, he saw the man
he wanted, riding on the fatal white horse at the head of a
small party of officers.   Vengeance was now within his grasp,
and he was not long in availing himself of the opportunity
fate had thrown in his way.   Levelling his piece, he took a
steady and deliberate aim at the supposed slayer of his child,
and as the report of the discharge rang out upon the still air,
and went echoing along the rocky shores of the loch, the officer
fell from his horse mortally wounded, and expired in a few
minutes.   Having avenged his son's death, Cameron fled,
satisfied that he had accomplished his vow.   But it was not
so.   The unfortunate man whose life-blood stained the verdant
turf of the *Mile Dubh* proved to be Major Munro of Culcairn,
the brother of Sir Robert Munro of Foulis, who had recently
met a soldier's death at Falkirk.   Chance had led the major to
exchange horses with the officer who had perpetrated the foul
crime, and thus it happened that the bullet that was intended
for his friend pierced his own heart.   To this day the place
where he fell is known as "Culcairn's Brae."

Prince Charles, after a series of remarkable adventures
among the desolate mountains of the west coast, and in the
society of the famous "Seven Men of Glenmoriston," returned
to Lochaber on the 20th of August, where he expected to meet
Cameron of Clunes, a kinsman of Lochiel's, from whom he
hoped to obtain some information as to the whereabouts of
that brave chieftain.   The place appointed for the meeting was
Achnasaul, near the foot of Loch Arkaig, and here the prince
waited in the pouring rain for the arrival of Clunes.   Drenched

to the skin, and without food of any kind, his condition was miserable indeed. His clothing, torn and soiled by the rough usage it had undergone, consisted of a dirty shirt, over which he wore a black Highland doublet much the worse for wear, and an old tartan kilt and plaid frayed and battered by the briars and thorns which had obstructed his path through the forest. For arms he carried a musket, and in his belt were thrust a pair of pistols and a dirk. His personal appearance was in keeping with his dress, and it would have been difficult to recognise in the rough-looking lad, with unkempt locks and red beard of a few weeks' growth, the gallant prince who, a few months before, had won the love and admiration of the bonnie lasses of old Dunedin who had attended his brief but brilliant court at Holyrood.

For some reason or another Clunes was unable to keep his appointment, and sent word by Peter Grant (one of the *PATRICK* Glenmoriston men with whom the prince had stayed) that he would come in the morning, and suggested that the fugitives should find shelter for the night in the adjoining wood. This they proceeded to do, and while following the path that led through a thick undergrowth of trees and bracken, a fine hart, startled at their approaching footsteps, bounded across the road and was promptly shot by Grant and converted into venison for the supper of the hungry prince and his half-starved followers. Upon arrival at Achnasaul, Glenaladale had despatched a messenger to MacDonald of Lochgarry, who was known to be hiding in the neighbourhood, to acquaint him with the news that the prince was close at hand and would be glad to see him. Immediately upon receipt of this welcome intelligence, Lochgarry started off in quest of the wanderers, and reached the wood where they lay concealed about nightfall. In the morning Clunes came in, and by his advice the party shifted their quarters to another part of the forest, where they were less likely to be observed by the military patrols from Fort Augustus or Fort William. On the evening of 21st August the heroes of Glenmoriston bade farewell to the "lad they should ne'er see again," and departed to their native glens, with the exception of their leader, Peter Grant, who was *PATRICI* left behind in order that he might receive a sum of money Prince Charles had promised to pay for their services.

About this time Lochiel, in the seclusion of his retreat among the mountains of Badenoch, received tidings of the prince's arrival in Lochaber, and he at once determined to open up communications with the royal fugitive. Sending for his brother Dr Archibald Cameron, and his kinsman the Rev. John Cameron,[1] he informed them of what he had heard, and expressed a wish that they should start off at once for Ach-na-carry, and endeavour to gain some reliable intelligence as to the prince's movements, and, if possible, obtain a personal interview, when plans for a suggested flight to France could be discussed.

In the hope of intercepting any messengers from the prince, it was thought advisable that Dr Cameron should proceed into Lochaber by one route, and the Rev. John Cameron by another; and the wisdom of this course was soon apparent, as before Dr Cameron had gone more than a few miles, he met one of his brother's tenants named MacCoilveen, who had been entrusted with a message from Prince Charles to Lochiel. As a proof of the fidelity of character possessed by the poor untutored Highlanders of that period, we are told that although MacCoilveen was perfectly well aware of the near relationship that existed between Dr Archibald Cameron and Lochiel, he could not be persuaded to give the doctor the slightest hint as to the nature of the communication, which he had been told was to be conveyed to none other than Lochiel himself. While Dr Cameron had been questioning the prince's messenger two strangers had approached, and as

---

[1] Although most histories of the '45 refer to the Rev. John Cameron as the brother of Donald Cameron, the younger of Lochiel, he does not appear in the list of the children of John Cameron, the titular chief, as given in "The Memoirs of Sir Ewen Cameron of Lochiel." There were five sons only, viz., Donald (of the '45), John of Fassfern, who certainly was not a minister, Dr Archibald, Alexander (afterwards a priest), and Ewen. Should it not be Alexander?

their appearance denoted their nationality, Dr Cameron stopped them, and after a few words had passed, extracted from them the information that they were two French officers who had been sent over from France with several others to assist the prince, and that, having landed at Poolewe in June, they had been wandering about ever since hoping to fall in with him, but had altogether failed to discover the whereabouts of the object of their search.

This unexpected occurrence caused Dr Cameron to alter his plans, and instead of proceeding farther on his way, he retraced his steps to Mellaneuir, where his brother was still residing, accompanied by the two officers and the trusty MacCoilveen. Lochiel, on being apprised of the arrival of the French officers, seems to have entertained some suspicions that they might be foes in the guise of friends, and had them conveyed to the abode of a neighbour, with injunctions that a strict watch was to be kept over their movements. The message that had been brought from the prince by MacCoilveen having been confided to Dr Cameron, he set off once more on his perilous errand, and making rapid progress, soon overtook his kinsman, the Rev. John Cameron, near the shores of Loch Lochy. Here they secured a boat in which they crossed the loch, and proceeded to explore the neighbourhood of Clunes, hoping they might secure the service of Cameron of that ilk to guide them to the prince's retreat. Fortune favoured them in their quest, for while rowing slowly near the mouth of the river Arkaig, they perceived two of Clunes's children; and shortly afterwards Cameron himself, having probably recognised the occupants of the boat, came down to the water's edge, and was soon in communication with his friends. Dismissing their servants, the three loyal Camerons made haste to gain the cover of the wood, in case their movements should be watched by some lurking enemy. With cautious footsteps they approached the rude hut which willing hands had erected to shelter the prince from the rain, and afford him some cover while he slept at night.

2 N

And here a strange contretemps happened, which might have proved fatal to Dr Cameron and his companions. The prince, not expecting to receive any visitors, had fallen asleep, and one of Clunes's sons shared his siesta, while the faithful Peter stood sentry over them by the door of the hut. Whether Peter had been imbibing too freely of the spirit that Clunes had provided, or whether the heat of the sultry August day had rendered him drowsy we know not, but certain it is that the usually alert Highlander slumbered at his post. He awoke, however, at the sound of the breaking twigs and moving branches, that betokened the approach of some intruders. Rushing into the hut, he unceremoniously awakened the prince and young Cameron, and implored them both to betake themselves to the hills while there was yet time. This the prince refused to do, as he considered it safer to remain in the hut and fire upon the party as they came within range of their weapons. Placing themselves under cover, with muskets primed and loaded, they awaited with some trepidation the arrival of the enemy, ready to fire at a signal from the prince. Fortunately for all concerned, Clunes was recognised the moment he emerged from the wood, and thus a terrible catastrophe was providentially averted.

Prince Charles was delighted to see Dr Archibald Cameron, and to hear from him that his brother's wounds were fast healing. A strong affection had sprung up between the young prince and his devoted friend and follower Lochiel, from that first eventful day when at Borrodale the young chieftain, with the spirit of his celebrated grandfather stirring in his breast, had enthusiastically declared that he would share the fate of the fearless lad who had come to win back his inheritance from the ravenous clutches of a German adventurer. The bonds of this friendship had been drawn closer by the sufferings and privations both had experienced during the long campaign, in which the devotion of Lochiel to the cause he had promised to support had never been known to waver. And now, like his prince, the "Gentle" Lochiel was an outcast and a

wanderer among his own people. The blackened pile of his
ancestral home stood gaunt and spectre-like amid the leafy
shades of Ach-na-carry, a grim and silent witness to the reality
of his loyalty to a fallen dynasty, and a standing memorial of
English barbarism. Well might Prince Charles thank God
that the life of his friend had been spared. Never was he in
greater need of his advice than at the present juncture, and
he could scarcely be restrained from setting out at once for
Badenoch in order to join the crippled chieftain. But wiser
counsels prevailed, and the attempt to reach Lochiel's hiding-
place was postponed until a more favourable opportunity
offered.

CHAPTER XXXIV.

THE lovely spot where Prince Charles was now lying hidden
merits some description, not only for its historical associations
but on account of the natural beauty of its surroundings. At
the present day, and notwithstanding its close proximity to
the great tourist route by which thousands of all nationalities
on pleasure bent pour northwards every year, Loch Arkaig and
its vicinity is almost as little known as if it were in Central
Africa. Solitude reigns supreme among its mountains and
glens, where the red-deer roam at will in undisturbed possession of Lochiel's great forest, and the eagle perches unmolested
among the rocky crags of Glas Bheinn, watching with its
cruel yellow eyes the unsuspecting rabbits, as they frisk and
play among the heather, all unconscious of the doom that
awaits some of their number. Here the Scots fir attains its
highest altitude, and the heather flourishes luxuriantly, its
gnarled and twisted stems affording splendid cover for all
kinds of game. Between thickly wooded banks, o'erhung
with fern and bracken, the noisy Arkaig flows with unceasing
murmur. Hoary trunks of ancient oaks and alders mingle with
the delicate silver and black branches of the birch, and the long

grey saplings of the ash trees—crabbed age and sprightly youth in picturesque contrast. Near this lovely spot the chieftains of Clan Cameron built their stronghold of Ach-na-carry,[1] and had dwelt there from the time that *Ailein MacDhomhnuill Duibh*, son of the famous *Dòmhnull Dubh*, had acquired the estates of Lochiel and Loch Arkaig by his adhesion to the cause of Celestine of the Isles, Lord of Lochalsh, nephew of John, Lord of the Isles, in 1491. At the present time nothing remains of the old castle but a few fragments of ivy-clad masonry, fast crumbling into decay. The dungeon to which the chief consigned his prisoners was hewn out of the steep bank of the loch, and was secured by a massive iron gate, which could only be approached by water. At the time of the construction of the Caledonian Canal, the waters of Loch Lochy increased in volume, and submerged not only the prison but also an island known as "*Eilean Mhic-an Toisich*" ("The Mackintosh's Island"), upon which stood some ancient ruins. The burial-place of the Cameron chieftains may still be seen on the small islet near the foot of Loch Arkaig.

Bitter indeed must have been the feelings of Dr Cameron when he surveyed the melancholy spectacle of his brother's devastated home, the cradle of his race. Here had lived and died his celebrated grandsire Sir Ewen, and it was doubtless some consolation to think of the severe punishment that bold chieftain had inflicted on a former generation of Sassenach intruders. The sight of the roofless walls, within which he had played when a child, must have caused a pang of sorrow to penetrate his soul, and stir up a spirit of intense hatred against the ruthless destroyers who had invaded the sylvan glades of Ach-na-carry, and left a path of desolation in their wake.

On 26th August another move was made by Prince Charles and his faithful attendants to the wood of *Torr a' Ghallain*, through which runs the beautiful avenue of the *Mile Dubh*. Here, in a cave, the fugitives found shelter for some days, while Dr Cameron and Lochgarry made several excursions

---

[1] "*Achadh-na-Cairidh*" ("Field of the Weir").

along the shores of Loch Lochy and Loch Linnhe, at imminent risk of capture, in order to make themselves acquainted with the movements of the troops which were quartered at Fort William and the temporary barracks that had been erected in the neighbourhood after Culloden. Glenaladale, who had remained with the prince since 16th July, was despatched to the west coast to watch for the arrival of some French ships which were daily expected.

As the month of August drew to a close, alarming news was brought to Prince Charles of the approach of a body of two hundred men of Lord Loudoun's Highlanders, commanded by Captain Grant of Cnoc-ceanach. These troops had been sent from Fort Augustus, with orders to search the shores of Loch Lochy in the neighbourhood of Clunes, as it was believed that the prince himself, or some of his principal officers, was in hiding there. This unwelcome intelligence was communicated by a little Highland lassie to the Rev. John Cameron while he was engaged in trying to obtain information, in company with one of Clunes's sons. The girl had seen the redcoats in the distance, and knowing only too well from her recent experiences that the presence of the *Saighdearan Dearg* portended evil, she hastened to the place where her friends were resting, and acquainted them with what she had seen. The minister immediately conveyed the news to Prince Charles, who was then sleeping in a hut on *Torr a' Mhuilt* in Glen Ciaig, about a mile from Clunes, and advised a speedy flight to the surrounding hills. Acting on this suggestion, the prince and his attendants, eight in all, armed themselves as rapidly as possible, and proceeded cautiously to the summit of *Meall-an-Tagraidh*, a mountain about 2000 feet high, and very difficult of access on account of its almost perpendicular ascent and the masses of pointed rocks which form its sides. Here they remained all day, almost dead with fatigue, and without a morsel of food to satisfy the cravings of hunger. At midnight one of Clunes's sons brought word that his father had set out with a supply of provisions to a remote spot some miles distant, where pursuit was well-nigh impossible, as the paths were inaccessible except to those who knew the locality. Tired as he was, the prince descended the mountain and started off in quest of the loyal Clunes. With indomitable pluck, and a dauntless courage which no amount of physical suffering could restrain, he pursued his toilsome way over rocks and stones, wading knee-deep through swift mountain torrents, traversing thick woods where the thorns and brambles tore his clothing and wounded his uncovered limbs, ascending and descending steep hillsides where a goat could scarce retain a foothold, and undergoing all this exertion without so much as a murmur of discontent.

> " The hills he trode were a' his ain,
> And bed beneath the birken tree ;
> The bush that hid him on the plain
> There's nane on earth can claim but he."

What real pathos is contained in the words of this old Jacobite ballad! The heart bleeds for the bonnie lad trudging footsore and hungry through the beautiful land that was his own rightful inheritance. Every mountain, every hill, every glen were his by Divine right ; the blue lochs sparkling in the bright autumn sunbeams ; the glorious pine woods scenting the air with resinous fragrance ; the shaggy moors, clothed at this season in a regal robe of purple—all were his ; but the relentless fate that had pursued his Stuart ancestors withheld the cup from his lips before he could taste of its contents. The land of promise was before him, but he could only enter it as an outcast and a fugitive.

After struggling on uncomplainingly for some hours, exhausted nature gave way, and the prince found himself unable to proceed further without assistance. Stalwart arms soon came to his aid, and, supported on either side by a muscular Highlander, Prince Charles was enabled to reach the place that Clunes had selected for a retreat among the recesses of the wild region that lies between Loch Arkaig and Loch Garry. Food was now plentiful, for the thoughtful

Clunes had driven in a cow which, with the help of his son, he had killed, and was soon engaged in cooking a portion for the use of the famished wayfarers. A hearty meal and a much needed rest soon restored the prince's drooping spirits, and he became quite cheerful and even merry in the society of his friends.

A day or two after his arrival at this place Dr Archibald Cameron and Lochgarry returned from their expedition of reconnaissance, and informed Prince Charles that he might now safely carry out his intention of joining hands with Lochiel and Cluny MacPherson in their retreat by the shores of Loch Ericht in Badenoch. This was welcome news to the prince. He had long wished to meet his faithful Lochiel, who had suffered so much in his cause; and so impatient was he to start at once, that he could not be persuaded to wait the arrival of Cluny, that chieftain having sent a message by Dr Cameron that he would meet the prince in the wood of Ach-na-carry, and conduct him to their hiding-place in Badenoch. Glad as Prince Charles would have been to welcome the brave Cluny, he was yet more eager to see and consult Lochiel, whose advice he much needed in the present emergency. Hoping to meet Cluny by the way, the prince set out for Mellaneuir attended by Dr Cameron, Lochgarry, and two servants; and such was the dilapidated condition of his clothing at the time of his journey into Badenoch, that we are told that while passing through Tullochcroam, near Loch Laggan, he was glad to accept from a gentleman of the name of MacDonald, who resided there, several articles of dress, among which were a coarse brown coat, a shirt, and a pair of shoes.

On 30th August the long looked forward to meeting with Lochiel took place in the small hut at Mellaneuir, near Loch Ericht. Lochiel, still lame from the effects of the wounds he received at Culloden, welcomed the prince with a most affectionate greeting, and was about to throw himself upon his knees with courtly reverence, when Prince Charles restrained him. "My dear Lochiel," he said, "you don't know who may be looking from the top of yonder hills; if any be there, and if they see such motions, they will conclude that I am here, which may prove of bad consequence."

A few days afterwards Cluny returned from Ach-na-carry, and was overjoyed to once more gaze upon the face of his gallant young prince, whom he had not seen for a long time. Owing to some unfortunate delay the Clan MacPherson had been unable to take part in the battle of Culloden. This unavoidable absence from the side of the prince on that fatal day was a matter of bitter regret to Cluny and his brave men, and he was almost ashamed to approach the royal presence, fearing he would be reproached for his apparent dereliction of duty. Probably Prince Charles guessed the thoughts that were troubling him, and with true magnanimity took him in both arms, and kissing him affectionately, said, "I'm sorry, Cluny, that you and your regiment were not at Culloden. I did not hear till lately that you were so near us that day." These thoughtful words put the chieftain's mind at rest, and he set to work to provide his guest with clothing and provisions.

All thoughts were now turned in the direction of effecting an escape into France, and many were the anxious discussions upon that all-important subject by the small band of faithful Jacobites. It was fully realised among them that for the time at least any further attempt at restoring the Stuart monarchy in Britain was out of the question, and that the only hope of ultimate success lay in the assistance they might be able to procure from the French king. Every day the prince remained in Scotland was fraught with the gravest risk to his person. The English blood-hounds were everywhere hunting down all those to whom attached the faintest suspicion of having taken part in the late rebellion, and if it was discovered in Fort William that the prince was in the locality, the whole country would be scoured to effect his capture. Terrible stories of the sufferings of his tenants in Lochaber reached the ears of Lochiel in his retreat in Badenoch. Atrocities of every description were daily perpetrated in the name of law; whole families were rendered homeless, and wandered through the depopulated glens of their native land in a starving and emaciated condition. The gentle heart of Lochiel was wrung by these harrowing accounts of the melancholy condition of his people, and so generous was his nature that he emptied his scanty purse of its contents and sent the money for distribution in Lochaber. This good example was followed by others, and among those who contributed to help the poor homeless creatures was Sir Stewart Threipland, who was for some time with Lochiel in Badenoch. With kindly sympathy he undid his purse strings and subscribed five guineas, saying as he did so, "I am sure I have not so much to myself, but then if I be spared I know where to get more, whereas these poor people know not where to get the slightest assistance." Noble words, and worthy of the cause in which he had embarked, and the heroes with whom he will ever be associated.

CHAPTER XXXV.

WHILE Prince Charles was enjoying the rude hospitality of his friends in Badenoch, Glenaladale was searching the horizon on the west coast for the sails of the French vessels which were to carry off the fugitives; nor had he long to wait. On 6th September two foreign ships sailed into Loch-nan-Uamh, and proved to be "La Princesse de Conti" and "L'Hereux," two well-armed sloops that had been despatched by king James to bring off the prince and his followers. Captain Sheridan was in command of the expedition, and upon landing he waited upon Glenaladale, and together they concerted measures for communicating the news to Prince Charles, who was supposed to be still lying hidden in the neighbourhood of Ach-na-carry.

As secrecy was of the utmost importance, Glenaladale set out himself for the hut of Cameron of Clunes, who, he naturally anticipated, would be able to direct him to the prince's retreat. Greatly to his disappointment, he found, on approaching the place where he expected to find that chieftain, that nothing was left of the hovel but a few charred fragments. Perplexed in mind, and fearing that some disaster had overtaken the prince and his party, Glenaladale wandered about the place in an aimless manner, not knowing what to do in order to obtain some tidings of the fugitives. Fortune, however, favoured him, and threw an old woman in his way who was able to tell him where Clunes was living. Proceeding hastily thither, Glenaladale communicated the news of the arrival of the French ships to Clunes, who, without the loss of an instant, despatched a message to Prince Charles by the trusty MacCoilveen, through the intermediation of Cluny MacPherson.

By a curious coincidence, on the very day that MacCoilveen departed on his errand, Cluny and Dr Archibald Cameron had been sent by the prince to Loch Arkaig, possibly for some of the buried treasure to replenish their now empty purses. Luckily, although the night was exceedingly dark, they met and recognised Clunes's messenger, and thus avoided a delay which might have proved fatal to the prince; for had MacCoilveen passed without being observed, he would, upon reaching Cluny's abode, have refused to deliver his message in the absence of the chief, and, by the time Cluny had returned from Lochaber, the French ships would probably have sailed. Thus, for once in his career, fortune smiled upon the unfortunate prince, and enabled him to avail himself of the opportunity offered of escaping from the clutches of his father's undutiful subjects. Immediately upon receipt of the welcome intelligence a start was made for Lochaber, and on 15th September Prince Charles, accompanied by Lochiel, Cluny, Lochgarry, John Roy Stuart, Dr Archibald Cameron, and several others, arrived on the east side of the river Lochy, near Mucomer.

It was at this place that the last battle was fought between the Camerons and Mackintoshes at the time of the ancient feud between those clans in the sixteenth and seventeenth centuries. Close by is the place of sepulture of the MacMartin Camerons of Letterfinlay, the oldest branch of that great Lochaber family. The burying-ground is remarkable, among other reasons, for the curious fact that, with only two exceptions, the names inscribed upon the tombstones are all of departed Camerons. So numerous were the members of that clan who lived in this locality, that there is a tradition that on one occasion a benighted traveller, who had dragged his weary way for many miles in the pouring rain, came late at night to Mucomer, and seeing a light in the window of a small bothy, knocked at the door and craved for shelter. Either the place was full, or the owner resented the intrusion of a stranger at such an unseasonable hour, for without further parley he proceeded to close the window he had opened to see who disturbed his repose. Dreading to be again exposed to the fury of the elements while shelter was within his reach, the tired wayfarer piteously entreated to be admitted, and cried, " Oh, if there is one Christian in the house, he will let me in!" This was too much for the owner of the bothy. Camerons he knew, MacDonalds he knew, Mackintoshes he knew, MacLeans and MacPhersons he was familiar with; but Christians were a clan of which he had no cognisance, and were probably hostile. Shutting the window with a bang, he shouted, " There are no Christians here ; we are all Camerons!"

The prince and his adherents having reached the banks of the Lochy were in a dilemma : between them and Ach-na-carry the river flowed swift and wide, and they had no means of crossing. At this juncture the faithful Clunes appeared and informed the prince that he had managed to secure a boat for his service; but so dilapidated and leaky did it appear, that the cautious Lochiel hesitated to risk the life of his beloved prince in so frail a craft. Clunes, however, was satisfied that there was no danger, and promised to cross first with some of the least important of the party, and then return for the prince and the other chiefs. Previous to embarking he produced six bottles of brandy which had been brought from the garrison at Fort Augustus; and amid much merriment, and many jokes at the expense of the enemy who had so kindly supplied the liquor, Prince Charles and his friends consumed the contents of three out of the six bottles, reserving the others for a future occasion. The ferrying was then proceeded with, Clunes going over first with some of the attendants, and having got safely to the other side, came back for the prince, and again for Lochiel and the remainder of the devoted band. The last crossing was attended with considerable danger, as the water came in so fast that it was only by dint of incessant bailing that the leaky old tub could be kept afloat. During this passage the remaining bottles of brandy were inadvertently smashed, and mingled with the water in the bottom of the boat, so that Lochiel and his servants were half-immersed in a pool of brandy and water. Such liquor was too good to be wasted, and by the time the opposite shore was reached most of it had found its way down the throats of the thirsty rowers. Ach-na-carry was reached on the morning of the 16th, and here, among the blackened ruins of Lochiel's ancient dwelling, the prince remained all that day, and at nightfall set out for Glen Camgharaidh, a small farmstead about two miles from Kinlocharkaig, where Dr Cameron and Cluny were awaiting his arrival with a good store of provisions.

The last night that Bonnie Prince Charlie was to spend in Lochaber was a memorable one; the brief drama in which he had played so conspicuous and noble a part had reached its termination; the curtain of destiny was about to descend upon the last tableau. Grouped around him were the principal actors in the thrilling scenes which had formed a terrible *dénouement* in the great tragedy of Culloden.

Foremost among the loyal band stood the "Gentle" Lochiel, his crippled limbs affording tangible evidence of the reality of his devotion. Attainted by the Government, his estates forfeited, the home of his ancestors a heap of ruins, his wife a fugitive, his tenantry dispersed or sleeping beneath Drummossie's fatal moor, and all that made life dear torn from his grasp, he stood there by his prince's side without a murmur, ready to follow him to the death if need be.

Mrs Grant of Laggan, writing twenty-eight years later, bears an honourable tribute to this gallant chief in the following words :—" I call him gentle, because he really was so. His disposition was milder, his manners softer, and his mind more cultivated than those of his companions in misfortune, to use a soft word. He was like Brutus among the conspirators. No man sacrificed more domestic comfort to mistaken principle. No man had clearer views of the fatal result."

These traits of character were reflected in a marked degree in the mind of Lochiel's brother, Dr Archibald Cameron: the same unselfish devotion to the prince he had sworn to support; the same gentle consideration for all his suffering kinsmen; and to these qualities was added a strong religious feeling, which was to support and comfort him in the hour of his great need, when the snares of the enemy had compassed him about. Like his brother, he had lost all his cherished possessions, and had nought to look forward to but a life of poverty in a foreign land.

With the two brothers was their uncle Ludovick Cameron of Torcastle, the youngest son of Sir Ewen Cameron of Lochiel. His military experience had been of great service to his nephew Donald, to whom he had acted in the capacity of major throughout the whole campaign, and was now about to share his exile. Few facts are recorded respecting this important member of Lochiel's family, but we know that he was a brave and capable officer, worthily fulfilling the traditions of his race.

Here also was the bold Ewen MacPherson of Cluny, whose good claymore, though absent from Culloden, had done good execution among the prince's enemies at Falkirk. " Touch not the cat but a glove" was the characteristic motto of his clan, and many Sassenach heads had received practical illustration of its truth. Cluny had determined to seek safety among his native hills of Badenoch with his kinsman Breakachie, and bade farewell to the prince on the next morning. Before he took his leave, Prince Charles gave him the following letter, which is still preserved in Cluny Castle. It runs as follows :—

"MR MᶜPHERSON OF CLUNIE,—As we are sensible of your and clan's fidelity and integrity to us during our adventures in Scotland and England in the years 1745 and 1746, in recovering our just rights from the Elector of Hanover, by which you have suffered very great losses in your interest and person, I therefore promise, when it shall please God to put it in my power, to make a grateful return suitable to your sufferings. CHARLES P.R.

"Diralagich in Glencamgier of Lockarkaig,
"18 *September* 1746."

This letter was lent by Colonel MacPherson of Cluny to the Stuart Exhibition of 1889, where probably some of my readers had the privilege of seeing it.

The only representative of the great MacDonald clan present at Glen Camgharaidh on the night of the 18th was Lochgarry,[1] who had joined the prince's army with six hundred men at the hill of Corrieyairack more than a year before, and had fought by his side ever since. Glengarry himself took no active part in the "Forty-Five," and his eldest son Alasdair, who had been in France, was captured by the English when returning to Scotland, and imprisoned in the Tower of London until after the rebellion was over. The sad death of his second son Æneas after the battle of Falkirk has already been described.

With well-tried friends around him, with abundance of good food to supply his wants, and with the prospect of a speedy escape from the clutches of his foes, Prince Charles spent his last evening in Lochaber in a happy frame of mind, such as he had long been a stranger to. His physical and mental sufferings were all forgotten in the congenial society of

---

[1] It was Lochgarry who uttered the famous curse upon the occasion of his son John embarking from Calais for Scotland. "My curse on any of my race who puts his foot again on British shore ; my double curse on he who of my race may submit to the Guelph ; and my deadliest curse on he who may try to regain Lochgarry."

the Highland gentlemen who on the morrow were to escort him to the friendly shores of France.

As the flowing bowl was handed round, the spirits of the party rose, and mirth and jollity prevailed in the humble farmhouse, which was for the nonce transformed into a royal palace. But with the dawn of the day that was to see that last farewell to their native shores, mirth gave way to sorrow; the Lochaber they loved with all the intensity of their Highland hearts was to be thenceforth but a memory,— the land of their infancy, their childhood, their manhood, was to be theirs no more. Never again were they to see the sun dispelling the morning mists from the mighty summit of Ben Nevis; never again were they to hear the music of the rippling waters of Loch Arkaig, or the roar of the cataracts that fall with headlong rush down the steep sides of the mountains of Loch Eil. No more would the evening breeze bring to their nostrils the sweet fragrance of the heather and the odour of the pine-groves. The lovely glens, where as youths they had often wandered with the maidens of their choice, and culled the scarlet rowan berries, or plucked the snowy blossoms of the hawthorn, were henceforth only to be seen in dreams. The great hills, among the crags of which they had, in boyish days, climbed to secure the prize of a callow brood of young eaglets, would still rear their everlasting pinnacles into the clouds, would still catch the last golden rays of the setting sun in the beautiful western land of old Albyn, while those who had been born under their shadows would gaze with yearning hearts across the main, and think what might have been.

"*Cha till mi tuille*" ran the words of the lament of Donald MacCrimmon, the hereditary piper of MacLeod of Dunvegan, when he started upon the dangerous expedition from which he was destined never to return. "*Cha till sinn tuille*" ("We return no more") must have been the refrain of the thoughts of the assembled exiles as they bade a last adieu to the land of their birth. "Lochaber no more, it's maybe we'll return to Lochaber no more," sung Allan Ramsay, the "Gentle Shepherd," in

1725, and the sweet words of this pathetic ballad may well
have occurred to the minds of the fugitives as they proceeded
on their way to join the French ships at Loch-nan-Uamh.[1]

On September 19th (or 20th) 1746 Prince Charles embarked on board " L'Hereux," accompanied by Lochiel and
Dr Archibald Cameron, Lochgarry, young Clanranald, Glenaladale, John Roy Stewart, and many other gentlemen who
had assembled on the west coast upon hearing of the arrival
of the French vessels.[2]   As the ship stood out to·sea, and the
coast-line of the land they all loved so well receded from their
gaze, sorrow fell upon the hearts of all, and strong men, who
had stood the brunt of many battles, were seen to weep like
children.

" Hame, hame, hame, hame fain wad I be,
O hame, hame, hame tae my ain countrie."

Prince Charles must have experienced something of the
mournful emotions that wrung the breasts of his faithful
Highlanders.   If they had lost a home, he had lost a crown.
The high ambitions and aspirations which had filled his soul
when, rather more than twelve short months before, he had
first placed his foot upon the rock-girt shore of his father's
kingdom, were dead within him.   Misfortunes, disappointments,
sufferings, had seared his heart and had left an ineffaceable
scar, which time might heal but could never obliterate.   The
cherished dream of his early youth, when he first began to
realise the splendid inheritance to which he had been born,
had vanished like a phantom of the imagination before the
stern realities of inexorable fate.   He must have felt, as he
stood upon the deck of the vessel that was bearing him away
from that Scotland which from earliest infancy he had learned
to love, all the sorrows of a young bridegroom from whose

[1] Dr Fraser Mackintosh, in his "Antiquarian Notes," p. 230, states that this
beautiful song was composed originally by Drummond of Balhaldie in honour of Jean
Cameron, one of the many daughters of Sir Ewen Cameron of Lochiel.

[2] Twenty-three gentlemen, and a hundred and seven men of common rank, are
said to have sailed with the prince in the two ships.—"Chambers's History of the
Rebellion of 1745–46."

arms his newly-wedded wife had been torn. But he did not repine. His mission had failed, crown and kingdom had slipped from his outstretched hands, but honour remained untarnished. Worthily had he supported the dignity of his royal ancestors in defending his birthright against the brutal might of Cumberland's serried battalions. His chivalrous bearing, his patience under adversity, his generous sympathy for those who had shared his perils and privations, had gained for him far more lasting honour than the perishable laurels that now decked the brow of the "butcher" of Culloden.

Deep in the hearts of thousands of the descendants of those brave men who fought by his side on Culloden's bloody field the memory of Bonnie Prince Charlie still lingers, notwithstanding all the long years that have passed since he dwelt among the mountains and glens of Lochaber, and added a glowing chapter to its already romantic history. Think of the poetry his deeds have inspired; and, anti-Jacobite though you may be, you must admit that to remove from our Scottish minstrelsy the many beautiful ballads which were the outcome of the "Forty-Five" would be to take away its very life-blood. Scotsmen are mostly Jacobite at heart, although they may not be members of the League of the White Rose; and in whatever part of the world they congregate, whether amid the eternal snows of the far north, or under the vertical sun of the tropics, there will you hear the praise of Bonnie Charlie sung with all the enthusiasm that is the outward sign of this latent racial sentiment which pervades all classes — Highlanders, Lowlanders, rich and poor alike.

For years after the escape of Prince Charles to France, the poorer and more illiterate Highlanders looked for his return to their shores with a sanguine expectancy which was only heightened by the cruel outrages committed every day in their midst by the English soldiery, who were quartered in forts and temporary barracks throughout the disaffected districts. They could not at first realise that all hope was gone, and that never again would they see the bonnie lad from whom so much had

2 P

been expected. The disaster at Culloden, terrible though it was, had not altogether crushed their proud and independent spirits. They knew the prince had escaped the snares of his enemies, and they rejoiced heartily; they knew also that many of their chiefs were with him in enforced exile; but with life there was hope, and with the help of their old ally France, the auld Stuarts would soon be back again. Even after his death in 1788, many of the more superstitious believed that he would, in some mysterious way, appear among them and regain the crown for his descendants. This longing for the return of their hero is pathetically expressed in the following verses of the old ballad, with which I will conclude the chapter :—

> " Bonnie Charlie's noo awa,
>   Safely owre the friendly main ;
> Mony a heart will break in twa,
>   Should he ne'er come back again.

> " Sweet the lav'rock's note and lang,
>   Lilting wildly up the glen ;
> And aye the o'ercome o' the sang
>   Is, ' Will ye no come back again ? ' "

"SOME 'FORTY-FIVE' SIGNATURES."

Charles P R

Prince Charles Edward.

Donald McDonell & off Lochgarry

Donald MacDonell of Lochgarry.

Alesr McDonell

Alexander MacDonell, XVI Chief of Keppoch. Killed at Culloden.

Angus MacDonell

Angus MacDonell of Greenfield.

Donald Cameron

Donald Cameron of Lochiel. (The "Gentle" Lochiel.)

Donald Cameron adjt of Lochiels Regt

Donald Cameron, Adjutant of Lochiel's Regiment.

John McDonell off Glengarry

John MacDonell, XII Chief of Glengarry.

was Donald MacDonald of Keppoch, the brother (or nephew) of the chieftain whose death at Culloden has been previously described. I have been unable to discover any account of his capture, but from the MS. notes in the possession of Mrs MacDonell of Keppoch, I find that both Donald[1] and his nephew Angus are stated to have been present at Culloden, and that Angus, escaping the fate of his brave father Alexander, who was slain before his eyes, succeeded to the chieftainship upon the field of battle, at the age of twenty-one.

Donald, after his capture, was taken to London, and tried before a grand jury at the Session House, St Margaret's Hill, Southwark, on 2nd August 1746. He was at the time of his trial a robust and good-looking young fellow of twenty-five years of age, full of youthful vivacity and of intrepid courage. When taken prisoner, he expressed his bitter regret that he had not been slain in battle. Upon being brought to the bar of the court to take his trial, he assumed an air of contemptuous disregard for the gravity of the situation, and the serious nature of the offence with which he was charged, and answered the questions put to him by the judge with humorous effrontery. When asked if his name was not Donald MacDonald, he replied, " I can't tell my name ; I don't know I ever was christened." To the question, if he was not a captain of Keppoch's regiment? he saucily answered, " I can't tell what I was, nor will I say any more ; for if you want to know my name, you may go ask my mother." Disdaining to plead for mercy, he was condemned to death, and conveyed to Newgate. While in prison his high spirits did not desert him, and he often tried to dance in his fetters. On one occasion he remarked to his jailers that, if they would only release him from his bonds and furnish him with bagpipes, he would give his comrades in prison a Highland fling. On 22nd August

---

[1] Most historians of the '45 state that Donald MacDonald of Keppoch was taken at Carlisle, and certainly this is corroborated by the fact that there is undoubtedly an officer of that name and clan among the list of prisoners who fell into the hands of the English there.

he was informed that his last hour had come, and, in company with two other Highlanders, Walter Ogilvie and James Nicolson, who had served in the prince's army, he was bound to a sledge, clad in his Highland dress of kilt and plaid, and dragged through the streets of London, surrounded by a strong escort of horse-grenadiers and a detachment of foot-guards.

The place fixed for the execution was Kennington Common, a large open space on the Surrey side of the Thames, where, about a month previously, several other unfortunate Jacobites had suffered the last penalty of the law. Upon arrival at the scaffold, MacDonald and his companions were allowed an hour in which to perform their devotions and prepare themselves for their dreadful fate. The allotted time having expired, they were seized by the executioner, and in a few brief moments the lifeless bodies of the unhappy men were dangling in the air. But Hanoverian justice was not yet satisfied, and the souls of the gallant Highlanders having fled, their poor clay still remained, upon which further vengeance could be wreaked. With horrible brutality the bodies were cut down and disembowelled, the heart and entrails taken out and burnt, and the heads struck from the still quivering trunks. This revolting spectacle was witnessed by thousands of men, women, and even children ; and it is some satisfaction to read that many expressions of sympathy for these victims of judicial barbarism were heard on all sides, and that the ribald jeers, so common on the occasion of an execution, were in this instance conspicuous by their absence. The mutilated bodies of the three Jacobites found their last resting-place in the Bloomsbury burying-ground of St Giles-in-the-Fields,[1] and I would draw the attention of the members of the Jacobite League to the fact that there is at present no memorial stone in the church to record the sad end of these loyal defenders of their prince.

The bloody work that was begun at Kennington Common was renewed at Tower Hill and Carlisle with relentless severity. All the world knows with what heroism the two Jacobite noble-

[1] The details of this execution are taken from the *Gentleman's Magazine* for 1746.

men, the Lords Kilmarnock and Balmerino, met their fate on
the spot where, in a previous age, the fair Anne Boleyn, the
gentle Lady Jane Gray, and the accomplished Earl of Surrey
had perished by the axe. To the shambles at Carlisle were
brought many Lochaber men, among whom was MacDonald
of Tirnadris, while the adjoining country of Moidart furnished
another victim in the person of MacDonald of Kinlochmoidart.

The Assizes for the trial of these prisoners and 128 others
were opened at Carlisle in September, and at the completion
of the proceedings 91 received sentence of death. About the
15th of October a warrant was sent to Carlisle for the
execution of ten of the condemned men, the list including
the two MacDonalds.

The circumstances of the capture of Tirnadris will be
fresh in the minds of my readers, and it will also be remembered that he had been the first to strike a blow in the
campaign which had ended so disastrously. After being taken
prisoner at Falkirk, he had been conducted to Edinburgh Castle
and imprisoned in the same room as the Rev. Robert Forbes,
afterwards Bishop of Orkney, whose MS. memoirs of the
"Forty-Five" have been brought to light by Mr Robert
Chambers, of Edinburgh, in his "History of the Rebellion
of 1745."

Bishop Forbes appears to have taken an affectionate interest
in the young Highland chieftain, and the chance acquaintance,
made under such peculiar circumstances, ripened into a close
friendship. The kindly minister thus describes the appearance
and character of MacDonald of Tirnadris :—" He was," he
writes, "a brave, undaunted, honest man, of a good countenance,
and of a strong, robust make. He was much given to pious
acts of devotion (being a Roman Catholic), and was remarkably
a gentleman of excellent good manners. He bore all his
sufferings with great submission and cheerfulness of temper."

Upon the removal of Tirnadris to Carlisle, during the
summer of 1746, a correspondence was kept up between the
two friends, and in a letter of August the 24th, Tirnadris,

after informing Forbes that his trial comes on on the 9th of September, and expressing a hope that God will stand by the righteous, proceeds as follows :—" The whole gentlemen who came from Scotland are all together in one floor, with upwards of one hundred private men, so that we are much thronged. They have not all got irons as yet, but they have not forgot me, nor the rest of most distinction; and the whole will be soon provided. You'll make my compliments to Lady Bruce and Mr Clerk's family, but especially to Miss Molly Clerk, and tell her that, notwithstanding my irons, I could dance a Highland reel with her."

Like his kinsman whose fate at Kennington I have just described, MacDonald of Tirnadris possessed the same fund of animal spirits and the same reckless daring as that un-daunted fellow-clansman had exhibited while in a similar situation. When his trial came on, he was strongly urged to plead guilty, and offer an humble submission to the usurper of his sovereign's throne; but his MacDonald blood would not permit such a traitorous act, and the suggestion was scorn-fully rejected. "Rather than do so, I would submit to be taken and hanged at the bar before the face of those judges by whom I am soon to be tried," were the words uttered by this loyal follower of the prince.

He seems to have thought much of his sorrowing wife, and makes frequent reference to her in his correspondence. On October the 17th he penned a sad farewell letter to a friend in Edinburgh : " My dear sir, I received yours yesterday, and as I am to die to-morrow, this is my last farewell to you. May God reward you for your services to me from time to time, and may God restore my dear prince, and receive my soul at the hour of death."

On the morning of the 18th of October 1746, in company with eight others, among whom was Kinlochmoidart, he paid with his life the penalty of his devoted fidelity to the House of Stuart. Consistent to the last, he uttered with his latest breath words of noble and affectionate loyalty, which are well worthy of record. "It was principle," he said, "and a thorough conviction of its being my duty to God, my injured king, and oppressed country, which engaged me to take up arms under the standard and magnanimous conduct of his Royal Highness Charles, Prince of Wales. I solemnly declare I had no by-views in drawing my sword in that just and honourable cause." Thus died the hero of High Bridge, having worthily fulfilled the traditions of his race, and proved himself a true son of loyal Lochaber.

Kinlochmoidart, who suffered at the same time, had never drawn his sword in the late rising, and his execution was a judicial murder for which no excuse can be offered. He was a cool-headed and plain-spoken gentleman, and although his sympathies were undoubtedly with the Jacobite party, he would probably have held aloof from active participation in the movement, had he not, like his neighbour Lochiel, come under the fascinating influence of Prince Charles. To a friend who visited him whilst a prisoner in Edinburgh Castle, and who had expressed some surprise at his engaging in so desperate an enterprise, he replied, "I myself was against it; but, Lord, man, what could I do when the young lad came to my house?"

So it happened that, in spite of his own better judgment, the cautious and far-seeing chieftain, having been drawn by fate into the sphere of the prince's attraction, found himself involved in an undertaking the issue of which was, to say the least, doubtful. He had been sent by Prince Charles, in the early part of the campaign, on an embassy to MacDonald of Sleat and the chief of MacLeod, with the object of trying to induce them to raise their clans for the service of king James. His persuasions were, however, of no avail, and it was while returning through Lesmahagow, in Lanarkshire, to join the Highland army in England, that he fell into the hands of a religious fanatic, who waylaid and captured him.

The executions at Carlisle were attended with the same unspeakable barbarities that had disgraced the previous ones at

Kennington, and the paid butchers of the English Government did their work with a callous indifference, begotten of constant practice. It was a poor revenge, and worthy of the inhuman wretches who planned it, to mutilate the inanimate bodies of these brave men, whose unselfish devotion to the rightful king had been their only crime. It is a lasting stain on the fair fame of England that such atrocities should have been committed in her midst. Where was her vaunted civilisation, her boasted magnanimity, her refinement, her religion, if such deeds could be tolerated by those who ruled the State? Surely the humane and generous treatment by Prince Charles of the prisoners taken by the Highland army at Prestonpans merited some return at the hands of the English, now that they were in a position to requite it. But it was not to be, and the fiat went forth that the unfortunate Highlanders were to be hunted down like beasts of prey, driven from their native glens, persecuted, slain, exterminated.

In the month of May 1746, a Bill of Attainder had been laid before the House of Commons, and many witnesses were examined to prove the guilt of the suspected Jacobites. After having passed the Lords, the Royal (?) assent was given on Wednesday, the 4th of June, and the persons mentioned in the Act were given until the 12th of July in which to surrender themselves, and if after the expiration of that period they had not done so, their estates were to be forfeited and themselves attainted of high treason.

Among those who ignored this unjust Act were all the Lochaber chiefs who had held posts in the prince's army, and who are thus named,—Donald Cameron, the younger of Lochiel; Dr Archibald Cameron, brother of Lochiel; Ludovick Cameron of Torcastle; Alexander Cameron of Dungallon; Donald MacDonald, the younger of Clanranald; Donald MacDonald of Lochgarry, Alexander MacDonald of Keppoch;[1] and of neighbouring chiefs we find Archibald MacDonald of Barris-

[1] From the fact that the name of Alexander of Keppoch appears in the list of attainted chiefs, it is probable that the Government were not aware that he had been slain at Culloden.

dale, Alexander MacDonald of Glencoe, Ewen MacPherson of Cluny, and Charles Stewart of Ardshiel. Only one member of the Mackintosh clan appears in the Act, viz., Lauchlan Mackintosh, merchant of Inverness.

Most of the proscribed chiefs had escaped with their prince to France, or followed him there as opportunity offered, but Cluny MacPherson remained behind in the security of his *Cage* (as his hiding-place was called) on the slopes of Ben Alder; and Keppoch, as we know, was beyond the reach of his foes.

CHAPTER XXXVII.

THE state of affairs in Lochaber immediately following the departure of Prince Charles and the chiefs was melancholy in the extreme, and to those of its inhabitants who had survived the massacre at Culloden, and the brutal outrages of the English soldiery during their frequent "rebel hunting" expeditions, the calm that succeeded the howling tempest of the battlefield must have seemed strange and unnatural. The wings of the Angel of Death were outspread over the land, and a great silence brooded in their shadow. By strath and glen, by moor and mountain, by clachan and shieling, the only sound that broke the mournful stillness was the wail of the newly-made widow, and the cry of her fatherless children, making their moan among the pile of blackened ruins that was once "home." It was as if some fearful whirlwind of destruction had passed over the country, some great convulsion of Nature which had swept the land bare of its inhabitants and devastated their dwellings making a wilderness of what was once a smiling landscape, and creating a vast solitude where but a short time before had resounded the mirthful sounds and joyous voices of a happy and contented people.

"*Bliadhna Thearlaich*" ("Charles's year"), which had begun so propitiously, had ended in disaster and misery, and it was perhaps only natural that the district of Lochaber,

where first the spark of disaffection had been fanned into the
flame of rebellion, should have been specially singled out by
the Whig Government for their severest and most vindictive
punishments. It is certain that no part of the Highlands
suffered more from the effects of the Jacobite rising of 1745
than the beautiful and historic country which forms the
subject of this work; and even at this day we are forcibly
reminded by the ruined Invergarry Castle, and the few fragments of masonry which are all that now remain of the old
castle of Ach-na-carry, and the once great stronghold of the
MacDonalds of Keppoch, how terrible was the vengeance of
the merciless Elector and his cruel son.

Although by the end of the year 1746 most of those
Jacobites who had been so unfortunate as to fall into the
hands of the English had perished on the scaffold, the blood-
hounds of the Government were still as active as ever in
hunting down any poor Highlander to whom the slightest
suspicion attached of having carried arms for Prince Charles ;
and from time to time a capture was effected among the
deep recesses of some scarce-trodden glen, or amid the thick
underwood of some unfrequented forest, where the fugitives
had made their abode after Culloden, hoping that by and by
the wrath of their enemies would be appeased, and that they
would then be able to return to what remained of their homes,
unmolested.

The *Scots Magazine* of the period gives many instances of
these later arrests and executions. In the month of December
1746, we are told that one Hugh Cameron of Anoch was
taken prisoner by a party of soldiers from Fort William.
Cameron had been an officer in Lochiel's regiment at Culloden,
and, after the escape of his chief, had taken refuge in a small
hut in a wood not far from the Fort. He is said to have
been a man of great stature, being six feet seven inches high,
and possessed of immense muscular strength. His capture was
due to strategy, for, fearing to tackle the giant when fully
armed the soldiers proceeded to the hut in the early hours of

the morning, hoping to find Cameron in bed. The plan was so far successful, that when the redcoats arrived at the retreat of the fugitive, they found him just awakened from his slumbers, and in a state of complete nudity. He had, however, time to arm himself with pistols and claymore, and made a most desperate defence before he could be taken. Eventually he was overpowered and bound with ropes, all naked as he was, and taken to Inverness, where I believe he was afterwards hanged.

Early in the following year (1747) Alexander Cameron, who with others was on parole at Inveraray, was cited to appear at Edinburgh before the Lord Justice-Clerk, and was confined in the Castle, but was liberated in June at the time of the general indemnity.

Angus Cameron, brother to Glen Nevis, was also taken prisoner at his house near Rannoch on 27th April, and brought to Edinburgh, but after having been imprisoned for some time regained his freedom.

It was about this time that the famous Sergeant Mòr made his appearance in Lochaber, with his band of daring freebooters, and for some years effectually resisted all attempts to capture him. He was the Rob Roy of Lochaber; and although he has not had the magic pen of the "Wizard of the North" to record his many bold adventures, his fame still remains among the mountains where his name once struck terror into the hearts of those who had cattle to lose, or property to be stolen.

Iain Dubh Cameron, commonly known as "Sergeant Mòr," had seen service in the French army, where he had been promoted to the rank of sergeant. While in France the news of the Jacobite rising reached him, and he determined to return to his native land and try his fortune in the army of Prince Charles. Probably he joined the ranks of his clansmen under the command of Lochiel, but of this I have no proof. After Culloden he appears to have skulked among the mountains of Inverness-shire, Perthshire, and Argyll, where he attached to his side several other reckless spirits of his own countrymen, and commenced a series of systematic cattle-lifting expeditions, or *creachs*, on a considerable scale, on the lands of all those who refused to pay him blackmail, or otherwise purchase their exemption from his midnight raids.

Robber though he was, his notions of honour remained unblunted, and he was never known to have betrayed a trust, or to have divulged a secret which had been committed to his charge. Many anecdotes are told of "Sergeant Mòr," in which these traits of character are conspicuous, as, for instance, the humorous story, recorded in General Stewart's interesting book, of the *rencontre* between the Sergeant and an officer of the garrison at Fort William, among the mountains of Lochaber.

The officer, who was proceeding to Fort William in charge of a considerable sum of money for the use of the garrison, had lost his way, and fearing that he might fall in with the dreaded freebooter, asked a stranger whom he met to accompany him to Fort William. The stranger assented; and as they proceeded on their way the conversation turned upon the Sergeant and his plundering proclivities, the officer describing him in no measured terms as murderer and thief. "Stop there," interrupted his companion, "he does indeed take the cattle of Whigs and you Sassenachs, but neither he nor his *cearnachs* ever shed innocent blood; except once," added he, "that I was unfortunate at Braemar, when a man was killed, but I immediately ordered the *creach* ('the spoil') to be abandoned, and left to the owners, retreating as fast as we could after such a misfortune!" "*You*," says the officer, "what had *you* to do with the affair?" "I am John Du Cameron, — I am the sergeant Mòr; there is the road to Inverlochy,—you cannot now mistake it. You and your money are safe. Tell your governor to send a more wary messenger for his gold. Tell him also, that although an outlaw, and forced to live on the public, I am a soldier as well as himself, and would despise taking his gold from a defenceless man who confided in me."

Sergeant Mòr continued to be the scourge of the district until the year 1753, when he was surprised while sleeping in a barn at Dunan in Rannoch, by a detachment of soldiers commanded by Lieutenant Hector Munro. He was brought before the Court of Justiciary at Perth, and tried for the murder of the man he had inadvertently slain at Braemar. His guilt having been proved to the satisfaction of the Court, he was condemned to death, and executed shortly afterwards.

It is a remarkable fact that, notwithstanding the losses many of the inhabitants of Lochaber had suffered at the hands of this notorious cattle-lifter, the news of his capture was followed by quite a storm of indignation against the person who, it was believed, had betrayed him. There was no crime so universally detested among the Highlanders as treachery, and the man who abused the confidence reposed in him, or who accepted a bribe for the betrayal of a fellow-man, was held worthy of expatriation and death. The ties of blood were very strong in the Highlands, and had been rendered even more binding by recent events. Fidelity to race was the *summum bonum* of the Highlander's creed, and had been instilled into his mind from earliest infancy: a thief he might be, a perverter of the truth he very often was, but a traitor, rarely. And so it happened, that when the stealer of his cattle and the disturber of his nightly repose was brought to justice, the knowledge that treachery was at the bottom of it produced a strong feeling of resentment against the man who had so far forgotten his national instincts as to play the unusual part of a Highland Judas; and it is said that from that time he was shunned by his neighbours, and that later, when poverty overtook him and he had to leave his native land, it was the general belief that his misfortunes were sent by heaven as a judgment for his deceit.

The vindictive spirit exhibited by the Government of the

Elector in their merciless treatment of the Jacobite prisoners soon began to create a feeling of disgust among the more humane of the Whig party, and it was felt that enough blood had been spilt to vindicate the outraged majesty of the law. By the month of June 1747, sufficient pressure had been brought to bear upon the Government to induce them to pass an Act of Indemnity, which granted a pardon to a large number of the proscribed noblemen and chiefs who had been previously named in the Act of Attainder. It was a step in the right direction, but it did not go far enough, for more than eighty persons were excluded from the provisions of the Act, and among them were the whole of the Lochaber chieftains who had taken an active part in the late rising.

This Act was supplemented by another, in which it was made penal for any Highlander to be found in the possession of arms after the 1st of August 1747. For a first offence against the Act the penalty was fifteen pounds, or, in default of payment, transportation to America as a private soldier.

At the same time, a further Act was passed, by which the distinctive dress that had been worn by the Highland race, with but slight alteration, for centuries, was proscribed, under the severest penalties. The preamble of this most arbitrary statute sets forth that "any person within Scotland, whether man or boy (excepting officers and soldiers in his majesty's service), who should wear the plaid, philibeg, trews, shoulder-belts, or any part of the Highland garb, or should use for great-coats, tartans, or parti-coloured plaid, or stuffs, should without the option of a fine, be imprisoned for the first conviction for six months, without bail, and on the second conviction be transported for seven years." The object of this Act is not very apparent; it was probably an ingenious effort on the part of the Government to abolish that national distinction which the Highland dress largely assisted in maintaining, while at the same time it offered a gratuitous insult to a large number of their late enemies, and afforded an excuse for the infliction of still further punishment.

This tyrannical enactment served to arouse the most intense feeling of shame and indignation among the Highlanders as soon as its clauses became known; and it would hardly be too much to say that nothing the Government had hitherto done in the way of reprisal was so keenly felt or so bitterly resented as this, their last, piece of spiteful legislature. To be forced to don the trews of the hated Sassenach was a degradation the proud Celt could not stomach, and many were the amusing methods he adopted to evade the obnoxious Act. Stewart tells us, in his "Sketches of the Highlanders," that "some wore pieces of a blue, green, or red thin cloth, or coarse camblet, wrapped round the waist, and hanging down to the knees"; others, we are told, "who were fearful of offending, or wished to render obedience to the law, which had not specified on what part of the body the breeches were to be worn, satisfied themselves with having in their possession this article of legal or loyal dress, which, either as the signal of their submission, or more probably to suit their own convenience, when on journeys, they often suspended over their shoulders on sticks." The utter impossibility of enforcing obedience to the Act brought it into ridicule, and in less than ten years it was practically a dead letter, although it was not actually repealed until 1782.

Another measure of the greatest importance to the Highlands, and Lochaber in particular, was an Act for the abolition of hereditary jurisdiction, passed in March 1747. It would take too long to explain here the various clauses and ramifications of a statute which was to revolutionise the whole system of judicature and civil government in the Highlands of Scotland, and break up for ever the last remnants of feudalism in Britain. In a few words, this Act was devised for the purpose of putting an end to the almost absolute power of the Highland chieftains over their vassals and clansmen, a power which had enabled them to set at nought for so long a period the authority of the pseudo-monarch who now sat on the throne of the Stuarts.

As several of the chiefs who would be affected by the provisions of this Act were friendly to the Government, some compensation had to be offered in return for the emoluments of the offices they were now called upon to resign. The principal of these was the Duke of Argyll, who, like his ancestors, preferred the loaves and fishes provided by his country's enemies to the frugal, but honourably earned, repasts of his more patriotic fellow-countrymen. The Duke of Argyll held the important office of Hereditary Justiciar of Scotland, and was also Sheriff of the county. As compensation for his resignation of the former post he demanded £15,000, and for the latter £5000, his total claim reaching the large sum of £25,000, of which a grateful Government paid him £21,000. The Duke of Gordon had the next largest claim of £22,300, part of which only was paid. In all, the sum granted by Parliament for the purchase of the whole of the heritable jurisdictions amounted to £150,000; and, as Chambers very truly remarks, the transaction was "one of the cheapest purchases of patronage and power ever made." The attainted Jacobite chiefs, having lost all their privileges and forfeited their estates, could make no claim for compensation; and so, without their being able to raise a finger in defence of their ancient rights, they were deprived of them for ever.

CHAPTER XXXVIII.

CŒLUM non animum, mutant, qui trans mare currunt. Under the blue skies of sunny France, the thoughts of the little band of loyal exiles who had accompanied their prince across the sea turned with a yearning longing to the mist - wreathed mountains and the wind-swept moorlands of Lochaber. Amid the palaces of the luxurious French nobles, and surrounded by all the gaiety and splendour of pleasure-loving Paris, their hearts were sad, and, like the Hebrews of old by the waters

2 R

of Babylon, they mourned when they remembered the land of their birth.

> " On Gallia's shore we sat and wept
> When Scotland we thought on,
> Robbed of her bravest sons, and all
> Her ancient spirit gone.
>
> . . . . . .
>
> " If thee, O Scotland, I forget,
> Even with my latest breath,
> May foul dishonour stain my name,
> And bring a coward's death." [1]

The career of Prince Charles, subsequent to his escape from Scotland, is too well known to need description here; but the purpose of this work would not be satisfactorily fulfilled if I omitted to give some account of the exiled Lochaber chieftains during their residence in France, in the years immediately following the " Forty-Five."

John Cameron of Lochiel, the son of the famous Sir Ewen, had dwelt in France for thirty years, subsisting partly on a pension allowed him by the French king, and partly on the income derived from his estates in Scotland. He frequently visited king James VIII. at St Germains, and was one of the most valued friends and counsellors of that monarch. Although the titular chief of the clan, he had, as we are aware, vested all authority in his son Donald, who now shared his father's exile, in company with his brother Dr Archibald Cameron and his uncle Ludovick Cameron of Torcastle. Alan Cameron, the other brother of the chief, after taking an active share in the preliminary intrigues that led up to the disastrous " Forty-Five," did not live to see the result of his labours. He died in France a short time before the prince departed for Scotland, and was thus spared the reverse of fortune which overtook his family after Culloden.

One of Prince Charles's first acts on reaching Paris was to

---

[1] From a parody on the 137th psalm, written about this period by William Hamilton of Bangour.

seek out his old friend, the elder Lochiel, and discuss with him the chances in favour of another expedition. It was, of course, impossible to make any further movement in this direction without some substantial assistance from the French king, and Charles determined to lose no time in seeking an interview, in order to lay before Louis the scheme upon which he had set his heart, and entreat his aid in providing men, ships, and money. Lochiel was invited by the prince to accompany him to Fontainbleau, where the king was then holding his court; and when the day arrived that had been fixed for the reception, Prince Charles arrayed himself in magnificent attire, such as he had long been a stranger to, and set out from the castle of St Antoine, surrounded by a numerous following of his friends, riding in splendid equipages, or mounted on gaily caparisoned steeds.

Over a waistcoat of gold brocade, upon which glittered the orders of St George and St Andrew in diamonds, he wore a coat of rose-coloured velvet, ornamented with a profusion of silver embroidery, and lined with silver tissue. Diamonds of great lustre gleamed in the cockade of his hat and in the buckles of his shoes, and his whole appearance was noble and distinguished, as became his royal birth and high pretensions. His principal attendants on this occasion were Lochiel, the Lords Elcho and Ogilvie, and his secretary Mr Kelly. The king received him with an outward show of most effusive affection, and addressed him in the most flattering language, but this was all. The discussion of the one great topic that was uppermost in the mind of the impetuous prince was indefinitely postponed; and notwithstanding the magnificent entertainment that was provided in his honour, he must have felt that his chances of obtaining any tangible assistance in furtherance of his bold enterprise were remote.

It is very much to the credit of the French Government that they should have so generously provided for the pecuniary wants of the unfortunate Highland gentlemen whom the adverse winds of fate had driven to their shores. The considerable sum of sixty-two thousand livres was distributed among the Scottish fugitives: John Cameron of Lochiel received three thousand; his son Donald, four thousand; Lochgarry, three thousand; and John Roy Stuart, three thousand; while all the others received various amounts in proportion to their rank and the services they had rendered to the Jacobite cause.

The brutal treatment of the Highland prisoners at the hands of their captors, and the melancholy accounts that reached young Lochiel of the state of Lochaber and its unhappy inhabitants, called forth his utmost indignation, and he chafed and fretted at his inability to shield his poor suffering clansmen from the vengeance of the Government. He had been offered the command of a regiment in the French service, and eventually accepted it; but in a letter that he wrote to king James on the 16th January 1747, he avowed his determination of sharing the fate of his people, and if they were sacrificed, to fall along with them.

In February of the same year he endeavoured, by every argument that he could command, to persuade Prince Charles to risk another expedition to Scotland, and gave it as his opinion that unless the attempt was made at once, while the clans were still thirsting for revenge on their cruel oppressors, it would probably fail, as, when once the Highlanders had been effectually disarmed and their spirits broken, it would be a task of the greatest difficulty to rouse them to further effort on behalf of the Stuarts. Prince Charles was only too ready to admit that he was fully convinced of the sound sense of Lochiel's reasoning, and that he was as anxious as his friend to try once more his fortune in Scotland among his brave mountaineers; but, eager though he was, he saw clearly that without the active support of the French king a successful issue of any such expedition could not be looked for. The death-blow to his hopes came during the early months of 1748, when the much-discussed treaty of peace between France and England had at last reached the preliminary stage of friendly negotiation between the two countries, with a proposal to hold a congress at Aix-la-Chapelle during the summer, at which it was expected the treaty would be formally ratified.

The noble and dignified protest made by the prince against the usurpation of his rights by the Elector George of Hanover is a matter of history, and redounds much to his credit; but it was of no avail. This was the end of all his cherished hopes and lofty ambitions; from henceforth his career was blighted by the freezing blasts of a pitiless fate, before which he succumbed both in body and mind. Repeated disappointments, the cold neglect and indifference of the French king, the life of forced inaction to which he was now doomed, all conspired to transform the bold, high-spirited prince of the "Forty-Five" into a morose and gloomy hypochondriac.

John Cameron of Lochiel died at Boulogne sometime during the year 1747, and was shortly followed to the grave by his brave son Donald, whose magnanimity and lovable disposition had earned for him the honourable appellation of the "Gentle" Lochiel. While in command of his regiment, military duty called him to Borgue, where he contracted a severe attack of brain fever, which proved fatal, and he expired on 26th October 1748.

Mrs Grant of Laggan tells us that when his estates were forfeited "his tenants paid the usual rent to the Crown, and besides this, they voluntarily paid a rent to support Lochiel's family abroad. When the demesne was taken by some friends for their behoof, the tenants stocked it with cattle of all kinds, and to this," she says, "my grandfather, one of that faithful band, amply contributed."

Even his political opponents bore tribute to his worth, for we find a poetical effusion of some merit in the *Scots Magazine* of 1748, evidently the work of a Whig poet who was honest enough to admit that one at least of the Jacobite leaders was worthy of admiration. The following extract from

of Dr Alexander Munro, one of the most clever surgeons of his day, who soon found that in young Archibald Cameron he had a pupil of more than average intelligence and ability. After acquiring a sufficient skill in anatomy and surgery, he commenced the study of physic with Dr Sinclair, a man of some eminence in his profession, under whose direction he made great progress. His education was completed by a tour on the Continent, where he probably made the acquaintance of his sovereign and prince. Upon returning to Lochaber, he had married a lady of the name of Campbell, who bore him several children, and at the time of which I write was residing with her husband in Lille.

In a later chapter I shall have occasion to describe the sad end of this brave gentleman, whose devotion to his young prince, and whose affection for his distinguished brother were the causes that produced a catastrophe such as neither he nor they had ever contemplated.

CHAPTER XXXIX.

THE estates of the attainted chiefs having been forfeited to the Crown, it became necessary to appoint persons of undoubted Whig proclivities to collect the rents and direct the agricultural operations on the various properties affected by the Act of Parliament, as it was feared by the Government, and not without reason, that the clansmen and tenants of the rightful owners of the land would endeavour, by every means in their power, to keep back a portion of the rent for the service of their exiled chiefs.

In the month of February 1748, Colin Campbell of Glenure, a brother of Campbell of Barcaldine, whose daughter Lucy was married to Ewen Cameron, son of Fassfern, was appointed by the Barons of Exchequer factor on the forfeited estates of Ardshiel, Mamore, and Callart. These agents of the Crown were naturally unpopular, and were subjected to many insults in the discharge of their objectionable duties. Glenure seems to have rendered himself especially odious to the tenants of Ardshiel, some of whom had been heard to threaten his life should he attempt any evictions on the property in question. One of these reckless individuals was named Alan Breck (*Breac*) Stewart,[1] son of Donald Stewart of Inverchromie, who had made himself conspicuous by his oft-repeated abuse of the obnoxious factor.

On Whitsunday 1751, Glenure evicted James Stewart,[2] known locally as "James Stewart of the Glen," from his farm in Glen Duror on the estate of Ardshiel in Appin, and it was known that he had taken measures for removing several other tenants in that locality. This action engendered much bitterness of feeling in the neighbourhood, and is thought to have incurred the special resentment of James and Alan Breck Stewart. The former is said to have exclaimed that he would go miles on his knees to slay the destroyer of his home.

On Monday, the 11th of May 1752, Glenure left his house in order to ride over to Fort William, where he had some business to transact. The same day Alan Breck Stewart went to the dwelling of his friend James, and exchanged the clothes that he was wearing, and which he had brought with him from France, for a dark-coloured short coat with silver buttons, and a blue bonnet. On the 14th of the same month, Glenure, having concluded his visit to Fort William, started on his homeward journey, attended by Donald Kennedy, sheriff-officer, and Mungo Campbell, writer, of Edinburgh, and his servant John MacKenzie. The party followed the road that leads from Fort William along the shores of Loch Linnhe, through the lovely wood of *Coire-Chaorachan*, past Corran, and the small clachan of Onich, till they arrived at Ballachulish ferry on Loch Leven. Here they crossed, and about five o'clock in the afternoon, just as they reached the gloomy shades of *Leitir Mhor*, on the

---

[1] This is the Alan Breck made famous in Louis Stevenson's story "Kidnapped."

[2] James Stewart was a natural son of Stewart of Appin, and was therefore related by ties of blood to Ardshiel.

Appin side of Loch Leven, the report of a musket rang out with startling effect upon the still air, and reverberated from hill to hill until the sound died away in the distance. The report was followed by another in rapid succession, and in the same instant Glenure was seen by his frightened companions to fall to the ground, apparently wounded. Upon coming up to the prostrate factor, they discovered that he had been shot right through the body by two musket balls, and was sinking fast. Assistance was sent for, but no medical skill could avail to staunch the life-blood that was flowing fast from those two terrible wounds, and in less than an hour from the time he was struck Glenure expired.

Suspicion fell at once upon Alan Breck Stewart, and immediate steps were taken by the authorities for his apprehension. All attempts to capture the supposed murderer were, however, fruitless, as he had absconded directly after the crime had been committed, and every effort to trace his whereabouts failed.

In a report from Captain Walter Johnstone, of Lord Bury's regiment, dated Invercomry, 7th June 1752, the following lines bearing on the subject appear :—" Next day Captain Campbell of Glen Lyon came here, and showed me two warrants from the Sheriff-Depute of Perthshire for apprehending Charles Stewart of Ardshiel, an attainted rebel, and Alan Breck Stewart, the supposed murderer of Mr Campbell of Glenure, upon which I gave the description of the two persons to all my parties, with orders to apprehend them."

A proclamation was issued by the Lords Justices on 28th May, offering a reward of £100 and a free pardon to any person concerned in the murder, other than the actual murderer, who would come forward with such information as might lead to the capture of the criminal. Twelve persons were arrested on suspicion, and among them was James Stewart, whose heedless words in connection with Glenure were now urged as evidence against him by his enemies, the Campbells. He was taken to Fort William on 2nd June, and examined before the sheriff, George Douglas, and committed for trial at Inveraray.

2 S

The proceedings in this *cause célèbre* were opened on Thursday, 21st September 1752, before a court composed almost entirely of Stewart's adversaries and political opponents. On the bench sat the Duke of Argyll and Lords Elchies and Kilkerran; the counsel for the prosecution were the Lord Advocate, Mr John Carmichael, Mr Simon Fraser, Master of Lovat, Mr James Erskine, Sheriff-Depute of Perthshire, Mr John Campbell, younger of Stonefield, and Mr Robert Campbell of Asknish, while the jury were Campbells almost to a man. The defence of the prisoner was undertaken by Mr George Brown, Sheriff-Depute of Forfar, Mr T. Millar, Mr Walter Stewart, and Mr R. Mackintosh. With such an array of legal talent against him, with a packed jury and partial judge, Stewart's conviction was a foregone conclusion. The evidence adduced by the prosecution was of the flimsiest description, and consisted principally of a reiteration of the foolish threat said to have been uttered by the prisoner against the murdered man; and, in addition to this, witnesses spoke to the fact that on the day following the murder the prisoner had sent Alexander Stewart, a packman of Appin, to William Stewart, merchant of Maryburgh (Fort William), with instructions to get from him the sum of five guineas, which he told the packman he wanted for his friend Alan Breck, who was, he said, about to leave the country.

The trial lasted from the Thursday until seven o'clock on the following Sunday morning, when the jury retired to consider their verdict, and were enclosed until twelve o'clock noon. Although the decision had been arrived at on Sunday, the formal verdict of "Guilty" was not pronounced until Monday morning. On 5th October, Stewart was bound to a horse and conducted to Fort William, guarded by a party of eighty soldiers.

He was carried from Fort William on 7th November, under a guard of one hundred men of Bockland's regiment, to the ferry of Ballachulish, but the night was so stormy that they could not cross until the following morning. Stewart was attended by Mr William Caskill, minister of Kilmallie, and

Mr Couper, minister of Fort William, and a few of his friends. A little after twelve o'clock, they arrived at the place of execution, which had been fixed at a spot close to the ferry at Ballachulish, where the murder was supposed to have been committed. Here a small tent had been erected, into which the prisoner was led attended by the two clergymen. After spending a short time in devotion, the unhappy man produced three copies of a speech he had prepared, one of which he gave to the Sheriff of Argyllshire, who was present in his official capacity, another to Captain Welsh, the commanding officer, and begged leave to read the third. The permission having been granted, he, with an audible and distinct voice, began to read a very extraordinary speech, in which he stoutly affirmed his innocence of any participation in the crime. "I positively deny," he said, "directly or indirectly being accessory to Glenure's murder, nor do I know who was the actor, further than my suspicion of Alan Breck Stewart, founded upon circumstances that have cast up since the murder happened." He complained bitterly of his treatment while in custody at Fort William, and suggested that his having taken part in the rising of 1745 was the cause of his unwarrantable arrest and unjust sentence. "When my trial came on, I found it was not only Glenure's murder I had to answer for, of which, I thank God, my conscience could easily clear me ; but the sins and follies of my forefathers were charged against me, such as the rebellion of 1715, of 1719, and 1745; so could not be allowed the character of an honest man."

He concluded this passionate harangue by commending his soul to his Creator in the following pious language: "I die in full hopes of mercy; not through any merit of myself, as I freely own I merit no good at the hand of my offended God ; but my hope is through the blood, merits, and mediation of the ever-blessed Jesus, my Redeemer and glorious Advocate, to whom I recommend my spirit. Come Lord Jesus, come quickly." He then took affectionate leave of his friends, mounted the ladder with the greatest composure and resolution, and read a short written prayer, together with the 35th Psalm, in a firm and audible voice. The storm all the time was raging furiously, so that the spectators could hardly stand on the hillside, and thus, amid the howling of the wind and the groans and tearful ejaculations of the assembled multitude, the spirit of James Stewart of the Glen sped to its Maker.

There is little doubt that Alan Breck Stewart was the real murderer of Glenure, and that James Stewart had been sacrificed, as he himself had truly said, on account of his connection with the Jacobite rising of 1745. The trial was a mere farce from beginning to end, and the arrest and execution of the unfortunate man was entirely due to the machinations of the Campbells, who, enraged at the escape of the guilty Allan, must needs make a scapegoat of his innocent namesake, as a blood-offering for their murdered clansman.

The following evidence, produced at the trial, will, I think, prove conclusively that Alan Breck was the criminal.

First. On the morning of the murder, Alan Breck was at the house of Alexander Stewart of Ballachulish, and left there about twelve o'clock, under the pretence of going fishing, having, as I have already described, changed his showy French clothes for less conspicuous ones on 11th May.

Second. On 15th May (the day following the murder) he arrived at the house of MacDonald of Glencoe at Carnach very early in the morning, before the family were up; and upon Glencoe and Alan's step-mother, Isabel Stewart, coming to the door, he told them that Glenure had been shot, and that he would have to leave the country. Glencoe asked him to take some refreshment, but he said he could not stop.

Third. On 16th May, while John MacColl, Appin's bo-man, was cutting firewood at Corrienakiegh,[1] near the farm of Caolasnacon, Alan Breck came up and asked him to go to Duror for some money, and to Glencoe's house for meal. He also wrote a letter to William Stewart of Fort William, with the quill of a

[1] Probably Corrie-na-Ciche.

wood-pigeon he had found, requesting him to give bearer some money.

Fourth. On 17th May Alexander Stewart, the packman, met MacColl, and requested him to seek out Alan, and deliver to him the parcel he was carrying, which contained the French clothes, and also give the fugitive the sum of five guineas, which he handed to MacColl with the bundle. That same evening, Alan Breck Stewart knocked at the window of MacColl's dwelling, and asked for the money and clothes, which were given him, and after partaking of some milk he departed, and was never again seen in that part of the country, although he was known to have visited some relatives in Rannoch.

These facts, sworn to by witnesses at the trial at Inveraray, speak for themselves.

Lochaber folk still speak of the 35th Psalm as "*Salm Sheumais a Ghlinne*" ("the Psalm of James of the Glen"), and the spot where the gallows stood is pointed out on the small fir-clad knoll of *Cnap-a-Chaolais*. For many years the mortal remains of this unfortunate victim of political injustice and clan hatred swayed to and fro above the dark waters of Loch Leven, a grim and ghastly spectacle, bearing silent witness to man's inhumanity to man, and helping to emphasise with their gruesome presence the gloomy traditions of drear Glencoe. The removal of the gallows and its burden was the work of a local character called *Donnachadh, an t-Sheana-Chinn,* who, with a dim perception in his half-witted brain that he was performing some heroic action, cut down the "wuddie," and threw it, together with the bones of James Stewart, into the loch.

Mrs Grant of Laggan visited the scene of the execution in the month of May 1773, and was shown the cairn that marked the spot where Glenure was murdered, upon which, she says, "every passenger throws a stone." In a letter written from Fort William, dated 14th May 1773, describing her visit, the following passage appears :—" I can't convey to you the impression which this assemblage of gloomy images

made at once on my mind, aided by the recollection that a
worthy and innocent gentleman related to my mother, suffered
death in consequence; though it appeared afterwards the
murder was committed by a soldier in the French service,
who lurked in the country since the year 1745 for that purpose."
The soldier referred to was evidently Alan Breck, who, as I
have already stated, had served in the French army. The
Scots Magazine of June 1752, from which I have taken the
main facts of the trial and execution of James Stewart, has
a short account of the execution of a notorious thief at Perth,
on 5th June of that year, and gives his name as Alan Breck
Stewart: there is, however, no reason for connecting him with
the murderer of Glenure.

The prefix Breck (Gaelic *breac*) is common in the Highlands, and means literally spotted or speckled, and is often
given as a nickname to a person pitted with small-pox.

CHAPTER XL.

THE year 1752 was marked in Lochaber by an increase of
military activity in connection with the enforcement of the
"Rebellion Statutes," as the new Acts of Parliament were
called, and strong garrisons of soldiers were posted at Laggan-
ach-Drom, between Loch Lochy and Loch Oich, and at various
places along the shores of Loch Arkaig. Captain A. Trapaud,
of Lord Bury's regiment, commanded at the former post, and
Captain John Beckwith, of the same regiment, at the latter.

Trapaud, who was afterwards governor of Fort Augustus,
was a great friend of General Wolfe, the hero of Quebec, and
it may interest some of my readers to know that this famous
officer had served as captain in General Barrel's regiment at
the battle of Falkirk, and having been promoted to the rank of
brevet-major, acted as aide-de-camp to the infamous Hawley
at Culloden, at which time Wolfe was but eighteen years
of age. Although he despised the Highlanders (*vide* his

letters[1]), and looked upon them as mere rebels, his mind
recoiled from the butcheries that took place after the battle,
and, as the following incident will show, he was able to administer a just reproof to no less a person than the commander-
in-chief.

Whilst engaged in riding over the battle-field in attendance
upon the Duke of Cumberland and his staff, a wounded man
was seen lying on the ground, who proved to be the young
chief of the Fraser regiment. The supercilious glance of
Fraser annoyed the duke, and turning to Wolfe, he said,
"Wolfe! shoot me that Highland scoundrel who thus dares
to look on us with so insolent a stare." Disgusted at the
wanton barbarity thus displayed by his commander, Wolfe
replied, with something of hauteur in his tone, that his commission was at his royal highness's disposal, but that he
would never consent to become an executioner.

Surely it was something more than a strange coincidence
when, after his last brilliant victory over the French on the
heights of Abraham (a victory largely due to the courage
and intrepidity of the despised Highlanders), the fatal bullet
had struck him to the heart, that the strong arms which
supported him as he breathed his last should have been
those of a Fraser.

The reports of the officers in command of the military posts
on Loch Arkaig and Loch Lochy are full of interesting details,
and we may learn much from them of the state of Lochaber
in the years following the "Forty-Five."[2] The harrying of
the Highlands appears from these despatches to have afforded
considerable sport to the ennuied subalterns of Lord Bury's
regiment, and they seem to have regarded the occasional arrest
of some offender against the new Act prohibiting the Highland
dress much in the same light as their modern representatives
do the capture of a notorious Burmese dacoit or troublesome

[1] Appendix XXX.
[2] A selection of the most interesting reports from the English officers stationed
in Lochaber during the years 1752-1755 will be found in Appendix XXXI.

Indian hill chief. These young English officers, habituated as they were to the dissipated and luxurious life of London, where they were able to enjoy to the utmost those questionable pleasures which were to be found amid the fashionable haunts of the great metropolis, resented bitterly their forced seclusion among the mountains of Lochaber, far away from the amorous glances of their Celias and Phyllises, and the almost equally seductive attractions of their favourite coffee-houses. Wolfe, in a letter written from Banff in 1751, says: " When I am in Scotland I look upon myself as an exile—with respect to the inhabitants I am so, for I dislike 'em so much." The dislike was mutual; but later Wolfe had reason to alter his opinion, and we know that before he died he had learned to admire and appreciate the character of his former enemies.

By far the larger number of the Highlanders arrested by the patrolling parties were poor men, of little influence in the country; but in the early months of the year 1753 two important captures were made, whereby two innocent Lochaber gentlemen were made to suffer all the indignities that a tyrannical and vindictive Government could heap upon them.

The first to fall into the clutches of the Elector's troops was the amiable Dr Archibald Cameron, who, probably thinking that the hue and cry was at an end, ventured to leave the safe seclusion of his retreat at Lille, and unwisely set out for his native Highlands, with the object, it is said, of recovering the remaining portion of the French gold that he had hidden by the shores of Loch Arkaig. In 1747 Dr Cameron had accompanied Prince Charles on his journey from Avignon to Madrid; and two years later, in 1749, he is believed to have paid a visit to Scotland, at the special request of the prince, in order to receive from Cluny MacPherson a large sum of money that had been left in his charge during the prince's wanderings. The first visit, risky though it undoubtedly was, appears to have been unattended with any unpleasant contretemps, and the doctor returned safely to France, having accomplished his mission. Whatever may have been the reason that prompted Dr Cameron to attempt another journey to the land of his birth we have no certain knowledge, but that it was fatal in its consequences we know, alas! only too well. The story of his capture, taken from a rare contemporary pamphlet, entitled "The Life of Dr Archibald Cameron, Brother to Donald Cameron of Lochiel, Chief of that Clan," and published in London at the time of his execution, is as follows:—

"He (Dr Archibald) was taken by a Party of Lord George Beauclerk's Regiment, who was detached from the Fort at Inversnaid in Search of him; this Detachment was commanded by one Capt. Graven: They had Information of the House where he was to stay some Days, but in their March to it, were obliged to pass through two small Villages; at the end of the first they saw a little Girl, who, as soon as she perceived Soldiers, ran as fast as she could; a Sergeant and two or three Men pursued her, but she reached the other Village before they could overtake her; and there she sent off a Boy, who seemed to be placed there to give Intelligence of the Approach of the Soldiers. The Soldiers then pursued the Boy, but finding they were not able to come up with him, the Sergeant called out to his Men to present their Pieces, as if they intended to shoot him. The Boy on this, turning round, begg'd his Life; they secured him, and then went to the House where the Doctor was, which they beset on all Sides. The Disposition the Captain made was admirable; he with some of his Men marched up to the Front of the House, but (Dr Cameron) was soon discovered from the Window, where he was immediately secured by the Sergeant who was placed there, as the Captain very judiciously suspected the Doctor might attempt to Escape from that Part of the House."

Brave little lassie! She did what she could to protect the good Highland doctor, whose kindness of disposition had doubtless touched the hearts of the children in the neighbourhood of the house in which he was residing. Unfortunately her efforts to draw the English redcoats off the scent were

2 T

unavailing, and the doctor fell an easy prey to the "admirable Dispositions" of the "judicious" Captain Graven.

The arrest of Dr Cameron took place at the latter end of March, and on the 26th of that month he was conveyed to Edinburgh Castle. It was during an interview he had while there with Lord-Justice Clark, that he indignantly denied having come to Scotland with any political object. "I did not come over with a political design," he said, "but only to transact some affairs relating to Lochiel's estate." About a month later the unlucky Doctor was removed to London and imprisoned in the Tower; and on 17th May was conducted by a strong detachment of Foot Guards, and several of the Tower warders, to the Court of King's Bench, where he was arraigned upon the Act of Attainder, for having taken part in the late rebellion, and not surrendering himself within the stipulated time. Dr Cameron made no attempt to deny his identity, but reiterated his previous statement that his visit to Scotland had no political significance; and he urged as a reason why sentence should not be pronounced against him, that he was a non-combatant in the rebellion, and had no military standing whatsoever; he also informed the Court that his medical skill had been used on many occasions to allay the sufferings of the English soldiers who had fallen into the hands of the Highland army at Prestonpans, Carlisle, and Falkirk, and also that it was partly due to his counsels that the City of Glasgow was not sacked by the Highlanders when it lay at their disposal.

Dr Cameron might as well have pleaded for mercy to a stone wall, as to have wasted his eloquence upon the adamantine hearts of English judges in the pay of a Whig Government. Mercy, indeed! mercy to a Highland rebel—perish the thought! Guilty or not guilty, he must hang, and so the atrocious sentence was pronounced by Lord Chief-Justice Lee, in terms that would have disgraced the tribunal of an Eastern despot :—
"You, Archibald Cameron of Lochiel, in that part of Great Britain called Scotland, must be removed from hence to His

Majesty's prison of the Tower of London, from whence you came, and on Thursday, the 7th of June next, your body to be drawn on a sledge to the place of execution, there to be hanged, *not till you are dead;* your bowels to be taken out, your body quartered, and your head cut off, and affixed at the king's disposal, and the Lord have mercy on your soul."

Dr Cameron heard this barbarous sentence with calm equanimity, and merely requested, in the most courteous language, that he might be allowed to send for his wife, who was then residing at Lille, in order that she might receive his last messages. This favour having been granted by his judges, Dr Cameron was again conveyed to the Tower to await his awful doom. His heart-broken wife, upon reaching London, strained every nerve to obtain a pardon for her unhappy husband, and is said to have personally petitioned the Elector and his son, but without effect.

The last terrible scene in the life of Dr Archibald Cameron is thus described in the *Scots Magazine* of May 1753:—"On Thursday, 7th June, about ten o'clock, Sir Charles Asgill and Sir Richard Glynn went to the Tower, and William Runford, Esq., the Deputy-Lieutenant, delivered the Doctor into the custody of Mr Missin, Deputy-Sheriff of the county of Middle-sex. Being put into the sledge, he requested of the Governor to speak to his wife, which being granted, and he being informed that she had left the Tower at eight that morning, he said he was sorry for it. On which the sledge drew away, among a great number of spectators, who all pitied his unfortunate circumstances. Sir Charles Asgill left the prisoner at the Tower, but Sir Richard Glynn followed the sledge, in his chariot, to Tyburn. The sledge was drawn by four horses, with black feathers on their head; and the Doctor was dressed in a light-coloured coat, red waistcoat and breeches, and a new bag-wig, without a hat. About a quarter past twelve he arrived at the place of execution, and having spent about ten minutes in devotion he was turned off. After hanging twenty-four minutes, he was cut down, his head cut off, and his heart taken out and burnt, but his body was not quartered. His body and head were afterwards put into a hearse, and carried to Mr Stephenson's, undertaker. On his way to the place of execution, he behaved himself with great composure and decency, and spoke often, with a manly cheerfulness and confidence. . . . A non-juring clergyman of the Episcopal Church of Scotland attended him, and he lived and died in that communion."

After the execution, we are told Dr Cameron's remains were carried from the undertakers on Saturday, 9th June, at twelve at night, and interred in the large vault in the Savoy Chapel. "Several gentlemen attended the funeral, who seemed greatly to lament his unhappy fate."

While imprisoned in the Tower, Dr Cameron employed his time in writing several interesting letters on any odd scraps of paper he could find, which he intended to have delivered to the Sheriff of Middlesex at the place of execution, but afterwards placed in the hands of his wife. In one of them he says: "Being denied the use of pen, ink, and paper, except in the presence of one or more officers, who always took away the paper from me whenever I began to write my complaints, and not even allowed the use of a knife with which I might cut a poor blunted pencil that had escaped the diligence of my searchers, I have, notwithstanding, as I could find opportunity, attempted to set down on some slips of paper, in as legible characters as I was able, what I would have my country satisfied of in regard to myself, and the cause in which I am now going to lay down my life. As to my religion, I thank God I die a member (though unworthy) of that church in whose communion I have always lived, the Episcopal Church of Scotland, as by law established, before the [1]

1688. And I firmly trust to find, at the most awful and impartial tribunal of the Almighty King, through the merits of my blessed Lord and Saviour Jesus Christ, that mercy (though undeserved) to my immortal part, which is here

---

[1] Blank space in text; probably the Doctor's writing was indecipherable.

denied to my earthly,—though it be well known I have been
the instrument of preventing the ruin and destruction of many
of my poor deluded countrymen, who were in the Government
service, as I shall make appear before I have done, if opportunities of writing fail me not."

Alas! the "poor blunted pencil" could not be sharpened,
and in the middle of a noble and pathetic letter to his son
it gave out, and the words he wished to write were never
written.

After the execution some other letters were found among
his personal effects, and one, in which he asks a friend to give
the steel shoe-buckles he was wearing to his wife, to be conveyed by her to his eldest son, is especially interesting, as
showing that to the last moment of his life he never wavered
in his loyalty to his rightful sovereign, and endeavoured, in
his last farewell message, to instil the same sentiments into
the breast of his son and heir.   The letter runs as follows :—
"These I send by you to my wife, as my last present to my
son, and bid her tell him from me that I send these, and not
my silver ones ; and that if I had gold ones, I would not send
him the gold, but these steel ones I wore when I was skulking ;
for as steel is hard and of small value, it is therefore an emblem
of constancy and disinterestedness ; so I would have him constant and disinterested in the service and defence of his king,
prince, and country, and neither be bribed or frightened from
his duty."

The execution of Dr Archibald Cameron was a wanton
act of unnecessary severity on the part of the English Government, for which it is impossible to find the slightest excuse.
That a benevolent and accomplished gentleman, whose noble
profession was to alleviate the pains of suffering humanity,
and whose only offence was that he had dutifully obeyed the
commands of his chief and brother, should have been dragged
to the scaffold and butchered with every detail of ingenious
brutality, under the warrant of a ruler professing Christianity,
is an ineffaceable stigma upon English justice.   Eight years

had passed since the Jacobite rising, and, secure behind the bayonets of his soldiers, the usurper of the throne of the Stuarts had no cause to fear any further attempt on the part of his royal rival to wrest the sceptre of Britain from his grasp. That he felt some qualms of conscience when signing the death warrant of Dr Cameron is certain, for we are told that when the fatal document was laid before him, he remarked, "Surely there has been too much blood spilt upon this account already." He, however, lacked sufficient moral courage to exercise his prerogative of mercy in opposition to the wishes of his inexorable ministers, and although, like Pontius Pilate of old, he saw no guilt in the person of the condemned man, he nevertheless signed the warrant and washed his hands of the responsibility.

In Dr Archibald Cameron, Lochaber men have a hero of whom they may well be proud, and it may interest them to know that in the heart of the great city of London, and within a few feet of one of its most noisy thoroughfares, the ashes of the good doctor rest in peace, beneath the altar of the ancient Chapel Royal of the Savoy. Here, in the year 1846, his grandson placed a small marble tablet inscribed with the date of burial and other particulars, but this was destroyed by the fire which occurred in 1864. Since the restoration of the building, a more worthy, and, I trust, more permanent memento of Dr Archibald Cameron has replaced the monumental stone. This has taken the shape of a magnificent stained-glass window, designed, I am told, by Rossetti and Burne-Jones. It is divided into six panels, the three upper ones containing representations of St Peter, St Philip, and St Paul; and the lower, St John, St James, and St Andrew. The inscription is as follows:—"In memory of Archibald Cameron of Lochiel, who having been attainted after the battle of Culloden in 1746 escaped to France, but returning to Scotland in 1753 was apprehended and executed. He was buried beneath the Altar of this Chapel. The window is inserted by Her Majesty's permission in place of a sculptured Tablet which was erected by his grandson, Charles Hay Cameron, in 1846, and consumed by the fire which partially destroyed the Chapel in 1864." The Register with the entry of the burial may still be seen.

CHAPTER XLI.

A MONTH after the capture of Dr Archibald Cameron at Inversnaid, his brother John of Fassfern was arrested by order of the Government, on a charge of having corresponded with attainted persons. The actual date of his apprehension was 28th April; and about the same time Alexander Stewart of Banavie, a Writer to the Signet, who had been employed by the late Lochiel, and who had been associated with Fassfern in various legal matters in connection with the estate, was also arrested and imprisoned with Fassfern in the jail at Fort William.

On 6th May these two innocent gentlemen were committed to the castle of Edinburgh, and on 3rd July Fassfern was liberated on bail, but was afterwards rearrested on a most unjust suspicion of having forged some documents relating to the property of his deceased brother Donald of Lochiel. Although there were not the slightest grounds for such a charge, Fassfern was subjected to every indignity that his enemies could heap upon him, and after a long period of imprisonment, he was brought up for trial at Edinburgh and acquitted of the charge of forgery; but on the other count, of having been in communication with the late Lochiel and other attainted chiefs, he was found guilty and sentenced to a term of exile.

After some years' residence in the West Indies, he was allowed to return to his beloved Fassfern, where he died. His son Ewen, who was married to Lucy Campbell, daughter of Campbell of Barcaldine, succeeded to the estates, and became the father of a large family. John, the eldest son, entered the army, and won honour and fame as Colonel John Cameron, 92nd Highlanders, of whose career I shall have more to say later.

The insulted majesty of the Whig Government having been appeased by the innocent blood of their latest victim, they began to relax their severity, and beyond the occasional arrest of some bold Highland reiver, who defied the provisions of the Act which forbade the wearing of the kilt, no further steps were taken to inflict punishment upon the unfortunate adherents of the Stuarts. This improved state of affairs was primarily due to the advice of the celebrated William Pitt, afterwards Earl of Chatham. Pitt had been one of the first English statesmen to recognise the martial spirit inherent in the Highlanders, and to perceive the immense advantage that would accrue to the British army by the infusion of their heroic blood into its somewhat effete ranks. With admirable sagacity he foresaw also that there could be no better antidote to their disaffection than honourable military service, under the command of officers who had accepted their commissions at the hand of that monarch against whose authority they had recently been in open rebellion.

With the splendid example of the Black Watch to point to, Pitt found little difficulty in persuading George II. to issue letters of service for the raising of several new regiments, whose ranks were to be exclusively filled with Highlanders, to whom special permission was granted to wear the proscribed Highland dress. The immediate outcome of this action on the part of the sagacious prime minister was the formation, in January 1757, of Montgomery's Highlanders, or the 77th Regiment of Foot ; and, a little later in the same month, the Fraser Highlanders, or 78th Regiment, were raised, and a lieutenant-colonel's commission given to the Hon. Simon Fraser, son of old Lord Lovat, whose double-dealing in connection with the late rising had been expiated on the scaffold at Tower Hill.

The opportunity thus afforded to the Highlanders for indulging their love for military exercises was eagerly taken advantage of, and the call to arms was responded to with an enthusiasm which was a source of wonder to the authorities, who were unable to understand the cause. The success of the policy that Pitt had inaugurated was due to the fact that the men who were to form the rank and file of the new regiments were given to understand that their commanding officers would be their own chiefs, and thus the ancient bonds of clanship were to be drawn closer, rather than loosened, by the change. Had the chiefs refused to accept the proffered commissions, the Highland regiments could never have been raised, and history would have many a blank page that is now filled with the glorious records of more than a century and a half of heroic actions, in which Highlanders have taken a lion's share.

It was only just that the man who called these regiments into being should be the first to sound their praise, and this he did in no measured terms during one of those splendid oratorical efforts with which he was wont to electrify the House of Commons, and strike terror into the hearts of his political opponents. "I sought for merit wherever it could be found," he said. "It is my boast that I was the first minister who looked for it, and found it, in the mountains of the north. I called it forth, and drew into your service a hardy and intrepid race of men—men who, when left by your jealousy, became a prey to the artifices of your enemies, and had gone nigh to have overturned the State, in the war before the last. These men in the last war were brought to combat on your side; they served with fidelity, as they fought with valour, and conquered for you in every quarter of the world." This noble tribute to the heroism of the Highland soldiers was uttered in the year 1766, and, to the honour of our Highland regiments, it is as true to-day as it was then.

The first list of officers commissioned in Fraser's Highlanders, dated 5th January 1757, contains the names of many gentlemen from Lochaber and its vicinity, among whom we find Captains Donald MacDonald, brother of Clanranald (killed at Quebec in 1760); John MacDonald of Lochgarry (afterwards Colonel of the 76th Regiment); Alexander Cameron of Dun-

2 U

gallon; and John MacPherson, brother of Cluny. Lieutenants Ranald MacDonell, brother of Angus, XVII. of Keppoch; Charles MacDonell, son of John MacDonell, XII. of Glengarry (killed at St Johns); Hector MacDonald, brother to Boisdale (killed 1759); Alexander MacDonald, son of Barrisdale (killed on the heights of Abraham, 1759); Ewen Cameron, of the Glen Nevis family (wounded at Quebec); Donald Cameron, son of John Cameron of Fassfern (died 1817); Alan Cameron (? of Errachd); and Hugh Cameron. The total number of men enlisted was fifteen hundred, of whom Colonel Fraser raised eight hundred, mostly of his own clan.

The uniform adopted by the regiment was the full Highland dress of kilt and belted plaid (*breacan-an-fheilidh*), and tartan or diced hose; for arms they carried muskets and the formidable claymore or broadsword; and those who could afford the expense were allowed to add to their equipment the dirk and sporran of badger skin. The headgear was a bonnet ornamented with two or three black feathers drooping over it, and decorated with the distinguishing badge of the clan to which the wearer belonged. Eagles' feathers were worn by the officers, as was the custom among the Highland chieftains.[1] Nothing could be more politic than the measures adopted by the authorities for rendering service in the army popular; Highland sentiment and tradition was respected; the wearing of the national garb was made a privilege which any able-bodied man could enjoy by joining the ranks of his comrades in the service of the State; due consideration was given to the antipathy that still existed between various clans, by the exclusion as far as possible of the elements of future discord; and, in fact, everything was done to avoid wounding in the slightest degree the susceptibilities of the newly-made soldiers.

The result was to popularise the army, and attract from every part of the Highlands a steady flow of recruits eager to take part in their country's service, and fight the French under the direction of their own chiefs.

[1] "Stewart's Sketches."

It would be well if some of our War Office authorities of the present day would study the early history of those gallant Highland regiments whose existence they periodically threaten, because, forsooth, they are utterly unable, owing to their crass ignorance of Celtic peculiarities, to obtain sufficient recruits to fill up the gaps that occur in the ranks. Let them but take a lesson from the book of England's greatest statesman, William Pitt, and they will find no difficulty in maintaining these historic battalions at full strength.

Fraser's Highlanders saw some hard fighting in Canada under General Wolfe, and were present at the taking of Quebec, where their courage and intrepidity contributed in no small degree to the brilliant victory of the British forces. The regiment was disbanded at the conclusion of hostilities in 1763; and many of the officers and men having expressed a wish to remain in America, the Government generously provided them with a grant of land, upon which they settled.

Captain Donald MacDonald, who was unfortunately slain at the taking of Quebec, was an officer of considerable ability, and had he lived would doubtless have attained high rank in his profession. His military career was begun in France sometime previous to 1745, and during that fatal year he had followed the fortunes of his prince in the ill-omened campaign which ended with Culloden. Like many other of his associates in that bold but fruitless effort to restore the Stuarts to power, he had suffered imprisonment, but was fortunate enough to regain his freedom without the ordeal of a trial. Returning to France after his liberation from captivity, he again sought to win fresh laurels amid the din of battle. In 1756 he returned to his native land, and in the following year received a captain's commission in Fraser's Highlanders. His keen military instincts and approved courage gained for him the confidence of General Wolfe, who rarely made any important strategical movement without first consulting Captain MacDonald.

Another officer of Fraser's Highlanders who merits some description was Ranald MacDonell, brother to Angus, seven-

teenth chief of Keppoch. Alexander, the sixteenth chief, who
fell at Culloden whilst endeavouring to rally his retreating
clansmen, had married Jessie, a daughter of Stewart of Appin,
by whom he had several children; but it is said that Angus,
who succeeded to the chieftainship, was not one of them, and
it is therefore assumed that he was illegitimate. That Angus
was the son of Alexander of Keppoch there is no possible
doubt, and it is also known that his mother was a native of
Skye, of humble parentage, whom Keppoch had met while
staying in the island at the house of his kinsman, Sir Alexander
MacDonald of Sleat, but no record exists of any marriage
having taken place.

It was during the period that Keppoch was serving in the
French army that Angus was born in Skye, and his mother
died shortly after bringing him into the world. Upon
Keppoch's return to Lochaber, he brought his son home, and
shortly afterwards married Miss Stewart. It is of course
possible that Keppoch had married Angus's mother whilst
he was living in Skye, but that, owing to her humble origin,
he had refrained from publishing the news abroad. This view
is the one taken by the present representatives of the family,
and is certainly not altogether an improbable or unreasonable
one, when looked at by the light of Keppoch's conduct to his
son, and the care he bestowed upon his education and up-
bringing. Angus was always treated as the heir and future
chief, and even after his father's second marriage, no distinction was made between him and his half-brothers, nor was
he in anyway slighted by his step-mother, which would most
certainly have been the case had he been illegitimate. It does
not seem at all probable that Keppoch, who was one of the most
polished and accomplished men of his day, the very soul of
honour and refinement, should have imposed upon his wife
the obligation of putting an illegitimate child upon the same
footing as her legitimate offspring. This, and the fact that
Angus's step-mother, so far from exhibiting any feelings of
aversion and resentment at his presence, was absolutely devoted

to him, and regarded him with a sincere affection which Angus
cordially reciprocated, appears to me strong proof that he was
not regarded as illegitimate. We have, moreover, the certain
knowledge that upon Alexander of Keppoch's death at
Culloden, Angus succeeded to the chieftainship as a matter
of course, and was accepted by the clan as their head without the slightest hesitation ; nor do we hear of any reference
or suggestion of illegitimacy being made at the time.

It is now, I fear, too late in the day to arrive at a satisfactory
settlement of the question, but after a close personal investigation of the various arguments *pro* and *con*, I lean to the belief
that Alexander of Keppoch legally married the mother of
Angus, and have little doubt that the child of the union was
legitimate. The circumstance of Angus's abdication of the
chieftainship to his half-brother Ranald in my opinion proves
nothing, as it was probably only a politic move to secure
the estates, for Angus, having been out in the '45, was
excluded from his patrimony by the Act of Attainder.

Ranald of Keppoch joined the ranks of Fraser's Highlanders upon their formation in 1757, and was at once
appointed lieutenant. He appears on the list of officers as
the *son* of Keppoch, a fact which tends to strengthen the
evidence in favour of the legitimacy of Angus. Ranald served
with distinction throughout the Canadian War, and was
wounded on the same day that saw the defeat of the French
under Montcalm and the death of the gallant Wolfe.

At the close of the war Ranald returned to his native
Lochaber, and occupied his time in superintending the erection of the present Keppoch House, a substantial building by
the side of the river Roy, and overlooked by the hill of Mulroy,
where his grandfather, the famous Coll of Keppoch, fought
the last clan battle against his old enemies the Mackintoshes.
Within a short distance is the dark wood of *Coille Diamhain*,
said to be haunted by the wraith of the wife of Alexander,
the fifth chief, 1497–1499. He was the second son of Angus,
the second chief, and succeeded his nephew Iain Aluinn, who

was deposed by the clan. Before being elected chief, Alexander
lived with his family at *Coille Diamhain* on the banks of *Allt
Ionndrainn*, a small burn that runs into the river Roy. He had
married a lady of Irish descent, the daughter of Donald Gallach
of Sleat by his wife, who was a daughter of MacDonell of
Antrim. When the lady came to Skye, she brought with her
a certain number of the Irish clans as a marriage portion; and
when her daughter married Keppoch, some of these wild
Irishmen came with her to Lochaber and settled there, some
taking the name of MacDonald, while others retained their
original surnames of Burke and Boyle; and to this day there
are families of these names in the neighbourhood of Glen Roy.
This lady disappeared in a mysterious manner, and her fate
has never been satisfactorily explained. Some thought she was
drowned in *Allt Ionndrainn* when it was in spate, and others
believed she had been foully murdered; but whatever may
have been the cause of her death, her spirit has haunted the
wood ever since, and even to this day many of the natives of
the locality fear to pass the place after nightfall, lest they should
see the ghastly form of "*A' bhaintigearna bheag*" ("the little
lady"), the name by which she was known among her people.
After building his house and being formally accepted as chief
of the clan in place of his brother Angus, Ranald rejoined
the army in Jamaica, where, about the year 1781, he married
a Miss Cargill, who bore him two sons and two daughters;
one of the daughters married a Mr Stewart, W.S., and their
family (I believe) are now in Edinburgh. Some years later
Keppoch retired from the army, and took up his residence at
Keppoch House, where, as we shall see later, he materially
assisted Cameron of Errachd in raising the 79th Regiment, or
Cameron Highlanders.

Angus of Keppoch married a daughter of MacDonell of
Achnacoichean, and had several children, one of whom, John,
wrote the MSS. notes that I have already referred to, and which
have proved of great value in connection with this work. When
a young man he visited Prince Charles Edward in Rome. The

prince was at that time an old man, and nearly blind; but,
notwithstanding his afflictions, he received young MacDonell
with great cordiality, and presented him with a piece of the
ribbon of his orders as a memento.

CHAPTER XLII.

THE death of Britain's second Hanoverian ruler, in the year
1760, was followed, in the month of December 1766, by the
decease at Rome of king James VIII. (commonly known as
the Old Chevalier). The exiled monarch of Britain had long
ceased to take more than a languid interest in the various
chimerical and visionary schemes for his restoration to the
throne of his ancestors. On the battle-field of Culloden the
ambitions and aspirations of his early years lay buried, without
hope of resurrection. He saw, what his impetuous and fearless
son would not or could not see, that the British people, as a
whole, were satisfied to endure the ills they had to suffer under
the rule of their Teutonic idol and his voracious parasites,
rather than flee for relief to the legitimate but papistical
Stuarts.[1] After suffering for many years from a chronic complaint, which was aggravated by the disappointments he had
so often experienced in his chequered career, king James
passed peacefully away, leaving to his two sons, Charles and
Henry, the mere insignia of royalty, unaccompanied by its
realities of throne and kingdom — a phantom legacy which
eluded, with a tantalising persistency, the hands that were
outstretched to grasp it.

Prince Charles, who, upon the death of his royal father,

---

[1] It has been often stated by the biographers of Prince Charles that he had
abjured Roman Catholicism, but there appears to be no absolute proof of this.
In a postscript to one of Dr Archibald Cameron's letters, written just before his
execution, he says: "I likewise declare, on the word of a dying man, that the
last time I had the honour to see his Royal Highness Charles, Prince of Wales,
he told me from his own mouth, and bade me assure his friends from him, that he
was a member of the Church of England."

became the titular king of Great Britain as Charles III., married, in the year 1772, the beautiful young Princess Louisa of Stolberg. This union, which was purely a *marriage de convenance*, contracted with the sole object of perpetuating the male line of the House of Stuart, was most unfortunate in its consequences. Unsanctified by the affections, it was a union only in name, and ended, as such alliances invariably do, in mutual recriminations and unseemly strife. Not only was the marriage an unhappy one, but it failed altogether to effect its purpose of providing an heir to the throne of Britain. The matrimonial fetters became so strained that, in the year 1780, they were broken asunder, and the youthful princess, whose happiness had been sacrificed upon the altar of political intrigue, left her royal spouse and sought shelter under the roof of her brother at Rome.

The spectacle presented by Charles at this period is melancholy in the extreme. Deserted by his wife, and almost forgotten by those who, but a few years before, would have been ready to lay down their lives in his service; afflicted in body, and troubled in mind; the companions of his youth dead, or living far beyond the reach of his call; with premature old age creeping slowly upon him, and the valley of the shadow of death looming dark across his path—his figure stands out against the background of history, eloquently speaking to the present and future ages in mute language the pathetic story of a disappointed and wasted life.

There is one touch of brightness in the gloomy picture of these later years of Bonnie Prince Charlie which must appeal to all hearts, whether Whig or Jacobite. To the side of that solitary figure, standing upon the brink of the grave, there comes, like a ministering angel, the form of a fair woman to soothe with her gentle presence the declining years of the lonely exile. With womanly tenderness and reverent care she attends to his many wants, and solaces his hours of ennui and suffering with words of comfort and affection. Father and daughter, they stand together united in a common bond of sympathy, for both had felt the buffetings of remorseless fate, and the sneers of an unkind and indifferent world.

The story of Prince Charles's *liaison* with Clementina Walkinshaw has been made the reason for much flinging of mud and pharisaical censure on the part of the "unco guid," who are always ready to perceive the mote in the eyes of their fellow-mortals, forgetting altogether the beam that obscures their own narrow field of vision. Looked at from the standpoint of strict morality, the guilty love of the prince for his mistress can only receive condemnation; but it must not be forgotten that the circumstances of his royal birth and princely position precluded him from choosing a consort at will, and, as the event proved, he was practically forced into a marriage with a woman who, beautiful and accomplished as she was, failed to kindle in his breast the slightest spark of the tender passion, without which the married state becomes the veriest hell upon earth. "Let him that is without guilt among you cast the first stone" was the stern rebuke of the God-man to the sanctimonious Jewish mud-throwers of eighteen centuries ago, and it would be well if the self-constituted judges of the erring prince had taken the Divine reproof to heart before seeking to blacken and defame his character. It was his daughter Charlotte,[1] by Clementina Walkinshaw, who watched by his bedside during those last terrible three weeks in January 1788, when, stricken by paralysis, he lay half-unconscious in his darkened room, within sound of the bells of the great cathedral of St Peter's; and when the last dread messenger came to bid him leave his shadowy earthly kingdom for an eternal and heavenly one, it was she who performed the last sad offices for her dead king and father.

The honours that were denied to him in life were showered upon the coffin that contained all that remained of what had once been Bonnie Prince Charlie. All the wealth and magnificence of the impressive Roman ceremonial were called into

---

[1] Before he died Charles legitimatised his daughter Charlotte, and created her "Duchess of Albany."

requisition, to render solemn impressiveness to his obsequies, and amid the chanting of white-robed priests, and the clouds of ascending incense, the body of Britain's legitimate king was laid to rest by the side of his royal father, under the shade of the mighty dome of St Peter's at Rome.

Upon the death of Charles, his only brother Henry, who had received the dignity of Cardinal from the hands of the Pope in the year 1747, succeeded to the empty title, but beyond having a medal struck, bearing the inscription, " Henry IX., King of England, by the grace of God, but not by the will of man," he did nothing to push forward his claim to the throne, being apparently too well satisfied with the high ecclesiastical position he filled, and the princely emoluments of the office, to embark in any risky political enterprise, such as had proved so fatal to his brother. He died in the year 1807, having attained the venerable age of eighty-two years, and was buried in the same vault that contained the mortal part of his father and brother. With Henry IX. the direct Stuart line came to an end,[1] and Jacobitism became merely a sentiment, a strong and lasting one nevertheless, and one that may yet bear fruit in the ages that are to come.

The accession of the third George to the throne that his great grandsire had wrested from the Stuarts, marked the commencement of a new and more enlightened policy on the part of the English Government towards the Highlanders, and Lochaber, in common with the other proscribed districts, benefited by the change. By the year 1760 militant Jacobitism was to all intents and purposes dead, and even the most fiery spirits among the adherents of the exiled Stuarts saw that it was useless to attempt to resuscitate it. Might had conquered right, as it always has done in the world's history, and all that the Jacobite chieftains could now do was to bow to the inevitable with as good a grace as possible, and outwardly, at least, to acknowledge George the Third as king.

A great deal of the prejudice that had existed against his

[1] Appendix XXXII.

Hanoverian predecessors had by this time died out; the fact that, unlike them, he had been born in the land he was to rule, materially assisted to add popularity to his name. "Born and educated in this country," said George, in his first speech to Parliament, "I glory in the name of Briton"; and it is much to his credit that he should have inaugurated his reign with such noble and patriotic words. Doubtless the gallant deeds performed during the Canadian war by the newly-raised Highland regiments had a great deal to do with the revulsion of public feeling in favour of the Highlanders, and the gradual relaxation by the authorities of those stringent and unjust measures which had been adopted at the close of the late rising of 1745.

Loyal as Lochaber had proved to the Stuarts, her sons were able to show, now that all hopes of a restoration of that ancient dynasty were at an end, that they could consistently, and without loss of dignity, help with their good claymores to fight the battles of their late enemies, and defend with their lives the honour of the United Kingdom, of which they formed a small but none the less important part. Under the folds of that standard, upon which was emblazoned not only the leopards[1] of England and the harp of Ireland, but the ruddy lion of Scotland, "ramping in a field of gold," they could take their stand, shoulder to shoulder, and perform prodigies of valour, as their ancestors had done in the days of Montrose and Dundee.

As Lochaber had been the birthplace of that last gallant effort to throw off the yoke of Hanoverian tyranny, so was it, by a strange coincidence, to be the nursery of those magnificent Highland battalions which were to add by their glorious victories over Britain's enemies a brilliant lustre to the reigns of the Elector of Hanover's descendants. The notable military successes of Fraser's Highlanders during the war in Canada, induced the Government, upon the outbreak

---

[1] Heraldically and originally leopards, but transformed by time and sentiment into lions.

of the American War of Independence in 1775, to repeat the
experiment; and letters of service were issued authorising
Colonel Fraser of Lovat to raise two fresh battalions for the
service of George III.   Colonel Fraser, whose exertions in
connection with the formation of the regiment in 1757 had
been rewarded by a grant of the family estates, threw himself
vigorously into the congenial task of enlisting recruits, and
was ably seconded in his efforts by Duncan MacPherson of
Cluny, John MacDonald of Lochgarry, Charles Cameron of
Lochiel, Charles Cameron of Fassfern, and Æneas Mackintosh
of Mackintosh.

Duncan MacPherson of Cluny was a son of the famous
Cluny of the '45, who, having skulked among the fastnesses
of Ben Alder for some years after Culloden, escaped to France
in 1755, and died at Dunkirk a year later.   Duncan was born
in 1750, at a time when the English redcoats were actively
engaged in their efforts to capture his father.   Upon the
destruction of Cluny Castle, Duncan's mother, who was then
daily expecting her confinement, sought shelter in a kiln used
for drying corn, and here it was that Duncan was born.[1]   His
uncle, John MacPherson, who had received a commission in
the 78th regiment, acted as guardian during the minority of
the young chief, and it was probably due to his influence that
Duncan was appointed major to the 71st.   Some years later
Duncan became lieutenant-colonel of the 73rd Foot (afterwards
the 71st Highland Light Infantry), and his ancestral estates
were restored to him as a reward for meritorious service.
He married, in 1798, Catherine, the daughter of Sir Ewen
Cameron of Fassfern, and sister of the brave John Cameron
who fell at Quatre Bras.   Cluny died in 1820, and was
succeeded in the chieftainship by his son Ewen.

John MacDonald of Lochgarry, who had been given a
captain's commission in the old 78th, was now promoted to the
rank of major in the 71st.   Later, in 1777, he was appointed to

---

[1] From this circumstance, Colonel MacPherson was known as "Duncan of
the Kiln."

the command of a regiment known as MacDonald's Highlanders, and, after a distinguished military career, died in 1789.

Charles Cameron of Lochiel was the second son of the "Gentle" Lochiel, and had succeeded to the chieftainship of Clan Cameron on the death of his brother John. Although the estates had been forfeited to the Crown under the Act of Attainder, Lochiel found little difficulty in obtaining leases of portions of the property on easy terms. Mrs MacKellar tells us that when the news of Lochiel's home-coming reached Lochaber, an aged clansman, who had probably taken part in the risings of 1715 and 1745, and who lay dying in his hut at high Achintore, near Fort William, was so elated at the joyful tidings that, notwithstanding his feeble condition, he raised himself in bed, "whilst his dim eye brightened and his shaking voice waxed strong as he shouted, '*Tha dia mòr nan Camshronach againn fhein tighinn dachaidh agus tòisichidh a mhèirle mar a bha i riamh*' ('Hurrah! our own great god of the Camerons is coming home, and the theft (forays) will begin again, as it always was before')."

Lochiel did come back, but instead of leading his bold clansmen in a marauding *creach*, as his ancestors oft had done, he enlisted them in the regiment he was helping Colonel Fraser to raise, and taught them to fight, not against their own kith and kin, but against the enemies of Britain. About one hundred and twenty of Lochiel's tenantry volunteered their services, and a company having been thus formed, their chief received a captain's commission, which was destined to be the indirect cause of his premature death.

The circumstances which led to that unhappy result were as follows:—In the month of April 1776, the men of the 71st Regiment, now numbering about 2300, were ordered to muster at Glasgow previous to embarkation for America, but Lochiel, who had been attacked by a severe and dangerous illness while in London, found himself totally unable to attend. When his clansmen arrived in Glasgow and discovered the absence of their chief, they one and all refused to embark without him. Fortunately for themselves, the refractory Camerons had Highland officers to deal with, who could not fail to respect the spirit of devotion and love which prompted an action which, in an English regiment, would have been considered rank mutiny. Threats of punishment would have been quite useless under the circumstances, and recourse was therefore had to persuasion, in the art of which Colonel Fraser was an adept. By a promise that Captain Charles Cameron of Fassfern, who had been appointed to the command of a company in the 2nd Battalion, should take the place of their invalided chief, Colonel Fraser succeeded in removing their objections, and they willingly consented to join their comrades on board the transport.

As soon as the tidings of his clansmen's mutinous behaviour reached Lochiel in London, he became alarmed for the consequences, and ill as he was, he started immediately for Glasgow, in order to induce them to return to their duty, and to plead for mitigation of any punishment they might have laid themselves open to. The long and fatiguing journey to the north caused a relapse, which proved fatal in the course of a few weeks. Lochiel had married a Miss Marshall, by whom he had a large family, but only two survived, viz., Donald, born in 1769 (to whom the estates were restored), and a daughter, Ann, who married Vaughan Foster, Esq.

It is no part of my scheme to include in this volume a history of the Highland regiments: the pleasant task of recording the gallant deeds of the hardy mountaineers of the north has been ably performed by other and more capable hands than mine. My self-imposed duty rests with Lochaber and Lochaber only; but as the history of a country is the history of its people, I have frequently to digress from the straight course of my narrative to follow the fortunes of those of Lochaber's distinguished sons who have made their mark in the world beyond the mountains, and added fresh honours to the annals of the land of their birth.

Captain Mackintosh of the 71st (the twenty-third chief of

the clan) narrowly escaped capture on the voyage out, for the ship which he and his company were in, having been detached from the rest of the fleet during a severe gale, was attacked by an American privateer carrying eight guns. The superior sailing powers of the British vessel, however, enabled her to get clear away, and after a short pursuit the enemy gave up the chase. Captain Cameron of Fassfern, who had by his bravery in action won the applause of his superior officers, met a soldier's death in a bold attack on a strong advanced post of the insurgent army at Sandy Hook, sometime during the month of December 1777. Lieutenant-Colonel MacPherson of Cluny had the honour of commanding the regiment at the affair of Boston Creek in 1779, in which the British forces gained a complete victory over a body of nearly three thousand of the enemy. After the close of the American War in 1783, the 71st returned to Scotland, and was disbanded at Perth[1] in the same year.

The heroism displayed by the Highland regiments in every campaign in which they had taken part, merited some recognition at the hands of the monarch they had so faithfully served, and it was felt on all sides that nothing the Government could offer in the shape of a reward would be so grateful to the brave officers and their intrepid clansmen, as the restoration of the estates their immediate ancestors had forfeited under the Act of Attainder. The thirty-seven years that had passed since Culloden had done much to heal the physical and mental wounds inflicted by English barbarism and Hanoverian tyranny, but the scars still remained, and often throbbed painfully, as those who bore them contemplated with tearful eyes the blackened ruins of a once happy home, or called to mind the act of cruel injustice which had driven them from their native land in sorrow and poverty. But brighter days were in store, and once again the sounds of mirth, which had been

[1] The old 71st Regiment must not be confounded with the present 71st, or Highland Light Infantry. The H.L.I. were originally the 73rd Regiment, or "MacLeod's Highlanders."

silent for more than a quarter of a century, resounded among Lochaber's romantic glens, and echoed from the sides of her ancient mountains, as with all the accompaniments of martial music and loyal acclamations, the chiefs returned to take their place at the head of their respective clans, in full possession of their ancestral estates. An old ballad thus describes the return of Lochiel :—

> " As o'er the Highland hills I hied,
> The Camerons in array I spied,
> Lochiel's proud standard waving wide,
>   In all its ancient glory.
> The martial pipe loud pierced the sky,
> The song arose, resounding high
> Their valour, faith, and loyalty,
>   That shine in Scottish story.
>
> " No more the trumpet calls to arms,
> Awaking battle's fierce alarms,
> But every hero's bosom warms
>   With songs of exultation ;
> While brave Lochiel at length regains,
> Through toils of war, his native plains,
> And won by glorious wounds attains
>   His high paternal station."

CHAPTER XLIII.

THE restoration of the forfeited estates took place in the year 1784, and, with the solitary exception of MacDonald of Keppoch, all the descendants of the attainted chiefs shared in the general amnesty. The fact that the chiefs of Keppoch had never had a charter from the Crown for the lands they had held by the sword for so many centuries was a stumbling-block in the way of their restitution, as no documentary evidence of legal ownership could be produced to support Ranald of Keppoch's claim to the property his ancestors had enjoyed. Had it not been for the influence of the Duke of Gordon, it is more than probable that Keppoch would have been altogether dispossessed of his patrimony; but having, by the advice of his brother Angus, applied to the Crown for a grant of the Keppoch lands, in which application he had the powerful support of the friendly duke, he was allowed, on payment of a nominal rent, to take up his residence in the land of his fathers, where, as I have already stated, he erected the mansion that still bears his name, by the side of the tumultuous Roy. Here, in 1793, he actively assisted Alan Cameron of Errachd (afterwards Sir Alan Cameron) in raising that splendid regiment of Cameron Highlanders, whose military achievements during the last hundred years have added additional prestige to our arms, and gained for the name of Cameron a deathless renown. Before proceeding to describe the circumstances attendant upon the formation of this essentially Lochaber regiment, I will give a brief account of the origin and history of its gallant founder.

The Camerons of Errachd (or Erracht) trace their descent from Ewen Cameron (*Eobhan MacAilein*), the tenth chief of Lochiel, by his second wife Marjory Mackintosh, and were known in Lochaber by their patronymic of "*Sliochd Eobhainn ic Eobhainn.*" The ancestral home of this sept of Clan Cameron was among the densely-wooded slopes of the beautiful *Gleann Laoigh* ("Glen of the Calf"), on the east bank of the river bearing the same name, and within a short distance of the Lochy. Here, under the shadow of the *Monadh Uisge Mhuillinn*, a hill of about 1500 feet in height, stands the house of Errachd, nestling amid the trees, which almost hide it from view, and here, a few months previous to the Earl of Mar's rising in 1715, Donald, the second Laird of Errachd, was born. Donald's father joined the Highland force under Mar, and was slain at Sheriffmuir. When Lochiel mustered the clan for service under Prince Charles, Errachd was selected by his chief to take the second place in command of the Camerons, as Fassfern (the *Tainistear*, or next heir to the chief), to whom the position belonged by ancient precedent, had decided not to join an enterprise which he considered both reckless and ill-timed.

2 Y

Donald of Errachd had married the only daughter of Coll, the fifteenth chief of Keppoch ("Coll of the Cows"), who was sister to the gallant Alexander of Keppoch slain at Culloden.[1] This lady had, a short time before the prince's arrival, presented her husband with a son and heir; and when he started with the clan for the rendezvous at Glenfinnan, she went out to the bridge of Laoigh, with her baby in her arms, to see the Camerons pass in all their martial array, and wave a sad adieu to her beloved husband. This child was Alan, who was thus early in his career an involuntary participator in a military parade.

For some time after Culloden, Alan's father was a fugitive among the hills of Lochaber, but upon the passing of the Act of Indemnity, he returned to his home in Glen Laoigh, and ended his days there in peace. As the young laird grew up he gave evidence that he possessed all the spirit and courage of his Cameron and MacDonald ancestors. With the blood of the Lochiels and Keppochs coursing wildly through his veins, he found himself unable to brook an insult or forgive an injury, and before he had attained to years of discretion he became involved in a serious quarrel with a neighbouring chieftain which led to a fatal termination.

The innocent cause of the dispute was the young widow of Cameron of Strone, a lady to whose many attractive qualities and great personal charms the impressionable Alan had early fallen a victim. From the ruddy hue of her tresses, the object of the young chieftain's affectionate regard was called by her neighbours "*A' bhanntrach ruadh*," or the "auburn-haired widow." This lady lived under the guardianship of one of her deceased husband's relatives, a tacksman of the adjoining clachan of Murshiorlaich, who belonged to that sept of Clan Cameron known as the MacGillonies (*Mac gille Onnaidh*) of Strone. This gentleman had been "out" in the "Forty-Five," and had after-

---

[1] I base this assertion on the MS. pedigree in the possession of Mrs MacDonell of Keppoch. Other authorities state that the Laird of Errachd married Marjory, daughter of MacLean of Drimnin.

wards escaped to Holland, where he had dwelt for some years. For reasons that do not appear, the continual visits of Alan of Errachd to the house of Murshiorlaich's fair kinswoman were distasteful to that chieftain, and high words ensued, which resulted in Errachd challenging his neighbour to meet him on the banks of the river Lochy, and there settle the dispute with the sword. At first Murshiorlaich refused to fight his boyish antagonist, whom he knew to be only an indifferent swordsman ; but the taunts of that fiery youth were of such a nature that his anger was aroused, and he agreed to meet him when and where he chose, with the stipulation that the fight should cease as soon as one or the other drew blood from his opponent.

Alan confided the arrangements to an old retainer of his late father, who at once proceeded to instruct his young master in the use of an old claymore, with which Donald, the late Laird of Errachd, had done good service at Culloden and elsewhere. With this powerful weapon in his grasp, Alan started for the spot by the banks of the river that had been appointed for the rencontre. Here he found Murshiorlaich waiting for him, and in a few moments the fight began. The superior skill of the elder combatant was soon apparent, as, notwithstanding the vigorous strokes with which young Errachd endeavoured to break down his guard, he received no hurt, and contented himself with merely parrying the blows which were aimed at him, without seeking to inflict a wound on his youthful adversary. They fought thus for a long time without result, until Murshiorlaich, wishing to bring the duel to a conclusion, made a thrust at Errachd's hand, and succeeded in drawing blood. This should have ended the combat, but the smart of the wound and the sight of blood so infuriated the impetuous Errachd that, regardless of the stipulation he had agreed to, he renewed the attack with such desperate strength that he quickly overcame the now fatigued tacksman, and, regardless of consequences, slew him with a terrible blow of his great claymore.

Now that it was too late, he gave way to bitter regrets,

and cursed the violent temper that had led him into such a scrape; and fearful lest the vengeance of the kinsmen of the dead man should fall upon his head, he fled to some relatives in Mull. Shortly afterwards we find him occupying the uncongenial position of clerk in the Greenock Custom House, an employment thoroughly unsuited to the lad who had never known restraint, and whose wild life among the heather-clad hills of Lochaber had quite unfitted him for the drudgery of an office. Military service was more to his taste, and vacating his stool in the Custom House, he started for America, and upon arrival joined the Royal Highland Emigrant Regiment (the old 84th), commanded by Colonel Alan MacLean of Torloisg. After serving for some years with this regiment, he unfortunately fell into the clutches of the enemy, and was imprisoned for two years in the prison of Philadelphia. Upon his release he was placed on half-pay, with the rank of lieutenant of Tarleton's Dragoons, and shortly afterwards returned to the home of his ancestors by the banks of the romantic Laoigh.

Alan Cameron was not the man to remain long inactive, and shortly after his return to Lochaber he conceived the idea of following the example of Fraser of Lovat by raising a regiment of Highlanders among the eligible men of his own clan.[1] Strife was in the air, France, Spain, and Holland had all declared war against Great Britain, and George III. stood greatly in need of soldiers to fight his battles and defend the honour of his kingdom. Errachd's offer to increase the military forces of the realm came at a most opportune time, and was eagerly accepted by the Government, who at once granted letters of service empowering him to raise a regiment for the king, but refused any pecuniary assistance. Undeterred by this ungenerous and scurvy treatment of his patriotic suggestion, Alan Cameron, with the assistance of several Lochaber gentlemen, among whom was Ranald, chief of Keppoch, succeeded in enlisting a fine body of Highlanders, who were recruited and equipped entirely at the expense of their chiefs

[1] Copy of Errachd's original recruiting poster will be found at Appendix XXXIII.

and officers. Keppoch, although he did not join the regiment himself, induced two or three hundred of his clan to swell the ranks of the 79th, or "Cameron Volunteers," as they were then called. It is one hundred and five years since this gallant regiment was raised, as Alan Cameron's commission of Lieutenant-Colonel Commandant is dated August the 17th, 1793, and it was probably shortly after this date that the first muster took place.

This notable event in the history of Lochaber was made the occasion of much festivity in the neighbourhood of Errachd. Highland games were held, and the newly appointed officers offered prizes for competition to the men and youths who took part in the various feats of skill. Among those who were fortunate enough to win prizes was Keppoch's valet, who, notwithstanding his very inappropriate costume of livery and top-boots, managed to secure the first prize for running and leaping. This man was Angus MacDonell (*Aonghas Mac-Raonuill*), and he was still living at Keppoch, as gardener, during the early married life of the present Mrs MacDonell of Keppoch, to whose husband, the late chief, he related the circumstances connected with the raising of the Cameron Highlanders; and it is from this source that I can give my readers an authentic account of the origin of the Errachd tartan, which was not long ago described by Mr Campbell-Bannerman in the House of Commons as a "spurious tartan of the MacDonald clan." There is a grain of truth in this assertion, but it was surely quite unnecessary for a Secretary of State for War to go out of his way to stigmatise a tartan as "spurious" that has been worn by one of Britain's most distinguished regiments during a century of honourable and gallant warfare.

Cameron or MacDonald, it is an historic garb, identified with many a brilliant victory and heroic action, and it would be a contemptible act of official vandalism to relegate it to the limbo of obscurity. The reason of its adoption by the Cameron Highlanders is as follows:—When the question of uniform was first discussed by the officers, it was, of course, a foregone conclusion that the Highland dress in its entirety of kilt, plaid, and bonnet would be unanimously selected, but the question as to which tartan should be worn presented some difficulty, as neither the Cameron or Keppoch varieties (being composed largely of red) looked well with the regulation scarlet tunics which were adopted by the regiments of the line.

The matter was at last settled by old Mrs Cameron of Errachd, Alan's mother, who suggested that by blending the tartan of the Clan MacDonald (which contains more green than that of Keppoch) with the yellow lines of the tartan of Clan Cameron, the difficulty would be solved, and that not only would the kilt and plaid harmonise better with the doublet, but the sentiment of both clans would be respected. Mrs Cameron's ingenious idea was warmly approved by the officers, and an experimental kilt and plaid were made (I believe, by the lady herself), which proved a complete success, and from that day the tartan now so familiar to our eyes has been worn by the 79th Cameron Highlanders.[1]

It was thus left to the daughter of Alexander of Keppoch (who died fighting against a British regiment at Culloden) to be the inventor of a dress with which another British regiment will always be associated. From that day in August 1793 this tartan has been known as the Cameron of Errachd, and has probably greater claims to be considered authentic than the majority of the modern clan tartans, many of which appear to have no authority whatever for their existence, other than the imagination of the manufacturer who benefits by their sale.

It was at this early period of the regiment's existence that the *Piobaireachd Dhomhnuill Duibh* (" Pibroch of Donald Dhu ") was first used as a march tune,[2] and it is probably owing to this circumstance that the Camerons have since claimed the

---

[1] The original contract for the manufacture of this tartan was placed with Messrs Holms of Paisley.

[2] When the Cameron Highlanders started on their march to Stirling from Fort William, the tune played by the pipers of the regiment was the old Highland air, "*Gabhaidh sinn an Rathad Mor*" ("We will take the high road ").

tune as the pibroch of their clan. I have stated elsewhere that this ancient pipe-tune was probably composed at the time of the first battle of Inverlochy, in honour of the victory gained by Donald Balloch, cousin of MacDonald of the Isles, over the royal forces. Whether this was so or not, it is an undoubted fact that this stirring old *piobaireachd* has for many centuries been in common use among the MacDonalds, especially those of Lochaber.

CHAPTER XLIV.

As a history of the "Cameron Highlanders" would fill a volume in itself, I can only give my readers a very brief account of the many brilliant campaigns in which that splendid regiment took so conspicuous and so honourable a part.

By January 1794, when the 79th was inspected at Stirling, it mustered nearly one thousand strong, and was composed almost entirely of Lochaber men, officered by gentlemen who were mostly cadets of clans belonging to the same locality. For a few months the regiment was quartered in Ireland, but returned in the autumn of the same year, and embarked in August for the seat of war in Flanders. In this most disastrous campaign the 79th lost nearly two hundred men, the majority of whom succumbed to the privations they were forced to undergo during the long and severe winter of 1794-95.

In April 1795 the Camerons were recalled to England, with a view to their joining the force about to be despatched to India, where Tippoo Sahib, with the assistance of his French allies, was waging war against Great Britain. Whilst waiting to embark, the regiment experienced its first taste of War Office interference, which, unfortunately, was only the commencement of a long series of vexatious official meddling and injudicious treatment that has not yet ceased.

This first grievance was the result of an order that was conveyed to Colonel Cameron from the military authorities, by which he was instructed to break up the 79th into four companies, and hold them in readiness for drafting into other regiments of the line. Such an order was a direct insult to Errachd and his brave Highlanders, and his pride of race was touched in its most tender place. Angered beyond measure, and with his temper at boiling-point, he sought an interview with the commander-in-chief, and with Highland boldness told him that "to draft the 79th is more than you or your royal father dare do." This blunt speech nettled the royal duke, and he expressed his opinion that the king would certainly send the regiment to the West Indies if they continued obstinate. Still further incensed by this threat, Errachd defiantly replied, "You may tell the king, your father, from me, that he may send us to hell if he likes, and I'll go at the head of them, but he dare not draft us."

This remarkable interview was so far successful that no further attempt was then made to draft the 79th, but as the commander-in-chief had intimated, an order soon reached Colonel Cameron to proceed with his regiment to Martinique, in the West Indies, a station rendered unpopular in the army on account of its unhealthy climate. For two years the 79th remained in this island of malaria and yellow fever, and so terrible were the effects of its prolonged stay in such an unwholesome atmosphere, that hundreds of the men were altogether incapacitated from further service, and many found an early grave under a tropical sky, far from the breezy hills and lofty mountains of their beloved Lochaber.

To remain longer in this death-trap would have meant annihilation, and now that the mischief was done, the authorities gave a tardy permission to those men who wished to leave the island, to join the ranks of their countrymen in the Black Watch. Over two hundred availed themselves of this offer, while the remnant of this once fine regiment, with their officers, returned to England, where they arrived in August 1797. The condition of the 79th was now deplorable, but Colonel Cameron was not disheartened, and took immediate steps upon his arrival to fill the ranks that had been thinned so sadly. Once again Lochaber responded to the call for loyal men to serve in the army of Britain, and by the month of June 1798, recruits to the number of 780 were enlisted to fill up the gaps that had been caused by death and removal.

The next destination of the Cameron Highlanders was Helder, in Holland, where it was brigaded with several other regiments, amongst which were the newly-raised 92nd Gordon Highlanders. The ranks of the 92nd were swelled by a fine company of Lochaber men, under the command of Captain John Cameron of Fassfern, a kinsman of Cameron of Errachd, and doubtless the meeting of the two chieftains in a foreign land was cordial in the extreme. On 2nd October 1799, the 79th and the 92nd, with the other battalions forming the fourth division of the army under Sir Ralph Abercromby, attacked and carried at the point of the bayonet an entrenched position of the enemy near Egmont-op-Zee, and, at the close of the engagement, both regiments were highly commended by the general commanding for their valour in the field. Among the list of wounded on this occasion, we find the names of the two gallant Camerons, Colonel Alan of the 79th, and Captain John of the 92nd, the former only slightly, but the latter severely, he having been struck by a bullet in the knee, which incapacitated him from further service for some time.

The Cameron Highlanders were quartered in England from November 1799 until August of the following year, when they were despatched to Ferrol in Spain, and after a few insignificant engagements with the Spanish troops, departed for the scene of Sir Ralph Abercromby's operations against the French in Egypt. In this campaign, which was destined to effect a total revolution in the government of the land of the Pharaoh's, the 79th played an important part, and shared with their comrades of the 42nd and 92nd in all the honours of the glorious victory of Alexandria. The great battle was fought on 21st March

2 Z

1801, and resulted in the complete overthrow of French authority
in the affairs of Egypt, an authority which they are now striving
hard to regain.

The splendid behaviour of the brave Camerons in Egypt
was rewarded by the thanks of George III. and the British
Parliament, and, as a lasting memorial of the services they
had rendered to their country, they were allowed to inscribe
the word "Egypt" on their colours, and use a figure of the
Sphinx on their arms and accoutrements.

At the close of the Egyptian War of 1801, the regiment,
after a short stay in the island of Minorca, returned to Scotland, where it remained until the early months of 1803, when
it was ordered to Ireland. About a year later a second
battalion was formed as a feeder for the first battalion, but
for some cause or another its existence was a brief one, as
in the year 1815 it was disbanded. During the time the 79th
was stationed in Ireland, the authorities, for lack of something
better to do, recommenced their meddlesome interference with
the affairs of the regiment, and began an organised attack upon
the kilt, which they considerately suggested should be abolished
in favour of the trews. With this object, a letter was addressed
to Colonel Cameron, dated 13th October 1804, in which he
was asked to give his "private opinion as to the expediency
of abolishing the kilt in Highland regiments, and substituting
in lieu thereof the tartan trews."

We may imagine the amazement and disgust with which
Alan of Errachd perused this practical illustration of War
Office imbecility. Abolish the kilt! preposterous! absurd!
suppress the ancient garb in which his ancestors and their
descendants had fought with distinction for centuries, ridiculous!
Never would Alan Cameron of the 79th give his consent to
hide the individuality of the Highlander in the trews of the
Sassenach, tartan though they might be. Doubtless he knew
by heart the lines in which Alexander MacDonald (*Alasdair
MacMhaighstir Alasdair*), the bard of Moidart, expresses so
forcibly his regard for the kilt and "*Am Breacan Uallach*"

("the noble plaid"); and it is more than probable that the following verses ran in his head as he penned his able reply to the official letter:—

> "Eilidh cruinn nan cuachan,
> Gur buadhach an-t-earradh gaisgeach;
> Shiubhlainn leat na fuarain,
> Feadh fhuar-bheann; 's bu ghasd 'air faich thu.
>
> "Flor chulaidh an-t-saighdear,
> 'S neo-ghloiceil ri uchd na caismeachd;
> 'S ciatach 's an adbhans thu,
> Fo shranntraich nam pìob 'nam bratach.
>
> "Cha mhios anns an dol sìos thu,
> 'Nuair sgriobar à duille claiseach;
> Fior earradh na ruaige,
> Gu luaths a chuir anns na casan!"

Thus literally translated by my friend Mr Lockhart Bogle:—

> "The circular kilt of the pleats,
> It's the dress of a victorious hero;
> In you I'd walk the bleak hills, full of springs,
> And you're fine on the plain too.
>
> "True garb of the soldier,
> Not useless to breast the alarm;
> You're beautiful in the advance,
> Amid the humming of the pipes and banners.
>
> "You're not worse in the going down,
> When the grooved sword is torn from the scabbard;
> True dress for the pursuit,
> You put swiftness into the feet."

Colonel Cameron's characteristic letter is too long for insertion here, but I cannot refrain from giving a few extracts from this most powerful defence of the national dress, which may be read to some advantage by its modern detractors. The letter is dated Glasgow, 27th October 1804, and after a preliminary statement that he will offer his sentiments upon the subject without prejudice either way, and from actual experience of over twenty years in all climates, the gallant officer goes on to say: "I have to observe progressively, that in the course of the late war several gentlemen proposed to raise Highland regiments, some for general service, but chiefly for home defence; but most of these corps were culled from all quarters, and thereby adulterated with every description of men, that rendered them anything but real Highlanders, or even Scotsmen (which is not strictly synonymous), and the colonels themselves being generally unacquainted with the language and habits of Highlanders, while prejudiced in favour of, and accustomed to wear breeches, consequently *averse* to that free congenial circulation of pure wholesome air (as an exhilarating native bracer), which has hitherto so peculiarly befitted the Highlander for *activity*, and all the other necessary qualities of a soldier, whether for hardship upon scanty fare, *readiness in accoutring*, or making *forced marches*, etc.; besides the exclusive advantage, when halted, of drenching his kilt, etc., in the *next brook*, as well as washing his limbs, and drying *both*, as it were, by constant *fanning*, without injury to either, but on the contrary, feeling clean and comfortable, while the buffoon tartan pantaloon, etc., with all its fringed frippery (as some mongrel Highlanders would have it) sticking wet and dirty to the skin, is not very easily pulled off, and *less so* to get on again in case of alarm or any other hurry, and all this time absorbing both wet and dirt, followed up by rheumatism and fevers, which ultimately make great havoc in hot and cold climates.

.   .   .   .

" I feel no hesitation in saying that the proposed alteration must have proceeded from a whimsical idea, more than from the real comfort of the Highland soldier, and a wish to lay aside that national martial garb, the very sight of which has, upon many occasions, struck the enemy with terror and confusion."

The colonel concludes as follows :—" I sincerely hope His Royal Highness will never acquiesce in so painful and degrading an idea (come from whatever quarter it may) as to strip us of our native garb (admitted hitherto our regimental uniform), and *stuff* us into a harlequin tartan pantaloon, which, composed of the usual quality that continues as at present worn, useful and becoming for twelve months, will not endure six weeks fair wear as a pantaloon, and when patched makes a horrible appearance, besides that the necessary quantity to serve decently throughout the year, would become extremely expensive, but above all take away completely the appearance and conceit of a Highland soldier, in which case I would rather see him *stuffed* in breeches and abolish the distinction at once."

A most logical and unanswerable letter, and one that all who have worn the kilt can thoroughly appreciate. Speaking from personal acquaintance with the national garb, having worn it during twenty-two years' service in the ranks of the London Scottish Volunteers and Glasgow Highlanders, as well as in private life, in all seasons and in all weathers, I can add my testimony to that of the brave colonel of the 79th, and stoutly affirm that for comfort, freedom of action, warmth in winter (owing to the continual chafing of the knees in walking, which circulates the blood and warms the whole body) and coolness in summer, there is no dress equal to it, and this apart altogether from the sentiment which necessarily attaches to an ancient and historical garment.

Colonel Cameron's arguments in favour of the kilt convinced the "auld wives" at the War Office that any attempt to abolish it would be the signal for a mutinous outbreak among the officers and men of the regiments interested, and so the "whimsical idea" was allowed to drop.

In August 1808 the 79th joined the army in Portugal, and in the following January were present at the battle of Corunna, but took no part in the actual engagement. It was during the time that the regiment was in Portugal that its founder and colonel retired from active command, upon his appointment to the post of Commandant of Lisbon. He was succeeded in the colonelship by his son, Lieutenant Philip Cameron, who faithfully followed in the steps of his gallant father, and gained for himself the love and admiration of his men and the regard of his brother-officers.

On the 25th of July 1810 Colonel Alan Cameron was promoted to the rank of major-general, and commanded a brigade under the Duke of Wellington at the action of Busaco, in which his old regiment distinguished itself by its usual intrepidity, and lost one of its bravest officers, Captain Alexander Cameron, who, being surrounded by a numerous body of the enemy whilst in charge of a picket, refused to surrender, and was instantly bayoneted. No less than seven wounds were afterwards discovered on his body.

After the battle of Busaco the health of Major-General Cameron began to fail, and misfortunes fell thick upon him. His second son, who was a major in his father's regiment, contracted a severe illness during the campaign, and died from its effects. Later, at the engagement of Fuentes d'Onor, on 5th May 1811, his eldest son, Lieutenant-Colonel Philip Cameron, who was then in command of the 79th, was struck by a bullet fired by a French soldier with the deliberate intention of slaying that brave officer. The wound proved mortal, and the heir of Alan of Errachd died, as his father would have had him die, amid the shouts of victory, and surrounded by his sorrowing clansmen.

In Colonel Philip Cameron, Wellington lost a gallant and capable officer; and to show his feeling of respect for the dead warrior, he attended the funeral with a brilliant staff, and having assisted at the last sad rites, which were, by his orders, conducted with all the military honours that time and place would permit, he penned a most kindly and sympathetic letter to Major-General Cameron, condoling with him on the great loss he had sustained, and eulogising in noble and eloquent language the character of the son whose death he was then mourning. The words with which the great duke concludes his letter are as follows:—" I cannot conceive a string of circumstances more honourable and glorious than these, in which he lost his life in the cause of his country"—words which should still find an echo in the breasts of Philip of Errachd's countrymen who now serve in the ranks of the grand old regiment which he commanded.

This second bereavement was a severe blow to Major-General Cameron, and finding his health growing gradually worse, he retired from the army with the rank of Lieutenant-General, and received the honour of Knight Commander of the Bath from the hands of George III. He died at Fulham on 9th March 1828,[1] having attained an age of over eighty years, and leaving behind him only one son, Lieutenant-Colonel Nathaniel Cameron of Errachd, who had commanded the 2nd Battalion of the 79th, and who, upon the death of his father, became the fourth Laird of Errachd. He married Lœtitia Pryce, the daughter of the Rev. John Curry, a lady descended from the ancient family of the Pryces of Glamorgan. She bore him ten children, the eldest of whom, Nathaniel Pryce Cameron, fifth of Errachd, born in 1814, is the living representative of this old Lochaber family.

The history of the 79th from the day on which Colonel Philip Cameron of Errachd fell mortally wounded at Fuentes d'Onor, is one glorious record of successive victories over the foes of Britain. Burgos, Toulouse, Peninsula, Waterloo, Alma, Sebastopol, Lucknow, Ashanti, Tel-el-Kebir,[2] are but a few of the names inscribed on the colours of the Cameron Highlanders, telling of great deeds and gallant actions performed amid the smoke of battle and in the face of death and danger.[3] By the indomitable pluck and dauntless courage of its officers and men, displayed in every action in which the regiment has

---

[1] The nickname of "*Cia mar tha*," given to Sir Alan Cameron by the men of the 79th, was due to his always using the Gaelic language when addressing his men.

[2] On 14th July 1893 Donald Cameron of Lochiel unveiled a beautiful monument at Inverness, erected in honour of the officers and men of the Cameron Highlanders who fell at Tel-el-Kebir.

[3] As these sheets are going through the press, I hear with sincere gratification how splendidly the Camerons maintained the honour of the regiment at Atbara and Omdurman.

been engaged, it has gained for itself immortal fame, and added fresh honours to the name of Cameron.

With such a history, it is incredible that in the very year of the centenary of the first muster of this magnificent regiment beneath the shadow of mighty Ben Nevis, there should have existed uncontradicted rumours that the War Office authorities had in contemplation its disbandment and utter annihilation as a distinctive battalion.[1] The mere suggestion of such an act of insensate officialism produced, I am glad to say, such an outcry of indignation from Highlanders and Low-landers, and even from Englishmen, that for the moment the matter has dropped, but we are promised a recurrence of it in the near future, and it behoves every one who has the welfare and honour of this historic regiment at heart to strive heart and soul to preserve it in its entirety. Lochiel, Lord Archibald Campbell, and many others have set a good example in this respect, and it is without doubt largely due to their efforts that the 79th is as yet untampered with. Upon the slightest symptoms of further meddlesome interference by that abstract entity, "the authorities," with the status of the Cameron Highlanders, the agitation must recommence with renewed energy, and be continued until the threatened catastrophe is averted.

The 79th is now "*The Queen's Own* Cameron Highlanders," and it would be strange indeed if Her Majesty, who perhaps understands Highland sentiment and Highland people better than any sovereign who has ruled the destinies of Britain, should allow a regiment whose career she has always followed with the greatest interest, and to whom, in the year 1873, she presented with her own royal hands the colours it now carries, to be effaced from her army at the will of unsentimental and unpatriotic ministers. It has been urged that the 79th is no longer a Highland, or even a Scotch regiment. If this is so, it is a disgraceful reflection upon the recruiting department

---

[1] I am glad to say that, since writing the above, a second battalion has been added to the gallant Cameron regiment.

of the War Office. If Highland regiments are to be recruited in Whitechapel or Portsmouth, better abolish them at once; but there can be no real necessity for this. Let the military authorities establish a properly organised recruiting depot for Highland regiments in Glasgow, and offer sufficient induce-ments to attract the numerous eligible young lads who are daily pouring into that city from the west coast in search of employment, and they will find ample material of the right sort for filling up the gaps in the ranks caused by the short-service system.

CHAPTER XLV.

WHILST Alan Cameron of Errachd was winning fame and honour at the head of the gallant regiment he had raised in Lochaber, his kinsman John Cameron, son of Ewen Cameron of Fassfern, was, as we have already seen, commencing his military career in the ranks of the 92nd Gordon Highlanders. This distinguished man was born at Inverscadale, a beautiful but lonely spot on the Ardgour shore of Loch Linnhe, over-shadowed by the fine conical-shaped mountain of Beinn-na-cille,[1] which rises from the plain to a height of about 2300 feet, between Inverscadale and Corran.

This property, which is now held by Lord Morton, whose residence of Conaglen House is close by, had in recent times belonged to MacLean of Ardgour, in common with the rest of that district; but at the time of which I am writing, it formed part of the Cameron estates, and was the abode of Ewen Cameron (afterwards Sir Ewen), the son of John Cameron of Fassfern, brother to the "Gentle" Lochiel of the '45. It is a wild, desolate place, well suited to be the birth-place of such a man as John Cameron. Seen in the cold, pale

---

[1] This mountain is a striking feature in the landscape as viewed from Fort William, and is regarded in the light of a barometer by the country folk, who foretell good or bad weather from the appearance of its summit. If enveloped in mist, rain may be expected; and if clear, a fine day is certain.

3 A

dawn of an autumn morning, when the huge hills loom through
the grey-skirted mists with ghostly indistinctness, Inverscadale
is gloomy in the extreme; but when the sun arises in his
splendour from behind the giant shoulders of the Glencoe
mountains, with his quiver full of golden beams, the phantom
cloud-forms disperse before the shafts of brilliant light that
are discharged among them from the celestial bow of Phœbus
Apollo, and, as they roll along the rugged hillsides in fleecy
masses, looking as though a herd of Brobdignagian sheep had
passed and left portions of their woolly covering entangled
among the jagged rocks and boulders, the sombre landscape
is transfigured, as if by the wand of an enchantress, into a
scene of surpassing loveliness. Often have I sat beneath
the leafy shades of Coire-Chaorachan, on the opposite shore
of Loch Linnhe, and watched with calm enjoyment the
glorious changes of sunshine and shadow among the hills of
Ardgour, the while I listened to the music of the rippling
wavelets, as, with ceaseless rhythm, they kissed the pebbly
beach at my feet. From this point Inverscadale may be seen
to advantage, and presents to the gaze a picture of typical
Highland scenery, its harsher features softened by the distance
from which we survey it.[1]

Here then, in the month of August 1771, John Cameron
was born, and here he spent the first few years of his life.
As was the common practice in the Highlands, a foster-
mother was selected from among the tenantry to rear the
young heir, and for this duty Mrs MacMillan was selected.
I mention this fact as her son, Ewen MacMillan, became
John Cameron's devoted personal attendant, and followed him
through the whole of his distinguished military career, which
ended at Quatre Bras. Before young Cameron was many
years old his father removed to Fassfern, the ancestral home
of the younger branch of the Lochiels, and here, under the

---

[1] On the Ardgour shore, a short distance from Inverscadale, the rock may be
seen upon which the unfortunate Glengarry met his death when jumping ashore
from the wrecked steamer "Stirling Castle" on 17th January 1828.

immediate supervision of his grandfather, John Cameron grew to manhood, surrounded by all the stirring associations of the '45 which yet clung to the district where Bonnie Prince Charlie had raised the standard of his royal father amid the shouts of the loyal clans.

At a very early age John Cameron displayed a love for outdoor exercises of all kinds, and showed a marked preference for those sports which demanded a quick eye and steady hand. Fishing in the blue waters of Loch Eil, or stalking the deer among the heather-clad hills that surrounded Fassfern, were his favourite amusements, and he excelled in both. He had been sent for a short time to the Grammar School at Fort William, and afterwards received some private tuition at his grandfather's house ; but study was not to his taste, and although he was by no means slow in attaining knowledge, he was glad when the time came for books to be thrown aside, and he could escape from his tutor into the open air, and, with rod or gun in hand, follow those congenial pursuits which strengthened his muscles and fitted him for the life he was destined to lead. John Cameron's educational career was completed at the University of King's College, Aberdeen, where he applied himself to more serious study, and acquired the tastes of a cultivated and polished gentleman.

Upon leaving the University he was apprenticed (articled we now call it) to Mr James Fraser of Gortuleg, a Writer to the Signet at that time practising in Edinburgh. The law had, however, no charms for John Cameron, and after a very short experience of its intricacies, he persuaded his father to purchase a commission for him in the army, where he hoped to emulate the gallant deeds of his famous ancestors and kinsmen. The regiment selected as the military seminary for young Cameron was the 26th, or Cameronians, but for some reason or another he preferred to join an independent company which had been recently raised by Campbell of Ardchattan. John Cameron's commission as Lieutenant was dated in the year 1793, and from this fact we gather that he was only

twenty-two when he started on that brilliant career of military
service which brought fame to his name, and added one more
hero of the Cameron clan to Britain's roll of honour.

The year following John Cameron's entry into the army,
the Marquis of Huntly applied to the Government for permission to raise a Highland regiment from among his father's
tenantry in Aberdeenshire and Lochaber, in which latter district
my readers will remember the Gordons had considerable possessions. Letters of service were granted on 10th February
1794, and Huntly immediately proceeded to enlist recruits,
aided by his mother, the beautiful Duchess of Gordon, who,
with a Highland bonnet on her head, and wearing a regimental
doublet over her dress, rode through the country, offering a
"gowden guinea and a kiss o' her bonnie mou," to any bold
fellow who would promise to join. Such a tempting offer
could not be resisted by the impulsive Highlanders, and
whether it was the kiss, or the guinea, or both, the result
proved that the Duchess's original method of recruiting was
a complete success, and men flocked in from all quarters.
Huntly journeyed to Lochaber to use his personal influence
among his tenants there, and endeavour to persuade them
to enlist in the new regiment. Knowing the esteem and
reverence all Camerons had for the members of the family
of Fassfern, he determined, if possible, to get young John
Cameron to accept a commission in the Gordon Highlanders,
feeling assured that if he did so, there would be no difficulty
in securing a large body of Lochaber men for the regiment.
With this object Huntly called upon Fassfern, and having laid
the matter before him, ended by offering a captain's commission to his son. The offer was a flattering one, and Fassfern
admitted that it was an honour he had not at all anticipated,
but as he doubted John's ability to raise sufficient men to
form a company, he reluctantly declined the proffered commission on that ground. Disappointed at the refusal, Huntly
exclaimed that he "would be glad to have John Cameron a
captain in his regiment, although he brought not a single man."

This kindly speech so pleased Fassfern, that he not only gave his consent to his son's acceptance of the captainship, but made personal efforts to enlist the necessary complement of recruits, efforts in which he was warmly assisted by his chief Lochiel, who, as we know, had only recently obtained possession of the family estates.

The result of these patriotic exertions was that, in the words of Dr Clerk of Kilmallie, "Cameron joined the regiment with a hundred men, as brave and true as any who ever fought under the British banner."[1]

To those of my readers who wish to follow in detail the career of John Cameron of Fassfern, from the day the Gordon Highlanders mustered at Aberdeen in June 1794, to its fatal but glorious termination at the battle of Quatre Bras in June 1815, I cannot do better than refer them to the excellent work on the subject, written in 1863, by the reverend Lochaber gentleman above-mentioned, who had exceptional facilities for obtaining information from Sir Duncan Cameron of Fassfern, the brother of the hero of Quatre Bras. It is a splendid record of meritorious service and knightly deeds of prowess in the face of the enemy, performed with all the traditional valour of his famous ancestor, Sir Ewen Cameron of Lochiel, but under very different circumstances, and with a totally diverse object.

The recital of these military episodes would fill a volume of some bulk, and any attempt to recapitulate them here would be to increase beyond all reasonable limits a work which is only intended to place before those interested in the subject, a brief outline of the history of a district comparatively unknown to the outer world. Leaving, therefore, the details of John Cameron's adventurous life to his talented biographer, I will proceed to give a short account of the fatal event which brought it to a close.

[1] "Memoirs of Colonel Cameron," by the Rev. A. Clerk, minister of Kilmallie.

CHAPTER XLVI.

THE year 1815 will ever be remembered by the British people
as an *année célèbre*, a year which will be associated for all time
with two great historical names—Wellington and Waterloo.
This was the year that saw the total downfall of the Napoleonic
despotism, which, having overspread almost the whole of the
Continent of Europe, threatened to crush the fair land of
Britain under its giant heel. At this period John Cameron
was Lieutenant-Colonel of the regiment, having been promoted
to that rank on 23rd June 1808. He had been thrice wounded
—at Egmont-op-Zee, at Arroyo, and at Maya, the latter
action having won the following flattering compliment from
Sir William Napier : "The stern valour of the 92nd," he writes,
"would have graced Thermopylæ."

In March 1815 the startling news reached Britain that
Napoleon Buonaparte, who, after his forced abdication at
Fontainbleau in 1814, had been imprisoned on the island of
Elba, had effected his escape, and after repossessing himself
of the imperial throne temporarily occupied by Louis XVIII.,
was engaged in the formation of an immense army to aid
him in his ambitious schemes. The allied Powers at once
determined to declare war against the would-be dictator of
Europe, and with that object immense sums of money were
voted by the British Parliament in order to assist in over-
throwing the obnoxious tyrant who had for so long disturbed
the public peace.

The great struggle for supremacy took place in June 1815,
and ended, as we all know, in the complete destruction of the
power of Napoleon. The night of 15th June of that celebrated
year found Colonel John Cameron at Brussels, where the 92nd
were quartered in expectation of the approaching conflict which
all knew would be most serious in its consequences. On this
night—the last which he was to spend on earth—Colonel
Cameron formed one among that brilliant company who graced

with their presence the historic ball given in honour of the allied army by the Duchess of Richmond.

> " The lamps shone o'er fair women and brave men;
> A thousand hearts beat happily; and when
> Music arose with its voluptuous swell,
> Soft eyes look'd love to eyes which spake again,
> And all went merry as a marriage bell.
> But hush! hark! a deep sound strikes like a rising knell."[1]

At ten o'clock, when the festivity was at its height, Colonel Cameron, by a preconcerted arrangement with the Duke of Wellington, quietly slipped from the ball-room and proceeded to his quarters, having received orders to march with his regiment early on the following morning to the farmhouse of Quatre Bras, that stood at the junction of four roads (hence its name) about ten miles from Waterloo, and was consequently a position of considerable importance, as it commanded the direct route to Brussels, or Nivelles, and opened a line of communication with the Prussian allies under Blucher.

At daybreak on the morning of the 16th June, amid torrents of blinding rain, Colonel Cameron started from Brussels at the head of his brave men of the 92nd, with a stern determination to conquer or die. "The war note of Lochiel, which Albyn's hills have heard," skirled out with shrill and piercing sound from the great war-pipes of the regiment, and awakened the echoes of Brussels' deserted streets, as the "Gordons" marched out to do battle with the formidable army that Napoleon had placed in the field. Shortly after their arrival at the position assigned to them, the Duke of Wellington and his staff rode up, and having complimented Colonel Cameron on the appearance and bearing of his men, dismounted, and stationed himself on a small elevation in the rear of the regiment, and waited the attack of the enemy.

In front of the farmhouse was a ditch, which Colonel Cameron directed his men to line, their rear being protected

[1] Byron's "Childe Harold's Pilgrimage," Canto III., stanza xxi.

by the walls and outhouses of the building. They had hardly got into position before the attack began, and the British force under General Sir Thomas Picton (to which the 92nd was attached) found itself confronted by the flower of the French army, led by the redoubtable Ney. For some time at the commencement of the action the Highlanders were subjected to a galling fire of shot and shell from the French artillery, which caused much havoc in their ranks, and exasperated the men beyond endurance. This was followed up by a series of desperate cavalry charges by the French dragoons, but they were unable to make any impression upon the 92nd, who, with their front rank kneeling with bayonets fixed, and their rear rank pouring volley after volley of well-directed fire into the advancing masses of the enemy, forced them to retreat with heavy losses. The blood of the Highlanders was now up, and it was only with the greatest difficulty that Colonel Cameron could restrain them from pursuing the Frenchmen.

Fearing that they would disobey his orders in the desire to inflict punishment on the slayers of their kinsmen, who now lay dead and dying in all directions, Cameron requested the duke for permission to charge the enemy. "Have patience," replied Wellington, "and you will have plenty of work by and by." The French infantry were now rapidly advancing, and began a simultaneous attack upon the right and front of the position, and a few of their number succeeded in obtaining a footing in the farmhouse. The duke observing this, and seeing the necessity for a bold effort, shouted, amid the din of the incessant musketry fire, "Now, Cameron, is your time—take care of that road!" This was sufficient for Colonel Cameron. In an instant he gave the order to charge, and with one tremendous shout the 92nd leaped the ditch and rushed with ungovernable fury among the enemy, driving them before them at the point of the bayonet, and hewing them down with the claymore. The French were quite unable to withstand the terrible onset, and gave way in all directions, and left the Highlanders masters of the field.

The victory had been won, but at what a cost! Thirty-nine of their number were lying dead where they fell, among whom were four officers; and one other—and he their brave leader—had received a wound which was known to be mortal. Almost in the act of giving the command to charge, Colonel Cameron had been shot through the body by a bullet fired from one of the upper windows of the farmhouse, while at the same instant the horse he was riding was struck and fell dead under its wounded master. The death of Colonel Cameron has been immortalised by Sir Walter Scott in the following lines :—

> " Through steel and shot he leads no more,
> Low laid 'mid friend's and foeman's gore—
> But long his native lake's wild shore,
> And Sunart rough, and high Ardgour,
> And Morven long shall tell,
> And proud Ben Nevis hear with awe,
> How upon bloody Quatre Bras,
> Brave Cameron heard the wild hurrah
> Of conquest as he fell."

The faithful Ewen MacMillan saw his chief fall, and immediately rushed to his side to render what assistance he could to the master he loved so well. But although Colonel Cameron still lived, he was beyond human aid; and as MacMillan saw the crimson life-blood flowing fast from the terrible wound the bullet had caused, he realised that in a few short hours he would be bereft of his best friend. Lifting the dying colonel from the sodden and blood-stained earth, with the help of a comrade of the 92nd he carried him to a sheltered spot out of range of the French bullets, and then set out to find a conveyance in which to carry the wounded officer to Brussels.

After some little difficulty a rough country cart was procured, and in this Colonel Cameron was tenderly placed, with his head supported on the breast of his devoted foster-brother, and, after jolting over the miry roads for ten miles, the village of Waterloo was reached. Feeling certain that

3 B

if he proceeded farther his master would die on the road, MacMillan halted and carried him into a small cottage by the roadside, where he made up a bed for him on the floor. Here, the stricken man was laid, and for a short time regained consciousness, and spoke of the events of the day with heroic disregard of his own sufferings. The news of the great victory, which his brave Highlanders had done so much to gain, was as balm to his soul, and he forgot his pain in the pleasure the intelligence gave him. He lingered for a brief space, surrounded by a few faithful clansmen, and attended by the sorrowing MacMillan. As death approached he bade the pipers play the tunes he loved, and which had been familiar to his ears from infancy. To the mind of the dying Highlander they brought tender memories of those boyish days when he had wandered, gun in hand, through the forests and over the mountains of his native Lochaber, free as the young roebuck he was stalking; or perchance there came a vision of the old home of Fassfern, standing amid the trees by the shores of blue Loch Eil, where as a lad he had listened with breathless interest to the tales his grandfather told of the gallant young prince who had slept beneath its roof. The weird and mournful music of the pipes was a fitting accompaniment to the scene that was being enacted in that obscure hut by the Charleroi road, where the Highland chief lay peacefully awaiting the call which was to summon him to his Creator. It came at last, and as the eyes of the valiant Fassfern closed for ever, he was heard to murmur by those who stood around, " I die happy, and I trust my dear country will believe that I have served her faithfully."

Lochaber did believe; and when, in the spring of the following year, the honoured remains of her brave son were disinterred from the temporary grave in the Allée Verte, and brought to Fassfern in a vessel specially lent for that purpose by the Government, such a funeral was seen as Lochaber has never witnessed before or since. Led by Sir Duncan Cameron, the brother of the deceased chieftain, as chief mourner, no less

than three thousand Highlanders followed the remains of
Colonel John Cameron to their last resting-place in the
ancient burying-ground of Kilmallie, where they were laid
to rest side by side with those of his famous ancestor Sir
Ewen Cameron of Lochiel, and his grandfather, John of
Fassfern. Among the kinsmen of the deceased officer who
attended on this occasion were Lochiel, MacDonald of Glencoe,
MacNeill of Barra, and Campbell of Barcaldine, besides many
others of more remote consanguinity, who came from all parts
of the Highlands to be present at the mournful ceremony, and
honour with their presence the obsequies of their distinguished
fellow-countryman.

To the wailing of the pipes, and amid the tears and
lamentations of sorrowing relatives, the coffin, which contained
all that remained of John Cameron's mortal part, was rever-
ently lowered into the kindly earth of that beautiful God's
acre by Loch Eil's silver shore, where, about a year later, a
fine obelisk was raised to his memory at the expense of the
officers of the Gordon Highlanders, and still stands a prominent object in the surrounding landscape.

The epitaph was composed by Sir Walter Scott, and may
still be read by those who can spare a few moments from
their hurried journey north to pay a visit to the spot where
the hero of Quatre Bras lies quietly sleeping. "Reader, call
not his fate untimely, who, thus honoured and lamented, closed
a life of fame by a death of glory." [1]

The distinguished services rendered by Colonel John
Cameron to his king and country had been inadequately
rewarded during his lifetime by a grant of certain armorial
bearings, "that is to say on a wreath, a demi-Highlander of
the 92nd Regiment armed and accoutred, and up to the
middle in water, grasping in his dexter hand a broadsword,
and in his sinister a banner inscribed 92nd, within a wreath
of laurel, and in an escrol above 'Arriverete,' in allusion to

---

[1] Concluding sentence of the inscription on the obelisk. The whole of Sir Walter
Scott's sculptured panegyric will be found in Appendix XXXIV.

the signal intrepidity displayed by him at the passage of the river Gava de Moulino;"[1] and, in addition, he was authorised to use two figures of Highlanders as supporters to the Cameron arms, and the name Maya as a motto, in recognition of his gallant behaviour in holding the Pass of Maya against an overwhelming number of French troops. The honour that should have been his guerdon while he lived, was now somewhat tardily bestowed upon his venerable father, who was created a Baronet of the United Kingdom in 1817. Sir Ewen enjoyed the title for eleven years, and died in 1828, leaving his son Duncan to succeed him.

There is an amusing story told by Dr Clerk of a meeting between Colonel Cameron and a Lochaber man, near Marmorice Bay, during the Egyptian expedition of 1801. Cameron and a brother officer, while taking a stroll in the country, saw coming towards them a Turkish officer of apparently high rank, surrounded by a considerable following of servants, who were most obsequious in their attendance, and were in evident fear of offending their master. The Pasha was dressed in the usual Eastern costume of flowing robe and costly finery, which to the eyes of the Highland officers appeared ludicrous in the extreme, and caused one of them to exclaim in contemptuous tones: "Do you see the fellow with the tail? it is easy telling who his mother was, the lazy dog." This remark was made in the Gaelic language, and we may therefore imagine the surprise of Cameron and his friend when the Turkish Pasha replied in the same language: "Ay, my man, and what sort of mother may own you for a cub?" Had this reply been uttered in any other tongue than the Gaelic, it is more than probable that blows would have ensued, but the mere sound of their ancient language instantly quelled all thoughts of retaliation. Explanations and apologies followed, and Cameron discovered that the Turkish officer was a native of Lochaber named Campbell, he having been born at Fort William. Dr Clerk made some inquiries among the old people at that

[1] Extract from the grant of arms, dated 20th May 1815.

place, and elicited the fact that, when a boy, Campbell had quarrelled with a schoolfellow, and in the fight which followed, managed to injure his antagonist so seriously that the lad died soon afterwards. This sad occurrence caused Campbell to flee across the sea, and having reached Turkey, he secured a commission in the army of the Sultan, and was rapidly advanced to the important post he was holding when Cameron met him under such extraordinary circumstances.

Ewen MacMillan, Colonel Cameron's foster-brother and faithful servant, procured a discharge from the army after his master's death, and turned his attention to agricultural pursuits on the farm of Carnas, belonging to Sir Ewen. Upon the death of that nobleman, he was generously provided for by Sir Duncan Cameron of Fassfern on his estate at Callart, where he died in the year 1840, and was buried near his old colonel in Kilmallie churchyard.[1]

CHAPTER XLVII.

THE early years of the present century saw a constant succession of military heroes bearing the name of Cameron in the ranks of the British army, men of fearless spirit and indomitable will, who, by their splendid loyalty of service at a time of great national peril, helped to build up and consolidate that magnificent empire over which our beloved Queen now holds benignant sway.

To recount the deeds of these famous soldiers would be a task of considerable magnitude, and I shall not attempt it here; but before closing the subject I cannot refrain from mentioning the names of two brave members of the Cameron clan, whose

[1] The MacMillans may be considered as a Lochaber clan, as, although little is known of their origin, it is certain that for many centuries they held possession of lands on both sides of Loch Arkaig, but eventually became absorbed in the Clan Cameron. There are, however, still many of the name in Lochaber. Skene considers it probable that the MacMillans were connected with the Clan Chattan.

deeds not only Lochaber but Britain should hold in honoured remembrance.

First in chronological order stands Major-General Sir Alexander Cameron, K.C.B., K.C.H., of Inverailort, near Fort William. He joined the army in 1799, and was appointed Colonel of the 74th Highlanders on 22nd July 1830. His service record is a splendid one, and shows that he was present at all the most important engagements in which the British army took part during those years that he was on the active list. It includes the campaign in Holland, 1799; Ferrol, 1800; Egypt, 1801 (he was severely wounded at the battle of Alexandria); Vimeira and Corunna, 1808; Peninsula, 1809 (received a severe wound at Vittoria, which incapacitated him for some time); and he concluded his military career by sharing the dangers and glorious victories of Quatre Bras and Waterloo. More fortunate than a great many of his comrades, who left their bones on the field of Waterloo, it was permitted him to return to his native land and end his days in peace among his kinsfolk in Lochaber. He died on 26th July 1850, and was buried near his relative, Colonel John Cameron, in the cemetery of Kilmallie, where a small monument has been erected to his memory.

Sir Alexander Cameron married Christina, a daughter of MacDonald of Barrisdale, by whom he had a son, Duncan, who afterwards accepted a commission in the Black Watch, and was appointed Adjutant to that distinguished regiment in 1838. Duncan retired from the army in 1840, and died on 24th June 1874. He married twice, his second wife being a daughter of Thomas Gillespie of Ardachy. The fruit of this marriage was a daughter, who is now Mrs Head of Inverailort.

The other brave Cameron, whose birthplace was among those giant mountains over which Ben Nevis reigns as monarch, was General Sir Duncan Alexander Cameron, G.C.B., who commanded the Black Watch for some years. He was born in 1807, and joined the regiment as ensign in 1825, and served with distinction through the Eastern campaign of 1854–55. At the famous battle of the Alma, it was Duncan Cameron's (then Colonel) glorious privilege to lead his regiment up the slopes of the steep hillside that was crowned by the great Russian redoubt, and gain immortal fame for himself and his countrymen. "We'll hae nane but Highland bonnets here!" was the proud exclamation that broke from the ranks of the 42nd, as with stately stride the kilted warriors swept onwards to victory with Cameron at their head, and were watched with feelings of mingled pride and admiration by the renowned Sir Colin Campbell, who commanded the Highland Brigade on that memorable 20th of September 1854. Later, Colonel Cameron was made Brigadier, and was present in that capacity at Balaclava and Sebastopol. After the conclusion of the Crimean War he returned to the Highlands, and in the year 1860 was appointed to the important post of Commander-in-Chief of Her Majesty's forces in Scotland. He afterwards filled several military positions of high rank, and commanded the British troops in New Zealand during the campaign of 1863–65; and when, later, he returned to his native land, he was made Governor of the Royal Military College at Sandhurst. Sir Duncan Cameron died on 8th June 1888 at Blackheath.

Whilst the sons of Lochaber had been fighting the battles of Britain in Spain, Belgium, and the Crimea, and earning fame for themselves and honour for the land of their nativity, changes of considerable moment had taken place in the government of the realm. Poor old George III. ("Farmer" George, as he was often called), after ruling the destinies of Britain for half a century, lost his reason and had to yield the reins of power to his son George, and retire to the obscurity of Windsor, where he died in 1820.

" Of kings the best—and last not least in worth,
For graciously begetting George the Fourth." [1]

---

[1] Byron, "The Waltz."

The prince regent ascended the throne as George IV., and was remarkable for nothing in particular, except that he arrogated to himself the grandiloquent title of "the first gentleman in Europe." Highlanders will be amused and interested to learn that his Celtic predilections were so strong that, at a levee at Holyrood Palace in the month of August 1822, he appeared in full Highland costume of Stuart tartan. Upon entering the reception-room to receive the homage of his Scottish subjects,[1] he was annoyed to find that he was not the only Englishman who had donned the kilt and plaid; for immediately in front of him stood the bulky figure of a corpulent city alderman, Sir William Curtis, his fat loins encircled by a kilt of startling tartan, in front of which hung a gorgeous sporan. A doublet and belted plaid covered his huge body, and his waist (if waist it could be called) was enclosed with a belt, from which hung various weapons which are usually associated (not always correctly) with the stalwart mountaineers of the north. The dress was completed by hose of a choice pattern, in which the "*sgian dubh*" was ostentatiously thrust. So satisfied was the worthy alderman with his appearance, that he had the cool insolence to ask the king if he did not think him well dressed. "Yes!" replied His Majesty, with sly allusion to the proverbial fondness of aldermen for turtle, "only you have no *spoon* in your hose." Byron thus humorously describes the scene :—

> " My muse 'gan weep, but ere a tear was spilt,
> She caught Sir William Curtis in a kilt !
> While throng'd the chiefs of every Highland clan
> To hail their brother, Vich Ian Alderman !

> " Guildhall grows Gael, and echoes with Erse roar,
> While all the Common Council cry ' Claymore ' !
> To see proud Albyn's tartans as a belt
> Gird the gross sirloin of a city Celt." [2]

---

[1] Glengarry was present on this occasion with his brother, Colonel MacDonell and twelve stalwart followers.

[2] Byron's "The Age of Bronze," stanza xviii.

George IV. reigned but ten years, and was succeeded by his brother William, Duke of Clarence, who took the title of William IV. He died in 1837 without issue, and thus the succession devolved upon our present gracious sovereign Queen Victoria, who was the daughter of Edward, Duke of Kent, the fourth son of George III.

Some of my anti-Jacobite readers, while perusing the earlier chapters of this work, may have taken exception to the prefix "*loyal*" which I have used in the title as a distinguishing adjective to the name of the district whose history and associations are here chronicled. The objection, at first sight, appears reasonable enough, when looked at from the standpoint of those who have been taught to call the last three Stuart's pretenders and impostors, and whose definition of the word "loyal" is biased by unreasonable prejudice and ignorance of historic facts. To such as these I would say that loyalty does not necessarily mean devotion to any *particular* ruler or dynasty, but fidelity to plighted faith, whether religious or political. The brave cavaliers of king Charles I., who were brutally murdered in cold blood after the battle of Philiphaugh, were every whit as loyal as those unfortunate Covenanters who perished by the stern orders of Dundee. Loyalty may quite as justly be claimed for the gallant Highlanders who fell at Culloden in defence of their rightful prince, or who were wantonly butchered by Cumberland because they would not swear allegiance to the Elector of Hanover, as for the English redcoats who were slain at Prestonpans by the claymores of their resistless foemen. In the past Lochaber had been loyal to the Stuarts, and only transferred her devotion to the House of Hanover when the last Stuart in the direct line of succession had passed away. Nearly a century elapsed before those brave Highlanders of Lochaber, whose ancestors had suffered exile and death at the hands of the Elector's Government, could quite forget all the cruelties of the '45; but having done so, they gave the same unswerving loyalty to their Hanoverian monarchs that their fathers had previously given to those of the Stuart dynasty. The splendid heroism exhibited by such men as Colonel John Cameron of Fassfern, and his kinsmen of Lochiel, Errachd, and Inverailort, in the ranks of the British army, and the equally meritorious though less prominent military services of Ranald MacDonell of Keppoch, John MacDonell of Lochgarry, Æneas Mackintosh of Mackintosh, and Duncan MacPherson of Cluny, fairly entitle the country that produced such illustrious soldiers to the honourable prefix of "loyal."

It has been left for our present beloved Queen to call forth in the highest degree those sentiments of loyalty and devotion on the part of her subjects in Lochaber which their forefathers had entertained for her Stuart ancestors ; for it must not be forgotten that in the veins of Queen Victoria, by her descent from Elizabeth, the daughter of James VI. of Scotland (I. of England), runs the blood of Robert the Bruce. By a long residence among her Highland people, she has learned to appreciate their true worth, to admire their many sterling qualities, and to understand something of their language and customs ; and in return for her kindly sympathy, her more than queenly benevolence to the poor and suffering among her tenantry, and her generous support of Highland institutions and charities, she has gained for herself and her sons and daughters the enduring affections of a warm-hearted and loyal people.

It was a proud day for Lochaber when, on Saturday the 21st August 1847, the gentle *Ban-righ*[1] Victoria first set foot on its classic shores, welcomed by the acclamations of a great gathering of Highlanders in tartan array, with Lord Lovat and Mr Stuart MacKenzie at their head. More than three hundred years had passed away since James I., the poet-king of Scotland, had come to Lochaber with sword in hand, to punish his proud vassal Donald Balloch for his contempt of the royal authority. This was in 1429, and from that time no sovereign of Britain had honoured Lochaber with his presence.

[1] Gaelic for "Queen."

The Queen's stay on the occasion of her first visit was a brief
but happy one; for by her side, in all the pride of his early
manhood, was her dear husband and consort, Albert "the
Good," upon whom she had lavished all that wealth of
affection that is inherent in the nature of our illustrious
sovereign. Fate was indeed unkind when it severed the tie
that bound together those two loving hearts, that seemed
formed only for each other. The high intellectual gifts
which distinguished the Prince Consort were reflected in a
marked degree by his royal spouse. Each was the complement of each. The tastes, the accomplishments, the
amusements of the one were shared in by the other. Love
of nature and the arts were deeply-rooted sentiments which
were mutually appreciated; and religion, which to many is
but an empty name, was to them a living reality, which gave
comfort and support in hours of trial and suffering. Is it to
be wondered at that, when the bolt of inexorable fate fell
from the blue sky that had up till that hour canopied their
lives with serene brightness, and tore from the arms of our
Queen the husband she loved as life itself,—is it to be
wondered at that she should withdraw herself from public
gaze, and, in the quiet of her Highland home, mourn for her
beloved dead amid those scenes which will for ever be
associated with his presence? On this, the Queen's first visit
to the Highlands, there were no painful memories to dim her
enjoyment of the romantic and sublime scenery which she
had come to see. "The scenery in Loch Linnhe was
magnificent—such beautiful mountains," writes Her Majesty
in the "Journal" which records her tour. The day following
the arrival at Fort William (described as "a very small place"),
the royal party drove to Ardverikie, Loch Laggan, occupied
at that time by Lord Abercorn, and was very much struck
with the wild picturesqueness of the road through Glen Spean.
Unfortunately for the comfort of the party, the weather was
extremely wet, and I fear that Her Majesty's first impressions
of Lochaber were not of the most pleasant.

CHAPTER XLVIII.

AT the time of the Queen's visit to Lochaber in 1847, the venerable Sir Duncan Cameron of Fassfern was still living at his house at Callart, by the shores of the beautiful Loch Leven, near North Ballachulish.   Unlike his famous brother, Colonel John Cameron, Sir Duncan was a man of peace, and lived among his people in true patriarchal style, fulfilling his duties of landlord with bountiful munificence, and devoting his time and money to the improvement of the social condition of those whom circumstances had placed under him.   He was born in the year 1775, and on attaining an age when it became necessary to choose a profession, he selected the law, and after a course of legal education, in which he greatly distinguished himself, passed his examination as Writer to the Signet in the year 1799. Upon the death of his father Sir Ewen, the first baronet of Fassfern, in 1828, he succeeded to the title and estates, and added to the latter the fine property of Glen Nevis, and became superior of the village of Maryburgh, adjoining Fort William, to which he gave the name of Duncansburgh —a name which now only exists as a parochial division of the flourishing town of Fort William.

Sir Duncan was a generous supporter of all the local charities, and among other philanthropic actions he built and endowed a church at a cost of £2000, which still stands. He filled the office of Deputy-Lieutenant for the counties of Argyll and Inverness, and several others of less importance. When Her Majesty visited Lochaber, Sir Duncan was growing old, and I believe his health would not allow him to be present to receive her when she landed at Fort William. He lived for sixteen years longer, and died at Callart on 15th January 1863, at the age of eighty-eight, but left no male issue, and so the title became extinct; his brother Peter, who commanded the "Balcarras" East Indiaman, having predeceased him.

By the death of Sir Duncan the male line of the historic

family of Fassfern came to an end, but fortunately it was not extinct, for a daughter was left to support the honour and dignity of the race, and prevent the ancestral estates passing into the hands of strangers. This lady married, in the year 1844, Alexander Campbell of Monzie, a cadet of the ducal family of Argyll (since deceased), and became known throughout Lochaber as Mrs Cameron Campbell of Monzie, a name which will ever be associated with deeds of charity and benevolence. She is the "Lady Bountiful" of the district that owns her for superioress, and in the discharge of those duties and responsibilities that her large possessions impose upon her, sets an example which other Highland ladies might do well to copy. I trust she may long be spared to carry on the good work so well begun by her amiable and large-hearted father.[1] Her eldest daughter, Christina, married in 1865 Henry Spencer Lucy, Esq. of Charlecote (a name famous in Shakespearian history), who died in 1890; their daughter, who married in 1892, is Mrs Ramsay Fairfax Lucy of Charlecote Park, and will, in all probability, succeed to the great Lochaber inheritance now enjoyed by her venerable grandmother.

Having thus brought the history of the Camerons of Fassfern up to the present day, I will pause in my genealogical ramblings, to describe in a few words that most interesting and picturesque district where old Sir Duncan ended his days, and which has been immortalised in the writings of the genial Dr Alexander Stewart, who takes his *nom de plume* of "Nether Lochaber" from the locality over which he exercises a spiritual authority of the most paternal kind. It is an unthankful task to follow after such a man as Dr Stewart, who knows and understands better than any living person the legends and traditions of his native country; and were it not that I have reason to believe that some of my English readers of the present and younger generation are unacquainted (to their loss be it said) with his writings, I should not attempt it.

[1] This hope was, I regret to say, not fulfilled. Mrs Cameron Campbell passed away on 28th July of this year (1898).

The district known as "Nether" Lochaber is that portion of Lochaber which is washed by the waters of Loch Leven, and comprises the villages or clachans of Corran, Onich, North Ballachulish, and Callart. It is approached from Fort William by one of two routes, both of which are distinguished by rare beauty of scenery, and the sublime environment of majestic mountains. The most frequently used road is the one that follows the coast-line of Loch Linnhe, and passes through the verdant shades of Coire-Chaorachan, a lovely wood of considerable extent that clothes the side of steep Beinn Bhàn with its fresh verdure, and which is the haunt of a variety of feathered songsters, whose harmonious notes fill the air with melody, while the rills of sparkling water that come splashing down from the heights above, murmur a sweet accompaniment. The sonorous voices of the ocean billows rolling on the beach below help to swell Nature's grand symphony, and lend an additional charm to the sublime surroundings. The banks on either side of the road are covered with dense thickets of hazel, rowan, and birch, the branches of which meet overhead and form a perfect tunnel of greenery, through which the sunbeams stream in long shafts of quivering light. Great clumps of feathery ferns cover the ground beneath the trees, shooting up their delicate fronds from the emerald green turf, through which the tiny rivulets trickle with ceaseless flow, keeping the soil moist and cool.

The yellow St John's Wort ("*Lus Chaluim-Chille*," as it is here called) trails among the brambles, and lights up the gloomy depths of the wood with its brilliant blossoms. Mosses of all kinds and colours thrive in the damp atmosphere, and form a soft carpet on which the tired wayfarer may rest his weary feet. Here that botanical curiosity the Sundew (Gaelic, "*Lus-na-fèarnaich*") may be found with its deadly red leaves covered with sticky hairs, expanded to catch the passing insects, that are attracted by the sweet honey-like substance exuded from its petals. Bog-myrtle (Gaelic, "*Roid*"), Wild Cress (Gaelic, "*Biolaire*"), and many other shade and moisture loving plants have their habitat in this sheltered spot, where the cushat dove coos to his mate the livelong day, and the mavis makes the very air melodious with his amorous trilling. As we pass along the road we may catch an occasional glimpse, through the interlaced branches of the trees on our right hand, of the blue sea and the mountains of Ardgour on the opposite shore of Loch Linnhe, with great Beinn-na-Cille towering above the white lighthouse at Corran, and the hills of ancient Morven looming grey and indistinct through the summer haze. A little farther on we get clear of the wood and emerge into the open road that is here close to the beach, and is protected by a substantial sea-wall, built of granite blocks, all yellow with stone-crop and lichen.

The high rocky cliff on our left is "*Druim-na-Birlinn*" ("the ridge of the Biorlinn, or galley"), and as we round the point we come in sight of Corran with its comfortable inn, where we may appease our hunger with a substantial meal of delicious High-land mutton—than which there is no daintier fare—and quench our thirst from a foaming jug of sparkling ale. Having refreshed the inner man, we proceed on our way, and upon regaining the road we pass Cuilchenna House, formerly the residence of Dr Norman MacLeod. A short distance farther is the picturesque village of Onich (an abbreviation of the Gaelic word "*Ochanaich*," which has reference to the lamentations for the dead), made famous by its talented minister Dr Alexander Stewart, who has his abode in the manse we may see among the trees.

There are many curious traditions extant respecting the ancient inhabitants of Onich, of which the following is one :— Many years ago one of the dairymaids of the chieftain of *Sliochd Shomhairle Ruaidh* became the mother of an illegiti-mate son, whose father was the aforesaid chief of the Glen Nevis Camerons. From this circumstance the boy was nick-named by his companions of more legitimate origin, "the hornless brown stirk," and when he grew up and took unto himself a wife, his children were known as "*Sliochd a ghamhna mhaoil Duinn*," and to this day the descendants of MacSorlie's

milkmaid are distinguished by that appellation, and their
children are rocked to sleep to the sound of a quaint lullaby
which has its origin in the same story, and runs thus :—

> " Pru dhé Mic a' Ghamhna.
> Pru dhé Mic a' Ghamhna chean-fhionn,
> Pru dhé Mic a' Ghamhna.
> Bhrist 'thu 'm braidein 's dh' òl thu 'm bainne,
> Pru dhé Mic a' Ghamhna.
> 'S dh' fhalbh thu 'n oidhche ris a' ghealaich,
> Pru dhé Mic a' Ghamhna.
> Ach ma dh' fhalbh 's ann duit nach b' aithreach,
> Pru dhé Mic a' Ghamhna.
> S' boidheach air lianaig ar n'aighean,
> Pru dhé Mic a' Ghamhna.
> S' boidheach balg-fhionn ar crodh-bainne,
> Pru dhé Mic a' Ghamhna.
> Chuala tu an damh donn ri langan,
> Pru dhé Mic a' Ghamhna.
> Ach ma chuala fhuair e'n t-saighead;
> Pru dhé Mhic a' Ghamhna chean-fhionn." [1]

The view from the end of Onich pier is simply unsur-
passable in its sublime grandeur.   I recall one glorious
September evening a few years ago, when, as the sun was
sinking behind the dark mountains of Morven, I waited for
the steamer that was to take me home to Fort William.
The whole of the western horizon was one blaze of yellow
light, suffused nearer the zenith with a flush of roseate pink;
the sky was perfectly clear, except for one or two fantastic
masses of indigo clouds that stretched their weird uncanny
shapes across the path of the setting sun.   Immediately in
front, across the calm, unruffled surface of Loch Leven, rose,
in all the beauty of their symmetrical outline, the green hills of
Appin, all aglow with luminous colour of ethereal radiance,
emphasised by the deep purple shadows that crept higher and
higher up their sides as the day waned.   Far away in the south
the mountains of Mull were clearly visible, apparently rising from
the bosom of Loch Linnhe, which stretched like a pathway of

---

[1] I have not inserted a translation, as the lines are merely intended to lull a child
to sleep, and are more or less nonsensical though pretty.

metallic green light into the remote distance. A faint line of black cloud lying between earth and heaven betokened the approach of the red-funnelled steamer, but as yet the vessel herself was invisible to my unassisted vision.

Turning to the east, the scene was indescribably grand, and even awesome, in its superb magnificence; for there, towering into the sky, the great Glencoe mountains reared their stately summits, all crowned and glorified with diadems of golden sunbeams which yet lingered upon them, while their bases were shrouded in Cimmerian gloom. Mountains piled upon mountains in stupendous masses of extraordinary configuration entirely shut out the view in that direction, and formed a background for the majestic Pap of Glencoe (Gaelic, "*Sgor-na-Ciche*"), which, with its sister "*Sgor nam Fiann*," guards the entrance to that wild pass, whose dark and blood-stained history is a blot upon our national records, which time and eternity can never remove.

Sir Duncan Cameron's house of Callart is invisible from Onich pier, as the projecting point of North Ballachulish, with its wooded slopes, hide it from view; but it is not far, and a short walk of a few miles will take the inquisitive pedestrian to its historic walls. The Camerons of Callart, like their kinsmen of Loch Eil, had fought on the side of the Stuarts, and had felt the yoke of English tyranny. Bishop Forbes, in his description of the brutalities that occurred after Culloden, writes:—"Among the wounded I pitied none more than one Cameron of Callort, who was a gentleman: he had his arm broke, a great many friends in the place (Inverness), even in our army; notwithstanding all, he could not have a surgeon to dress him for ten days."

In front of Callart, Loch Leven, which is very narrow at the ferry (Gaelic, "*Caolas mhic Phadruig*"), widens considerably, and is studded with beautiful green islands, the two largest of which are Kenneth's Isle (Gaelic, "*Eilean Choinnich*") and the Isle of St Mun (Gaelic, "*Eilean Munde*"); the latter being the ancient place of sepulture of the Camerons of Callart and the MacDonalds of Glencoe. I was once told a curious story relating to this island,

3 D

which I have since seen in print, but slightly altered in detail.
The tale, as I heard it, was as follows:—

In the days of old, the son of one of the chieftains who
dwelt at Calart became enamoured of a maiden of the adjoining clan of *Mac Mhic Iain*, or the MacDonalds of Glencoe. The
girl was passionately fond of her handsome lover, but fearing
that his good looks might attract others of her sex, she requested
him to bind himself by a sacred oath to remain faithful. This
he promised to do, and on the occasion of their next meeting
swore that while his head remained upon his neck he would
never swerve from his fidelity to the maiden of his choice. The
vow was, however, soon broken, and the fickle Cameron transferred his affections to a girl of his own clan, in utter disregard
of his solemnly-pledged word. A few months afterwards he
died suddenly, and was buried in the island, but was not allowed
to rest in peace while his vow remained unfulfilled.

Some time after the burial, a boatman passing the spot at
night heard piercing shrieks as of a soul in agony, but dared
not land to ascertain their cause. These heartrending cries
were now repeated every night, greatly to the terror of the
frightened inhabitants of the surrounding district. At last they
became quite unbearable, and one man, braver than the rest,
determined to visit the island and unravel the mystery. Taking
a boat, he rowed cautiously round the sacred spot upon which
stood the chapel built by "*Ailein nan Creach*" as a peace-
offering for his sins. With trembling steps he landed, and, with
his heart in his mouth and sword in hand, proceeded to the place
from which the blood-curdling sounds issued. As the moon broke
through the drifting clouds, he saw with horror that the head of
the recently-buried man was protruding from the earth, and from
its cold, clammy lips came the awful wailings that had terrorised
the neighbourhood. Approaching nearer, he was able to distinguish the meaning of the supplications that rent the air, which
were to the effect that the uneasy spirit of the perjurer could not
rest until his head was taken from his shoulders, in accordance
with the terms of the vow he had so recklessly made while in

the flesh. Emboldened by this extraordinary request, the bold intruder raised his great claymore high in air, and with one sweeping blow of his strong arm cut off the head of the deceased Cameron; and as the grisly object rolled away among the long, dank grass, its glassy eyes gleaming in the cold moonlight, the earth closed over the body, and the cries were heard no more.

While I thought on the strange traditions associated with this beautiful corner of Lochaber, the sun had set behind a great bank of clouds that now obscured the whole of the western sky, presaging a wet and stormy night. The shadows which had been stealthily creeping up the hillsides had now gained their summits, wrapping them in a mantle of gloom, save where, high above all, the peak of Creag Ghorm flamed out with ruddy glow. The thud, thud, thud of the "Chevalier's" paddles echoed loudly from the opposite shore as she glided swiftly over the bosom of the loch, her masthead light glimmering like a star amid the black smoke that belched out from her red funnels. And now, where silence had reigned supreme, all was bustle and noise. Piermaster Cameron shouted directions to his men in guttural Gaelic; Cockney tourists strutted about in suits of fearful and wonderful pattern, and discoursed in even more wonderful language of the relative merits of the various brands of whisky they had sampled since they left "Hobàn," or of their many hairbreadth escapes in this land of barbarians. Groups of Highland lasses waited on the pier, gossiping merrily in their native tongue, their heads and shoulders enveloped in tartan plaids, from under which shone eyes of lustrous black.

Leaning against the small shed which serves to shelter passengers from the rain was a typical Highland shepherd and his shaggy collie, in charge of a small flock of mountain sheep with great curled horns, that he was taking home to Fort William. As the steamer approached, it became evident that mirth and revelry prevailed on board, for surely that was the "Reel of Tulloch" I could hear the pipers playing to the accompaniment of dancing feet. Soon the vessel was alongside and the ropes made fast to the pier; and while the passengers went on shore, those who, like myself, wished to proceed to Fort William took their place on the steamer. Cheery Captain MacMillan, a true son of Lochaber, stood on the bridge, giving his orders in stentorian tones, and welcoming his friends from Onich with a hearty hand-shake, as he uttered the Gaelic greeting of *"Ciamar tha sibh an dingh?"* ("How are you to-day?"); to which came the reply, *"Tha gu math, ciamar tha sibh fèin?"* ("I am well; how are you?"). Down by the gangway, genial Mr Lawson was prominently visible, scrutinising through his inevitable eye-glass (which, rumour says, is a fixture, and is worn sleeping and waking) the faces of the incoming passengers as they filed on board, with an eye to tickets. Mr "Purser" Lawson is an important personage on the "Chevalier," and all those who have travelled frequently by the West Highland route must have learned to appreciate the bluff heartiness of manner which is his distinguishing characteristic, and will, I am sure, bear a willing tribute to those excellent qualities which have gained for him the respect of Mr MacBrayne's patrons.[1]

Night is fast closing in as we leave Onich, and to the sound of the pipes and the shouts of the dancers—among whom I noticed MacColl, from Oban, and poor MacLennan, whose sad death in Canada all Highlanders deplore—we steam out into the darkness, with the threatening storm-clouds lowering overhead, and thread our way through the narrows of Corran to our destination of Fort William.

CHAPTER XLIX.

My pleasant task now draws to its conclusion, but before finally laying down my pen and saying farewell to my patient readers, it will be necessary to glance briefly at some of the more important events that have occurred in Lochaber during

[1] This chapter was written some time ago. I am not aware whether Mr Lawson still retains his post on the "Chevalier."

the last half decade, events which, though not possessing that romantic interest that attaches to her earlier history, are yet of sufficient consequence to arrest the attention of all who can appreciate the more prosaic records of those great commercial undertakings and social improvements which have so materially assisted in revolutionising the West Highlands, and bringing them in touch with the centres of civilisation and culture. To the skill and perseverance of the celebrated engineer Telford, in successfully carrying out the oft-discussed project of cutting a canal from Loch Linnhe on the west coast to the Moray Firth on the east, is due much of Lochaber's modern prosperity; and although the Caledonian Canal can hardly be classified as a recent undertaking, seeing that it was commenced as far back as the year 1803, and had been taken into consideration by the Government as early as 1773, it was not until April of the year 1847, a few months before the Queen's first visit to Lochaber, that the canal became available for continuous traffic.

Mrs Grant of Laggan, in a letter dated 24th May 1773, makes reference to the scheme that was then engaging the attention of no less a person than James Watt, whose inventions in connection with the application of steam as a motive-power have rendered his name immortal. Mrs Grant, in describing the beauties of Glen More, writes as follows:— "What gives it interest is that when you arrive at the end of it (Loch Lochy), you see and feel yourself in the centre betwixt the two seas, and see at once the Lochy and the Oich on each side of you, running in different directions; one making its way through Loch Linnhe to the west sea, and the other through Loch Ness into the Moray Firth on the east. It is these fast following lakes, linked by filial streams, that form the opening which the three forts were meant to guard, and which they say invites art to the aid of Nature in forming a canal that should in a manner divide Scotland, but that will be the business of a wiser and richer century."

James Watt was employed by the trustees of the forfeited estates to survey the ground and furnish a report and estimate of the cost of a canal with a uniform depth of ten feet. This he did after some months of careful investigation, and gave it as his opinion that such a canal would cost £165,000. Whether the estimate was considered excessive, or the necessary funds were not forthcoming, I am unable to say, but until 1803 the matter remained dormant. In that year a Parliamentary commission empowered Messrs Telford & Jessop, civil engineers, to make a series of careful surveys on a much more important scale than those of their predecessor Watt. The canal was to be deeper and wider than he had suggested, and was to be made to carry a frigate of thirty-two guns throughout its whole length. A much larger expenditure of money was of course demanded by the contractors for the additional labour which the increased size would necessitate, and the result of Telford's survey was an estimate of £474,531; and this did not include the purchase of any lands or proprietary rights, as it was thought that the benefits resulting from the canal would more than compensate the owners of the property which it would traverse, for any loss they might sustain during its construction. This estimate was accepted by Parliament, and the work commenced under the entire control and superintendence of Telford, who, notwithstanding the many almost insuperable natural obstacles he had to contend against in this stupendous undertaking, was entirely successful, though not before many years of incredible toil had been gone through. The poet Southey, who was a personal friend of Telford's, thus bears metrical testimony to his skill in overcoming the many physical difficulties that stood in his way. The lines were written at Banavie in 1819.

> " When these capacious basins, by the laws
>   Of the subjacent element receive
>   The ship, descending or upraised, eight times [1]
>   From stage to stage with unfelt agency
>   Translated; fitliest may the marble here
>   Record the architect's immortal name—
>   TELFORD it was by whose presiding mind
>   The whole great work was plann'd and perfected."

---

[1] This refers to the eight locks at Banavie, known as " Neptune's Staircase."

The Caledonian Canal was opened for navigation on the 24th October 1822, and the event was made the occasion for much rejoicing in Lochaber and the adjacent districts which were traversed by it. At the invitation of Charles Grant, Esq., who represented Inverness in the House of Commons, and who was one of the most energetic and zealous of the canal commissioners, a number of the local gentry met on board a small steamer, which started from the Muirtown locks at Inverness, and proceeded down the canal to Fort William, where a substantial dinner and unlimited supplies of the national beverage were provided at the expense of Mr Grant. This triumphal excursion took two days, Fort Augustus being the first stage of the journey. Salutes were fired as the steamer passed the house of any chief or nobleman, and the pipers on board struck up appropriate tunes. Glengarry went on board at Invergarry, and joined heartily in the festivities, whilst the ladies on shore waved their handkerchiefs, and the male portion of the MacDonalds made the welkin ring with their cheers as the little craft continued its journey to Fort William. Thus joyfully was this important waterway opened to the world; and it is not too much to say that from that day Lochaber saw the commencement of a new era, which was destined to transform an almost trackless and unknown country into an important and flourishing district, and wipe out, as it were, the scars of the terrible "Forty-Five."

The transition was not rapid, as, although the much-looked-forward-to canal was at last an accomplished fact, unlooked for difficulties soon began to appear, and want of adequate funds rendered their removal impossible. In the first place, the expenses exceeded the revenue by a considerable amount, and in consequence the works were allowed to fall into premature decay, a state of things that soon rendered the canal unnavigable except by vessels of the smallest tonnage. So bad was the condition of Telford's great work in 1838, that Mr Walker, the president of the Institute of Civil Engineers, who had been deputed by the Government to examine the canal, reported that nothing short of its entire renovation would be of any use. Money at this period was scarce, and the ministry of the day did not feel justified in recommending the large expenditure of public money that such a scheme demanded ; so the subject was allowed to drop, and the navigation of the canal practically ceased.

From time to time surveys were made with a view to commencing the partial reconstruction of the canal, but beyond an Admiralty investigation, which was carried out by Sir Edward Parry of Arctic fame, nothing was done until 1843, when the Government at last awoke to the importance of maintaining in an efficient condition this great national highway of commerce, and provided the funds required for the purpose. Mr Walker was instructed to prepare plans, specifications, and estimates according to his original survey, with the result that a contract was made with Messrs Jackson and Bean, by which they were bound to execute the necessary repairs in three years. Work was at once begun, and within four years the canal was put into thorough repair, at a cost of about £1,200,000 to the nation. Traffic was resumed in April 1847, and now not a day passes without an almost continuous stream of vessels, many of large size and heavy tonnage, finding their way through its narrow channel, while many thousands of tourists are by its aid enabled to survey from the decks of one or other of Mr MacBrayne's comfortable steamers some of the finest and most sublime scenery in the Highlands, without the slightest inconvenience or fatigue.

Fort William has to thank the Caledonian Canal for its present thriving condition, for had it not been for the existence of that important work, few visitors would have found their way to its hospitable shores. One can hardly realise that within the memory of living persons the only regular communication by sea with Fort William was that afforded by a small sailing vessel named "The Kitty and Lucy," that plied at stated intervals between that place and Glasgow, carrying goods and an occasional passenger or two.

Probably before this book is published the Caledonian Canal will have a powerful rival in the West Highland Railway, which will bring Fort William within a few hours' journey of Glasgow and Edinburgh, and will, I have little doubt, in the course of a few years entirely change the character of Lochaber. The historic fort of which I have had so much to tell has already fallen a victim to the encroachments of the iron horse, and nothing now remains of it but part of the old barracks, where the Highland games were annually held, and where, but a few years ago, I saw poor MacLennan dancing a reel with inimitable grace, in all the exuberance of vigorous health and gaiety of spirit. It is sad to think that he has passed away, and that his cheery presence and the sound of his pipes will enliven us no more.

The new line, which is to do so much for the West Highlands, branches off from the Caledonian system at Crianlarich, and after traversing the desolate moor of Rannoch, reaches Fort William *via* Loch Laggan, Loch Treig, and Spean Bridge, passing quite close to the old ruin of Inverlochy Castle, and, proceeding along the sea-shore in front of the Alexandra Hotel, finds its terminus near the pier. The work has been well and ably carried out by the famous firm of contractors, Messrs Lucas & Aird, who, in spite of the arduous nature of the task, due to the mountainous character of the country through which the railway passes, have succeeded in bringing their engineering labours to a satisfactory conclusion. The line is now to be extended to Mallaig on the west coast, and open up direct communication with Skye.

Such a railway cannot but prove of immense advantage to the islanders, as by its means they will be enabled to transport their fish and other native products to the markets of Glasgow and Edinburgh in much quicker time than they can do now by the Strome Ferry route. I do not hesitate to prophesy great things of the West Highland Railway both socially and commercially, as not only will the outer islands be brought into closer communication with the great educational centres, and

3 E

thus enable the inhabitants of those remote portions of Great Britain to share with their more fortunate brethren of the mainland in the many facilities offered in this enlightened century for self-improvement, but they will also attract to their shores many visitors who are at present deterred from visiting them on account of the long and tedious journey involved; and thus money will circulate freely, and much of the misery caused by poverty be removed.

As far as Fort William itself is concerned, I have every reason to believe that, in the course of a few years, it will rival Oban as a tourist resort: and although it is with some regret I make this statement of my convictions—for I like not the genus— I nevertheless feel that advantages will accrue from the presence of the stranger that will go far to outweigh any objections that can be raised to his national peculiarities and prejudices.

Of those two important legislative measures which have recently engaged the attention of Parliament, viz., the Crofters Act and the Deer Forest Commission, it will be unnecessary to speak. They are fresh in the minds of all, and until some years have passed the results will not become apparent; but that they will effect a radical change in Lochaber and the whole of the district affected by their operations is certain. It behoves landlord and tenant alike to see that the clauses of the new Acts are carried out in a conciliatory spirit, so that neither the pride of the one nor the susceptibilities of the other will be wounded. If this is not done, bad feelings will be engendered and deplorable consequences ensue: a state of things which God forbid!

CHAPTER L.

AND now I must hasten on to an ending, bearing in mind the old Greek proverb, "Μέγα βιβλίον, μέγα χαχόν" ("A great book is a great evil"), a maxim which, I fear, we slaves of the pen are too apt to forget when riding our favourite hobbies roughshod over the necks of a much-enduring public, and altogether over-looking the fact that topics which to us possess a real and engrossing interest do not necessarily awaken the same sympathies in the minds of our readers. It will be remembered that this volume commenced with an account of a royal visit to Inverlochy in those almost prehistoric days when the Pictish kings ruled the destinies of ancient Caledonia. It will therefore be quite in keeping with the fitness of things if I conclude it with a short description of another royal visit to the modern castle of Inverlochy, in the year of our Lord 1873; but before proceeding with the narration of that event, a few words are necessary to explain the more important changes that had taken place among the landed proprietors in Lochaber since the restoration of the forfeited estates in 1784.

I have already stated that the lands which from time immemorial had been held by the chiefs of Clan Cameron, and which had been forfeited to the Crown after the "Forty-Five," had been restored to Donald, the son of Charles Cameron of Lochiel, and grandson of the "Gentle Lochiel." Donald married the Hon. Anne Abercromby, and at his death the chieftainship devolved upon his eldest son, also named Donald, who held a captain's commission in the Grenadier Guards, and afterwards married Lady Catherine Vere Louisa Hobart, daughter of the Hon. George Vere Hobart, and sister of the fifth Earl of Buckingham. In the year 1835 this lady gave birth to a son, who was christened Donald, and who, when his father died in 1858, succeeded to the chieftainship of Clan Cameron, being twenty-first in direct descent from Angus, the first chief.

Donald Cameron of Lochiel received an English education at the famous public school of Harrow, and at the age of seventeen entered the diplomatic service, and subsequently received an appointment as first attaché to the Earl of Elgin's special mission to China in 1856–58, and afterwards to Her Majesty's Legation at Berlin. His father's death in 1858 caused him to resign his appointment, but he continued to serve his sovereign by fulfilling the duties of Deputy-Lieutenant for Inverness-shire, and as a magistrate for the counties of Argyll and Buckinghamshire.

Lochiel married in 1875 the amiable and accomplished Lady Margaret Scott, second daughter of the Duke of Buccleuch, a lady who shares with Mrs Cameron Campbell of Monzie the love and respect of all Lochaber. Many are the acts of unostentatious charity performed by Lady Margaret Cameron that are unheard of beyond the confines of her husband's estates; many are the poor widows, the aged men, the young children, who have received benefits at her hands. Wherever want and suffering exists in Lochaber, there will Lady Margaret be found, ministering to the one and relieving the other, with kindly words of comfort and the more substantial assistance of money, food, and clothing. Schools, Bible-classes, Dorcas societies, hospitals, all find a supporter in the lady who brightens with her presence the gloomy shades of Ach-na-carry. It is a great name she bears, and she bears it nobly; and with such a mother, the sons she has brought into the world cannot but prove themselves worthy of the great name of Lochiel.

Lochiel himself is at one with his wife in all her charitable schemes, and finds both time and money to help them forward. A good landlord and chivalrous gentleman, the present chief of Clan Cameron is generally beloved and respected by his tenants and fellow-clansmen, and in all things bears himself as becomes the representative of a glorious line of heroic ancestors. It is sad to think that, although Lochiel still holds in undisputed possession the estates of his forefathers by the shores of Loch Arkaig, and maintains with quiet dignity his position as head of his clan, the lands of those ancient neighbours and allies of his clan, the MacDonells of Keppoch, no longer own as lord any descendant of that bold and fearless race who for centuries had held them by the sword against all claimants.

When Ranald, the eighteenth chief of Keppoch, died, some-

where about the year 1798–99, the grant of lands which he
had obtained from the Crown, by the assistance of the Duke
of Gordon, was not renewed, and the estates gradually passed
into the hands of Mackintosh of Mackintosh, whose family, it
will be remembered, had always laid claim to them. Ranald
was succeeded in the chieftainship by his nephew Donald,
the son of Angus the seventeenth chief, by his wife, who was
a daughter of MacDonell of Achnacoichean.   Donald married
a granddaughter of Alexander, of Culloden fame, and thus,
whatever may have been his father's origin, there can be no
question as to the legitimacy of his descendants. The blood
relationship was still further strengthened when Donald's son
Angus chose for his wife Christina MacNab of Innisewan,
whose mother was a granddaughter of Charlotte, daughter of
Alexander of Keppoch.   Angus was therefore related in every
way to his brave ancestor; for not only was he a great-
grandson, both on his father's and his mother's side, to the
hero of Culloden, but by his marriage with Miss MacNab he
forged another link in an almost unique pedigree, which
removed once and for all any possibility of disputed succession to the barren but honourable title that was all he had
to leave his children.   His married life was spent at Keppoch,
which, by the cruel irony of fate, he had to rent from a
descendant of the old enemies of his race; but "*autres temps
autres mœurs,*" the Mackintoshes of the nineteenth century
have little in common with their progenitors who fought at
Mulroy, and so, until he died in February 1855, Angus of
Keppoch lived on the best of terms with his neighbour
Mackintosh, and brought up his family ·in the old house by
the side of the rushing Roy, whose turbulent waters had often
run red with the blood of heroes, and whose rocky banks had
echoed the shrill notes of the war-pipes of Mac Mhic Raonuill
in the days that were gone for ever.   And now, in the peaceful
retirement of a quiet London suburb, far away from the
Lochaber she loves so well, dwells the venerable widow of the
last chief of Keppoch, contentedly spending the evening of

her life in the society of two of her accomplished daughters, and surrounded by the relics and mementos of a glorious past.

It may be as well to state here that the Sir John MacDonald of Dunalastair, Perthshire, who styled himself chief of Keppoch, had no real claim to that honour, although he was to a certain extent connected with the family, owing to his descent from an illegitimate son of Ranald Mòr, the seventh chief, who fought at *Blàr-nan-leine*, and who was afterwards executed at Elgin. This son was called Iain Dubh, and his descendants (many of whom still exist in Lochaber) were known as the Black Tribe.

Another change of importance that had taken place in the landed proprietorship of Lochaber, after the restoration of the forfeited estates, was the transfer of the Duke of Gordon's property of Inverlochy to the first Lord Abinger, about the year 1837–38. When the duke died without issue in 1836, his cousin, the Earl of Aboyne, purchased this portion of the Gordon estates from the duke's trustees, with the right of salmon fishing in all the rivers of Lochaber; but, owing to financial difficulties, he found himself unable to retain possession of the property, and after about a year's occupation, sold it, together with the valuable fishing rights, to Lord Abinger (the representative of the English family of Scarlett), who had been raised to the peerage in 1835. The other portion of the duke's Lochaber estates, Inverlair, Loch Treig, and Strathossian, were sold to Colonel Walker of Crawfordton, but were afterwards purchased by Lord Abinger, and now form part of the immense property owned by the young lord, who has only recently succeeded to his inheritance. Thus it came about that the lands which had formed part of the territory over which the mighty Lord of the Isles once held sway fell under the subjection of a stranger.

[1] The next in succession to the chieftainship of the MacDonells of Keppoch is a cousin of the Miss MacDonells, now residing in India. The Marchioness D'Oyley, who is a daughter of Alexander Angus MacDonell, is also closely connected with the family of Keppoch.

It was to the fine residence built by Lord Abinger under the western slopes of Ben Nevis, and called by him Inverlochy Castle, from its close proximity to the ancient ruin of that name, that the Queen came on the 9th September 1873, when she paid her second visit to Lochaber. Accompanied by Princess Beatrice and a small suite of attendants, Her Majesty drove from Kingussie station on the Highland Railway, whither she had come from Balmoral, taking the same route she had traversed in a contrary direction in 1847 with her beloved husband. Tender recollections of that happy journey must have passed through the Queen's mind as familiar objects were passed on the road, which were now rendered sadly interesting from the fact that *he* had noticed them on that last memorable occasion. A rock, a mountain, a waterfall that had been pointed out for her admiration; the tiny burns, the rushing rivers, the mighty granite crags frowning from their dizzy height upon the road beneath—all were sacred because they had attracted *his* attention, and, inanimate though they were, they became living memorials of him who slept.

There is something peculiarly touching in the many pathetic allusions made by the widowed sovereign in her "Journal" to that former visit, when, with her noble consort by her side, she drove along the same road from Ardverikie on her return to Balmoral. Twenty-six years had passed since then, a quarter of a century of a nation's history, and now once again Lochaber welcomes with enthusiastic loyalty the sovereign of Britain to its hospitable and romantic shores. Entering this most picturesque portion of her realms by Glen Spean, Her Majesty passed under a triumphal arch erected by Mrs MacDonell of Keppoch, who was at that time residing at Keppoch House. The arch was composed almost entirely of heather, and bore as an inscription the words — " Loyal Highlanders welcome their Queen" on one side, and on the other the same phrase in Gaelic. A considerable concourse of people were assembled at this spot to catch a glimpse of their royal visitor, and as the

Queen passed the pipers struck up their most joyful tunes, and shouts of welcome resounded through the pine wood which here lines the road. "Unfortunately," says Her Majesty, "we drove past them too quickly." At Spean Bridge Lord and Lady Abinger met their distinguished guests, and accompanied them to Inverlochy, where rooms had been prepared for Her Majesty's accommodation.

As on her previous visit, so on this occasion, the Queen's pleasure was marred considerably by bad weather. "Mist on all the hills and continuous rain! Most disheartening," is the first sentence in Her Majesty's "Journal" of 10th September; but with a plucky determination not to let the disloyal state of the elements interfere with her arrangements, carriages were ordered to be got ready, and a start was made for an excursion to Fassfern. The Queen was delighted with the beautiful scenery of Loch Eil and the lovely woods that clothe its banks, at that time in all the beauty of their autumn foliage, and as the sun came out at intervals, everything was seen to the best advantage. Two days later Her Majesty and Princess Beatrice drove over to Ach-na-carry *viâ* Banavie and Gairlochy, on a visit to Lochiel. This was the first occasion on which the Queen had set foot on the ancestral estates of the chief of Clan Cameron, and it was with a feeling akin to reverence that she approached the spot so intimately associated with the name of her unfortunate kinsman Prince Charles, in whose melancholy history she had always taken a warm and sympathetic interest. Lochiel, dressed as became a Highland chieftain in the picturesque tartan of his clan, received Her Majesty with courteous dignity, and conducted her on board his steam launch, which was to take the royal party on a short voyage up Loch Arkaig. For once the sun deigned to gladden Lochaber with his presence, and lit up the glorious scenery with golden radiance as the tiny vessel with its precious freight glided over the sparkling waters of the loch. The hidden beauties of Coille a Ghiubhais, that clothes, with a garment of leafy verdure, the southern shore, were revealed in all their entrancing loveliness, while high over all rose majestic mountains, their rugged peaks standing out clearly against the celestial blue of the sky.

The Queen, with that innate love of the beautiful which has always distinguished her, found here much to admire, and her interesting "Journal" is full of graphic descriptions of the charming environs of Ach-na-carry. But there was something that filled her soul with a deeper emotion than the mere natural beauty of the surroundings could awaken within her royal breast, something that thrilled every nerve and stirred every fibre of the gentle heart of Britain's Queen, something that is reflected in the mind of every true-born Briton, be he Highlander, Lowlander, Gael, or Sassenach, who has the true love of his country at heart, and who rejoices to hear of the great deeds, the noble actions, the gallant exploits of those of his fellow-countrymen who have gained honour and prestige for the land of their birth among the nations of the world. It is the spirit of patriotism that forms the connecting link between sovereign and people, and binds them together in a union more sacred than the marriage tie. It is the spirit of patriotism that creates a national bulwark a thousand times more effective than mighty armaments and costly ironclads, a bulwark from behind which Britain can regard without apprehension all attempts to undermine her greatness or destroy her influence. It was the spirit of patriotism that welled up in the Queen's mind when, standing on the deck of Lochiel's steamer, she surveyed the beauteous scene of mountain and moorland, of loch and stream, that was spread out like a vision before her. Proud, indeed, might she be to govern such a land and such a people; "*Tir nam beann, nan gleann's, nan gaisgeach*" ("land of mountains, glens, and heroes") it truly was, as these pages bear witness, and no one was more ready to acknowledge this than she who now ruled its destinies.

Modern Jacobites, and members of the League of the White Rose, may scoff if they will (I respect their sentiments, while disagreeing with many of their theories and modes of procedure),

3 F

but I boldly maintain that there exists in the whole of Britain no such ardent Jacobite as the Queen herself. Interested in everything that appertains to that stirring period of Scottish history known as "The Forty-Five," and openly admitting her sympathy for Bonnie Prince Charlie and his ill-starred undertaking, Her Majesty has won the hearts of her Highland subjects; for Jacobitism as a sentiment is not yet dead among them; and there still lingers in many a remote clachan and in many a quiet Lochaber glen, a strong feeling of reverence for the old House of Stuart, and for the memory of the gallant young prince who strove bravely to restore its ancient glories.

The Queen's own sentiments are summed up in the following touching words, which I take by permission from her "Journal," describing the visit to Ach-na-carry. They were called forth by a remark made by one of her suite, who, struck by the historical association of ideas that the Queen's presence as the guest of Lochiel engendered in his mind, said that "it was a scene one could not look on unmoved." "Yes," writes Her Majesty, when describing in her "Journal" the day's proceedings, "and *I* feel a sort of reverence in going over these scenes in this most beautiful country, which I am proud to call my own, where there was such devoted loyalty to the family of my ancestors—for Stuart blood is in my veins, and I am now their representative, and the people are as devoted and loyal to me as they were to that unhappy race." What better testimony can there be to the loyalty of Lochaber than these noble and patriotic words of our beloved sovereign, words with which I am proud to conclude this work.

Reader, farewell! I have rambled with you over Lochaber's heather-clad braes, by moorland and river, by strath and glen. I have trod with you the classic ground upon which her ancient heroes fought and bled in their struggle for freedom against the might of the oppressor. I have endeavoured, I trust not unsuccessfully, to awaken your interest in her history, her people, her traditions. I have conducted you to lands beyond the seas,

where her sons have gained a deathless renown in the ranks
of the gallant defenders of Britain's honour. I have told you
something of those great chieftains whose valorous deeds are
writ large upon the scroll of fame; and of their faithful clansmen, who followed them with unquestioning obedience and
staunch devotion even unto death itself. And now I have
come to my journey's end, having fulfilled my long meditated
task of adding a page to the history of the beautiful Lochaber
I love so well. *Vale.*

Monument to Colonel John Cameron of Fassfern at Kilmallie.

APPENDIX.

APPENDIX.

I.

ORIGINAL GAELIC VERSION OF
PIOBAIREACHD DHÒMNUILL DUIBH.

Piobaireachd Dhòmnuill duibh, piobaireachd, Dhòmhnuill,
Piobaireachd Dhòmnuill duibh, piobaireachd, Dhòmhnuill;
Piobaireachd Dhòmnuill duibh, piobaireachd, Dhòmhnuill,
Piob agus bratach air faich' Inbhirlochaidh.

Chorus—Piobaireachd, piobaireachd, piobaireachd, Dhòmhnuill,
Piobaireachd, piobaireachd, piobaireachd, Dhòmhnuill,
Piobaireachd, piobaireachd, piobaireachd, Dhòmhnuill,
Piob agus bratach air faich' Inbhirlochaidh.

Chaidh an diugh, chaidh an diugh, chaidh an diugh oirnne,
Chaidh an diugh, chaidh an diugh, chaidh an diugh oirnne,
Chaidh an diugh, chaidh an diugh, chaidh an diugh oirnne,
O, chaidh an diugh, 's chaidh an de' le Clann-dònuill.

Theich gu'n do theich iad, O, theich Clann-an-Toisich,
Theich gu'n do theich iad, O, theich Clann-an-Toisich;
Theich gu'n do theich iad, O, theich Clann-an-Toisich,
Dh' fhalbh Clann Mhuirich, 's gu'n d'fhuirich Clann-dònuill.

Theid 'us gu'n teid sinn, O, theid sinn Srath-Lochaidh,
Theid 'us gu'n teid sinn, O, theid sinn Srath-Lochaidh;
Theid 'us gu'n teid sinn, O, theid sinn Srath-Lochaidh,
Choinneamh Mhic Dho'uill duibh, choinneamh Mhic Dhònuill.

II.

EXTRACT FROM SKENE'S VERSION OF "THE PROPHECY OF ST BERCHAN."

Fiche[1] bliadhna is deich m- bliadhna
For Albain in airdri riaghla
For Iar Scoine sceithfidh fuile
Fescur oidhche iar n- iomargain.

Iar sin nos geabha Tairbidh[2]
Mac laidh as aedhidh
Bu lana fir domhain de
'S co *Loch Debhra* a librine.

Translation.

Twenty years and ten years
Over Alban the sovereign reigned ;
On the middle of Scone it will vomit blood,
The evening of a night in much contention.

Afterwards the Tairbith will possess
Son of death and slaughter,
The men of the world were full of him,
And at Loch Deabhra his habitation.

III.

EDINBURGH, *Octr. 24th* 1495.

Rex confirmavit cartam Celestini de Insulis domini de Lochalch (qua concessit consang suo *Alano Donaldi Duff* [*Ailein Mac Dhòmhnuill Duibh,* XII Chief of Lochiel], capitaneo de Clan Camroun,—constabulariam castri de Strome, et terras

---

[1] *Fiche,* which might be taken for *fichead* ("twenty"), is probably *seachd* ("seven"), as *seachd bliadhna diag* would be seventeen years, the length of Macbeth's reign ; the *is* being an abbreviation of *agus.*
[2] Skene thinks this refers to Macbeth's son, Lulach.

12 merc, de Kysryner in dominis et comitatu Rossie vic Invernes,
—pro sustentatione ac fideli custodia dicti (castri) Tenend. dicto
Alano Donaldi et heredibus ejus masculis inter ipsum et
Mariotam Angusii de Insulis legitime procreatis, quibus deficientibus heredibus aliis quibuscunque ipsius Alani, viz.,
masculis de corpore ejus legitime procreatis, quibus def.,
heredibus masculis Eugenii Donaldi prefati Alani fratris
germani quondam legitime procreatis, et eorum heredibus
masculis procreatis :—

Reddend. relevium dict. terrarum tantum : Insuper voluit
quod deficientibus dicto Alano, etc., dicto constabularia et
terre sibi reverterentur :—

Test. Lachlano juvene Makgilleoun magistro de Doward,
Eugenio Donaldi Lachlani de Ardgoir, Hectore Torquelli
Negelli constabulario castri Swyne, Donaldo Cristini Makduff,
Jacobo de Weik rectore de Kilmure secretario dom. comitis
Rossie domini et fratris dicti Celestini :

Apud Inverlocha, 29 Novr. 1472):

Necnon cartam Alexandri de Insulis de Lochalche,—(qua,
unacum consensu concilii sui, concessit consang. suo *Eugenio
Alani* capitaneo de Clan Camroun, heredibus ejus et assignatis,
—terras hereditarias 14 mercarum in dominio de Lochalche, viz.
Achenadariache et Lunde, estimatas ad duas mercas ex antiqua
consuetudine, Fairnamore ad duas merc, Culwoyr et Achemoir
ad duas merc, Fayrinneagveg et Fudanamine et Acheache ad
duas mercas, Achechoyuleith et Brayeintraye ad duas mercas,
Culthnok et Achenacloich et Blaregarwe et Acheæ ad duas
merc, Awnernis et Wochterory ad duas merc., in dominio de
Lochalche; ac etiam in Strome, Carranache 20 sol, Slomba
20 sol, quarterium de Doun ad 10 sol, Achinche cum tribus
quarteriis ad 30 sol., in dominio Locharran, vic Rossie :—

Tenend. a dicto Alex, pro fideli servitio :

—*Test.* Rodrico Alexandri M'Aleod, Colino Nigelli Gewa,
Angusio Mertini, Duncano Mertini et Joh. Duff Duncani :—
Apud Collensay 29 July 1492.): Necnon aliam cartam dicti
Alexandri de Insulis de Lochalche ac de Lochheil,—qua

3 G

concessit Eugenio Alani Donaldi, capitaneo de Clan Camroun, heredibus ejus et succesoribus, terras 30 merc. de Lochheil, viz., Cray, Salachan, Banwe, Corpoch, Kilmalyhe, Achedo, Anat, Aychetilay, Drumfermalach, Fanmoyrmell, Fassefarne, Corebeg, Owechane, Aychetioldown, Chanlaycheil, Kowilknap, Drum-nasall, Clachak, et Clachfyne in Lochheil; et terras unius marse de Gastomoir, terras 3 merc de Clanyn, 3 merc de Mescherleith, 3 merc de Thomecarech, in dominio de Lochabria, vic Invernes: Test. Joh. Alani Donaldi, Alex. Hectoris, Martinio Duncani, Angusio Duncani, et M. Alex. Auchinlek notario publico:— Apud Insulam de Hie 26 Aug. 1492.

IV.

GRANT OF LANDS IN LOCHABER TO DUNCAN MACKINTOSH,[1] Captain of Clan Chattan, by James IV., 5th January 1493.

Rex confirmavit cartam Johannis de Ila comitis Rosse et domini Insularum, qua concessit consang. suo Duncano Makkintoische, capitaneo de Clanchattane et heredibus ejus,— terras de Keppach, Inverroygur, Achnacrose, duas Bointynnis, Bohene, Murvalgane, Tullach, Daildonedarg, Achderre, Inver-royg - minor, Mischoralich, Achynnellane, Leyndale, Cloynis, Glastormore, Mucomer, Leachturynnich, Cloynkallich, Stron-enbay, Tornessa, Blarrobhir, duas Ratullichys, Achmesk, Inverglie, et Achrone, in dominio de Lochabhria, vic. Invernes unacum officio ballivatus dictarum terrarum necnon officio ballivatus terrarum dicti comitio sibi reservatarum, viz., Achdrome, Glengarre, Lettirfinlai et duarum villarum de Lanachynnis; proipsius heredumque ejus homagio et servitio fideli, etc., etc.

Vide also a similar grant by James III., dated 4th July 1476.
—*Registrum Magni Sigilli Regum Scotorum.*

---

[1] The original grant of these lands by the Lord of the Isles to Malcolm Mackintosh was in the year 1447, when he was also appointed bailie or steward of the lordship of Lochaber, an office which descended to his son Duncan.

V.

GRANT OF THE CASTLE OF INVERLOCHY TO ALEXANDER
GORDON, Third Earl of Huntly, by James IV.,
22nd March 1505.

Rex pro bono servitio, concessit Alexandro Comiti de
Huntlie, et heredibus ejus, — Castrum et locum Castri de
Inverlochy, cum antiquis bondis, fossis, stagnis ortis, clausuris
et viridi, viz., *le grene* ejusdem castri vic. Invernes; — cum
potestate reformandi in altum erigendi et edificandi dictum
castrum cum propugnaculis vectibus ferreis, *la machcoling*,
drawbriggis, etc., et capitaneos, constabularios, janitores, etc.,
ordinandi: Reddend. annuatim unum denarium nomine albe
firme.—*Registrum Magni Sigilli Regum Scotorum.*

VI.

GRANT OF LANDS IN LOCHABER, ETC., TO EWEN M'ALLAN
CAMERON (*Eobhan MacAilein,* XIII Chief of Lochiel),
9th January 1527.

Rex cum avisamento thesauraii, confirmavit Eugenio
Alansoun de Lochiell, et ejus heredibus,—12 marcatus terrarum
de Kysyrn, cum constabularia castri de Stroime, in comitatu
Rossie, vic. Invernes; 14 marcat antiqui extentus in dominio
de Lochalche, viz., Achenadariach et Lundy estimat, ad 2
marcat Cuylohir et Achmoir ad 2 marcat, Fayrnaegveg, et
Fynimain, et Acheachye ad 2 marcat; Achchonelyth et
Brayeyntrahe ad 2 marcat Culthnok et Achnacloich, Blare-
garrewe et Achiae ad 2 marcat, Awnarnys et Ochtertere ad
2 marcat in dominio de Lochalche: ac in Strome-Carranache
20, solidatas Slomba 20 solidat quartrium de Doune, 10 solidat,
cum tribus de Locharrane, vic. Ros; 30 marcatas de Lochiell,
viz., Creiff, Salachan, Banwye, Corpoch, Kilmalye, Achedo,
Annat, Achetilye, Drumfermalach, Fainmormeyll, Fassefarne,

Correbeg, Owechan, Achtyeldown, Chanlochiell, Knowilknap, Drumnasallye, Clachak, et Clachfyn, in Lochiell; 1 marcat de Glastirmore, 3 marcat, de Cloynyn 3 marcat, de Moyscheralich, et 3 marcat, de Thomacherech, in dominio de Lochabria, vic. Invernes; — quas idem Eug; personaliter resignavit, et quas rex pro bono servitio univit in liberam baroniam de Lochiell. ·

GRANT OF LANDS ON LOCH ARKAIG—*same date.*

Rex pro servitio impenso et impendendo et pro compositione thesaurario persoluta concessit Eugenio Alani heredibus ejus assignatis; 40 marcatas terrarum de Glenlie et Lochirbaig (Loch Arkaig?) cum dimedietate ballivatus de Lochaber, vic. Invernes que fuerunt quondam Alani Donaldi patris dicti Eug; et in manibus regis per 50 annos ratione nonintroitus per decessum dicti Alani exiterunt.—*Registrum Magni Sigilli Regum Scotorum.*

VII.

Novr. 8th 1537.

Rex concessit Donaldo Cameroun (*Domhnull Dubh Mac Dhòmhnuill*, XV Chief of Lochiel), filio et heredi apparenti Ewgenii Alansoun capitanei de Clancameroun 60 denariatas terrarum de Knokdert (extenden ad 10 libras annuatim), 20 denariar. de Glenneves (ad 10 marcus annuatim) vic Invernes;— que (de rege tente per servitum warde) fuerunt in manibus regis, viz. Knokdert per 70 annos, Glenneves per 42 annos, a tempore obitus postremi legitimi possessoris nonintroitu earundem dicto Don. donato: et (bonus mobilibus per Andream Pap serjantum perquisitis et non compertis), 4 Maii 1537 coram Johanne Cuthbert vicecomite deputato de Invernes appreciate sunt et dicto Donaldo vendite pro 700 lib. et 420 marc. Faciend. jura et servitia debita et consueta :—et voluit rex quod domini veteres dictarum terrarum, heredes regressum quandocumque dict. summas persolverent infra septennium.— *Registrum Magni Sigilli Regum Scotorum.*

VIII.

AGREEMENT BY SORLE M'CONILL MAKLANE, TUTOR OF GLEN NEVIS.

Apud Edinburgh primo die mensis Novembris anno lxiiijo.

The quhilk day in presence of the Lordis of Secreit Counsall comperit Donald Dow M'Conill M'Ewin of Locheld (*Domhnull Dubh Mac Dhòmhnuill*, XV Chief of Lochiel), capitane of the Clanchamroun on that ane part; and Sorle M'Conill Maklane, tutour of Gleneves for himself and in name of Alester M'Alester, oy and apperand air of umquhile Alester M'Alester M'Donald of Gleneves, on that uther part; ather of thame having divers actionis and causis to persew aganis utheris as thai allegeit, and wer contentit and consentit to ansuer uther befoir the Lordis of Counsall and Sessioun, summarlie, but diet or tabill upoun summondis of sex dayis warning. And in consideratioun, that thai bayth dwell in the far Hielandis, and may nocht await of ony lang continewance upoun pley, quhilk forme and ordour thai acceptit and allowit to be als sufficient in all respectis as gif thair saidis actionis wer intentit upoun xxi or xv dayis warning, and baid the course of tabill as utheris dois; and this consent to be extendit to all and quhatsumevir actionis to be intentit be ony of the saidis personis aganis utheris, for quhatsumevir caussis or occasionis bipast.—*Register of the Privy Council.*

IX.

OBLIGATION OF LAUCHLAN MACKINTOSH OF DUNAUCHTANE TO RANNALD M'RANNALD (IX Chief of Keppoch) OF KEPPOCH, 1569 A.D.

At Invernes the xx day of Junii, the yeir of God j^{m}v^{c}lxix yeris, in presence of my Lord Regentis Grace and Lordis of Secreit Counsale, comperit Lauchlane M'Yntosche of Dunnauchtane and gaif in his obligatioun following subscrivit with his hand . . .

" I, Lauchlane M'Yntosche of Dunnauchtane, be the tennour heirof bindis and obleissis me and my airis, that I sall mak securitie to Rannald M'Rannald of Keppach of sic landis and rowmes as he hes of me, at the sicht of my Lord Regentis Grace according as his Grace sall think ressonabill and equitabill; and quhatevir his Grace willis me to do in that behalf I sall fulfill the samyn without contradictioun." Signed, etc.

X.

COMPLAINT BY JOHNNE DUNBAR OF MOYNES, GEORGE DUNBAR IN CLUNE, AND WILLIAME FALCOUNER IN LETHINBAR, as follows :—

William Ros of Kilraak, Hutcheoun Ros, his son and apparent heir, David Ros of Holme, at least Johnne Ros of Cantray, Johnne Ros of Ballivat, David Ros in Lyne, David Ros Williamestoun, Lauchlan Ros in Leanuraddich, Hutcheoun Big, Ros his brother, Alexander Ros in Ardrie, Johnne Watt, and David Rossis his brothers, etc., etc. . . . as also Allane Camroun of Locheldy, Allaster M'Allaster V^cConeill of Glenneves, Ewene M'Coneill V^cEwene V^cConeill of Blarmascylach, Johnne Badach M'V^cEwene of Errach, his brother, Ewne ——, Duncane M'Mertine of Letterfindlay, his brother, Donald M'Mertine, Ewne M'Mar M'Martine, Donald M'Anduy V^cEwne, Allan M'Anduy V^cEwne, Allane M'Ane of Innerloch, Johnne Moir M'Allane V^cEane of Callardy, Allaster Dow M'Allane V^cEane of Culchinny, etc., etc., with convocation of the lieges to the number of 200 " broken hieland men and sorneris, all bodin in feir of weir, with bowis, darlochis and tua handit swordis, steilbonnettis, haberschonis, hacquebutis and pistolettis," —came upon 8th October last, " undir cloude and silence of nicht, be way of briggancie, to the said George Dunbaris duelling house in Clune, pertening heretablie to the said Johnne

Dunbar of Moynes, and thair tressonablie rased fyre in the
said house, and in ane uther cotter house of the said George
Dunbaris, brynt and distroyit the same, putt violent handis in
Marjorie Dunbar spous of the said George Dunbar, and in
Issobell Dunbar spous to the said Williame Falcouner, tirvit
thair claiths af thame, and schoit thame naiked furth of thair
houssis, the said Issobell Dunbar being then lyand bedfast in
grit disease and dolour, scho being bot tuellf dayis befoir
delyverit of a bairne; quhilk bairne thay maist barbarouslie, but
pitie or compassioun, threw oute of hir arme and kaist furth in
the midding. And not satisfeit thairwith, thay at the same
tyme reft and awaytuke fra the said George, furth of his
houssis, his haill insicht, plennesching movabilis, guidis and
geir, togidder with thre scoir ten hors and nolt; and sa mony
of the same nolt as wald not dryve, to the nowmer of auchtene,
thay barbarouslie hocht and slew; committing heirthrow oppin
and manifest tressoun, concovatioun of his Hienes leigis, reiff
and brigancie, and hocheing of oxin, besydis the beiring and
weiring of hacquebùtis and pistollettis.—*Register of the Privy
Council, James VI.*, 1598.

XI.

ORDER DENOUNCING JOHN CAMERON OF ERRACHD AND OTHERS for refusing to assist the Government in their Action against the Clan Gregor.

EDINBURGH, 25th Feby. 1612.

Although Allan Camroun of Lochyell (*Ailein Mac Iain
Duibh*, XVI Chief of Lochiel) and Allaster M'Donald (*Alasdair
nan Cleas*, X Chief of Keppoch) of Gargavach, who have been
employed by his Majestie against the "rebellious thevis and
lymmaris of the Clan Gregour," and in some other services
concerning the "peace and quietnes of the Heylandis" had
expected that their kin and friends would have joined them
with their forces for prosecuting that service, yet Johnne
Camroun M'V^cEwne in Errache, Ewne Camroun his brother,

Donald M'En (duy?) Vic Donnald Camroun, Allaster M'Allaster
V^cDonald Camroun of Gleneves, Donald and Angus Camronis,
his sons, Donald M'Sourle Camroun in Auchintourmoir, Ewne
M'Donnald V^cEwne Camroun in Blairniscalloch, Donald
M'Martyne and Duncane M'Martyne, all of the Clan Chamroun,
and Ronnald M'Donald of Insche, and Donald M'Donnald in
——, both brothers of the said Allaster M'Donald of Gargavach,
—said persons having been formerly assisters of the said Allan
and Allaster in all their private affairs but now " being offendit
with thame becaus thay have randerit thair obedience to his
Majestie and tane upoun thame the executioun of some of his
Majesteis directionis aganis the Clan Gregour and some uther
brokin men of the Heylandis " and being " loath that ony suche
course sould tak effect in thair personis, bot that rather the
saidis Allane and Allaster M'Donnald sould have followit the
wicked and unhappie trade of the rebellious lymairis of the
Heylandis and Illis, that thairby thay micht have bene the
more able undir thair patrocinie and protection to have con-
tinewit in thair iniquitie and wickednes, fra the quhilk thay feir
now to be reclamed be thame "—have not only refused to assist
the said Commissioners in his Majesty's service, but avowedly
oppose them, declaring themselves to be friends of the Clan
Gregour and of all broken men, so that the execution of the
said service is frustrated. Charge has been given to the said
defenders to answer ; and, none of them now appearing, they
are all to be denounced rebels.—*Register of the Privy Council
of Scotland.*

XII.

EDINBURGH, *May 19th* 1613.

For attempting to reset and encourage the proscribed Clan
Gregor in the year 1613, the Privy Council issued a proclamation
in which those persons who had done so were fined, among the
names are " Allaster Camroun Laird of Glenneveis in the soume
of fyve hundreth merkis; Allane M'Inteoch in Inverlochie in the
soume of ane hundreth merkis; Ronnald M'Ronnald in Inche

of Loichquhaber, in the soume of ane hundreth' merkis," etc., etc.
—*Register of the Privy Council of Scotland.*

XIII.

Troubles in Lochaber in September 1613, from information given by James Primrose, Clerk of the Council.

"The haill continent adjacent to the Ilis is lykewayes peacable except Lochquhaber; quhair thair is a grite dissessioun and trouble now arissin amangis the Clanchamroun thameselffis, and proceding upoun this occasioun;—The Erle of Ergyle at the sighting of his chartour kist, findis some evidentis whairby his umquhile fader, uncle and utheris his predicessoris were infeft, retourit, and seasit in a twentie merk land in Lochquhaber possist to Allane M'Coneill Duy. Having advisit heirupoun with his procuratoris he uses a wairning aganis Allane for removing frae the landis; and upoun the wairning he intentis ane actioun of removing befoir the Sessioun.

"Allane, being twitcheit with this unlooked for proces, come to this burgh to advise with his procuratoris quhat course he sould tak thairin; and meeting with the Erle of Ergyle the Erle shew to him that, althoght to his opinion he had the undoubtit right to the landis, yitt he wes content, for eschewing of contestatioun and proces, that both thair rightis sould be judgeit be thair aune procuratoris. Allane yeilding heirunto, and thair procuratoris haveing sene the writtis produceit, thay fand that the Erll had the best right. Whairupoun Allane aggrees with the Erll and takis ane new right halding of him.

"The Marques of Huntlie being informit heirof, and taking offence that Allane sould acknowledge ony superiour within Lochquhaber bot him, he delt with Allane to renunce the securitie he had tane of the Erll of Ergyll, and to tak ane new right and securitie of the same landis fra· him. Allane refusit this conditioun with mony protestations that althoght he held that xx merk land of the Erll of Ergyll, yitt that sould be no prejudice to his obedience and service to the Marques of Huntley,

3 H

scoir men, that same very day of the meeting of his adverse
freindis, and within half a myle to the place of meeting.

"Allane, when he mett with his company, tauld thame that
that day he wald haif his freindis to renounce his landis, or then
he wald tak his advantage the best way he might of thame; and
for this effect desyrit thame to derne thame selfis in a wode
neirby, and that he him self accompanyit with sax personis
allanerlie, wald go agaitward to the place quhair his freindis
keept tryist, and desyre thame to send sax of thair nomber to
confer with him upoun all materis contravertit betuix thame;
and gif thay aggreit, he bad his company keepe thame quiet; yf
thay aggreit not, and that thay intendit ony harme to him, he
tauld thame that he sould tak the flight hard by the wode
quhair thay lay, and desyrit thame, quhen his enemeyis in the
chaise come by the wode, that then they sould ishe oute and
persew thame on thair bakis. According to this appointment,
Allane and sax with him in company gois fordwart, and sendis
ane of thair nomber to his freindis, desiring thame to send sax
of thair company to confer with him. Thay persaving Allane
so single accompanyed, thinking that he had bot new come in
the cuntrey, and that he had no mo company bot the sax that
wer with him, they all brak at him, resolveing then to haif his
lyfe. He flees hard by the wode quhair his ambusche lay. Thay
follow him that same way with schouteing and shoiting of
arrowis, and when thay ar all by the ambusche comes furthe.
Allane, persaveing, he turnis, and thay upoun the bak, and he
upoun the face, makis ane cruell and bloodie onsett upon thame,
slayis tuentie of the chief and principallis of thame, takis aucht
prisonarris, and sufferis the rest to eschaip. And then he
possessis him self of his haill landis agane,—learneing ane
lessone to the rest of his kin who ar alyve in quhat forme thay
sall carye thame selffis to thair Cheif heirefter."

N.B.—The Erll of Enzie mentioned was George Gordon,
Earl of Enzie, son of the Marquis of Huntly, and brother-in-law
to the Earl of Moray.

XIV.

PROCLAMATION AGAINST ALAN, XVI CHIEF OF LOCHIEL
(*Ailein MacIain Duibh*).

EDINBURGH, 9*th* *Decr.* 1613.

Forasmekle as Allan Camroun of Lochyell haveing of laite committit most detestable and cruell murthouris and slauchteris upoun diverse of his Majesteis peciable and good subjectis, and haveing treasounablie rissin fyre, brynt houssis, cornis, and barnis, besydis diverse utheris insolencyis and villannyis committit be him, to the offence of God, contempt of his Majestie, and misregaird of law and justice, for the quhilk he is denunceit rebell and put to the horne. . . .

Forasmekle as Allan Camroun of Lochyell being unmyndfull and ungrait of the mony benefiteis and favouris quhilkis he has ressavit frome the Kingis Majestie, especialie by ressaveing of him into favour and mercy quhenas he stood in dainger of the lawis for diverse haynous crymes and offenceis comittit be him, and he haveing maid shipwraik of his faith and promisit obedience, shaiking af all feir of God and his prince and reverence of the law, and preferring the mishevous and unhappie course of his bypast wicked lyff, to godlines, civilitie, good reule and quietnes, he and the persons underwrittin, thay are to say:—Ewne Camroun in Culdoir; Allane Dow in Cluishepharnie (here follows a long list of names,) hes in a most cruell detestable and schamefull maner, yockit with hes awne kynnismen and friendis, and hes barbarouslie murdreist and slayne umquhill Johnne Camroun *alias* Bodache Allaster Camroun of Glenneves and utheris his Majesteis good subjectis, to the nombir of twenty personis or thairby: hes treasounablie reased fyre, brynt diverse housis and barnis with a grite quantitie of cornis being in the barnis and barnyairdis, and hes committit diverse stouthis, reiffis and utheris insolencyis. For the quhilkis crymes he and his compliceis foirsaidis being callit to thair tryall before his Majesteis Justice, thay, takand upoun thame the ignominie and guylt of the saidis crymes, absentit thame selffis frome thair tryall, and are thairfore lauchfullie and ordourlie denuncit rebellis and put to the horne; quhair thay remaine as yit unrelaxt, in heich contempt of oure Soverane Lord, his auctoritie and lawis; lykeas, to the fordir contempt of his Majestie, thay have associate unto thame selffis diverse utheris disordourit and brokin men, by whose concurrence and assistance they intend ane oppin rebellioun within the cuntrey of Lochquhaber, to the encouragement of uther Heyland people to brek louse, and sua to disturb the policie and quiet of the Heylandis.—*From the Register of the Privy Council of Scotland.*

This proclamation, which is very long, finishes by the offering a reward of "ane thousand poundis" for the capture or slaying of Alan Cameron of Lochiel, and "fyve hundreth poundis" for the "taking, exhibitioun, or slauchter" of any of the other persons mentioned. Letters of fire and sword are granted to George, Marquis of Huntly, with full power to take summary vengeance upon Lochiel and his adherents.

XV.

COMPLAINT BY THE KING'S ADVOCATE AND LAUCHLANE M'INTOSCHE OF DUNNAUCHTANE, Heritable Bailie and Steward of the Lordship and Stewartry of Lochaber, as follows:—

June 10th 1617.

In July last the said Lauchlane proclaimed courts to be held for the administration of justice to the inhabitants within the bounds of the said Lordship. On   July he went to his house of Keppache on the water of Spean, where he stayed till the day fixed for the holding of the Courts. Meanwhile Allan Camroun of Lochyell (*Ailein Mac Iain Duibh*, XVI Chief of Lochiel) assembled together Duncane Camroun *alias* M'Mertene, Dougall Camroun, Dougall Camroun *alias* M'Allaster M'Coull, Donald Camroun *alias* M'Martene, Ewne Camroun *alias* M'Martene,

M'Condochie M'Ewne, Johnne V^cCoull, Camroun, son
of Ewne V^cCondochie V^cEwne, and Allan Moir M'Invich, with
others to the number of 200 armed with "bowis, darlocheis,
durkis, Lochaber aixis, tua handit swordis, haberschonis," and
hagbuts and pistollets; and, "concurring togidder in a most
wicked and rebellious societie," they resolved to withstand the
holding of the said courts. They understanding that the said
Lauchlane must cross the water of Lochy at the ordinary fords,
resolved to guard the same and stay his passage. "And for this
effect thay be the haill space of aucht dayis togidder preceiding
the day foirsaid appointit for halding of the saidis courtis, causit
a nomber of thair saidis compliceis cast and dig up trinsches and
strong fortis of stone and feall alongis the fuirdis of the said
watter of Lochy upon the syde thairof, and placeit and plantit
the name (nomber?) of fyftie muscataris in the saidis trinsches.
And the said Allan Camroun ranked the remanent of his saidis
compliceis in battall array outwith the said trinsches and fortis.
And thair, upoun the day foirsaid appointit for halding of the
saidis courtis as said is, howsoone the saidis personis persavit the
said Lauchlane M'Intosche approtcheing agaitward toward the
said watter, and the fuirdis thairof, of purpois to haif corsit the
same for halding of the saidis courtis, thay schote and dischargit the haill nomber of thrie hundreth schote of muscat and
hagbute over the said watter; and the said Lauchlane haveing
come unto the watter syde of Lochy and being entiring in the
fuirdis thairof, the saidis personis of new agane schote and
dischargit at him and his saidis compliceis and servandis the
haill nomber of four hundreth schote of muscat and hagbute,
of purpois to haif schote and slane him thairwith; and thairby
violentlie stayit the said Lauchlane M'Intosche fra passing
throw the saidis fuirdis and fra halding the said courtis."

Pursuers appearing and defenders not appearing the Lords
find the charges proven, and order the said defenders to enter
their persons within the Tolbooth of Edinburgh within fifteen
days, and to remain there at their own expense until further
order be taken.—*Register of the Privy Council, James VI.*

XVI.

LATHA INBHER-LOCHAIDH
(*Battle* [literally "*day*"] *of Inverlochy*).

FOUGHT 2ND FEBRUARY 1645.

Hi rim h-ŏ-rò, h-ò-rò leatha
H-i rim h-ŏ-rò, h-ò-rò leatha

   "   "   "   "   "
Chaidh an latha le Clann-Dòmhnuill.

An cuala 'sibhse 'n tionndadh duineil,
Thug an camp bha 'n Cille-Chuìmein ;
'S fad chaidh ainn air an iomairt,
Thug iad as an naimhdean iomain.

    H-i rim, etc.

Dhirich mi moch madainn dhòmhnaich,
Gu barr caisteil Inbher-Lochaidh,
Chunna 'mi 'n t-arm a dol an ordugh,
'S bha buaidh an là le Clann-Dòmhnuill.

Direadh a mach glun Chuil-eachaidh,
Dh' aithnich mi oirbh sùrd 'ur tapaidh ;
Ged bha mo dhuthaich na lasair,
'S eirig air a chus mar thachair.

Ged bhiodh Iarlachd a bhraghaid,
An seachd bliadhna so mar tha e,
Gun chur, gun chliathadh, no gun àiteach,
'S math an riadh bho 'm beil sinn paighte.

Air do laimhse Thighearna Lathair,
Ge mor do bhosd as do chlaidheamh ;
'S ioma oglaoch chinne t-athar
Tha 'n Inbher Lochaidh na laidhe.

'S ioma fearr goirseid agus pillein,
Cho math 'sa bha riamh dheth d' chinneadh,
Nach d' fhoad a bhotann thoirt tioram,
Ach faoghlum snàmh air Bun-Neimheis.

Sgeul a b'àite 'nuair a thigeadh,
Air Caim-beulaich nam beul sligneach,
H-uile dream dhiu mur a thigeadh,
Le bualadh lann an ceann ga 'm bristeadh.

'N latha sin shaoil leo dhol leotha,
'S ann bha laoich ga'n ruith air reothadh,
'S ioma slaodanach mor odhar,
Bha na shineadh air ach'-an-tothair.

Ge be dhireadh Tom-na-h-aire,
Bu lionor spog ùr ann air dhroch shailleadh,
Neul marbh air an suil gun anam,
'N deigh an sgiùrsadh le lannan.

Thug sibh toiteal teith ma Lochaidh,
Bhi ga 'm bualadh ma na srònan,
Bu lion 'or claidheamh clais-ghorm comhnard,
Bha bualadh an lamhan Chlann Dòmhnuill.

Sin 'nuair chruinnich mor dhragh na fhalachd,
'N am rusgadh na 'n greidlein tana,
Bha iongnan nan Duimhneach ri talamh,
An deigh an luithean a ghearradh.

'S lionmhor corp nochte gun aodach,
Tha na 'n sineadh air chnocain fhraoiche,
O'n bhlar an greaste na saoidhean,
Gu ceann Leitir blar a Chaorainn.

Dh' innsinn sgeul eile le firinn,
Cho math' sa ni cleireach a sgrìobhadh ;
Chaidh na laoich ud gu'n dicheall.
'S chuir iad maoim air luchd am mì-ruin.

Iain Mhuideartaich nan seol soilleir,
Sheoladh an cuan ri la doillear,
Ort cha d' fhuaradh briste coinnidh,
'S ait' leam Barra-breac fo d' chomas.

Cha b' e sud siubhal cearbach,
A thug Alasdair do dh' Albainn,
Creachadh, losgadh, agus marbhadh;
'S leagadh leis coileach Strath-bhalgaidh.

An t-eun dona chaill a cheutaidh,
An Sasunn, an Albainn, 's 'n Eirinn
Is it e curr na sgeithe
Cha miste leam ged a gheill e.

Alasdair nan a geur lann sgaitheach,
Gheall thu 'n dé a bhi cuir as daibh,
Chuir thu 'n retreuta seach an caisteal,
Seoladh gle mhath air an leantuinn.

Alasdair nan geur lann guineach.
Na 'm biodh agad armuinn Mhuile;
Thug thu air na dh' fhalbh dhiu fuireach,
'S retreut air prabar an duileisg.

Alasdair Mhic Cholla ghasda
Lamh dheas a sgoltadh nan caisteal;
Chuir thu 'n ruaig air Ghallaibh glasa,
'S ma dh-ol iad càl gun chuir thu asd' e.

'M b' aithne dhuibse 'n Goirtean-odhar,
'S math a bha e air a thothar,
Cha 'n inneir chaorach no ghobhar;
Ach fuil Dhuimhneach an deigh reothadh.

Bhur sgrios mu 's truagh leam 'ur caradh
'G eisdeachd an-shocair 'ur pàistean
Caoidh a phannail bh' ann 's 'n àraich
Donnalaich bhan Earraghàël.

—*From MacKenzie's Beauties of Gaelic Poetry.*

XVII.

LETTER FROM GENERAL MONK TO SIR EWEN CAM
OF LOCHIEL, subsequent to the Treaty of Peace
the Garrison of Fort William.

DALKEITH, *5th June*

SIR,—I have received your letter, dated the 26th Ma
which I perceive you have confirmed the Articles conc
upon your part by Lieutenant Collonel Duncan Campbell
I have spoken to Captain Bryan to examine the business
hath happened between Collonell Allen and some of
friends. I hope that you will see your people to live or
and peaceably, and to pay their cess as the rest of the cou
does, and to be careful that your Clans keep no broken p
among them, nor disturb the peace of the countrey. This
at present from, etc.,

(Subscribed)　　GEORGE MON

XVIII.

INSCRIPTION ON THE MONUMENT AT TOBAR NAN CEA
LOCH OICH.

As a Memorial of the ample and summary Venge
which in the swift course of Feudal Justice, inflicted by
orders of the Lord MacDonnell and Aross, overtook the
pretrators of the foul Murder of the Keppoch Family, a bra
of the Powerful and Illustrious Clan of which his Lordship
the Chief, this Monument is erected by Colonel MacDor
of Glengarry XVII Mac - mhic Alastair, his Successor
Representative, in the year of our Lord 1812. The head
the Seven Murderers were presented at the feet of the N
Chief in Glengarry Castle, after having been washed in
Spring, and ever since that event, which took place earl
the Sixteenth Century, it has been known by the nam
" Tobar nan Ceann," or " The Well of Heads."

XIX.

CUMHA DO MHAC MHIC RAONAILL NA CEAPICH AGUS A
BHRATHAIR, A CHAIDH A MHORT 'SA BHLIADHNA
1663. (*Lament for the two murdered Chiefs of
Keppoch, who were assassinated in the year* 1663.)

'S mi am shuidh' air bruaich torrain
Mu 'n cuairt do Choire-na-cleithe ;

Ged nach h-'eil mo chas crubach,
Tha lot na 's mu orm fo m' leine ;

Ged nach h-eil mo bhian scracte,
Tha fo m' aisne mo chreuchdan ;

'S cha n e curam na h-imrich,
No iomagain na spreidhe ;

No bhi gam chur do Cheann-taile,
'S gun fhios cia 'n t-aite do 'n deid mi ;

Ach bhi 'n nochd gun cheann-cinnidh ;
'S tric 's gur minig leam fein sin ;

Ceann-cinnidh nam Braigheach
'Chuireadh sgath air luchd-Beurla.

Tha mo choill air a maoladh,
Ni a shaoil leam nach eireadh.

Tha mo chnothan air faoisgneadh,
'S cha bu chaoch iad ri 'm feuchinn.

Cha n fheil ann diu ach tuaileas,
Dh' fhan iad bhuam am barr gheugan.

Cha b 'e fuaim do ghreigh lodain
'Gheibht 'a sodrich gu feilltean ;

No geum do bha tomain
'Dol an coinnimh a ceud laoigh ;

No uisge nan sluasid
Bharr druablas na feithe.

'S e be mhiann le d' luchd-taighe,
'Bhi gan tathich le beusan ;

Mu dha thaobh Garbh-a-chonnidh,
Far 'm biodh na sonnanich gle mhor.

Le am morgha geur, sgaiteach,
Frith bhacach, garbh leumnach,

'S beag an t-ionghnadh leam t' uaisle
'Thigh 'nn an uachdar ort 'eudail ;

Is a liuthad sruth uaibhreach
As 'n do bhuaineadh thu 'n ceud uair.

Ceist nam fear thu bho 'n Fhearsit
Is bho Cheapich nam peuran ;

Bho Loch-Treig an fheoir dhosrich,
'S bho Shrath-Oisein nan reidhlean

'S bho cheann Daile-na-mine
Gu Sron na h-iolaire leithe.

Sliochd an Alasdair Charrich
'Rachadh allail 'na eideadh ;

Sar mhac an Iarl Ilich
Ceannard mhiltean is cheudan.

'S ro mhath shloinninn do shinnsreadh,
Fuil dhireach Chuinn-Cheud-chathich ;

Bho mhac an righ Spaintich,
A rinn tamh ann an Eirinn.

Siol Mhilidh nan cathan
A bha grathun 'san Eiphait.

B' e mo chreach is mo ghonadh
Nach d' fhuair thu cothram na Feinne.

Gun tigh 'nn ort 's tu 'nad chadal
Ann an leaba gun eirigh,

'S ann air maduinn Di-domhnaich
'Rinn na meirlich do reubadh ;

Da mhac brathair t' athar
Gum bu scrathail leam fein sud.

Agus seachd de shiol Dughaill
Luchd spuilleadh nan ceudan.

Ach thig Sir Seumas nam bratach
'S bheir e 'm mach dhuinn bhur n eirig ;

Agus Aonghus bho Ghairidh
Leoghann fathramach gleusta

'S gun a choimeas air thalamh
An am tarruinn nan geur-lann

Thig na cinn dibh a chonaibh
'S ann leam 'bu torlicht 'an sgeula.

—*From the Rev. A. MacLean Sinclair's*
edition of the Bard's Poems, 1895.

XX.

A Proclamation anent some Rebels, Robers, and
Thieves who are, or have been lately in arms in the
Braes of Lochaber.

August 15th, 1688.

James by the Grace of God, King of Great Britain, France and
Ireland, Defender of the Faith. To all and sundry our loving
Subjects to whose knowledge these presents shall come Greeting.

Forasmuch as we have granted a Commission of Fire and
Sword to the Laird of M'intosh for recovering possession of his
Lands of Keapoch and others, detained from him illegally by
Coll M'donald and his Adherents ; and having joyned with the
Laird of M'intosh a Company of our Forces under the Command

of Captain M'kenzie of Suddy, the said Coll having associate to himself all the Outlaws and other desperate Thieves and Robers bearing the Sirname of M'donald, and others their Associates and Accomplices, to the number of Seven or Eight Hundred men ; they did in a most Treasonable and Rebellious manner, dare to Invade and Suprize such as were cloathed with Our Authority, and to Murder and Assasinat many of them. And We being fully Resolved in all Cases to Defend and Maintain our Subjects in their just Rights, Properties and Possessions, and to punish severely such as either oppose Our Authority or injure them, We have thought fit and necessary to Commissionat others of Our Forces, under the Command of Captain Charles Straiton to repair to the said place and to reduce by all possible means and methods the said Rebels, and to require the Chiefs of all the Neighbouring Clanns to be ready with such numbers of their Clanns, Friends, and Followers, as shall be desired and required to assist them in the way and manner exprest in Our respective Letters to them.

And for the more speedy and effectual suppressing of the said Rebels, We do hereby declare, that whoever shall Maintain, Harbour, or Resett them, by themselves or others, give the least Assistance, by Meat, Drink, Money, or other supply, or shall omit to do their utmost endeavour for apprehending them, or shall any manner of way Intercommune with them, shall be punished as accessaries to their Crimes and Accomplices thereof, with the utmost severity of Our Laws. We do also hereby Order and Command all the said Chiefs of Clanns, Heretors, Woodsetters, Liferenters, Tacksmen, Chamberlains and others, Bordering upon any part of Our Seas, Firths, or Isles; to secure all their Boats and Passages, to the end that none of the said Traitors be ferried over, and that, as they shall be answerable upon their highest peril.

And for the better Prosecution of all the said ends and designs, We hereby discharge any of our Subjects to Travel in the Highlands without Passes from their Landlords and Masters, and that ay and while the said Rebels be fully reduced : Impowering hereby any having Commission from Us, or any under their Command, to seize and apprehend such as want Passes, ay until they be able to give a sufficient account of themselves.

Expecting that all Our good Subjects will concurr in suppressing and rooting out the said Barbarous and Inhuman Traitors, to their utmost power, which We will look upon as most acceptable Service; Indemnifying all such who shall act or concurr in the prosecution of this Our Proclamation. And to the end, Our Royal Pleasure in the Premises may be made publick and known, Our Will is, and We Charge you strictly, and Command that incontinent, these Our Letters seen, ye pass to the Mercat Cross of Edinburgh, and whole remanent Mercat Crosses of the Head Burghs of the Shires of the Kingdom, and other places needful, and there, in Our Name and Authority make Publication of Our Royal Pleasure in the Premises, that none pretend Ignorance.

Given under Our Signet at Edinburgh, the Fifteenth day of August, one thousand six hundred, eighty eight Years, and of our Reign the Fourth Year.

Per Actum Dominorum Secreti Concilii.

(Signed)   COLIN M'KENZIE,

Cls. Sti Concilii.

God Save the King.

[Copied from an original printed Proclamation in the British Museum Library.]

XXI.

LETTER FROM J. MACKINTOSH OF TORCASTLE TO THE EARL
    OF PERTH complaining of the behaviour of Keppoch
    and his Associates, previous to the battle of Mulroy.

KEPPOCH, *August* 3, 1688.

My Lord,

    I came to this place six dayes agoe, and the first two nights these rebells in this countrey lay darned and did not appear, but since, they, with ther wicked accomplices

and ther broken relations from all the countreyes about, have
convocate themselves to a great number, and doe behave themselves most contemptuously, insomuch that this same day, they
have seased on some of the King's souldiers, and his Messenger
at Arms, disarmed, threatened and ffettered them. My friends
and I are here making up a little fort in which we are to leave
some men for secureing me in my possessione, this being the
only most probable means for reduceing the rebells, and had it
not been for this, we had been at them ere now ; besides that
the spates here are impassible ; but how sone as the waters fall,
we hope to make some accompt of them. All my concurrence
from the severall shyres, allowed by the Councell did faill me,
except such of my own relations as are with me, and Captain
Mackenzie of Siddy and his company.

The M'Phersones in Badinoch after two citationes disobeyed
most contemptuously. I thought it my duty to acquaint you
heirof, quhairby your Lordship may tak any course your Lordship pleases, by making it knowen to the Councill and I am

Your Lordship's most humble and obedient servant

(Signed)   J. MACINTOSHE

(Addressed)   of Torcastell.

For the Earle of Perth
Lord Hich Chancellor
off Scotland
These."

XXII.

LETTER IN ANTIQUARIAN MUSEUM, EDINBURGH.

Addressed on Back "To our Trustie and well beloved M'Donell
of Cappagh."

"James R.

"Trustie and well beloved, Wee greet you well,
The behaviour of your selfe and family since th malise of our
unaturall enemies have prevailed against us, shews us that in
supporting you and doeing you Justice against the oppression

of Anti-monarchiall and ill men, wee shall add a lasting prop to the hereditary succession of our Crowne, and that as Innate Loyalty cannot be Debotched soe a Rebellious race by noe faire or Gentle means can be reclaimed, You may therefore Reckon upon it, That as soon as God shall please to putt itt in our power we will putt the experience wee have at so cleare a Rate acquired into practice and that you shal be one of the first that shall find th effects of it. The news we have recieued of the Brave Viscount Dundees death has mos sinseably afflicted us, Butt as he has perpetuated his Memorie by falling in soe Just a Cause, Soe wee are resolued by extraordinarie marks of our favour to make his family conspicuos, that th world may see Lasting Honnor and Happiness are to be acquired, by th Brave and Loyall onely; What he has soe happily begun and you soe Successfully maintained by a Thorough defeat of our Enemies, wee shall not doubt a Generous prosecution of, when wee consider that th Highland Loyaltie is inseparably annexed to th person of their Hereditary King: nor noe wayes feare the Event whilst the Justice of our Cause shal be seconded by soe many bold and dareing Asserters of our Royall Right. If their Couradge and your and th rest of th Commanders conduct were not Steddy th loss you had in a Generall you loved and confided in, at your verie entrance into action with so great inequality were enough to Boffle you Butt you have shewed your selves above surprize and given us proofe that wee are in a great measure like to owe you th Reestablishment of th Monarchy to your vallour, Wee are therefore resolued to send imediately our R^t Trustie and R^t well beloved the Earle of Seafort to head his friend and followers and (as soone as th season will permitt th Shipping of Horse) our R^t Trusty and intirely beloved naturall sone th Duke of Berwicke with considerable succors to your assistance, wch the present good posture of our affaires here will allow us to spare, ffor th Immediate hand of God appeares Signally to bess th Justice of our Cause, there haveing already fallen above tenn thousand of our Enemies by distemper and want, Wee must above all things recommend unto you a thorough union amongst

3 K

yourselves and due obedience to your Superior officers and that you look with the greatest indignation upon any body that under any pretence whatsoever shall goe about to disunite you, Such an one being a more dangerous enemie to our interest, then those that appeare in open Armes against us, Wee refer to the bearer to give you a full accompt of our fforce and the present condition of our Enemies wch is such as will putt our affaires here soone out of all doubt, and soe wee bidd you heartily farewell, Given at our Courte at Dublin Castle th Last day of November 1689 and in the fifth yeare of our Reigne.

"By His Maties Command.

" Duplicat to M'Doniell of Cappagh."

XXIII.

Extract from a Letter written by Major-General Mackay to the Duke of Portland, dated from Perth, 26th July 1690.

" J'ay a presant dans le sud nos trois regimens entiers, celluy de Leslie, et neuf compagnies fort foibles d' Argyll et autant d' Angus, les autres quatre de chacun ayant esté laissées a Inderlochy nommé *Fort William*, avec neuf compagnies de Grant, et deux cent montaignards, qui se sont deja mis au solde du Roi."

XXIV.

Copy of an Agreement entered into by Lochiel, Glengarry, and Keppoch, in the year 1744, for the Prevention of Crime among their Dependents.

" We Donald Cameron of Lochiel, John M'Donnell of Glengarry, and Alexander M'Donnell of Keapoch taking to consideration that severals of our Dependents and followers are too guilty of theft, and depredations, and being sensible of the bad effects and consequencies of such pernicious praticis, and in order to put an entire stop to such villany, as far as ly in our power, Have jointly agreed and resolved upon the following articles which we faithfully promise upon honour to observe and fulfil.

" 1ᵐᵒ· That any of our Dependents, Tenants, or followers guilty of such thefts as by law may be capitally punished, we hereby oblidge ourselves jointly to contribute a sum of money necessary to prosecute such person, or persons, and to convey him, or them, to the next and most convenient county goall within whose jurisdiction he resides, and their adduce such evidence against him as may legally convict him, or be assolized in course of process.

" 2ᵈᵒ· That any of our Dependents, Tenants, or followers, guilty of theft receipting, or outhounding, so far as we judge the same may infer a corporall punishment, are to be confined, and incarcerate by us respectively within a lockfast and secure ward, when we think most convenient to appoint, and such a criminall be publickly at sight of a number of the neighbouring tenants, so often as is thought sufficient to punish him for his crime.

3ᵗⁱᵒ· That we appoint sufficient and sponsall persons, or men of authority within proper districts of our estates (or where our authority among our followers and Dependents will extend and reach), to apprehend and incarcerate any person or persons guilty of the above crimes, and impowering our respective Deputes, to use such criminalls, by scourging, jugging, stocks, and other punishments in as rigorous a manner as any of us their constituents might have done ourselves, and this power to continue no longer with any of those our Deputes than he duly puts to execution this our authority committed to him.

" 4ᵗᵒ· That any notorious and infamous villain guilty of the above crimes, flying from, and deserting any of us, to the protection of any of the other two of us, or privately lurking within any part of our estates, any one of us in whose estate such a fugitive resides, is hereby oblidged, upon proper application, to deliver him up to the one of us who has a right and title to punish him.

" 5to. and lastly.   We hereby consent and agree that these our articles and resolutions are to be lodged in the custody of Sir Alexander M'Donald of M'Donald, Baronet, with power to him to severely reprimand upon the most publick occasion, one and all of us failing in the strict observance of all and every the above articles ; in witness whereof, we subscribe these presents at Keappoch, the thirteenth day of October, one thousand seven hundred and fourty four years.

" DONALD CAMERON

" JOHN M'DONELL, of Glengary

" ALEXR. M'DONELL.

" Follows a list of deputies appointed in the following districts—

" By Lochiel :—John Cameron of Fasfern, for the lands of Lochiel ; Dr Archibald Cameron, for Locharkaig, Glenluy, and Stralochy ; Glenevis and Callart, for Mamore, Glenevis, and Garghaick ; Dungallon, for Suinart and Ardnamurchan ; John M'Evan-ic-Allan, and John Ban M'Ian for Morven ; John Cameron of Kinlochliven, and Donald Cameron of Clunis, for Dochinassie ; Torcastle, for Ardgour.

" DONALD CAMERON.

" By Glengary :—Donald M'Donnell of Scothouse, and Coll M'Donnell of Barrisdale, for Knoydart, equally betwixt them ; Allan and John M'Donnells, sons to Scothouse, for Morror ; Donald M'Donnell of Lochgary, John M'Donnell of Arnabeé, Angus M'Donell of Leeak, and Angus M'Donell of Greenfield, for Glengary and Abertarph.

" JOHN M'DONELL of Glengary.

" By Keappoch :—Donald M'Donnell, brother to Keappoch, Donald M'Donnell of Tirnadrish, Donald M'Donnell of Crain-ichan, and Alexander M'Donnell of Tulloch for the Braes of Lochaber ; Ronald M'Donell of Aberador for the Braes of Badenoch.

" ALEXR. M'DONELL."

N.B.—The document from which the foregoing is a copy is in the possession of Lord Macdonald, and was lent with others to Mr Lachlan Macdonald of Skaebost for the purpose of a very interesting paper, read before the Gaelic Society of Inverness on December 7th, 1887, entitled " Gleanings from Lord Macdonald's Charter Chest."—*Gaelic Society's Transactions*, vol. xiv. p. 75.

XXV.

FROM INFORMATION NOTED DOWN BY JOHN MACDONELL OF KEPPOCH, which he had obtained from his father Angus, who had fought at the battle of Culloden with his father Alexander, Chief of Keppoch, who was killed there.

I. " As soon as Prince's landing was known council held at Keppoch amongst the Chief's friends. Keppoch said, ' That as Prince Charles had risked his person among them and generously thrown himself into the hands of his friends, they were bound in duty at least to raise men instantly for the protection of his person, whatever might be the consequences.' He departed to join him at once with a few followers, while he left his brother Donald and his cousin Donald of Tirnadris to raise men and watch movements of the enemy. On his way Keppoch took an English officer (who was on his way to inspect the garrison at Fort William) prisoner, and took him along with him to Glenfinnan."

II. " A plan between the Highlanders and Low Country Royalist going on in '43. Stewart of Appin and M'Donell of Keppoch attend meeting, were both sent to France with proposals to the Prince and Court of France in '43 or '44 (I do not know which of these years). I do not know any of the stipulated conditions, but the Prince should land on the Western Coast attended with at least five thousand regular troops. Murray of Broughton comes to Highlands in Summer '45, and I have cause to imagine that he was employed to prepare the Chieftains, and his coming was then known. The Prince lands in South Uist, accquaints his friends ; Sir Alexr. MacDonald of

Sleat advises him not landing without the stipulated number of troops from France. But the Prince seemed determined to try his fortune. Young Clanranald accompanies him to Borrodale. The preconcerted signal of his landing the firing of one gun. Nothing known about the invasion by any but the Chiefs until Murray's arrival in the country. The signal commanded the leaders then prepare their followers. All engage in the cause. The landing at Arisaig. The affairs of the two companies from Fort Augustus. Twelve men and a piper sent to Highbridge to stop their gaining Fort William until a sufficient force could be gathered first; an express sent to Lochiel. Capt. Scott retreats from Torness; and pursued, overtaken near Laggan Achdrom, a party having got before him on the military road on the north side of Loch Oich. Scott's party formed; fired one platoon. The Highlanders, after firing, attacked with their swords. Their attempt to go by Invergarry; are obliged to lay down their arms. The Brae Lochaber men joined at Low Bridge only by a few men of the Camerons of Dochanassie. After the surrender Lochiel and some of his men joined. The Prisoners were then placed in the centre between the Mac-Donell's and Camerons, and conducted back to Achnacarry, Lochiel's place of residence. Lochiel took charge of the prisoner; allowed his friends to return home in order to prepare for marching immediately to join the Prince. Lochiel conducts prisoner to Glenfinnan. The M'Donells arrive without any regular form. The Prince meets (them?) at Glenfinnan; attended by Clanranald, Glenaladale, and a few more gentle-men without any men. The two small parties passed the night at Dalnieu; killed some cows, made belts of raw hides; the two leaders formed their men opposite to one another. The Royal Standard displayed at the small hut of Slatach, and delivered to Donald MacDonell, Brother to Keppoch, and carried to Dalnive. Prince made his appearance among the men, and distributed some broadswords to such as wanted them. Clanranald returns from Glenfinnan in order to bring forward his men. The Prince in the meantime, with the small body of MacDonells and Camerons, began his march to the head of Lochiel. Second night at Fassiferne. Third Stage, Erracht, passing by the Moss of Corpach a few guns were fired from the garrison of Fort William; from Erracht marched to the west end of Loch Lochy, passed over Gairlochy, and passed the night at Low Bridge; from Low Bridge the Prince arrives at Laggan Achdrom. Here the Stewarts of Appin, commanded by Ardshiel; Clanranald and his men, Glengarry men, commanded by Angus Og M'Donell, second son of John of Glengarry, the eldest son being in France. Here information was received that General Cope with the army was in the Braes of Badenoch, and intended to cross Corriegherraig. Then set off with his men through the night for Corriegherraig; arrives next day at Garvamore. General C. marches down through Badenoch and by Aviemore to Inverness. In Badenoch M'Pherson of Cluny joins with his followers. From Badenoch they march to Dalwhinnie; to Dalnacardoch to Blair in Athole. The Marquis of Tulliebardine rose the Athole men, and plentifully treated the army. From Blair they march to Dunkeld; here the Prince was proclaimed Regent from Dunkeld to Perth."

III. "After the battle of Falkirk it was resolved to march north and establish their headquarters at Inverness, with the intention of securing the supplies of money sent from in the " Hazard " sloop of war. . . . In the meantime the siege of Fort William and Fort Augustus was undertaken. Clanranald, Earl of Cromarty, Barisdale, and several others were sent to Sutherland and Caithness with a very strong detachment. The attempt on Fort William failed; what else could be expected without experience, engineers, or proper artillery? Le Despair—money—Fort William."

IV. "The march to England was conducted in a very regular manner. From the reception the army met with in England it was evident that a great number wished well to the cause, tho' few had the courage or resolution to join."

" At the battle of Preston Pans the Highlanders were allowed to charge with their usual impetuosity."

XXVI.

Inscription on Prince Charles's Monument, Loch Shiel.

" On this spot, where Prince Charles Edward first raised his standard, on the 19th day of August, 1745 : when he made the daring and romantic attempt to recover a throne lost by the imprudence of his ancestors ; this column is erected by Alexander M'Donald, Esq. of Glenalladale, to commemorate the generous zeal, the undaunted bravery, and the inviolable fidelity of his forefathers, and the rest of those who fought and bled in that arduous and unfortunate enterprise."

XXVII.

Copy of a Letter written by Lochiel in conjunction with Keppoch, from the Headquarters of the Highland Army in Glen Nevis, to Stewart of Invernahayle, protesting against the action of the Campbells.

"Glen Nevis, 20th March 1746.

" Yesterday we received a letter from Clunie, giving an account of the success of the party sent by His Royal Highness, under the command of Lord George Murray, a copy of which we think proper to send you enclosed. And as you happen for the present to be stationed contiguous to the Campbells, it is our special desire that you instantly communicate to Airds, the sheriff, and other leading men among them, our sentiments, which, God willing, we are determined to execute, by transmitting this our letter and the enclosed copy to any most convenient to you. It is our own opinion that, of all men in Scotland, the Campbells had the least reason of any to engage in the present war against His Royal Highness's interest, considering that they have always appeared against the royal family since the reign of James the Sixth, and have been guilty of so many acts of rebellion and barbarity during that time, that no injured prince but would endeavour to resent it when God was pleased to put the power into his hand.

"Yet his present Majesty and His Royal Highness the Prince Regent were graciously pleased, by their respective declarations, to forgive all past miscarriages to a most violent and inveterate enemy, and even bury them in oblivion, provided they return to their allegiance; and though they should not appear personally in arms to support the royal cause, yet their standing neutral should entitle them to the good graces of their sovereign.

"But in spite of all the clemency that a prince could show or promise, the Campbells have openly appeared, with their wonted zeal, for rebellion and usurpation in the most oppressive manner. Nor could we form a thought to ourselves that any men endowed with reason or common sense could use their fellow-creatures with such inhumanity and barbarity as they do; of which we have such daily proofs, by their burning houses, stripping of women and children, and exposing them in the open field to the severity of the weather, houghing of cattle, and killing of horses; to enumerate the whole would be too tedious at this time. They must naturally reflect that we cannot but look on these cruelties with horror and detestation, and with hearts full of revenge, and we will certainly endeavour to make reprisals, and are determined to apply to His Royal Highness for an order to enter their Country, with full power to act at discretion.

"And if we are lucky enough to obtain it, we will show them that we do not make war against women and the brute creation, but against men. As God was pleased to put so many of their people into our custody, we hope to prevail upon his Highness to hang a Campbell for every house that will hereafter be burned by them. Notwithstanding the many scandalous and malicious aspersions industriously contrived by our enemies against us, the world never—hitherto since the commencement of the war—could impeach us with any acts of hostility that had the least tendency to such cruelty as they exercise against

3 L

us, though often we had it in our power, if barbarous enough to execute them. When courage fails against men, it always betrays cowardice to a degree to vent spleen against women and children, brutes and houses, who cannot resist them. We are not ignorant of their villainous intentions! The intercepted letters of the Sheriff Airds, etc., will plainly discover that it was on their application that their General Cumberland granted orders for burning, etc., which he could not be answerable for to any British Parliament, it being most certain that such barbarities could never be countenanced by any Christian senate. —We are, etc.,

(Signed) "DONALD CAMERON, of Lochiel.
"ALEXANDER MACDONELL, of Keppoch.

"*P.S.*—I cannot omit taking notice that my people were the first to feel the cowardly barbarity of my pretended Campbell friends. I shall desire to live to have the opportunity of thanking them for it in the open field.

(Signed) "D. C."

XXVIII.

FOOTNOTE TO SIR WALTER SCOTT'S "LADY OF THE LAKE," CANTO III., STANZA V., referring to the building of the Church of Kilmallie by "*An Gille dubh Mac Gille Chnamhaich*," taken from "Macfarlane's Geographical Collections."

"There is bot two myles from Inverloghie (Inverlochy), the church of Kilmalee, in Loghyeld (Loch Eil). In ancient tymes there was ane church builded upon ane hill, which was above this church, which doeth now stand in this toune; and ancient men doeth say, that there was a battell foughten on ane litle hill not the tenth part of a myle from this church, be certaine men which they did not know what they were. And long tyme thereafter, certaine herds of that toune, and of the next toune, called Unnatt (Annat), both wenches and youthes, did on a tyme conveen with others on that hill; and the day being somewhat cold, did gather the bones of the dead men that were slayne long tyme before in that place, and did màke a fire to warm them. At last they did all remove from the fire, except ane maid or wench, which was verie cold, and she did remaine there for a space. She being quyetlie her alone, without anie other companie, took up her cloathes above her knees, or thereby, to warm her; a wind did come and caste the ashes upon her, and she was conceived of ane man-chyld. Severall tymes thereafter she was verie sick, and at last she was knowne to be with chyld. And then her parents did ask at her the matter heiroff, which the wench could not weel answer which way to satisfie them. At last she resolved them with ane answer. As fortune fell upon her concerning this marvellous miracle, the chyld being borne, his name was called '*Gili-doir Maghrevollich*,'[1] that is to say, the 'Black Child, Son to the Bones.' So called his grandfather sent him to schooll, and so he was a good schollar, and godlie. He did build this church which doeth now stand in Lochyeld, called Kilmallie."

XXIX.

PRINCE CHARLES AND FLORA MACDUGALD, daughter of "Ailean Dall."

"Flora Macdugald, a daughter of 'Ailean Dall' the poet, told me that she spoke often to an old woman who had given a drink of milk from her cog to the beloved but unfortunate Prince Charles Stuart—the 'Bonnie Prince Charlie' of song and story. She was a young girl at the time, and in her return from the 'buaile' she had to walk over a plank that bridged a foaming burn. The plank was unsteady, and a gallant-looking gentleman, who stood on the opposite bank, jumped into the water and held it firmly until she had passed over. He had wet his feet, and she felt ashamed and sorry, and when she got

---

[1] *Note by the Author.*—Macfarlane either did not understand Gaelic or is making fun of the legend; for the Gaelic name he gives to the lad of such questionable parentage, means something quite different to his translation of it.

near him, after he came out of the burn, she offered him her
cog that he might have a drink. He took it freely, and, having
unbonneted, he shook hands with her, and they parted. She
saw him again when he was in hiding, and knew that it was
Bonnie Prince Charlie who had stepped into the foaming brook
to steady the plank for her. She spoke of it always until her
death in old age. She could never forget his kind face and
smiling eyes, when, regardless of his wet hose, he took off
his bonnet, and shook hands with her."—*Transactions Gaelic
Society of Inverness*, Vol. XIV., p. 136. Extract from a paper
by Mrs Mackellar, entitled "The Sheiling: its Traditions and
Songs."

XXX.

EXTRACTS FROM LETTER OF GENERAL WOLFE TO HIS
　　　FRIEND CAPTAIN RICKSON, of Colonel Lascelles's
　　　Regt., stationed at Fort Augustus.

"EXETER, *7th March* 1755.

"MY DEAR FRIEND,

　　　　　　　" Just as I received your letter, the
drum beat to arms, and we have been in a bustle ever since.
Now that it has become a little calm again I will gather my
wits together, and collect my friendly sentiments (a little dispersed with the sound of war) to answer it. Be so good, for
the time to come, to presume with yourself that you have a
right to correspond with me whenever you please, and as often ;
and be persuaded that you cannot do me a greater favour than
by writing to me. . . .

　　　"Since I began my letter to you, yesterday, there's a fresh
and loud report of war. More ships are ordered to be fitted
out ; and we must expect further preparations, suited to the
greatness of the occasion. You in the north will be now and
then alarmed. Such a succession of errors, and such a strain
of ill behaviour as the last Scotch war (1745–46) did produce,
can hardly, I believe, be matched in history. Our future annals
will, I hope, be filled with more stirring events.

"What if the garrisons of the forts had been under the orders of a prudent, resolute man (yourself for instance), would not they have found means to stifle the rebellion in its birth? and might not they have acted more like soldiers and good subjects than it appears they did? What would have been the effects of a sudden march into the middle of that clan that was the first to move? What might have been done by means of hostages of wives and children, or the chiefs themselves? How easy a small body united prevents the junction of a distant corps; and how favourable the country where you are for such a manœuvre. If notwithstanding all precautions they get together, a body of troops may make a diversion by laying waste a country that the male inhabitants have left to prosecute rebellious schemes.

"How soon must they return to the defence of their property (such as it is), their wives, their children, their houses, and their cattle? But above all, the secret, sudden night march into the midst of them; great patrols of 50, 60, or 100 men each to terrify them; letters to the chiefs, threatening fire and sword, and certain destruction if they dare to stir; movements that seem mysterious, to keep the enemy's attention upon you, and their fears awake; these and the like, which your experience, reading, and good sense would point out, are means to prevent mischief. . . .

"If there's war, I hope the General in the north will not disperse the troops by small parties, as has been practised hitherto; but rather make choice of certain good stations for bodies that can defend themselves, or force their way home (to the forts), if occasion require it. At Laggan Achadrum, for example, they should build a strong redoubt, surrounded with rows of palisades and trees, capable to contain 200 men at least. This is a post of great importance, and should be maintained in a most determined manner, and the MacDonalds might knock their heads against it to very little purpose. Mr M'Pherson (Cluny) should have a couple of hundred men in his neighbourhood, with orders to massacre the whole clan, if they show the least symptom of rebellion. They are a warlike tribe, and he is a cunning fellow himself. They should be narrowly watched; and the party there should be well commanded.

.   .   .   .

"Pray ask Trap. (Genl. Trapaud, Governor of Fort Augustus) if he knows anything of Lady Culloden, how she is in health? for I have a particular esteem for her, am obliged to her for civilities shown me, and interest in my welfare. She seemed, poor lady, to be in a very ill state of health when I was in that country.

"I could pass my time very pleasantly at Fort Augustus, upon your plan, and with your assistance. There is no solitude with a friend. . . .

"Your faithful and affectionate servant,

"JAMES WOLFE."

XXXI.

EXTRACTS FROM REPORTS ADDRESSED BY MILITARY OFFICERS STATIONED IN THE HIGHLANDS TO LIEUT.-GENERALS CHURCHILL AND BLAND, Edinburgh Castle, after the "Forty-five," the principal stations in the Lochaber district being at Laggan Achadrum (between Loch Lochy and Loch Oich) and on an island at the east end of Loch Arkaig.

Captain Walter Johnstone, of Lord Bury's Regiment, reports on 7th June 1752 :—" Soon after my coming here (Invercomrie, Loch Rannoch) I had a letter sent me by Lord Breadalbane, wrote by Colonel Lafaupille, to the Serjeant of the King's Regiment, who was here before I came, ordering him to give assistance when required in apprehending such persons as he should be directed; and next day Captain Campbell of Glen Lyon came here, and showed me two warrants, from the Sheriff Depute of Perthshire, for apprehending Charles Stewart of

Ardshiel, an attainted rebel, and Allan Breck Stewart, the supposed murderer of Mr Campbell of Glenure; upon which I gave the description to all my parties, with orders to apprehend them, or give their assistance in apprehending them when required."

Captain John Beckwith, of Lord Bury's Regiment, stationed at Loch Arkaig, reports on 11th June 1752:—"Having, conformable to my orders, made the detachments to Bonarkaig, head of Loch Arkaig, Glen Dissery, Glenfinnon, head of Loch Yeal (Loch Eil), Strontian, Inversanda, Glen Scaddle, and the four posts under the command of the officers at Tray, the South Moyrer detachment marched from and received my orders at Fort Augustus.

"I quartered the moving patrol at Moy, and took post myself at Erroch (Erracht) with a sergeant and three men. This house belongs to Ewin Cameron, head of a tribe, and a near relation of the late Lochiel. This glen runs pretty nearly north and south about seven miles. The post is a quarter of a mile from the river Lochy, exactly opposite to the Long Ford, on the south of which is the Duke of Gordon's lands, possessed by Allan Cameron. On the east side of my post is the mountain Bennane (probably *Beinn Bhan*); on the west Draenfatch Glenlee (probably *Druim Fada, Glen Laoigh*), and it's five miles from Fort William."

The same officer reports from Strontian, that he had patrolled to Glenscaddle (Ardgour), and that on the 26th May he had sent a patrol to Achason, where the corporal took up a man of the name of Cameron (servant to Mrs Jane Cameron), with a piece of tartan wrapped round him like a philabeg. "This man I sent to the Sheriff Substitute at Fort William, who confined him." From Inversanda the corporal reports that the party had been well supplied with milk, butter, and cheese; but at a great price. The milk twopence the Scots pint, the butter sixpence per lb., and cheese in proportion.

From Laggan Achadrum Captain A. Trapaud reports on 25th June 1752:—"William Cameron, taken up on the 6th June by the Glenmorriston party for wearing the Highland dress, is sentenced to six months' imprisonment by the Sheriff of Inverness-shire. The sergeant commanding at Knockfin reported that on the 17th inst. he had an information of four thieves driving cattle within two miles of his post—that they were well armed and in Highland dress. He immediately pursued them, and recovered four çows and one horse, and followed the track of the thieves several miles. . . . On the 16th inst. I had an information given to me, by Alex. M'Marten in Glencog, that Donald Burk and Angus Campbell were concerned with some others in stealing some of the battlement stones from High Bridge. I had the two fellows apprehended and sent to Mr Douglass, the Substitute Sheriff at Fort William. The corporal stationed at High Bridge, who received the prisoners, reported to me that when he came to the gates of Fort William they were shut, and as he was stepping forward to call the sentry, Donald Burk slipped to one side and made his escape, and took the chance of the three men firing upon him."

Report from Captain Walter Johnstone, dated Invercomrie, 22nd June 1752:—"On the 8th inst. I received a letter from Colonel Crawford telling me that when the bearer pointed out any man to me I might be sure that there was something very material against him. Upon my asking him what he designed, he told me he knew where there was a thief who had fled from Lochaber, and desired a party to apprehend him, so I gave him a sergeant and six men, who marched that night, and returned to me on the 11th with one Cameron a prisoner, whom they took in a shieling near Crieff. On the 12th I sent a fresh party with him to Colonel Crawford, who writes me that he is a most notorious plunderer, and that he used to leave Lochaber and fly into the low country when the troops went to their summer stations."

On 13th July the same officer reports :—"On the 28th June, Colonel Crawford, to whom I had wrote as reported in my last, sent me Allan Cameron and Angus M'Donald. The first, he tells me, was living very quietly within two miles of Fort William, and the other near Fort Augustus. So he sent to

Captain Trapaud at Laggan to apprehend him, which he did. I sent them both to Perth on the 29th, and it seems they are of consequence, for the Sheriff writes me a letter of thanks for apprehending them."

Report from Captain Trapaud, dated Laggan-Achadrum, 9th October 1752:—"On the 28th of September, having received intelligence that the famous thief, John Brec Kennedy was in Glen Glye, 'twixt Nine Mile Bridge and Glenroy, the party at this post met in said glen and took Kennedy. The serjeant from this post cut him through the skull in two different places before he could take him. He is now confined in the hospital at Fort Augustus, and likely soon to recover from his wounds."

Report from Captain-Lieutenant George Sempill in Lord George Beauclerck's Regiment, dated Locharkaig, 13th October 1755:—"I have a report from the officer commanding in North and South Morer, that the inhabitants of those countries begin to wear instead of breeches, stuff trousers, much after the form of those the seamen use, but not longer than the kilt or philabeg. I am at a loss whether to look upon that as part of the Highland dress, and take notice of such people as offenders against the law."

XXXII.

THE HEIRESS OF KING CHARLES I., AND THE HEIRESS OF THE ROYAL HOUSE OF PLANTAGENET AND STUART.

James II. died at St Germain-en-Laye, 16th September 1701. By his second wife, Mary of Modena, he left a son, James Francis Edward, and a daughter, Louisa Maria, who died unmarried in 1712. The son—James III. as he styled himself, the Chevalier de Saint Georges, or the "Old Pretender," as others styled him—married Clementina, grand-daughter of John Sobieski, King of Poland, by whom he left at his decease, 1st January 1766, two sons. Charles Edward, the elder, known as the "Young Pretender" and "Young Chevalier," whose hopes

3 M

of becoming King of England were shattered by his defeat at Culloden in 1746, died without legitimate issue, 31st January 1788. His brother, Henry Benedict, was raised to the purple in 1747, and subsequently bore the designation of Cardinal of York. His death at Rome, in June 1807, extinguished the descendants of James II. The legitimate succession then opened to the descendants of James II.'s sister, the Princess Henrietta Maria, wife of Philip, Duke of Orleans; she died in 1670, leaving two daughters. Mary, the eldest daughter, married Charles II., King of Spain, but died without issue; her sister, Anne, married Victor Amadeus, King of Sardinia, from whom was descended Francis V., Duke of Modena, who married, 30th March 1842, Adelgonde, daughter of Louis I., King of Bavaria, and died without issue, 20th November 1875. His younger brother, Ferdinand, Archduke of Austria, had married, 4th October 1847, Elizabeth, daughter of the Archduke Joseph of Austria, and left at his death, 15th December 1849, an only daughter, Mary Theresa, who, born 2nd July 1849, and married 20th February 1868, to Louis, Prince of Bavaria, eldest son of Luitpold, Prince Regent of Bavaria, is now the unquestionable heiress of the House of Stuart.—*Extract from Whitaker's Almanack for* 1887, *pp.* 86 *and* 87.

With Cardinal York expired all the descendants of King James II., and the representation of the Royal Houses of Plantagenet, Tudor, and Stuart thereupon vested by inheritance in Charles-Emanuel IV., King of Sardinia, who was eldest son of Victor-Amadeus III., the grandson of Victor-Amadeus, King of Sardinia, by Anne, his wife, daughter of Henrietta, Duchess of Orleans, daughter of King Charles I. of England. Charles-Emanuel IV., died *s.p.* in 1819, and was succeeded by his brother, Victor-Emanuel I., King of Sardinia, whose eldest daughter and co-heiress, Beatrice, Duchess of Modena, was mother of Francis V., Duke of Modena, present Heir of the Royal House of Stuart.—*From "The Royal Stuarts" by the late Sir Bernard Burke, Ulster King of Arms, author of "The Peerage," etc.,* 1859 *Edition.*

XXXIII.

G. III R.
LXXIX. REGIMENT.
OR,
CAMERON VOLUNTEERS.

All VOLUNTEERS, who wifh to Serve his Majefty
KING GEORGE THE THIRD,
Have now an opportunity of entering into prefent Pay, and free Quarters, by Enlifting into
The LXXIX Regiment, or, Cameron Volunteers.
COMMANDED BY
Major *A L L A N   C A M E R O N* of *E R C H T*.

Who has obtained his *Majefty's* Permiffion to raife a
Regiment of *Highlanders;* which he does at his own
private Expence having no other View connected with
the undertaking, except the Pride of Commanding a
Faithful and Brave Band of his Warlike Countrymen,
in the Service of a King, whofe greateft Happinefs is to
reign as the Common Father and Protector of his People.

ALL ASPIRING YOUNG MEN
Who wifh to be ferviceable to their *King* and *Country* by Enlifting into the *79th
Regiment*, or, *Cameron Volunteers*, will be Commanded by the *Major* in *Perfon*, who
has obtained from his Majefty, that they fhall not be draughted into any other
Regiment ; and when the Reduction is to take place, they fhall be marched in to
their own Country in a Corps, to be therein difembodied.

The paft and well known Generofity of Major *Cameron* to all his *Countrymen* who
have applied to him on former occafions, is the ftrongeft Pledge of his future Goodnefs
to such as fhall now ftep forward and Enlift under his Banner.

Any Young Man who wifhes to Enlift into the *Cameron Volunteers*, will meet with
every Encouragement by applying to the Major in Person, or, to any of the Officers,
Recruiting for his *Regiment*.

GOD SAVE THE KING
AND
CONSTITUTION AMEN

[I have to thank Lieut. Angus Cameron, Acting Adjutant, Depot, Cameron
Highlanders, Inverness, for the above. Owing to the absence of the Battalion
in the Soudan, I was unable to procure a photographic reproduction of this
interesting poster.]

XXXIV.

Inscription on the Monument erected at Kilmallie in Memory of Colonel John Cameron of Fassie-fern.

"Sacred to the Memory of Colonel John Cameron, eldest son of Ewen Cameron of Fassiefern, Bart., whose mortal remains, transported from the field of glory where he died, rest here with those of his forefathers. During twenty years of active military service, with a spirit which knew no fear and shunned no danger, he accompanied, or led, in marches, sieges, and battles, the 92nd Regiment of Scottish Highlanders, always to honour, and almost always to victory ; and at length, in the forty-second year of his age, upon the memorable 16th of June 1815, was slain in command of that corps, while actively contributing to achieve the decisive victory of Waterloo, which gave peace to Europe. Thus closing his military career with the long and eventful struggle, in which his services had been so often distinguished, he died, lamented by that unrivalled General, to whose long train of success he had so often contributed ; by his country, from which he had repeatedly received marks of the highest consideration ; and by his Sovereign who graced his surviving family with those marks of honour which could not follow, to this place, him whom they were designed to commemorate. *Reader, call not his fate untimely, who, thus honoured and lamented, closed a life of fame by a death of glory!*" [1]

---

[1] The above epitaph was composed by Sir Walter Scott.

ADDENDA.

ADDENDA.

I.

CAMERON GENEALOGY, FROM GAELIC MSS. OF 1450.

Genelach Clann Maclanſhaig z. Eoghan ic Domnaill dubh
mc Ailin Macilanfaig ic Poil ic Gillapatruig mc Gillamartain ic
Poil ic Maclanfaig mc Gillroid agus Clann Gillcamsroin agus
Clann Maclanfaig o fuilid Clann . . . z. Clann Maclanfaig
. . . sron ic Gillaanfaig ic Gillamartun og ic Gilla . . .
ic Gillamartan moir ic Gilla camsroin.

Translation.

Genealogy of Camerons (*Siol ic Malonoy* or *ic Gillonoy*)
Cameron of Strone, a sept) Ewen son of Donald du son of
Alan the servant of the Prophet, son of Paul son of Patrick son
of Martin son of Paul son of Mullony son of Gillroid from whom
descended Clan Cameron and Clan Millonay the Clan . . .
or children of Millonay of Stron son of Gillony son of Martin
Og son of . . . son of Martin Mòr son of Gilla Cameron.

II.

NAMES IN THE BRAES OF LOCHABER BESIDES MACDONALDS AND MACKINTOSHES.

MacArthurs, about whom there is a saying,

> " Cnoic's uillt's Alpanaic
> Ach cuin a thainig Artairaic,"

seem to have been long in Braes.

MacKillops, several in Braes, but I do not know if they are old inhabitants.

MacKerracher, supposed to be M'Donalds, but kept patronymic of some Farquhar from whom they came.

MacGillivantaig, from Mac Gille Mhanntaich (or the Stutterer), originally M'Donalds.

Burke, }
Boyle, } All came over with Lord M'Donald's daughter, who married Alasdair, Vth of Keppoch; her mother
Kelly, } brought them from Ireland as her tocher.

Kennedey, long in Lochaber. Buchanan says the first of them came from Ireland with Robert the Bruce. Buchanan says that the Lochaber Kennedys are descended from an Ulrick Kennedy of the family of Dunures, who for slaughter fled to Lochaber many years ago; his progeny, from the proper name of their ancestor, deriving their surnames of MacWalricks, the principal person of whom is MacWalrick of Lismachan in Lochaber, who with his sept are dependents on the family of Keppoch.

MacMasters, originally proprietors of Ardgour.

Stewarts came with Stewart of Appin's daughter, who married Ronald, IXth of Keppoch.

Campbells, a sept of them who fought under Keppoch.

Boyds, came from Ardgour.

Grants,
M'Innes, } Stray individuals who settled there in later times.
Camerons,
M'Phersons, }

M'Phee, were originally proprietors of Colonsay, but being expelled from there by the MacNeils, some took refuge in Lochaber, and fought under the banner of Lochiel.

[Information furnished by Miss Josephine MacDonell of Keppoch.]

III.

Poets belonging to Keppoch Family.

Alasdair-nan-Cleas, made witty and sarcastic verse, but I have no trace of any.

A daughter of Bohuntine, married to Alasdair Buidhe of Keppoch (no trace of any extant).

Archibald, Chief of Keppoch, son to above (I hope to get trace of some of his).

Angus, 3rd son of above Archibald; his songs said to be in "Leabhar Raonuill Duibh," but I don't know where to find it.

Silis, daughter of Archibald, married Gordon Wardhouse.

Catharine, daughter of Archibald, married at Strathmasie her grandson Lauchlan MacPherson, a poet (no trace of her poems).

The Sister of murdered chiefs composed lament. I have a short piece, but do not know if it is complete.

A granddaughter of Angus, youngest son of Alasdair-nan-Cleas (*Achnancoichean*). I have one poem of hers.

Donald Donn, son of Bohuntine of Keppoch descent (I have two short ones of his contemporary of Iain Lom).

Domhnuill MacFhionnlaidh (a MacKillop) was of the followers of Keppoch, and composed the well-known song the "Comhachag," and lived at Fersit. He is buried at Cill a' Choireil, and it is over his grave Dr Fraser Mackintosh erroneously placed a tombstone to Iain Lom.

[Information furnished by Miss Josephine MacDonell of Keppoch.]

3 N

IV.

LIST OF THE CAMERON CHIEFS.

I. ANGUS, married Marion, daughter of Kenneth, Thane of Lochaber, and sister of Banquo.

II. GILLESPICK, eldest son of Angus, assisted in the restoration of Malcolm Canmore, 1057 A.D.; said to be the progenitor of the MacMartins of Letterfinlay. Created "Lord Baron," 25th April 1057.

III. JOHN, eldest son of Gillespick; lived in the reign of David I.

IV. ROBERT, son of John, died early. *Tempus*, reign of Alexander II.

V. SIR JOHN DE CAMBRON, eldest son of Robert; said to be the progenitor of the Camerons of Glen Nevis. Died during the reign of Alexander II.

VI. SIR ROBERT DE CAMBRON, eldest son of Sir John; lived during part of the reign of Alexander III.

VII. JOHN, son of Sir Robert; lived during the time of Bruce, and probably led the clan at Bannockburn.

VIII. JOHN (*Ochtery*), son of John; lived during the reign of David II.; fought at Halidon Hill. Married Ellen de Montcalto.

IX. ALAN (*MacOchtery*), son of John. It was during his chiefship that the feud with Mackintosh began, and the battle of Invernahavon fought. Married a daughter of Drummond of Stobhall, whose sister was Annabella, Queen of Robert III. and mother of James I.

X. EWEN, son of Alan. He was chief at the time of the battle of the North Inch, 1396.

XI. DONALD (*Domhnull Dubh MacAilein*), brother of Ewen. This was the famous Donald Dubh, who

fought at Harlaw in 1411. Married the heiress
of the MacMartins of Letterfinlay.

XII. ALAN (*Ailein MacDhomhnuill Duibh*), eldest son of
Donald Dubh. Married Mariot, daughter of Angus
MacDonell (*Aongas na Feairte*), II Chief of
Keppoch; known in Lochaber as "*Ailein nan
Creach*" ("Alan of the Forays"). *Tempus,* James III.

XIII. EWEN (*Eobhan MacAilein*), son of Alan. Rebuilt
Torcastle, fought at Blar-nan-Leine, 1544. Married,
first, a daughter of Celestine of Lochalsh, and second,
Marjory, daughter of Lauchlan, chief of Mackintosh.
He was outlawed and executed at Elgin in 1547.

XIV. EWEN (*Eobhan Beag*), grandson of Ewen; said to have
been assassinated by order of MacDougal of Lorne
in 1554. His illegitimate son, by MacDougal's
daughter, was the renowned "*Taillear Dubh na
Tuaige.*"

XV. DONALD (*Domhnull Dubh MacDhomhnuill*), uncle of
Ewen Beg; died about 1564, reign of Queen Mary.

XVI. ALAN (*Ailein MacIain Dubh*), nephew of Donald. He
married a daughter of Stewart of Appin. Lived to
a great age.

XVII. SIR EWEN (*Eobhan Dubh*), grandson of Alan. He
was born at Kilchurn Castle in February 1629, his
mother being a daughter of Robert Campbell
of Glenfalloch, afterwards Lord Glenorchy. He
married in 1657 the sister of Sir James MacDonald
of Sleat.

XVIII. JOHN, eldest son of Sir Ewen; fought at Sheriffmuir,
but was not popular with the clan. Died in France.

XIX. DONALD ("The Gentle Lochiel"), eldest son of John;
supported Prince Charles, and fought in all the
battles of the "Forty-Five." Died in France.

XX. JOHN, eldest son of Donald.

XXI. CHARLES, eldest surviving brother of John.

XXII. DONALD, eldest surviving son of Charles.

XXIII. DONALD, eldest son of Donald.

XXIV. DONALD, the present Lochiel, eldest son of Donald.

V.

LIST OF THE CHIEFS OF KEPPOCH, from the Family MS.

JOHN, 1st LORD OF THE ISLES, died about 1386.	MARGARET STEWART, daughter of Robert II., who founded the Stuart dynasty. Margaret was his second wife, his first being Amy nic Ruari, sister of Ranald of the Isles, by whom he had issue—(1) John, who died without issue; (2) Godfrey of Uist and Garmoran, whose descendants are said to be extinct; (3) Ranald, progenitor of the MacDonalds of Clan Ranald; (4) Mary, who married twice, first to one of the MacLeans of Duart, and secondly, to MacLean of Coll.

DONALD, 2nd LORD OF THE ISLES, married Lady Mary Leslie, only daughter of the Countess of Ross, by right of which union he claimed the Earldom of Ross. Died between 1420-1423.	JOHN (Mòr Tanastair), ancestor of the Earls of Antrim. Father of Donald Balloch.	ALEXANDER (Alasdair Carrach), 1st Chief of Keppoch.	DONALD, a natural son; one of the hostages mentioned in the Treaty of 1369.

I. ALEXANDER (Alasdair Carrach), married daughter of the Earl of Lennox. Fought at Harlaw, 1411; first battle of Inverlochy, 1431. Burnt Inverness, for which his lands were forfeited.

II. ANGUS (*Aongas na Feairte*), son of Alexander. Fought on the side of the Lord of the Isles. Seized the Castles of Inverness, Ruthven, and Urquhart. Was present with Donald Balloch at the raid upon the Ayrshire coast. Stormed Brodick and Rothesay Castles, and was with Angus of the Isles at the Battle of Bloody Bay. Married a daughter of MacPhee of Glen Pean. His daughter Mariot married Alan Cameron, XII Chief of Lochiel (*Ailein nan Creach*).

III. DONALD, son of Angus. Supported Alexander of Lochalsh. Took the castle of Inverness, and plundered the lands of Urquhart. Made his peace with James IV. at Mingarry, 1495. Married a daughter of Lochiel.

IV. JOHN, son of Donald, called *Iain Aluinn*, was deposed by his clan because he delivered one of them to the Chief of Mackintosh, who had him hanged. John left a son, Donald, from whom descended the famous bard, Iain Lom. *Tempus*, 1496-1498.

V. ALEXANDER, uncle of John, selected by the clan upon the deposition of his nephew. Married a daughter of Donald Gallach of Sleat. Her mother was a daughter of MacDonnell of Antrim, and brought to Skye some Irish clans, some of whom her daughter took with her to Keppoch, and their descendants are still in Lochaber. Of this stock come the Burkes and Boyles, who took the surname of MacDonell. *Tempus*, 1498-1500.

VI. DONALD (*Glas*), son of Alexander. Built Keppoch Castle on Tom Beag. Aided Donald Dubh of the Isles. Huntly sent against him, and peace was restored after two years. Married a daughter of Lochiel. *Tempus*, 1500-1513.

VII. RANALD (*Raonuill Mòr*), son of Donald. From this chief the family of Keppoch take the patronymic of "*Mac Mhic Raonuill.*" Fought at Blar-nan-Leine on the side of Iain Moydartach against Ranald Gallda and the Frasers. Was captured owing to the treachery of Mackintosh, who handed him over to Huntly. Was executed at Elgin along with Lochiel. He married a sister of Mackintosh.

VIII. ALEXANDER (*Alasdair*), son of Ranald, was killed at Boloinne. Never married. *Tempus,* 1547-1549.

IX. RANALD, brother of Alexander. Fought under the banner of James V., who promised to restore the lands of Keppoch, but was prevented by death from doing so. The Regent Murray commenced negotiations for the same purpose, and would probably have carried them through had he not met an untimely fate by assassination. Ranald married a daughter of Stewart of Appin.

X. ALEXANDER (*Alasdair-nan-Cleas*), eldest son of Ranald. Supported Sir James MacDonell of Islay in his rebellion. Fled to Spain, but was afterwards pardoned and received a pension from the king. He was constantly embroiled in feuds and wars during the many years of his chieftainship. He married a daughter of MacDougall of Lorn, by whom he had several sons. The story of the "Chieftain's Candlesticks" is associated with this Keppoch. *Tempus,* 1591-1640.

XI. DONALD (*Glas*), second son of Alexander; his eldest brother Ranald was living in exile in Spain, and never became chief. Assisted his father in the Islay rebellion, and later joined the army of Montrose, and fought at the battle of Inverlochy, February 1645. His name appears among the

Colonels of Foot in the army of Charles II. Took
part in Glencairn's rising. He married a daughter
of Forrester of Kelbeggie. *Tempus*, 1640-1656.

XII. ALEXANDER, son of Donald, minor at his father's death,
the command of the clan being held by his uncle
Alexander. It was this young chief and his brother
Ranald who were so treacherously murdered at
Keppoch. There is a tradition in the family that
Alexander's father Donald (*Glas*) had warned the
Government of the intended Spanish invasion of
Britain, and that as a reward for the information the
Keppoch lands were to have been legally restored to
the family, but owing to the murder the matter fell
through. *Tempus*, 1656-1663.

XIII. ALEXANDER (*Alasdair Buidhe*), uncle to the murdered
chiefs. He married first a daughter of MacDonald
of Bohuntine, who was drowned on Christmas night
in the river Roy, at a place still called *Linne na
h-ighnean*, whilst she was returning from Loch Treig.
He then married a daughter of Glengarry. *Tempus*,
1663-1670.

XIV. ARCHIBALD, second son of *Alasdair Buidhe*. His elder
brother was not allowed to assume the chiefship, as
he was suspected of having taken part in the murder
of his cousins Alexander and Ranald. This chief
was a celebrated poet and famous warrior. He
fought under Viscount Dundee when he raised the
clans for Charles II., and is said to have been
present at Killiecrankie (*Raon Ruari*) with his son
Coll. He married a daughter of MacMartin of
Letterfinlay; with issue Coll, Ranald (of Tirnadris), Alexander, Angus, and nine daughters, the
eldest of whom, Juliet, was a poetess of some
repute.

XV. COLL ("Coll of the Cows"), son of Archibald. He was only twenty-one years of age when he led the clan at Mulroy (*Meall Ruadh*) against Mackintosh and the Government troops. Laid siege to Inverness to punish the inhabitants for aiding Mackintosh; compelled them to ground their arms before any man wearing the MacDonald tartan, and exacted a heavy fine from them. When Dundee arrived, Coll joined him, and fought at Killiecrankie. Dundee was at Keppoch before this, when the plan of his campaign was arranged. Iain Lom composed a song at the time to try to rouse the chiefs to prompter action, as he thought they were loitering too long idle in Lochaber. Received letter from James II. after Killiecrankie, commending the devotion of the Keppochs to the Stuart cause ever since their greatest misfortunes began. Coll joined Colonel Cannon, Dundee's successor; but with the other chiefs, who lost confidence in him, Coll retired after signing the agreement to meet together to concert other measures. He signed the letter of the chiefs in answer to MacKay's offer to lay down their arms, in which they refused to do so. When Cannon was succeeded by Buchan, there was a meeting at Keppoch of the chiefs to decide what course they would pursue. It was unanimously decided to continue the war. Coll was outlawed for Mulroy, did not make his peace for seven years; was marked for destruction before massacre of Glencoe, but made his peace before. In 1715 Coll joined Earl of Mar; was at Sheriffmuir, where the MacDonells particularly distinguished themselves on the right. After the clansmen were compelled to deliver their arms, the chiefs retired, Coll going to France, where he remained a year in the service of James VIII., and was one of the principal movers in planning the last final struggle of the Stuarts, which was undertaken in the '45. Coll married Barbara, daughter of Sir Donald MacDonald of Sleat ; her mother was daughter of the Earl of Morton. He had issue Alexander, Donald (executed at Kennington Common in 1746), and Archibald. A daughter married to Cameron of Errachd, whose son raised the 79th Cameron Highlanders.

XVI. ALEXANDER, succeeded his father, was ten years in the French army. In 1743 went to France with proposal to Prince Charles's French Court; was one of the first to join the prince at Glenfinnan. On hearing of prince's arrival, held council at Keppoch, and gave it as his opinion that their duty was to raise men instantly for the protection of his person, *whatever* might be the consequences. He was the attached friend as well as the devoted follower of his prince, whom he had known from his childhood. About an hour after standard was raised in Glenfinnan, the remainder of Keppoch clan arrived. It was by Keppoch's advice battle was given to General Cope at Prestonpans (see Home's " Works "). After Falkirk, Tirnadris taken, then executed at Carlisle. When it was found necessary to retreat north, as the army was much diminished by desertion after Falkirk, Prince Charles would not consent, and it was Keppoch who was sent to persuade him, because of the prince's confidence in his judgment and tried affection, and to Keppoch he yielded where others had failed (see note, Home's " Works "). Prince Charles spent a night at Keppoch before the attempt to surprise him at Moy Hall, and that night Keppoch's youngest daughter was born, and named Charlotte after the royal guest. It was on this occasion that the prince received the tartan

3 O

plaid which had been spun and dyed by Mrs
MacDonell of Keppoch. He left it at Moy Hall,
and it was always kept over the bed on which he
slept by the late Lady Mackintosh. He married
Jessie, daughter of Stewart of Appin. The manner
of his death at Culloden is well known. Was succeeded by Angus.

XVII. ANGUS, his son, who had fought at Culloden with his
father, took his place at the head of the clan. He was
only twenty-one. He was not the son of Miss Stewart
of Appin. Some have doubted his legitimacy, on
account of his resigning the chieftainship later, but
there is no proof that such was the case, and he was
always treated as the chief's eldest son, and remained
at the head of the family when he died. At the
meeting held on the 8th May 1746 by the chiefs, who
entered into a bond for their mutual defence never
to lay down their arms or make a general peace
without the consent of the whole, Angus was present
as representative of his clan. By this bond they
solemnly promised to raise, on behalf of their
prince, as many able-bodied men as they could
on their respective estates, and agreed that the
following chiefs, viz., Lochiel, Glengarry, Clanranald,
Stewart of Appin, Keppoch, Barisdale, MacKinnon,
and MacLeod, should assemble on Thursday, 15th
May, at Ach-na-carry in Lochaber, etc., etc., and that
anyone engaged in the association making terms for
himself would be looked upon as a traitor to his
prince, and treated as an enemy by his associates
(see Appendix, Home's " Works "). The chiefs had
been too sanguine, for not one of them, for various
reasons, was able to meet on the appointed day.
Lochiel later wrote a circular to his brother chiefs,
advising them, under existing circumstances, to

disperse their people; but as expectation of assistance from France was still entertained, he requested
them to preserve their arms as long as possible.
Angus then was in hiding near Loch Treig. Then
he and MacNab of Innisewen were with the prince
through some of his perilous wanderings. It was
the relation of some of these adventures then, that
awakened the prince's memory to those times which
he had completely forgotten, when Angus's son
John (writer of MSS. notes), as a young man, went
to see his prince at Rome, when the latter was an
old man and almost blind. He gave John a piece
of the ribbon off his orders. Angus married a
daughter of MacDonell (*Achnancoichean*). Their son
Donald married the daughter of Barbara (the eldest
daughter who left issue, of Keppoch of Culloden's
six daughters); and their son Angus, who married
the granddaughter of Charlotte, Keppoch's youngest
daughter, was the late chief of Keppoch. Angus
resigned the chieftainship to his brother Ronald, who
was between nine and ten years old at Culloden.
By Angus's advice his brother applied for a grant
of the Keppoch lands through the Duke of Gordon,
as Angus's life being under attainder for his share
in the rising of '45, he could not do so himself.
His brother having the lands, he also gave up his
place as chief.

XVIII. RANALD, second son of Keppoch of Culloden, succeeded
as chief about 1759, after he had been serving in the
1st battalion of the 78th or Fraser's Highlanders,
which he entered as lieutenant when it was raised in
1757. His name is entered as *son* of Keppoch, not
as chief. He built the present Keppoch House about
this time; returned to active service in Jamaica and
America later on. In Jamaica he married a Miss

Cargill 'about 1780-82; had two sons who left no
issue, and one daughter unmarried. One daughter
married, whose family are now in Edinburgh. She
was married to a Mr Stewart, W.S. After Ranald
retired from the army, the 79th Cameron Highlanders
were raised in 1793, principally by Alan Cameron
of Errachd (Keppoch's first cousin), who was colonel
of the regiment. Keppoch did not join himself, but
raised about two hundred of the Keppoch clan to
swell the ranks. Athletic sports were held on the
occasion, and the first prize for running and leaping
was won by Keppoch's valet, though he wore his livery
and top boots. This man was called Angus Mac-
Donell, known as *Aonghas Mac-Raonuill*, and was
still alive and gardener at Keppoch during the early
married life of Angus MacDonell (my father), to
whom he related the circumstances. The tartan for
the regiment was designed by Mrs Cameron of
Errachd (sister of Keppoch of Culloden), as the
Cameron tartan or the Keppoch tartan did not look
well with the scarlet jacket. The tartan designed
was a blend of ordinary MacDonald tartan with a
yellow stripe taken from the Cameron tartan. The
march of the regiment was "*Piobaireachd Dhomhnuill
Duibh*," composed for Donald Balloch at the first
battle of Inverlochy. From the patronymic of the
Camerons being " *Mac Dhomhnuill Duibh*," and the
Cameron regiment having the tune as their march,
many people lately have thought it was a Cameron
pipe tune; but it is, and always has been, a Mac-
Donald *piobaireachd*. Ranald's two sons were in
the army (Gordon Highlanders, Richard's regiment;
Alexander, I am not sure which regiment), and were
in the Peninsular war wounded several times; both
died unmarried. The youngest son of Keppoch
of Culloden, Alexander, was major in the army;

married daughter of Tirnadris. His son Chichester left two sons, who were both killed in the war in Canada; both unmarried. The son John and two daughters never married. Major Alexander emigrated to Canada, where he died. He has no descendants extant.

ANGUS was great grandson of Keppoch of Culloden twice over, as his father was son to Angus, Keppoch's son, and his mother was daughter to Barbara, Keppoch's daughter (the eldest who left issue). He was next in succession. He married Christina M'Nab, whose mother was the daughter of Charlotte, Keppoch of Culloden's youngest daughter. The old man, who related about the raising of the 79th, was their gardener for some years after they married. The lands of Keppoch had passed finally to Mackintosh of Mackintosh at the death of Ranald, the chief who was at the raising of the 79th, as the grant he had obtained was not renewed, as the Duke of Gordon, through whom it had been obtained, had lost his hold of Lochaber and his influence. So they lived at Keppoch as Mackintosh's tenants.

DONALD, their son, three times descended from Keppoch of Culloden, was the next Keppoch, and died in 1879 unmarried. He was our only living brother. A cousin in India is the next in succession.

[This MS. was kindly furnished by Miss Josephine MacDonell of Keppoch, and was copied by herself from an original MS. in possession of her mother, Mrs MacDonell of Keppoch (née M'Nab), wife of Angus, chief of Keppoch.]

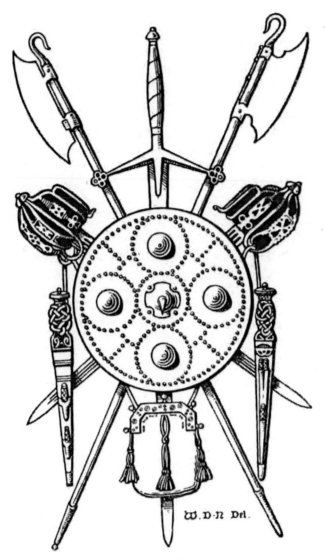

Lochaber Weapons.

INDEX.

A

	PAGE
A' bhaintigearna bheag,	342
A' bhanntrach ruadh,	354
Abinger, Lord,	406
Achdalieu,	83
Ach-na-carry,	115
Act of Attainder,	305
Act of Indemnity,	311
Ailein Mùideartach,	151
Ailein nan Creach,	30, 246, 249, 394
Alasdair Carrach,	21, 22, 23, 26, 93
Alasdair nan Cleas,	46, 470
Albannach,	9
Alford,	67
Antrim, Earl of,	40, 44, 51, 54
Aonghas Mac-Raonuill,	357
Aonghas na Feairte (Angus of Keppoch),	30, 469
Aonghas Og,	21
Argyll, Earl of,	39, 44, 51, 54
Argyll in 1715,	150
Argyll, John, Duke of,	99
Argyll's Flight from Inverlochy,	65
Auldearn,	67

B

	PAGE
Baillie, Major-General,	55
Balloch, Donald,	25, 26, 415, 476
Banavie,	12
Bannockburn,	21
Banquo,	13
Bard of Keppoch—*see* Iain Lom,	58
Battle of the Shirts,	36, 37

PAGE

Ben Nevis—the name, ... 71, 174
Berchan, St, ... 12, 416
Bill of Attainder, ... 305
Black Lord of Badenoch, ... 16
Black Tailor of the Axe, The, ... 41, 43
"Black Watch," 170
Blarmachfhuildaich, ... 13
Blàr nan leine, ... 36, 37
Boyds of Ardgour, ... 33, 464
Brae Lochaber names, ... 463
Bruce, Robert, ... 15, 16
Burt's Letters, Captain, ... 172, 173

C

Cailein Uaine, ... 251
Caithness, Earl of, ... 27
Caledonian Canal, ... 397
Callart, ... 12
Cameron—Origin of Name, ... 17, 18
     Genealogy, ... 218, 463, 466
     Pibroch, ... 81
Cameron, Alan, ... 79
Cameron, Angus, ... 18
Cameron, Charles, ... 349
Cameron, Donald, the "Gentle" Lochiel, . 154, 163, 184, 265, 268, 287
     Death of, ... 317
     Present Chief, ... 403
Cameron, Dr Archibald, . . . 201, 202, 293, 328, 335
Cameron, Ewen, of Lochiel, ... 40
Cameron, John, ... 154, 163
Cameron, John, of Fassfern, ... 369
     Death of, ... 377, 406
Cameron, Lady Margaret, ... 404
Cameron, Ludovick, of Torcastle, ... 163, 293
Cameron, Major-General Sir Alexander, ... 382
Cameron, Miss Jenny, ... 192
Cameron of Errachd, Alan, ... 353, 354
Cameron, Sir Duncan, ... 388
Cameron, Sir Ewen, . . 58, 75, 76, 82, 113, 146, 155, 156, 161, 434
Cameron Highlanders, Sketch of, ... 359, 459
Cameron Volunteers, ... 357, 459
Camerons of Glen Nevis, ... 218
Campbell-Bannerman on Tartan, ... 357

PAGE

	PAGE
Campbell, Mrs Cameron,	389
Campbell of Ach-na-breac,	57, 65
Campbell of Fonab,	169
Campbell of Glenure, Murder of,	321
Campbell of Monzie,	389
Camus nan Gall,	251
Caolas mhic Phadruig,	393
Carnich,	26
Castle Tioram,	36
Charlemagne,	7, 10
Charles II., Death of,	87, 145
Chronicle of St Berchan,	12, 416
?"	367
Cille-Chuimein,	17
Clach-an-turramain,	221
Clach na h-Annait,	246
Clach nan Caimbeulach,	64
Clach Shomhairle,	214
Clan Battle, The last,	100
Clan Chattan,	17–18
Clanranald, Origin of,	21
Claverhouse,	106, 115
Death of,	124
Clayton, Colonel,	160
Cluny,	201
	221
Coll of the Cows,	95, 354, 472
"Colonel Anne" Mackintosh,	203, 261
Comyn, Black and Red,	16
Comyn, Sir John,	16
Comyns of Lochaber and Badenoch,	15, 17
Cope, Sir John,	199
Corpach,	12, 30
Craigs, The,	131
Cromwell,	72, 73
Culloden, Battle of,	253
Cumberland, Duke of,	252, 261, 265

D

Dàn Chloinn Uisneachain,	227
Davidsons,	19
Deirdre, Legend of,	228
Disarming Act,	311
Dòmhnull nan Ord,	251

PAGE

Donald Glas, ... 88
Donald, King, ... 7
Donald of the Isles, ... 7
Druim-na-Birlinn, ... 391
Drummond, Lady Mary, ... 137
Drummossie Muir, ... 253
Duncan I., ... 12

E

Eilean Mhic-an Toisich, ... 284
Eobhan MacAilein, ... 353, 419
Eocha, King, IV., ... 7, 8, 10, 12
Errachd Camerons, ... 353
Ethodius, King, ... 6
Ewin, King, ... 6

F

Falkirk, Battle of, ... 206
Farquharson of Invercauld, ... 203
Fassfern, John Cameron of, ... 71, 335, 377
"Florida," The, ... 120
Fordun, ... 6, 7
Fort Augustus, ... 17
Fort William, ... 12, 64, 127, 130, 134
  Burning of, ... 213
  Railway to, ... 401
  School, ... 142
  Siege of, ... 241, 245
Fraser Highlanders, ... 337, 347
Frasers, ... 36, 37
Freiceadan Dubh, The, ... 170

G

Gardiner, Colonel, ... 204
George III., ... 346
George IV., ... 385
George, Prince, ... 144
Glenaladale, ... 190, 275
Glencoe, Massacre of, ... 132
Glenfinnan, ... 190
Glengarry, Origin of, ... 21
Glen Nevis, ... 213
Glen Roy, ... 56
Gonranus, King, ... 7

PAGE

Gordon, Duchess of, ... 372
Gordon Highlanders, ... 369, 372
Gordons of Huntly—their Origin, ... 34
Gormshuill, ... 120
Graham, James (Montrose), ... 49
Graham of Claverhouse—*see* Viscount Dundee, ... 104

H

Harlaw, Battle of, ... 23
Head, Mrs, of Inverailort, ... 382
Henry IX., ... 346
Hereditary Jurisdiction, Abolition of, ... 312
High Bridge, ... 186
Highland Garb in 1688, The, ... 101
Hollinshed, ... 6, 7, 11
Huntly, ... 27, 34

I

Iain Aluinn, ... 58
Iain Dubh Cameron, ... 308
Iain Garbh, ... 30
Iain Lom, Bard of Keppoch, . . . 58, 98, 119, 128, 142, 435
Inveraray, ... 54
Inverlochy, ... 5, 12, 26
    Battle of, ... 26, 55, 57, 60, 69
    Garrison, ... 75, 112
    Newport, ... 129, 143, 431
Inverlochy Castle, ... 16, 69
Invernahavon, Battle of, ... 19

J

James I., ... 24
James II. and VII., ... 139
James III. and VIII., . . 139, 147, 148, 155, 158, 177, 298, 343

K

Keppoch Chiefs, ... 468
Keppoch Family Poets, ... 465
Keppoch Murder, The, ... 58, 88, 91
Keppoch, Origin of Family, ... 21
Keppoch's Candlesticks, ... 257
Kill a Choireil, ... 249
Killiecrankie, ... 121, 122, 123

PAGE

Kilmallie,	. . . .	71, 250
Kilsyth,	. . . .	. 67
Kilt, Defence of,	. . . . . .	. 363
Knox, John,	. . . .	47, 48

L

Last execution in Scotland under feudal laws,	. . .	. 165
Latha Inbher-Lochaidh,	. . . . . .	. 431
Laud, Archbishop,	. . . . . .	. 48
Lesly, Bishop of Ross,	. . . . .	. 10
Livingstones at Ardgour,	. . . . .	. 33
Lochaber, meaning of name,	. . . . .	. 1, 11
In 1689,	. . . . . .	. 111
"Lochaber no more,"	. . . . .	. 295
Lochan a Chlaidheamh,	. . . . .	. 120
Lochgarry,	. . . . . .	. 294
Lochiel's family in 1719,	. . . .	. 163
Loch-nan-uamh,	. . . . .	183, 289
Lochy, River,	. . . . . .	. 5, 12
Lords of the Isles,	. . . . .	. 21
Lundavra, meaning of name,	. . . .	12, 13

M

MacAindrea, Iain beag,	. . . . .	. 237
Macaulay, Lord,	. . . . .	114, 122
MacBane, Donald,	. . . . .	. 98
Macbeth,	. . . . .	12, 13, 14
Mac Cailean Mòr,	. . . 44, 54, 56, 63, 116, 143, 151
MacCrimmon,	. . . . . .	. 211
Mac-Dhomhnuill Duibh,	. . . . .	. 30
MacDonalds of Keppoch—their Origin,	. .	37, 92, 95, 405
Alexander,	. . . . .	. 46
Cicely, the poetess,	. . . .	. 93
Coll,	. . . . . .	. 92
Ranald,	. . . .	339, 341, 352, 421
MacDonald, Alasdair, of Antrim, "*Mac Colla Ciotach,*"	.	53, 57
MacDonald, Flora,	. . . .	. 274
MacDonald of Glenaladale, Alexander,	. .	. 197
MacDonald of Glengarry, Alexander,	. . .	. 89
MacDonald of Tirnadris,	. . . .	. 302
MacDonald of Tulloch,	. . . .	. 96
MacDonalds of Isla,	. . . .	. 53
MacDonald, Strontian,	. . . .	. 39
MacDonwald, The Merciless,	. . .	13, 14

PAGE

MacDougall of Lorne, ... 41
Macdugald, Flora, ... 451
MacGille Chnamhaich, ... 246
MacGillivray of Dunmaglass, ... 203
MacGillonies, ... 19, 20, 354
MacIain of Ardnamurchan, ... 26
MacIain of Glencoe, ... 133, 394
Mac ic Eobhainn, ... 33
MacKay, Angus Dubh, ... 23
MacKay, General Hugh, ... 108, 119, 127, 243
MacKellar, Mrs Mary, . . . 12, 82, 90, 239, 349
Mackintosh, ... 17
    Origin, ... 18, 92
    Tradition, ... 259
Mackintosh, Captain, ... 350
Mackintosh, Dr Fraser, ... 5, 142, 219
MacLean, Charles, ... 22
MacLean, Ewen, ... 32
MacLean of Ardgour, ... 31
MacLean of Coll, Lachlan, ... 30
MacLean of Duart, ... 30
MacLean, Red Hector, ... 31
MacLeans at Harlaw, The, ... 23
MacLeod of MacLeod, ... 120
MacMartins of Letterfinlay, ... 218, 291
MacMasters, ... 31, 32, 33
MacMillans, ... 381
M'Nicol, Rev. Donald, ... 10
MacPhersons, ... 19, 99
    Cluny, ... 19
    Duncan, of Cluny, ... 348
    Ewen, of Cluny, ... 293
Malcolm II., ... 12
Mamore, ... 5, 12, 13
Mar, ... 26, 28, 147, 154, 157
Mary Queen of Scots, ... 47
     1
     284
Monk, General, ... 73
    of, ... 49, 50, 68
Morris, Mowbray, ... 51
Mort-na-Ceapach, ... 91
Moy Castle, ... 209
    Rout, ... 210

PAGE

N

Nether Lochaber, ... 389
Nevis, Ben,—*see* Ben Nevis, ... 71

O

O'Birrin, ... 28, 29
Ogilvie, Sir Thomas, ... 65
Onich, ... 392
Orange, William, Prince of, ... 138, 139

P

Perth, North Inch of, ... 20
Philiphaugh, ... 67
Pibroch of Donald Dhu, ... 5, 358, 415, 476
"Pickle the Spy," 273
Picts' name and dress, ... 8, 9
Piper story, ... 239
Pitt, William, ... 336–337
Prestonpans, ... 204
Prince Charlie, ... 117, 272, 275, 283, 297, 343
Prince of Orange, The, ... 103

Q

Queen Victoria at Lochaber, ... 386, 407

R

Ranald Galda, ... 38
Ranald of the Hens, ... 36
Recruiting in Highlands, ... 369
Recruiting poster of Cameron Volunteers, ... 356
Robert II., ... 18
Rob Roy, ... 152
Ruthven Castle, ... 40

S

Scott, Captain, ... 186
Seaforth, Earl of, ... 55
Sheriffmuir, ... 150
Silver Shoe, Ailein nan Creach's, ... 249
Skene, Dr, ... 218, 233
Sliochd a ghamhna mhaoil Duinn, ... 391
Sliochd Eobhainn ic Eobhainn, ... 353
Sliochd Shomhairle Ruaidh, ... 218, 226, 391

PAGE

Sons of Uisnach, ... 227
Speed, John, ... 12
St Andrew's Cross—Badge of Scotland, ... 10
Stapleton, ... 242
Stewart, Alan Breck, ... 320
Stewart, James, of the Glen, ... 320, 324, 325
Stewart ("Nether Lochaber"), Dr, ... 143

T

Taillear Dubh na Tuaige, ... 41, 226
Tartan, Cameron of Errachd, ... 358, 476
Tau Ghairm, ... 247
Telford, ... 397, 398
Thane of Lochaber, ... 14
The "Forty-Five," 177
Tobar nan Ceann, ... 91
Tom-eas-an-t-slinnein, ... 217
Tor Castle, ... 24
Tor-nan-cor, ... 226
Torran-na-brataich, ... 64
Tullibardine, Marquis of, ... 195

U

Urquhart Castle, ... 22, 37

V

Viscount Dundee—see Claverhouse, ... 104, 105, 115

W

Wade, General, ... 167
Walkinshaw, Clementina, ... 345
Walter, Steward of Scotland, ... 15
Well of Heads, ... 91
White Rose League, ... 297, 409

Printed by M'FARLANE & ERSKINE, Edinburgh.

Lightning Source UK Ltd.
Milton Keynes UK
02 September 2009
143304UK00001B/84/A